Software Project Effort Estimation

Adam Trendowicz • Ross Jeffery

Software Project Effort Estimation

Foundations and Best Practice Guidelines for Success

 Springer

Adam Trendowicz
Fraunhofer Institute for
Experimental Software Engineering
Kaiserslautern
Germany

Ross Jeffery
The University of New South Wales
Sydney
New South Wales
Australia

ISBN 978-3-319-35359-3   ISBN 978-3-319-03629-8 (eBook)
DOI 10.1007/978-3-319-03629-8
Springer Cham Heidelberg New York Dordrecht London

Foreword

Software effort estimation is one of the oldest and most important problems facing software project management; being able to plan correctly is the basis for all project management activities. One cannot manage a project without the knowledge of what resources are needed to achieve the project goals. It is an area where there has been a great deal of research in the development and fine-tuning of new models and encoding of experience in applying these models.

Today, there are a large number of models, each having different strengths and weaknesses in general and, more importantly, different strengths and weaknesses relative to the environment and context in which they are to be applied, for example, the historical data available and the kinds of factors that are relevant. At the start of a project, it is difficult to understand all the influencing factors and risks; there is a minimal amount of information available. Effort needs to be reestimated at various points in time as the project progresses. And how do you balance early effort commitment against new estimates? What trade-offs are possible?

Which models to apply under what conditions is difficult and requires a great deal of insight into the environment. As with all software engineering approaches and models, it is critical to understand the context in which the approach is to be applied, the model assumptions and context for which the model was developed (not always made clear by the model developer), and how to apply and tailor the model to your context.

This book addresses all these points and provides a large set of model types and classes, focusing on what you need to understand about your environment, what information you need to be able to apply the model, what models are most effective for a particular environment, and how you can learn from the model's application so you can evolve and improve your model over time.

The book is full of insights and useful advice on what to do and how to do it, what to be wary of, and the limitations of effort estimation. Just reading the tips contained in each chapter is a valuable experience.

The book goes beyond effort estimation and provides enormous insights into project management, in general, discussing such issues as project trade-offs, risk assessment, and organizational learning.

This is the most complete work on all aspects of software effort estimation that I have seen and provides an excellent reference for the field. It belongs on the bookshelf of every organization that needs to manage a software project. At the same time, it is an excellent text for a university course on software effort estimation, a topic that is typically insufficiently treated in most curricula.

December 2013

Victor R. Basili
University of Maryland
College Park, MD, USA

On True Success

Past successes, no matter how numerous and universal, are no guarantee of future performance in a new context.

– Henry Petroski

Failure is success if we learn from it.

– Malcolm Forbes

Success consists of going from failure to failure without loss of enthusiasm.

– Winston Churchill

To be defeated and not submit, is victory; to be victorious and rest on one's laurels, is defeat.

– Józef Piłsudski (First Marshal of Poland)

Preface

The time for action is now. It's never too late to do something.

—Antoine de Saint-Exupery.

What Is This Book About?

In this book, we focus on the estimation of software development effort. Three aspects are considered important for the proper handling of effort estimation: (1) *foundations* of software effort estimation, (2) selecting the most suitable estimation *approach*, and (3) successfully using effort estimation in specific *contexts*.

What Is This Book NOT About?

This book does not include project planning activities that typically follow effort estimation. We do not discuss such aspects as how to allocate project resources to work tasks, how to sequence work activities, how to determine critical paths, and how to resolve resource conflicts. Finally, we are not addressing project scheduling or budgeting. We refer readers interested in these subjects to books that address project management topics, for example, the PMI's (2013) Project Management Body of Knowledge (PMBOK Guide) or OGC's (2009) PRINCE2, which offer very useful overviews of common project management practices.

To Whom Is This Book Addressed?

In its very early stage, this book was intended as a collection of notes, where the most relevant estimation principles, definitions, and empirical observations, found in the literature and from experience, were gathered. In the course of time, this was shared with others. This book aims to inherit the intention of these initial notes and the needs of people they were shared with. It is addressed to those who want to take actions in order to improve their estimation practices, yet are missing (1) the necessary knowledge and understanding of estimation principles and (2) a concise reference of best practices and most common estimation approaches they can start with and adapt to their particular needs. This book assumes one prerequisite about its intended audience: it assumes that readers believe that it is never too late to do something about your estimation practices, irrespective of whatever shape they are now in.

Software Practitioners

This book is intended for all software practitioners responsible for software effort estimation and planning in their daily work. This includes primarily, but is not limited to, those who are responsible for introducing and maintaining estimation practices in a software development organization.

Students

In this book, we also appreciate the value of the old saying "as the twig is bent, so grows the tree" and address the content to students of software engineering programs, particularity project and process management courses.

How to Read This Book

We anticipated this book to be a reference guidebook you can grab whenever you need to learn or recall specific aspects of effort estimation. The way you read the book depends on your particular needs at a given moment. So before you start, think for a moment—what do you want to achieve?

- *If you want to understand the basic challenges and principles of software effort estimation*, read Chaps. 1 and 2.
- *If you want to master* the *principal concepts and techniques of existing estimation methods*, read Chaps. 3–5 and the Appendix.
- *If you want to select the most suitable estimation method for estimating software development effort in your specific context*, read Chaps. 6 and 7.
- *If additionally you want to get a quick insight into the most common estimation methods, including their prominent strengths and weaknesses*, read Chaps. 8–15, or only some of them if you are interested in any specific method we present there.
- *If you want to introduce a new estimation approach or improve the one you have been using*, read Chap. 16.
- *In any case, read the best-practice guidelines* we present in Chap. 17.

Moreover, each part of the book begins with a brief summary of the chapters it encompasses. Refer to these summaries to quickly decide which chapter to read.

Key Terminology Used in This Book

In this book, we use several basic terms, which in other literature and in practice are often used interchangeably. In order not to confuse the reader, we would like to start by clarifying the most important terms we will use throughout the text.

Cost Versus Effort

Although principally and intuitively different, the terms "cost" and "effort" are often used as synonyms in the software project management area. The Webster dictionary defines cost as "the amount or equivalent paid or charged for something" and effort as "conscious exertion of power" or "the total work done to achieve a particular end". In the software engineering domain, cost is defined in a monetary sense, and with respect to software development projects, it refers to partial or total monetary cost of providing (creating) certain products or services. Effort, on the other hand, refers to staff time spent on performing activities aimed at providing these products or services. In consequence, project cost includes, but is not limited to, project effort. In practice, cost includes such elements as fixed infrastructure and administrative costs for example. Moreover, dependent on the project context (e.g., currency or cost of staff unit) despite the same project effort, project cost may differ.

In the software engineering literature and practice, "cost" is often used as a synonym for "effort." One of the ways to notice the difference is to look at units used. Cost in a monetary sense is typically measured in terms of a certain currency (e.g., \$, €, ¥, etc.), whereas cost in an effort sense is typically measured as staff time (e.g., person-hours, person-days, person-months, etc.).

In this book, we focus on estimating software development effort, and we consistently differentiate between cost and effort.

Estimation Versus Prediction Versus Planning

In software engineering, effort estimation, prediction, and planning are related to each other; yet, they have different meanings, that is, they refer to different project management activities. Actually, the dictionary definitions perfectly reflect the differences between these three processes:

- *Estimation*: "the act of <u>judging tentatively or approximately</u> the value, worth, or significance of something"
- *Prediction*: "the act of <u>declaring or indicate in advance</u>; especially: <u>foretelling</u> on the basis of observation, experience, or scientific reason"
- *Planning*: "the act or process of <u>making or carrying out plans</u>; *specifically*: the establishment of goals, policies, and procedures for a social or economic unit"

Estimation Versus Prediction

Both estimation and prediction contain an element of uncertainty; the first refers to approximating an actual state, whereas the latter refers to a future state. Simplifying, we may define prediction as estimating in advance. Since in software engineering, effort estimation refers to approximating development effort in advance, before development is completed, it should actually be called effort prediction. Yet, in practice, both terms are used interchangeably. In this book, we will follow this practice and use estimation and prediction as synonyms for foretelling the effort required for completing software development projects.

Prediction Versus Planning

There is, however, a significant difference between prediction and planning. Prediction refers to an unbiased, analytical process of approximating a future state. Planning, on the other hand, refers to a biased process of establishing goals with respect to the future state. Although predictions form a foundation for planning, plans do not have to be (and typically are not) the same as predictions. In the case of software development, the goal of prediction is to accurately foretell resources (such as effort) required to provide project outcomes. The goal of effort planning is, on the other hand, is to plan the project in such a way that the project goals are achieved. In other words, we plan means within a project to achieve a specific project's end.

Kaiserslautern, Germany   Adam Trendowicz
Sydney, NSW, Australia   Ross Jeffery

Acknowledgments

A number of great people and organizations have made their explicit or implicit contribution to this book by inspiring us, contributing to our knowledge, or helping us in the creation of this book. Hereby, we would like to express our gratitude to these people and organizations.

We would like to thank the reviewers of the book manuscript, Yasushi Ishigai and Mirosław Ochodek, for their valuable remarks.

Adam Trendowicz would like to express special thanks to Yasushi Ishigai for recent years of collaborative work in industrial contexts and great discussions on the industrial challenges regarding effort estimation and potential solutions to these challenges. Moreover, he would like to thank Fraunhofer Institute for Experimental Software Engineering (IESE), Kaiserslautern, Germany, for giving him an opportunity to develop their professional expertise, including software effort estimation.

Ross Jeffery would like to thank National ICT Australia (NICTA) and the University of New South Wales, who have supported his research for many years. He would also like to thank the many academic and industry colleagues who have assisted with the research in effort estimation.

We would like to convey special thanks to Mr. Ralf Gerstner and Ms. Victoria Meyer from Springer for their great support in copyediting this book.

Last but not least, we seek forgiveness from all those whose names we have failed to mention.

Disclaimer

Any of the trademarks, service marks, collective marks, registered names, or similar rights that are used or cited in this book are the property of their respective owners. Their use here does not imply that they can be used for any purpose other than for the informational use as contemplated in this book. Rather than indicating every occurrence of a trademarked name as such, this report uses the names only with no intention of infringement of the trademark. The following table lists trademark names used in this book.

Trademark	Subject of trademark	Trademark owner
CoBRA®	Cost Estimation, Benchmarking, and Risk Assessment	Fraunhofer Institute for Experimental Software Engineering (IESE)
GQM⁺Strategies®		Fraunhofer Institute for Experimental Software Engineering (IESE)
CMMI®	Capability Maturity Model Integrated	Software Engineering Institute (SEI)
MS Office®	MS Word®, MS Excel®, and MS PowerPoint®	Microsoft® Corporation
PMBOK®	Project Management Body of Knowledge Guide	Project Management Institute (PMI)
PRINCE2™	Projects in Controlled Environments 2	Office of Government Commerce (OGC)

Acronyms

AC	Actual cost
ACWP	Actual cost of work performed
AHP	Analytic hierarchy process
ANGEL	Analogy estimation tool
ANN	Artificial neural networks
AVN	Analogy with virtual neighbor
BBN	Bayesian belief network
BCWP	Budgeted cost of work performed
BCWS	Budgeted cost of work scheduled
BRACE	Bootstrap-based analogy cost estimation
BRE	Balanced relative error
CART	Classification and regression trees
CASE	Computer-aided software engineering
CI	Confidence interval
CMMI	Capability maturity model integrated
CoBRA	Cost estimation, benchmarking, and risk assessment
COCOMO	Constructive cost model
COTS	Commercial off-the-shelf
DAG	Directed acyclic graph
DBMS	Database management system
EF	Experience factory
EQF	Estimating quality factor
EO	Effort overhead
ESA	European Space Agency
EV	Earned value
EVM	Earned value management
FP	Function points
FPA	Function points analysis
GAO	US Government Accountability Office
GP	Genetic programming
GQM	Goal-question-metric
IEEE	Institute of Electrical and Electronics Engineers
IFPUG	International Function Point Users Group

IRQ	Interquartile range
ISBSG	International Software Benchmarking Standards Group
JPD	Join probability distribution
KPA	Key process area
LAD	Least absolute deviation
LMS	Least median of squares
LOC	Lines of code
MCDA	Multi criteria decision analysis
MIS	Management information systems
MMRE	Mean magnitude of relative error
MRE	Magnitude of relative effort
MSE	Mean squared error
MSWR	Manual stepwise regression
NPT	Node probability table
OEM	Original equipment manufacturer
OLS	Ordinary least squares
OS	Operating system
PDCA	Plan-do-check-act
PDR	Product design review
PERT	Program evaluation and review technique
PI	Prediction interval
PMI	Project Management Institute
PMBOK	Project Management Body of Knowledge
POP	Predictive object points
PRINCE	Projects in controlled environments
PROBE	Proxy-based estimation
PV	Planned value
QA	Quality assurance
QIP	Quality improvement paradigm
QSM	Quantitative software management
RE	Relative estimation error
ROC	Rank order centroid
RR	Robust regression
SEER-SEM	Software Evaluation and Estimation of Resources-Software Estimating Model
SEI	Software Engineering Institute
SLIM	Software lifecycle management
SLOC	Source lines of code
SMART	Specific, measurable, attainable, relevant, timely
SPI	Software process improvement
SPR	Software productivity research
UCP	Use-case points
WBS	Work breakdown structure

Contents

About the Authors

Adam Trendowicz is a senior consultant at the Fraunhofer Institute for Experimental Software Engineering (IESE) in Kaiserslautern, Germany, where he leads the team of "Measurement and Prediction." He received his Ph.D. in Computer Science from the University of Kaiserslautern (Germany). Dr. Trendowicz has led software cost estimation and software measurement improvement activities in software companies of different sizes and from various domains (e.g., in Germany, Japan, and India). He has been involved in functional software size estimation (Function Point Analysis) and productivity benchmarking in organizations from both industry and the public sector. Dr. Trendowicz has taught several tutorials on software cost estimation and supervised the "Software Economics and Risk Management" module within the distance master studies program "Software Engineering for Embedded Systems"—a program developed jointly by the University of Kaiserslautern and Fraunhofer IESE. Finally, Dr. Trendowicz has authored the book titled *Software Cost Estimation, Benchmarking, and Risk Assessment. The Software Decision-Makers' Guide to Predictable Software Development.* Moreover, he has coauthored more than 20 international journal and conference publications. Dr. Trendowicz's other software engineering interests include (1) project management, (2) software product quality modeling and evaluation, and (3) technology validation by means of empirical methods.

Ross Jeffery is Emeritus Professor of Software Engineering in the School of Computer Science and Engineering at the University of New South Wales and research consultant in the Systems Software Research Group in National ICT Australia (NICTA). His research interests are in the software engineering process and product modeling and improvement, electronic process guides and software knowledge management, software quality, software metrics, software technical and management reviews, and software resource modeling and estimation. His research has involved over 50 government and industry organizations over a period of 20 years and has been funded by industry, government, and universities. He has coauthored 4 books and over 190 research papers. He has served on the editorial board of the *IEEE Transactions on Software Engineering*, the *Journal of Empirical Software Engineering*, and the Wiley International Series in Information Systems. He was a founding member of the International Software Engineering Research Network (ISERN). He was elected Fellow of the Australian Computer Society for his contribution to software engineering research.

Part I

Foundations

A problem well stated is a problem half solved.

—Charles F. Kettering

In this part, we introduce the topic of software effort estimation as one of the basic elements of planning and managing software development undertakings.

Chapter 1 provides a brief introduction to software development and the application of quantitative approaches for managing software development projects. In this chapter, we also summarize typical effort estimation threats and challenges of software development projects.

Chapter 2 introduces terminological and methodological principles of software effort estimation. In this chapter, we position effort estimation within the software development environment and sketch the basic estimation process including its primary inputs and outputs.

Chapter 3 overviews common factors influencing software project effort. In this chapter, we discuss three principal groups of factors—context factors, scale factors, and effort drivers—and consider examples of the most common factors from each group. Moreover, we provide guidelines on how to reduce their negative impact on project effort in practical situations.

Chapter 4 discusses information uncertainty and estimation inaccuracy as two critical aspects of software effort estimation. In this chapter, we discuss basic types of uncertainty and common sources of uncertainty. Moreover, we provide guidelines for how to represent and handle uncertainty in effort estimation and how to reduce any negative influence of uncertainty on effort estimates. In this chapter, we particularly discuss how to handle the imperfect information upon which estimates are based. Finally, we discuss the relationship between uncertainty and change in the context of software development projects.

Chapter 5 summarizes top-down and bottom-up estimation strategies. In this chapter, we overview the strengths and weaknesses of each strategy and provide guidelines on which strategy should be used, depending on the particular estimation situation. We also discuss an estimation strategy in which multiple estimation methods are used to develop the effort estimate. Finally, we answer the question of how to aggregate multiple estimates produced by the application of either a bottom-up estimation or multiple estimation methods.

Challenges of Predictable Software Development

1

Failing to plan is planning to fail.

—Winston Churchill

Effort and cost estimation are of paramount importance for the success of software development projects. Everyday practice shows that many software organizations still propose unrealistic software costs, work within tight schedules, and finish their projects behind schedule and budget, or do not complete them at all.

In this section, we introduce software effort estimation as an essential element of a successful software development project. We look at the characteristics of software and the software engineering environment that make estimation a particularly challenging task. Finally, we try to answer the basic question of estimation, namely, "what is a good estimate?"

1.1 Software Is Getting Complex

The creation of genuinely new software has far more in common with developing a new theory of physics than it does with producing cars or watches on an assembly line.

—Terry Bollinger

Software is everywhere. Most of today's goods and services are realized, at least partially or completely with the help of software systems. Our dependency on software increases continuously. On the one hand, progress in the domains where software has traditionally been playing a key role entails increasing pressure upon software to progress. On the other hand, in domains that were traditionally reserved for hardware, software has become the major driving force of overall progress. For example, it is said that 60–90 % of advances in the automotive domain nowadays are due to software systems. Some products and services that would have traditionally been realized through "hardware" solutions are now realized through software systems. Other products and services are only possible through software systems

A. Trendowicz and R. Jeffery, *Software Project Effort Estimation*,
DOI 10.1007/978-3-319-03629-8_1, © Springer International Publishing Switzerland 2014

and could not have been realized by other means. In this way, the size and complexity of software systems in various domains has increased rapidly.

This increasing complexity of software systems entails a fundamental shift in their cost, time-to-market, functionality, and quality requirements. Software is required to support a wide variety of domains; must always be faster, more intelligent, more dependable; must require less hardware resources and be ever easier to maintain; and, and, and. The wish list is typically quite long and ends up with: "The software must cost less and come to the market before our competitors even think about something similar."

1.2   Software Development Is Getting Complex

Better, faster, cheaper. Choosing to concentrate on two of these concepts made accomplishing the third difficult or impossible.
—James E. Tomayko and Orit Hazzan

When looking at the traditional manufacturing disciplines, software practitioners may ask themselves: "If most manufacturing industries are able to control cost, schedules and quality—at least most of the time—why can't we?" One simple answer is: "because software development differs from classical manufacturing." Let us briefly go through several aspects that distinguish software development from traditional manufacturing.

Development Technologies and Paradigms Change Rapidly. Software development teams must strive to achieve software development objectives by exploiting the impressive advances in continuously changing—and thus often immature—technologies and development paradigms. In fact, mastering rapidly changing technologies and processes is often considered as the most important challenge differentiating software development from other domains. Without counting the minor changes in methods and tools, throughout the past 50 years, the software industry has roughly gone through at least four generations of programming languages and three major development paradigms.

Development Distribution Increases. Together with the increased variety of software products, technologies, and processes, development distribution is growing constantly. Development is shifting from single contractors to distributed projects, where teams are scattered across multiple companies, time zones, cultures, and continents. The global trend toward software outsourcing has led to software companies needing a reliable basis for making make-or-buy decisions or for verifying the development schedule and cost offered by contractors if they decide to buy parts of a software product.

Software Development Is Still a Largely Human-Intensive Process. Moreover, software development is a human-based activity with extreme uncertainties from the outset. Robert Glass (2002) reiterated this fact by saying: "Eighty percent of software work is intellectual. A fair amount of it is creative. Little of it is clerical." Software development depends on the capabilities of developers and on the capabilities of customers and other involved parties.

Software Products Have an Abstract Character. Probably none of the afore-mentioned aspects has as large an impact on the difficulty of software production as does the abstract character of software products. It is this "softness" of software products that makes software engineering differ from other, "classical," engineer-ing domains. To create software, developers start with customer requirements and go through a sequence of transformations during which all involved parties create, share, and revise a number of abstract models of various, usually increasing, complexity. In addition, individual project tasks in a transformation sequence are usually highly interdependent. The intangible and volatile character of software products—especially requirements—makes them difficult to measure and control. This contributes to software development being a mixture of engineering, science, and art.

1.3   Project Management and Estimation Are Key Success Factors

Understanding the importance of accurate estimation, and a willingness to put in the resources ... are vitally important to a company's success.
                                                                              —Katherine Baxter

The complex and multidependent character of software development makes man-aging software projects a challenging task. A software project should, like any other project, be considered in terms of a business case. It should therefore lay out the reason(s) for the investment, the expected benefits of the initiative, the costs to make it happen, an analysis of the risks, and the future options that are created. A software project also requires, as one of its key success factors, effective manage-ment. It must focus on areas critical for financial success, the effective use of resources, an analysis of market potential and opportunities for innovation, the development of a learning environment, and so on.

Criteria of Project Success

The classical definition of "project success" is "a project that provides software of required functionality and quality within cost and schedule." Except for the meaning of "quality," which has been a subject of discussions for years, it is perhaps a clear definition of project success. But is it really?

In practice, success has a number of faces. Although perhaps not deemed "a success," a project that has not met some of the classical success criteria can still be far from a complete disaster. For example, if the project is canceled in a timely manner because it cannot meet the functionality and quality requirements within a reasonable budget and time, it could be classified as not having failed—under the condition that lessons learned can be applied in future projects to avoid a similar situation.

Software project management is a key project success factor, and, as aptly noted by Barry Boehm, "Poor management can increase software costs more rapidly than any other factor." A number of bad management practices may lead to failed projects, and one of the most common aspects of poor project management, which typically results in a project crisis, is poor effort estimation. Glass (2002) points to poor effort estimation as one of the two most common causes of runaway projects, besides unstable requirements. Rosencrance (2007), in her survey of more than 1,000 IT professionals, reports that two out of the three most important causes of an IT project failure are perceived to be related to poor effort estimation, in particular insufficient resource planning and unrealistic project deadlines.

Effective project management requires reliable effort and schedule estimation support. On the one hand, project managers need a reliable basis for developing realistic project effort, schedule, and cost plans. On the other hand, as project management is to a large extent a political game, they need a reliable and convincing basis for negotiating project conditions with project owners and/or customers. In the latter scenario, simple, gut-feeling estimates are definitely insufficient to justify realistic project plans against demands and expectations of other project stakeholders.

Yet, independent of these findings, many software organizations still propose unrealistic software costs, work within tight schedules, and finish their projects behind schedule and budget, or do not complete them at all.

1.4   What is a "Good Estimate"?

A good estimate is an estimate that provides a clear enough view of the project reality to allow the project leadership to make good decisions about how to control the project to hit its targets.

—Steve McConnell

The basic question of software effort estimation is "What is a good estimate?" Traditionally, effort estimation has been used for planning and tracking overall resources, such as staff required for completing a project. With this objective in mind, over the years, researchers have been pursuing an elusive target of getting 100 % accurate estimates in terms of the exact number of person-hours required to complete on a software project. Effort estimation methods that grew up on this goal focus on providing exact point estimates.

Yet, software practitioners nowadays require from effort estimation comprehensive decision support for a number of project management activities. They noticed that even the most accurate estimates are worthless if they cannot be reasonably justified to a project sponsor and customers or if they do not provide guidelines on what to do if the project is not going to meet estimates. From this perspective, one of the critical characteristics of good estimates is the additional information provided to support project decision making. Firstly, project decision makers need to identify the project areas that are responsible for increased development effort in order to have a transparent and convincing basis for renegotiating project resources and/or scope with the project sponsor. As aptly concluded by Tom Demarco (1982), the purpose of estimation "is not to solve any of the problems of actually getting a system built, but rather to make sure you encounter the fewest number of surprises as you undertake this work." Secondly, they need an indication of the effort-related development processes that can potentially be affected in order to improve productivity at low overhead—"low-hanging fruits."

Summarizing, a good estimate is one that supports the project manager to achieve successful project management and successful project completion. Thus, a good estimation method is one that provides such support without violating other project objectives such as project management overhead.

Tip

▶ A good estimate is one that supports project management activities such as planning and negotiation of project resources, managing changes and risks, etc. A good estimation method should thus provide—in addition to single point estimates—transparent information on project-related factors affecting development effort.

Further Reading

- R. Charette (2005), "Why software fails [software failure]," *IEEE Spectrum*, vol. 42, no. 9, pp. 42–49.

  This article looks at the status and the future of software. In the context of trends in size and complexity, it gives an overview of famous software disasters and their reasons. Among the most relevant causes of failed software projects are unrealistic or unarticulated project goals, inaccurate estimates of needed resources, and inability to handle the project's complexity.

• L.J. Osterweil (2007), "A Future for Software Engineering?," *Proceedings of the 29th International Conference on Software Engineering*, Workshop on the Future of Software Engineering, Minneapolis, MN, USA: IEEE Computer Society, pp. 1–11.

  This article identifies common trends and key challenges of software engineering practice and research. Among other items, it asks about the future of design, modeling, and quantitative quality control of something as intangible as software.

• Y. Wang (2007a), *Software Engineering Foundations: A Software Science Perspective*, CRC Software Engineering Series, vol. 2, AUERBACH/CRC Press.

  In Sect. 1.3 of his book, the author discusses general constraints of software and software engineering. He distinguishes three interrelated groups of constraints: cognitive, organizational, and resources constraints. For each group, the author lists and specifies in detail several basic constraints.

• E. Yourdon (2003), *Death March, 2nd Edition*, Prentice Hall.

  This book is one of the software engineering and project management classics, which, although not being technologically completely up-to-date now, discusses timeless traps of software project management. The author discusses reasons for software projects being what it calls "death march" projects; that is, projects that are sentenced to fail from the very beginning because of their unrealistic set up. Typical symptoms of a "death march" project are: (1) schedule, budget, and staff are about half of what would be necessary, (2) planned product scope is unrealistic, and (3) people are working 14 h a day, 6 or 7 days a week. Author suggests a number of useful solutions to avoid and, if this is not an option, to rescue death march projects.

• S. McConnell (1997), *Software Project Survival Guide, 1st Edition*, Microsoft Press.

  The book provides a set of guidelines on how to successfully perform software projects. For each major stage of software development, the author refers to the most common weaknesses that software projects typically face and discusses ways of addressing them in order to successfully get through the project.

• T. DeMarco and T. Lister (1999), *Peopleware: Productive Projects and Teams, 2nd Edition*, Dorset House Publishing Company, Inc., p. 245.

  This book discusses human aspects of software engineering. Authors show that the primary issues of software development are human, not technical.

• F. P. Brooks (1995), *The Mythical Man-Month: Essays on Software Engineering, Anniversary Edition, 2nd Edition*, Addison-Wesley Professional.

  This book discusses human aspects of software engineering. Fred Brooks makes a simple conjecture that an intellectual job, such as software development, is completely different from physical labor jobs, such as traditional manufacturing—although both jobs may be human-intensive. Using this assumption, the author discusses in a number of short essays people- and team-related aspects of software development projects. The book discusses many important issues of managing human resources, such as work environment, team building, and organizational learning. Finally, the author outlines important pitfalls of managing software projects and development teams and suggests a number of interesting solutions to these pitfalls.

- J. E. Tomayko and O. Hazzan (2004), *Human Aspects of Software Development*, Charles River Media Inc., p.338.

  The authors devote their book to software engineering as a human-intensive activity. They discuss a number of social and cognitive aspects of software engineering such as teamwork, customer–developer relationships, and learning processes in software development.

- T. DeMarco (1982), *Controlling Software Projects: Management, Measurement, and Estimates*, Prentice Hall.

  This book is another software engineering and project management classic. It discusses timeless aspects of managing software projects on the basis of quantitative information. The author devotes three out of four parts to project estimation and measurement. The first part of the book addresses the issue of project estimation as a key element of project control. The author discusses the typical challenges of estimation and shows examples of how to implement successful estimation processes within a software organization.

- Project Management Institute, Inc. (2013), *A Guide to the Project Management Body of Knowledge (PMBOK® Guide), 5th Edition*.

  The PMBOK provides a collection of best practices on professional project management. The body of knowledge presented in the book includes well-recognized and widely applied project management processes and associated techniques. Among other project management processes, the PMBOK provides standard procedures and guidelines regarding project estimation. Moreover, relationships of estimation to other project management processes are well illustrated and comprehensively explained.

- S. Berkun (2008), *Making Things Happen: Mastering Project Management*, *Revised Edition*, O'Reilly Media.

  This book is a collection of essays, each of which addresses selected aspects of project management. The essays are organized around three major project aspects: plans, skills, and management. For each, it discusses key success criteria, associated challenges, and best-practice solutions. Moreover, he illustrates issues with a number of real-life examples.

- M. Lopp (2012), *Managing Humans: Biting and Humorous Tales of a Software Engineering Manager, 2nd Edition*, Apress.

  The book comprises a number of essays devoted to the subject of managing humans and work activities in software development projects. He discusses typical behaviors of managers and engineers, and typical problems of interactions between these two groups of project members. The author specifies, in a very expressive manner, the skills a manager should possess to deal with these issues in everyday life. For each challenge, the author sketches an example situation and suggests best-practice solutions.

- S. McConnell (2006), *Software Estimation: Demystifying the Black Art*, Microsoft Press.

  In the first chapter of his book, McConnell presents his view on what constitutes a "good estimate." He starts with two basic aspects: (1) distinguishing between estimates, plans, and bids and (2) accounting for estimation uncertainty and considering estimates in probabilistic terms. Next, he takes a critical look at the common definitions of good estimates dominated by estimation accuracy perspective.

Principles of Effort and Cost Estimation

2

Plans are nothing; planning is everything.
—Dwight D. Eisenhower (quoting 19th-century Prussian General Helmuth von Moltke)

One of the reasons for failed estimates is an insufficient background of estimators in the area of software estimation. Arbitrary selection and the blind usage of estimation methods and tools often lead to disappointing outcomes, while the underlying reasons remain unclear. In discussions with corporate management, it is not uncommon to hear the phrase "think of a number and multiply by three." Deliberate decisions regarding the particular estimation method and its knowledgeable use require insight into the principles of effort estimation.

In this chapter, we introduce the basic methodological concepts of software effort estimation. We introduce basic terminology and characterize typical estimation stakeholders. Next, we describe the typical context of software effort estimation and associated aspects of optimizing software project scope and resources. Further, we summarize typical purposes of effort estimation met in practice, and we sketch a basic estimation process including its primary inputs and outputs. Finally, we overview the project estimation life cycle and illustrate components of project effort estimation.

2.1   Basic Concepts of Effort Estimation

An estimate is the most optimistic prediction that has a non-zero probability of coming true. Accepting this definition leads irrevocably toward a method called what's-the-earliest-date-by-which-you-can't-prove-you-won't-be-finished estimating. What's a better definition for "estimate"? An estimate is a prediction that is equally likely to be above and below the actual result.

—Tom DeMarco

A. Trendowicz and R. Jeffery, *Software Project Effort Estimation*,
DOI 10.1007/978-3-319-03629-8_2, © Springer International Publishing Switzerland 2014

2.1.1   Basic Terminology

Software effort estimation is often confused with project planning and bidding. These processes, although related to one another through overlapping activities, differ with respect to their objectives and the outputs they are supposed to deliver.

Tip

▶ Do not commit to estimates as internal project targets and do not provide them to customers as bids. Use estimates as a basis for creating internal project targets; that is, realistic estimates, increased by contingency reserves needed for dealing with anticipated project risks. Use targets as a basis for bidding processes.

Estimate

Project Management Institute (2013) defines the estimation objective as providing an approximation (estimate) of the amount of the resources needed to complete project activities and to deliver outputs—products or services—of specified functional and nonfunctional characteristics.

Traditionally, an estimate is considered in deterministic terms, that is, as a single value. In order to account for inherent estimation uncertainty, range estimates are alternatively proposed. Instead of a single effort value, estimates are represented by a range and/or distribution of possible effort values. In order to account for estimation uncertainty, known project risks, such as little domain experience of the development team, are taken into account. Point estimates often implicitly incorporate acceptable project risk as they are derived from range estimates through discretization. Traditionally, an estimate is considered in deterministic terms, that is, as a single value. But as DeMarco suggests, using an estimate that represents "the most optimistic prediction that has a non-zero probability of coming true" may, in practice, have fatal consequences. Uncritically selecting the most optimistic prediction may easily result in running a software project into high risk of over-running initial estimates. In the light of practical experiences, estimates should rather be defined as the predictions with highest probability of becoming true instead of the most optimistic ones. In the case of projects that are considered very risky, estimates should even be "biased" toward pessimistic predictions that have nonzero probability of coming true. For example, PMI (2103) recommends explicit inclusion of contingency and management reserves in order to account for known and unknown risks, respectively. In order to account for inherent estimation uncertainty, range estimates are alternatively proposed. Instead of a single effort value, estimates are represented by a range and/or distribution of possible effort values.

Tip

▶ Estimates should always be represented as a range of possible values. If a point estimate is required, it should represent the prediction that has the highest probability of coming true.

Scope

In project management (PMI 2013), *scope* may refer to

- *Product scope*: the features and functions that characterize the product, service, or result and/or
- *Project scope*: the work that needs to be accomplished to deliver the product, service, or result with the specified features and functions.

In software engineering, adjusting project scope in response to scarce project resources typically refers to reducing the product scope by cutting the functionality of a delivered software product. In consequence, the project scope is automatically reduced by the activities needed to deliver the excluded functionality. The project scope can also be indirectly reduced through reducing software quality in that specific quality assurance activities are not performed; this saves required project resources but decreases the quality of resulting software products.

Target

The objective of internal project planning is to set up a target for the resources needed to complete project activities. Such a target is also commonly referred to as project budget—although it does not refer to money but to effort. Project target represents an ***internal commitment*** and consists of estimated resources increased by so-called contingency reserves[1] (PMI 2013). These reserves are resources, such as effort, that are used at the discretion of the project manager to deal with anticipated but not certain events—"known unknowns." Contingency reserves typically cover rare events that are not included in the project plan or its work breakdown structure because under usual project conditions, they are very unlikely to occur. Examples of such events are loss of critical project staff or collapse of subcontractor's business. A realistic project plan should always have room in it for unforeseen events. Project managers should anticipate possible risks, evaluate their

---

[1] Note that in addition to *contingency reserves* for addressing impacts of anticipated project risks, PMI (2013) recommends planning *management reserves* to cover unforeseen risks and changes to the project. Both contingency and management reserve are included in the target.

impact on effort, and adjust project plans appropriately. Yet, they should take care not to double-count risks by considering them in both estimation and project planning. During estimation, project managers should consider the uncertainty of estimated values or the impact that known environmental factors may have on effort. Estimates of resources will be available to a project manager during the project, independent of anticipated project risks. During project planning, on the other hand, project managers assign each identified risk with specific resources (contingency reserves) needed for dealing with risks in case they occur. Contingency reserves may then be utilized only if the risk to which they are assigned occurs.

Tip

▶ When preparing estimates and project targets, remember not to double-count the same risks. Consider them either during estimation, by means of uncertainty, or during project planning, by means of contingency reserves.

Identifying targets that have potentially been set up already for a project is one of the essential aspects of project estimation. When asked for estimates, we should first establish whether any project targets have already been defined—for example, based on the customer's preferences. If this is the case, "estimation" may in fact mean figuring out how to fit the project to the target—especially when, for a given project scope, the target imposed upon the project is smaller than any realistic estimate.

Tip

▶ When you are asked to provide an estimate, make sure you are aware of any target already specified—especially when the target is smaller than any reasonable estimate for a given project scope. In such a case, "estimating" will actually mean determining how to meet the target.

In practice, targets—if actually predefined—and estimates should be aligned in an iterative process, with both being subject to potential adjustments. Adjusting estimates does not mean manipulating them to fit targets—particularly if they are unrealistic. It means adjusting project-related factors affecting effort. In the first instance, project characteristics such as team capabilities or tool support should be optimized—to the extent feasible—in order to improve development productivity and thus reduce effort. If adjusting the project characteristics does not bring the expected effect, then modifying the project scope, that is, the functionality and quality of the project's work products, may be necessary. Each time we adjust the project scope, we need to repeat the estimation in order to prove that we are still aligned with the project target. But adjusting a project is not always possible, particularly when the project scope is also fixed by a customer and is not subject to negotiation. In such cases, the targets must be adjusted; otherwise, we face what Yourdon (2003) calls a *death march project*: a project that is destined to fail, with the probability being proportional to the discrepancy between targets and realistic estimates. In one large financial organization where we worked, there was a business manager who regularly set the target for developers at half their calculated point estimate with the words "take it as a challenge."

Tip

▶ If there are predefined targets, perform estimation as an iterative process in which targets and estimates are aligned by negotiating other components of the project. For a fixed project target, try negotiating the project scope. Alternatively, the project's environment characteristics that have an impact on development productivity may be adjusted appropriately in order to meet the target.

Bid

The objective of bidding is to agree on the project resources with external contractors of a software product or service. Bids typically rest on a point value and refer to the software product price and project duration offered externally.

Tip

▶ Typically, we don't need an accurate estimate; we need an accurate commitment (Armour 2008). Yet, it is always worth trying to be fair and propose to customers a range of bids that reflect the inherent project's uncertainty. If a customer is not willing to accept such "imprecise" range bids, then you still can give a "precise" one taken from a range that accounts for project risks and profits.

Bids include the internal target and profit, where profit might also be considered in nonfinancial terms. Kitchenham et al. (2003, 2005) note, for example, that in a competitive situation, the lowest compliant bid typically wins the contract. In consequence, knowledge of the extent and capability of competitors usually affects—at least to some extent—the pricing decision represented by the bid. A company may, for example, decide to take on a project below the planned cost in order to win a contract and expand its market share by gaining a new customer.

Work Plan vs. Commitment Plan

Armour (2005) points out that the difference between internal and external commitments is so important that it should be natural to prepare two project plans, one each for internal and external commitment. He calls them work plan and commitment plan, respectively.

Work plan reflects the resources the project will need according to internal estimates and targets, based on incomplete knowledge of the project and risks

(continued)

Work Plan vs. Commitment Plan (continued)

anticipated at the time the work plan is created. This corresponds to what is traditionally understood under the project plan and is what the project team works with. For example, a work plan includes uncertainty about the skill level of the team or the potential risk of losing critical team members during the project. Such internal issues are typically not presented to the customer.

Commitment plan is the plan presented to the customer. It incorporates the work plan plus a contingency buffer to account for uncertainty at the time of creating the commitment plan. This uncertainty may have a number of different sources: On the one hand, incomplete knowledge of the project environment; on the other hand, known and unknown risks accounted for through contingency and management reserves (PMI 2013).

As pointed out by Armour (2008), in practice, it may not really matter if we can provide an accurate point estimate. What matters is that we can provide an accurate commitment. In other words, it is important that we can commit ourselves to a certain amount of resources and that we are aware of the risk of exceeding these resources. From this perspective, commitment is the point on the estimate probability distribution curve which we promise to the customer.

Summarizing, a bid represents a combination of three elements: estimated cost, contingency margin, and profit. It represents an *external commitment*, that is, a commitment to an external project stakeholder, such as a contractor.

Tip

▶ Commitments are negotiable. Estimates are not negotiable. If a fixed bid or target is less than the estimate, then other project constraints such as functionality and quality should be adjusted.

Actual

Actual is the true value of the project resources that are actually needed to successfully complete project activities. Actual resources are known after project completion.

Estimates vs. Target vs. Bid

The practical consequences of confusing estimates, targets, and bids are unrealistic internal and external project commitments, which lead to failed projects. One of the common sources of such a situation is a lack of estimation/planning competencies and conflicts of interest between project stakeholders.

For example, typical software developers tend to be relatively young and, although having software project competence, they do not have much decisive power. On the other hand, although lacking software project knowledge, sales personnel or business managers tend to have more decisive power than developers. In consequence, developers fit their estimates to—often unrealistic—expectations of a sales department or business manager.

Although in this book we focus on estimates, keep the aforementioned differences in mind in order to avoid confusion when estimating and when using estimates for creating project budgets and bids.

Tip

▶ Do not allow a sales department to provide estimates for software projects instead of developers.

2.1.2 Effort Estimation Stakeholders

As for any project activity, there are a number of individuals that have interests in effort estimation. We distinguish several roles associated with effort estimation, depending on their stakes and exact involvement:

- *Estimation Process Owner*: This role is responsible for introducing and maintaining estimation processes, methods, models, and data within an organization. This person has in-depth knowledge of the estimation method and manages estimation initiatives and activities within the organization. The estimation process owner is typically a dedicated full-time position within an organization.
- *Estimator*: This role uses estimation methods and models existing within an organization for estimating particular development projects. A project manager, who estimates and manages projects, typically plays the role of the estimator.
- *Domain expert*: This role provides input information for building an estimation model when measurement data are missing or insufficient. Domain experts should be knowledgeable in project effort dependencies within the context for which the effort estimation method is applied. Domain experts do not have to be knowledgeable in effort estimation. They should have a basic understanding of estimation and know which factors and to what extent they influence effort in the project, within this context. In the case of estimation based on human judgment, however, domain experts play the role of estimators and thus should be additionally knowledgeable in project effort estimation.
- *Decision maker*: This role represents other project stakeholders who are not directly involved in the estimation process but who have the power to affect the project, including the performance of estimation. For example, a project owner (also referred to as a project sponsor) may place pressure on estimators with respect to project resources and thus bias estimates. An example of this situation from practice might be a Scrum planning meeting (Rubin 2012) during which a

powerful product owner biases estimates of the Scrum team. In the extreme case, it is enough that the product owner raises an eyebrow or shakes his/her head and the Scrum team then bias their estimates in order to please the product owner.

In reality, the role of the estimation process owner and the estimator is often played by the same person who is then responsible for both effort modeling and estimation.

2.2   Effort Estimation in Context

Early in the project you can have firm cost and schedule targets or a firm feature set, but not both.

—Steve McConnell

2.2.1 Project Equilibrium Triangles

A typical question that software project managers need to answer is how to provide a product of required functionality and acceptable quality with limited resources? In Fig. 2.1, this project management dilemma is illustrated by means of two so-called project equilibrium triangles.

The project scope triangle represents a trade-off between project outputs and inputs. The three competing objectives are: software functionality, software quality, and resources needed to accomplish the former two. The resources triangle represents a trade-off between project resources, namely, staffing, duration, and effort.

For example, if the customer requires project completion within a fixed effort and/or duration, then the overall project equilibrium can be accomplished through affecting other dimensions, that is, staffing within the resources triangle and/or functionality and quality within the scope triangle.

A key to project success is to achieve equilibrium in both scope and resource triangles. The element that connects the project scope and resources is productivity, traditionally defined as a ratio of project outputs to its inputs. One practical consequence is that depending on productivity, the same project scope may require different amounts and abilities of resources, and vice versa, the same amount of resources may deliver different amounts of functionality and quality.

The exact trade-offs within and between project scope and resource triangles depend on the particular project context, which consists of multiple environmental characteristics, called context factors. Example context factors are capabilities of involved personnel or technologies employed (for a detailed discussion of context factors, refer to Sect. 3.1).

Project Staffing, Duration, Time, and Budget

Staffing refers to the number of persons required to complete a certain project work, task, or activity. The unit of staffing is the number of persons. As we discuss in the subsequent paragraphs of this chapter, the magnitude of staffing is closely related to, and depends on, the time and effort planned for the work.

Duration refers to the <u>total elapsed time</u> needed to complete a particular work, <u>including nonproductive time</u> such as breaks, holidays, and sick leave. Typical units for project duration are hours, days, months, or years. For example, one person may need 5 days to complete a task that requires 5 h of fully productive work, because the person can work on the task for only 1 h per day.

Effort is a combination of person and time. It refers to the amount of <u>fully productive work time</u> one person would need to complete a certain work. If multiple persons work on the same task, each for different amounts of fully productive time, then the total work effort is computed by summing the working time for all persons. Typical units of work effort are person-hours, person-days, person-months, and—for large projects—person-years. For example, if completing a certain work task requires three persons working on it for 5 h each, then the total work effort for this task will be three persons multiplied by 5 h of productive work per person, which equals 15 person-hours of effort. In practice, time is often confused with duration (elapsed time). In consequence, task duration is often estimated as a direct derivative of the estimated effort, which is required for completing the task. This would be correct under the assumption that all task activities were performed one after another, without breaks, by equally performing personnel. Project management practice teaches that project duration is a derivative of a task's effort and staffing with consideration of dependencies between task activities, availability and performance of personnel assigned to tasks, project scheduling, and additional internal and external project constraints. Since effort, persons, time, and duration are interrelated, in practice, planning project duration is an iterative process that starts from initial effort estimates and continues with scheduling work tasks, assigning resources, and computing task duration. If the performance of the assigned human resources differs from that assumed initially, or the resulting task duration is not acceptable, then the initial effort estimate needs to be revised, and the planning cycle must be repeated.

Budget refers to the amount of money available for project realization. Besides this monetary meaning, the term budget is also used to refer to the project target, that is, to the total amount of effort needed to complete project activities.

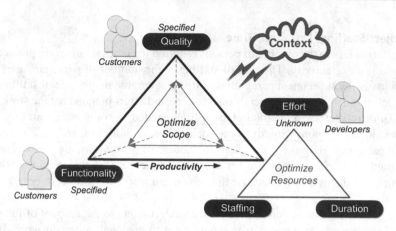

Fig. 2.1 Project equilibrium triangles

Tip

▶ "Projects must meet the needs of customers and users in order to be successful. It
is possible to meet budget and time goals but still be unsuccessful if customer
needs have not been met." [Anonymous]

In industrial practice, two project optimization situations typically take place.
Figure 2.1 may illustrate a so-called *fixed-scope project*, in which the contractor
specifies—at a more or less fixed level—functionality and quality the software
project should deliver. Project resources are then estimated to meet the project
scope objectives defined by the contractor. In a *fixed-budget project*, on the other
hand, the contractor specifies one or more project resources—typically project
duration or cost, or both. In this case, the project scope—functionality and quality—
needs to be optimized to meet the fixed resource requirements. In fixed-scope
projects, if the contractor does not specify any particular requirements concerning
the level of effort, staffing, and duration, the provider may decide about specific
trade-offs between these three aspects of software project resources (as represented
by the small triangle in Fig. 2.1). Typically, a provider estimates project effort first
and then, based on the available human resources (staffing), determines a reasonable project duration. In fixed-budget projects, where the contractor determines the
cost and/or duration of the project, the basic strategy of the provider is to optimize
project scope (functionality and quality) in order to fit predefined resources (large
triangle in Fig. 2.1). Yet, a provider may additionally optimize the detailed project
resources (small triangle in Fig. 2.1). The scope of possible optimization between
effort, staffing, and duration depends to a large extent on (1) whether a contractor
fixes only one or both cost and duration aspects and (2) whether cost has been
expressed in monetary terms or effort. If only one aspect, duration or cost, is fixed,
the other can be adjusted by appropriately adjusting staffing level on the project. If
fixed cost is expressed in monetary terms, then a provider has the additional

possibility of adjusting project effort (i.e., variable cost) by manipulating the fixed cost of the project, for instance, infrastructure costs. In some cases, typically public projects, a contractor fixes cost in terms of effort. In this situation, the provider has less room for optimization within the small triangle (Fig. 2.1).

Tip

▶ Before starting estimation, determine first if you are expected to estimate project resources for a fixed project scope (product's functionality & quality) or to estimate the feasible project scope to fit fixed (target) project resources.

Release planning is an example of optimizing the project scope to fixed resources in the context of incremental or multirelease software development. The goal of release planning is to optimally distribute product functionalities—at required quality—throughout a sequence of development projects of limited size in terms of effort or duration. Priorities assigned by a contractor to individual software functionalities and interdependencies between functionalities are additional constraints to release planning. Each project is optimized by maximizing benefit in terms of the product's functionality and quality within acceptable cost—effort or duration.

2.2.2   Optimizing Project Resources Triangle

As John Boddie noticed, "Everybody wants things good, wants them fast, and wants them cheap. Everyone knows you can actually achieve any two of the three." Software engineering is not different. People expect software of high quality, available quickly, and at low budget. The resources equilibrium triangle in Fig. 2.1 represents the inherent association between project effort, staffing, and duration. Based on multiple industrial experiences, the relationship between software development effort, staffing, and duration forms a bell-shaped curve. Particular functional forms used for modeling staffing distributions are represented by Rayleigh (Norden 1958; Putnam and Myers 2003), Gamma (Pillai and Nair 1997), or Parr's (Parr 1980) curves. One of the practical consequences of the effort-staffing-duration relationship is that after fixing the functional and nonfunctional scope of a software product, one of the project resources may still be affected—at least to some extent—by manipulating other resources. For example, for a fixed project scope, we may adjust development effort by affecting project staffing level and/or its duration.

Figure 2.2 illustrates example distributions of staffing across the software life cycle in two different types of projects. The solid curve represents a so-called build-quality-in type of project where major effort is spent in early development phases, such as requirements specification and design. The main purpose of focusing project effort in its early phases is to avoid rework during its later phases such as

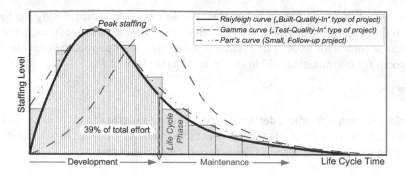

Fig. 2.2 Distribution of software life cycle staffing

verification, validation, and maintenance. Observations from practice show that defect prevention is much less expensive than rework. Moreover, the longer the time span between injecting a defect and reworking it, the more effort it takes to correct (Boehm and Basili 2001). For example, it is observed that finding and fixing a software problem after delivery is often 100 times more expensive than finding and fixing it during the requirements and design phase. The dashed curve is a test-quality-in type of project, in which little effort is spent on early development phases, which typically results in major rework overhead during later project phases such as verification, validation, and early maintenance. Finally, the dash-dotted line represents projects for which some staff are already working at the beginning of the project. One such case would be a follow-up project where some work has already begun in the previous project.

How to Interpret the Staffing Curve? The staffing curves represent time-sensitive effort models, that is, effort models that represent the effect of trading off project staffing against project time and effort You may agree with particular shapes of the staffing curves or consider them as mathematically and practically bizarre. Yet, you need to remember that they only represent empirical observations that authors have made in particular contexts and tried to approximate with mathematical equations. But these curves do not necessarily correspond to your specific project environment. Thus, as with any other fixed-model approach to effort estimation, staffing curves should not be reused uncritically, without adapting them to the particular context. They can and should, however, be considered as representing universally true consequences of staffing-time-effort trade-offs.

The Rayleigh and Parr's curves represent multiple observations from practice. They suggest that investments in software quality assurance practices in the early stages of a software development process contribute to increased overall project performance, that is, efficiency and effectiveness of development activities (e.g., Wang et al. 2008).

Tip

▶ One of the essential practical consequences of the effort-staffing-time dependency
   is that without the appropriate resources available on time, the project is actually
   doomed to fail.

Time-Effort Trade-Offs

Independent of the assumed functional form of the project staffing distribution,
effort, time, and staffing levels always stay in a close dependency with each other.
In other words, you cannot manipulate one of these parameters without affecting
others—an eye must always be kept on the trade-off between these three. One
practical consequence of this observation is that there is no single pair of effort-
time values for developing a software product of a given functionality and quality
within an organization with certain productivity of the development process.
In other words, we may choose from among multiple options of effort-duration
pairs, which create a curve of the project effort-time trade-offs. Yet, although we
may expect so, the curve does not represent a straight line, but is nonlinear. This also
means that the effort area under the staffing curve in Fig. 2.2 does not remain
constant, although it may seem so at first glance. In practice, effort may increase
as the time is compressed through putting more staff into the project. This loss in
process productivity is caused by a factor Ross (2008) calls *management stress*.
In essence, management stress comprises constraints on a software development
process with respect to increasing levels of project staffing. In software development
practice, several project characteristics are used to indicate management stress. The
most common are size of the project measured in terms of size of its deliverables or
size of the project team. All of these indicators are, however, proxies for the amount
of project coordination and communication. The inevitable overhead associated
with project coordination and communication is the main factor responsible for
increasing effort as project staffing increases, for example, to shorten project
schedule. Wang (2007a, b) expresses this effect formally in his law of work coordination. In the research carried out by He Zhang (2008), it was shown that variation in
staff assimilation rates on a project when new staff are added will either cause the
project to finish later, finish earlier, or not impact the completion time. The critical
factor is the rate at which staff can be successfully and productively assimilated.

The solid line in Fig. 2.3 illustrates the management stress phenomenon by
example using the functional form[2] of the effort-schedule dependency observed
by Putnam and Myers (2003) and Jensen (1983). We have extended these observations (dotted line) by the hypothesized effects of extremely low project staffing.

Minimum project time represents minimum development time achieved by
putting maximal reasonable staffing into the project, that is, staffing that shortens

---

[2] In practice, other functional forms of the effort-schedule dependency are possible.

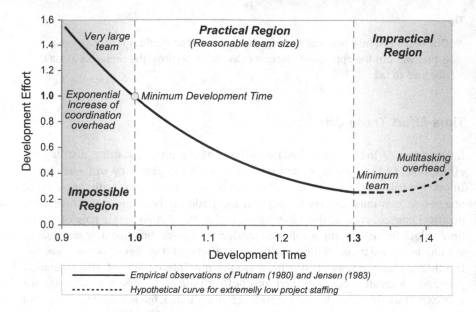

Fig. 2.3 Effort-time trade-off for a given project size and process productivity

project time with an acceptable increase in the project effort overhead needed to coordinate work. Project coordination comprises such aspects as team communication or simultaneous work on multiple project tasks.

Impractical region represents the situation where project staffing is reduced beyond a minimal reasonable level, such as one person per independent work item. Periods of effective work in the project in this case will be much shorter compared to time spent outside the project. The time required for switching back to the project is in this case relatively large compared to the very short duration of effective project work. In consequence, the large overhead for multitasking will again be disproportional to potential gains in project duration. Moreover, reducing the project team may require that one person is assigned to multiple work items, some s/he has little experience with. This would cause further productivity loss and increase of overall project effort.

Impossible region represents the situation where increasing project staffing—team size—entails an increase in project coordination overhead that is disproportional to gains in project duration. In other words, reduction in project time does not compensate for an enormous increase in project effort overhead. A critical consequence of this observation is that one cannot compress estimated, reasonable schedules indefinitely by simply putting additional resources into the project without increasing development effort.

Tip

▶ Never shorten a schedule estimate without considering the resulting possible increase in effort.

For example, if 10 developers can create a software product within 10 months, can 100 developers deliver the same product within 1 month, or can 2,000 developers do it within 1 day? Probably not, and there are several reasons why it is impossible in practice. For example,

- Larger teams require more overhead for work coordination and management.
- Larger teams increase complexity of communication paths, which not only require more communication overhead but also increase the chance of miscommunication.
- Shorter project durations require more work to be done in parallel, which is not always possible and increases the chance that some products are based on incomplete or erroneous components—thus increasing the amount of rework.

The negative effect of increasing a team in order to shorten the project schedule is even more severe if we add people during the project runtime, especially when the project is already late. Such attempts to rescue late projects may in practice have a totally opposite effect. Brooks (1995) addresses this phenomenon in a law (so-called *Brook's Law*), which says that adding new personnel to a late project makes it even later. In this case, we need to consider the extra overhead for introducing new staff into the already running project—in addition to the overhead on communication and coordinating parallel tasks within a larger team. When introducing new staff into the project, project performance suffers in two ways: (1) team members need a certain effort to introduce new staff into project activities and (2) team members who introduce new staff cannot work on the project activities at that time. As mentioned above, the effect will depend on the staff assimilation rate.

Summarizing, there are several practical implications of the effort-time trade-off. First, there is an impractical effort-time region representing an extremely slow project. An extremely stretched schedule does not make economic sense in practice because the delivery time is too long to be accepted by a customer, compared to possible cost savings. Moreover, there is an impossible effort-time region representing an extremely fast project.

Tip

▶ In practice, planning to operate with a smaller development team over a longer project schedule gives better results in terms of product quality than planning a larger team over a shorter schedule.

Wang (2007a, b) formally formulated empirical observations of the time-effort-staffing trade-offs in his laws of work coordination, which we summarize briefly in Table 2.1. For a detailed discussion of the laws and rationale behind them, refer to Wang (2007a, Sect. 8.5) or Wang (2007b).

Table 2.1 Wang's laws of work coordination

Law	Definition
The law of coordinative effort in engineering	The actual effort of a coordinated project is a product of effort needed to complete the work by one person (ideal effort) and the effort overhead needed for interpersonal coordination of the complete project team
	The coordination overhead is the product of the interpersonal coordination rate for individual team members and the number of pairwise coordination interactions among all team members
	Finally, the interpersonal coordination rate of an individual team member is an average ratio of the time the person spends on interpersonal coordination activities and the total working time of the person in a given project
The law of incompressibility of effort	In cooperative work, a given ideal project effort—that is, the effort one person would need to complete the project—cannot be compressed by any kind of staff allocation. This indicates that
	• The duration of the project may be reduced via cooperative work of multiple personnel, but the total effort cannot be reduced below the minimum effort a person would require to complete the project
	• The total effort in any type of cooperative staff allocation will be larger than the minimum effort
The law of interchangeability of labor and time	For a given effort, staffing and duration are transformable. This law indicates that the duration of a cooperative project is a function of staffing and the interpersonal cooperation rate for the given project
Law of the shortest duration of cooperative work	There exists the shortest duration under the optimum allocation of staff for a given ideal project effort with a certain interpersonal cooperation rate

In general, there are a number of other ways to shorten project duration besides assigning additional staff to the project. Most, if not all of them, boil down to improving performance of an existing project team. Example means to achieve this include introducing additional tool support or improving software development or project management methods and processes. However, we need to keep in mind that every organizational change, even though it should contribute to long-term performance gains, requires investment, which typically results in a short-term performance drop.

Effort-Time Trade-Off for Interdependent Work Tasks

In project management practice, dealing with effort-time trade-offs is quite complex and involves more aspects than simply effort, duration, and staffing. In reality, software projects consist of multiple, mutually interrelated work tasks. In consequence, project duration is a function of individual task durations and their distribution—scheduling—within the whole project.

Total project duration can thus be affected not only by manipulating the duration of individual work tasks but also by the way these tasks are distributed within the project. Yet, a number of nuances need to be considered before playing with project effort-time trade-offs. For example, we may want to affect project duration by changing the duration of individual work tasks. For this purpose, we manipulate staff assigned to selected work tasks, that is, we affect their duration at the expense of changed effort. Now, if these individual work tasks are not located on the project's critical path, then the manipulations will likely not have any effect on total project duration—although it will affect the total project effort.

Potential project resource manipulations—either on individual work tasks or on their distribution within the project—are limited by a number of project constraints. One of the most relevant constraints includes project internal and external restrictions on the sequence and timeline of project work tasks. External to the project, the sequence of work tasks or their exact point in time may be determined by customer-defined project deadlines or by the availability of external inputs or resources. Internal to the project, the sequence of work tasks is typically limited by the availability of intermediate project outcomes and the availability of shared project resources.

Therefore, using a simple functional form curve for dealing with effort-time trade-offs within a project that consists of multiple interrelated tasks might lead to failed estimates. In such a case, the project manager needs to additionally consider a number of project aspects such as constraints on task scheduling.

2.3   Objectives of Effort Estimation

Methods and means cannot be separated from the ultimate aim.

—Emma Goldman

Software effort estimation has been traditionally associated with simply planning the amount of resources required for completing project activities. Recently, however, software practitioners require effort estimation to support them with a number of project decision-making tasks. It is a very important aspect of effort estimation that should be kept in mind when selecting an appropriate effort estimation approach.

From a short-term perspective—a single project—effort estimation should provide comprehensive decision support for managing project risks, whereas from a long-term perspective—multiple projects—it should guide process improvement initiatives aimed at increasing efficiency of work. Simultaneous to any newly arising estimation objectives, there is also continuous pressure to improve the cost-effectiveness of estimation itself. In practice, software decision-makers require estimation and planning not to take more than say about 5 % of the total project effort.

In the next few paragraphs, we summarize briefly the most common objectives of effort estimation followed in the software industry.

2.3.1 Managing and Reducing Project Risks

A common observation in the software industry is that project management decisions often fail because effort estimation methods do not provide sufficient insight into resource-related sources of project risks (Charette 2005, Jones 2006, Cerpa and Verner 2009). Project managers need to know not only, say, that a project is going to overrun an agreed budget—typically based on simple resource estimation—but they also require insight into potential causes of project overruns in order to timely and effectively mitigate the related project risks. For instance, studies performed by Jørgensen and Sjøberg (2001, 2004) as well as by Kitchenham et al. (2005) underlined the essential role of early and accurately identifying relevant factors influencing software development productivity and project effort—commonly referred to as *effort drivers*. It was observed that driven by irrelevant information, software managers tend to provide inaccurate estimates and fail to effectively justify and negotiate project cost and scope. When project target and bids are accepted based upon unrealistic estimates, they have a negative impact on the quality of project work—due to tight schedules and budget shortages.

Effort estimation is thus required to provide transparent information on relevant effort drivers and their mutual relationships in order to support decision-makers in understanding what may go wrong, why it may go wrong, and what can be done to prevent it.

A systematic estimation method should force project managers and the project team to critically review completeness and consistency of available project information. It is also required to bring together various project stakeholders, representing different knowledge, perspectives, and interests, for the purpose of identifying information that would not probably be identified otherwise. Information considered during the estimation process should include such aspects as software functionality and quality, internal and external project constraints, and assumptions that need to be made implicitly because actual project knowledge is missing.

It is important that there is a mutual connection between project estimation and risk management. On the one side, effort estimation should provide information on potential project risks. On the other side, it should use outcomes of other risk analysis activities as part of the input to project estimates. Since uncertain and incomplete information is an inherent source of risk in software project management, effort estimation is expected to handle it. In Sect. 4.4, we discuss in more detail handling estimation uncertainty.

2.3.2 Process Improvement and Organizational Learning

Software development is characterized by human-intensive processes and rapid technological advances. This means that successful software projects, like in any other domain, require continuous process improvement and organizational learning.

Industrial experiences gained by Jørgensen et al. (2002) and Jørgensen (2004a) show limited ability of software organizations to learn from estimation experience. Typically, the most probable effort is estimated at the project beginning and compared against the actual effort at the project end. If the estimated most likely effort deviates from the actual one, software practitioners usually do not learn more than that they were wrong. From this perspective, information on effort-related risks provided as output of effort estimation across multiple projects forms a basis for determining critical process deficiencies and learning from experience. For example, a recurrent negative influence of poor team qualifications on increased development effort may be an indicator of poor team selection and/or team training processes. Yet, comparing risks identified in different projects requires that they can be compared. In order to ensure comparability across projects, we must consider explicitly their environment. It is thus particularly important that a potential effort estimation approach not only provides information on relevant effort drivers but also explicitly considers critical characteristics of a project context. Finally, when talking about learning and improvement, we must remember that effort estimation itself is a part of organizational processes and, as such, is subject to learning and improvement. Therefore, an estimation method should support improving the overall estimation process and the method itself, for instance, by identifying the causes of poor estimates.

2.3.3   Baselining and Benchmarking Productivity

In industrial practice, software decision-makers often require a reliable basis for managing development productivity. Example productivity management activities include establishing productivity baselines, identifying productivity improvement potentials, or comparing a project's productivity against baselines or against other projects. Improving productivity is a critical aspect of successful software projects, not only because it implies reduction in project effort, but also because of its indirect impact on the quality of delivered software products. As shown in the most recent industrial survey of Emam and Koru (2008), between 24 % and 34 % of software projects are considered unsuccessful—10–12 % canceled—due to low performance. On the other hand, benchmarking of software projects between different organizations is gaining increasing attention in the context of rapidly growing global development. Comparing a project's performance in the context of software within outsourcing—near- or far-shoring—supports make-or-buy decisions and facilitates choosing between potential software suppliers.

A typical situation in the software engineering domain is the existence of large discrepancies between project contexts—domain, technology, team capabilities, and so on—which results in large variations in development productivity across projects. One of the most critical practical consequences of this fact is that simple software productivity metrics based solely on software size and project effort are hardly comparable. In order to compare productivity, a number of factors influencing productivity must be considered.

As productivity is closely related to software development effort (as illustrated in Sect. 2.5, Fig. 2.5), factors influencing productivity are at the same time factors influencing development effort. Effective management of both development effort and productivity requires considering these factors in an explicit and understandable manner. For example, when benchmarking software projects, we must ensure that we do not compare apples and oranges and that we consider as many factors as possible, which may potentially contribute to the observed productivity discrepancies. In other words, we must ensure that the rationale behind the observed discrepancies is clear. In that sense, effort modeling can potentially support the baselining of productivity, which we can then use for the purpose of benchmarking software projects.

2.3.4 Negotiating Project Resources and Scope

Poor communication among customers, developers, and users during the project bidding phase and during project realization is one of the major sources of troubled and failed software projects. Jørgensen (2004a), for instance, observed that experienced project managers always require justification of cost estimates so that they can be reviewed. Salas (2004) observed that estimates in the context of government/military software acquisition were lacking clear and detailed justification. Moløkken et al. (2004) in their industrial survey observed that besides previous experience with an estimation method, its ability to support justification of project cost was a significant argument to select a certain estimation method. They observed that the proper support for communicating and justifying development costs is a particularly critical success factor in the case of external (outsourced) software projects.

In consequence, price-to-win estimation strategies, demands to cut project costs, as well as political interests lead to unrealistic project schedules and budgets. Yet, effort estimation methods commonly used in the software industry do not support sufficient insight into cost-related factors that would provide a detailed and precise explanation of project estimates. In consequence, software project managers lack sufficient and reliable information for communicating software costs to customers and managers.

2.3.5 Managing Project Changes

Agile software development has recently gained much industrial attention as an alternative to traditional "heavyweight" development processes. Consequently, increased flexibility is expected from the effort estimation process in order to support in software projects organized upon iterative and agile development processes, such as implemented in Scrum (Rubin 2012). This requires, for example, continuous accommodation by an estimation model to the changes in the set of predictive variables and in their relative impact on effort in each development iteration. In addition, there is a need for systematic feedback from the estimation process across development iterations in order to learn about the reasons for potential discrepancies between estimates and effort actually spent in a project.

Finally, as one of the primary reasons for failed software projects is frequent change to project scope, software estimation methods should provide extensive support for managing those changes—in addition to supporting negotiating changes to the project scope. For example, by carrying out function point sizing (e.g., ISO 2005, 2009) at different points during software requirements analysis and design, it is possible to have a quantitative measure of any changes to the project scope (size) that are occurring as the work continues. Note that measuring scope should be a part of the systematic change management process, where the impact of change on the scope (and other project constraints) must be assessed and accepted before it is implemented.

2.3.6 Reducing Management Overhead

Last but not least, one of the primary business objectives of commercial organizations traditionally is minimizing costs. Therefore, software practitioners expect effort estimation not to impose much overhead on the project and development team, for example on average, 6 % of total project cost (Trendowicz 2008, Sect. 2.3).

2.4   Estimation Life Cycle

> *Your task is not to foresee the future, but to enable it.*
> —Antoine de Saint-Exupéry

Following well-defined systematic development processes is considered key to successful software development. Yet, the key role of well-defined and lived project management processes is typically not as obvious nowadays. Too many projects still fail because estimation and planning are treated as a necessary evil and performed in an ad hoc manner. Project managers seem to be oblivious about the existence of estimation processes and their key role in overall project success. In this section, we introduce a basic estimation process and discuss its key elements in the context of associated project management activities.

2.4.1   Defining Estimation Process

Figure 2.4 illustrates an abstract software effort estimation process.

In the *define project* step, a project manager defines the scope of the software project. User requirements regarding the expected development outputs and characteristics of a project environment are the starting points for defining a project's scope. Based on this information, the project manager specifies detailed development

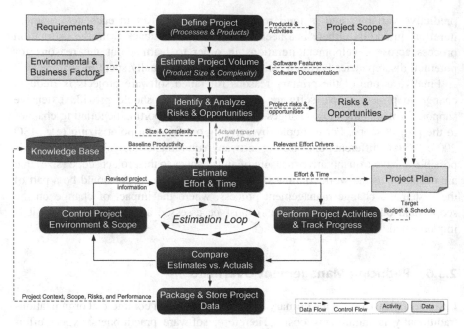

Fig. 2.4 Phases of the estimation life cycle (based on Stutzke 2005)

outputs and required project activities, for example, using the Work Break-down Structure (WBS) technique. In the context of defined organizational processes,[3] project activities—engineering and management—are typically a result of adapting the organizational process to the specific characteristics of the project context. Detailed product definition includes, on the one hand, determining specific functional and nonfunctional features of an expected software system and, on the other hand, specifying additional development deliverables, such as associated software documentation.

In the *estimate project volume* step, the project scope is a basis for estimating the volume of a project, which is typically quantified in terms of size of major development products. Measuring software size is one of the most important and, at the same time, one of the most difficult-to-determine elements of effort estimation (Sect. 2.5). Yet, investing effort for these initial activities pays off through better initial project estimates and reduced risk of project overruns.

Tip

▶ Project environmental factors and expected deliverables are essential determinants of project effort. Remember to invest proper effort to specify these elements thoroughly before starting estimation.

---

[3] For example, starting from level 3 on the SEI's Capability Maturity Model (CMMI 2010).

Even for the same project volume, effort required to complete the project may, and typically does, differ depending on the project context. Therefore, in the next step—*identify & analyze risks & opportunities*—a project manager identifies potential project risks, that is, events that may have a negative or positive impact on project success. Factors having a direct impact on project effort are then considered as effort drivers in the effort estimation.

Risk and Opportunity

Detailed discussion on the project risk management is beyond the scope of this book. Let us only note that risk refers to an event and consists of the probability of an event and its consequences (effect) on a project. In principle, an event may have a negative or positive effect on a project; in the first case, it is referred to as risk, in the latter case, as opportunity.

In the context of effort estimation, only a limited number of the most relevant risks are typically considered. These are risks that are the most probable and have the greatest impact on development effort. In practice, events that are de facto facts about the project environment—100 % probability—are often the inputs to effort estimation. Yet, their exact value may still be uncertain. For example, we may know from the very beginning of the project that low capabilities of the development team will surely have a significant negative impact on project effort; yet, at that point in time, we may still not be sure how low these capabilities will actually be.

Other risks, not considered directly in effort estimation, are usually input for project planning. There, an appropriate response is associated with each risk. Example responses may mean planning actions that help mitigate risk, that is, reducing its probability of occurrence. Another kind of response is planning contingency reserves to the overall project budget to deal with potential consequences of risk, if it occurs. As noted earlier, project managers must be careful not to include the same risk twice in effort estimation (as an effort driver) and in the project plans (as a contingency factor).

Example 2.1. Relation Between Effort Estimation and Risk Management

Let us consider an example project at the beginning of which the project manager identified potentially insufficient domain experience of the development team as a risk to project success. He decided to include the team's domain experience as a relevant effort driver in the effort estimation process.

After quantifying actual domain experience of team members and estimating development effort, it occurred that (1) effort exceeds a customer's acceptable level and (2) low domain experience of the team has the greatest impact on the increase in project effort from among all effort drivers considered. This information is provided back to risk management to plan appropriate response actions. The objective of risk response is to reduce its impact on project effort and thus to ensure that the project will be finished within acceptable effort.

A response to insufficient domain experience may be to involve experienced personnel in the critical phases of software production, such as requirements specification and design.   ■

Estimation loop forms the basic project estimation cycle, in which project resources are estimated, planned, controlled, and revised on a regular basis. The central activity of the estimation cycle is effort and time prediction—*estimate effort & time* step. The objective of this activity is predicting the effort and time required for completing the remaining project work using actual project information. Besides software size and effort drivers, a baseline development productivity observed in similar historical[4] projects is the third fundamental input to effort estimation. Based on these three inputs, development effort is estimated using a particular estimation method. In Sect. 2.5, we sketch and discuss an abstract estimation procedure that represents elements common to most effort estimation methods.

In the *perform project activities & track progress* step, the project manager executes the project plan and monitors the progress of project work and resource consumption against that plan. As the project work progresses, the project manager compares estimates against actual project values and clarifies potential sources of deviations—*compare estimates vs. actuals* step. Discrepancies from the plans and changes to the project scope and environment during the project run time are the basis for project control activities—*control project environment & scope*. Based on the revised information regarding the actual project environment and scope, re-estimation takes place in order to account for potential changes in project environment and scope.

At the project finishes, the project manager stores actual project data such as size, effort, and effort drivers for future estimations—*package & store project data* step. In addition, the project manager analyzes experiences gained with respect to the estimation approach applied and documents these for the purpose of future improvements. For more details on introducing and continuously improving estimation technologies, refer to Chap. 16.

2.4.2 Implementing Estimation Process

In order to properly guide engineering activities, effort estimation needs to be integrated with development processes throughout the whole software life cycle. At the organizational level, the base estimation process and methods must be a part

---

[4] Historical projects are already completed projects, for which actual data on size, effort, and effort drivers are available.

of a defined software engineering—development and management—process. At the project level, estimation, as with any other organization-wide process, potentially requires adjusting to the specific project context.

Tip

▶ Define estimation process as an integral part of standard organization-level project management processes, integrate it into standard development processes, and adjust it to particular projects depending on their specific characteristics.

Finally, even the best process will not bring any effect if it is not "lived," that is, if it is not used for guiding everyday project work. Two crucial prerequisites for "lived" processes are (1) communicating processes to affected project stakeholders and (2) getting their commitment prior to project planning.

Tip

▶ Communicate the planned estimation process (e.g., schedule, expected inputs, and involved personnel) to project stakeholders and get their commitment in advance.

Steve McConnell once concluded that *"in software, the chain isn't as strong as its weakest link; it's as weak as all the weak links multiplied together."* This observation applies to project estimation and planning, where, in the worst case, errors made in single activities multiply into an overall project management failure.

2.5   Basic Components of Project Effort

The problem with quick and dirty, as some people have said, is that the dirty remains long after the quick has been forgotten.

—Steve McConnell

At the abstract level, an estimation process comprises a few standard elements, which principally can be found in almost any existing estimation method. We illustrate these basic elements in Fig. 2.5.

To assist understanding of the basic elements of the estimation process, let us first look at Example 2.2, where we use a metaphor to everyday life and compare estimating software development effort to planning a car trip.

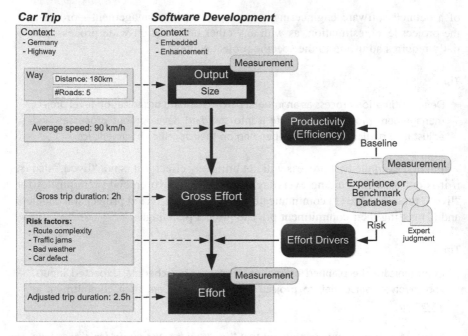

Fig. 2.5 Components of project effort and effort estimation

Example 2.2. Estimating Duration of a Car Trip

Figure 2.5 presents a car trip metaphor of the estimation process. In the first step of planning the trip, we define the context. We assume that we are traveling in Germany and we want to use highways for that purpose. Selection of a certain context has, in practice, a number of implications on the detailed conditions, which in turn determine baseline efficiency, that is, the speed of our car trip. German traffic regulations with respect to highways, for example, determine the admissible speed, which, in turn, determines the range of speed as well as the feasible average speed on the trip route. The output of the car trip is the route covered. We characterize the "size" of the route using standard distance metrics such as kilometers (km). We measure trip efficiency as a distance covered per unit of time. For that purpose, an average speed metric defined as km per hour (km/h) is adopted.

The gross estimation of trip duration equals the time required to cover a route distance with an average speed based on past experiences. Yet, in order to accurately plan the actual trip, we must consider a number of potential risks that may cause our average speed to differ from the one we typically observed in the past. In other words, we should consider trip characteristics that may differentiate the actual trip from analogous trips taken in the past in the same context. Example risk factors to consider include: route complexity, traffic situation, weather conditions, or possible car defects. The final estimate is the result of adjusting gross trip duration with respect to actual values of potential obstacles. ■

In the next few paragraphs, we discuss the individual elements of software development effort in more detail.

2.5.1 Context

The context of estimation refers to a set of project environmental factors—so-called *context factors*. In the software engineering context, the characteristics of the development environment have a number of practical implications for effort estimation. Therefore, we need to consider context whenever we design an estimation process, select estimation methods, and interpret estimation results. An example context factor might be the software application domain. Industrial observations show that baseline productivity as well as factors influencing development productivity and effort differ between various application domains. For instance, we may expect that "typical" development productivity and relevant factors influencing productivity will be different for office desktop software and for safety-critical embedded software. In this case, embedded software development imposes certain basic requirements on quality assurance processes that typically decrease the rate of development compared to desktop software. Another example of a relevant context factor is development type. For instance, enhancement projects typically imply software reuse, which, dependent on the quality of reused software artifacts, distinguishes development productivity from new development projects, in which complete software is created from scratch. Application domain and development type are examples of categorical context factors, that is, qualitative factors, which are assigned labels instead of numerical values. In fact, context factors typically represent categorical characteristics of a project environment. Since their quantitative impact on effort is difficult to determine, it is convenient to keep them constant within the scope of effort estimation rather than to consider them as variables or effort drivers. In Sect. 2.2, we provide a brief overview of the most relevant context factors.

Tip

▶ While determining relevant context factors, focus on categorical project environment characteristics, such as application domain, development type, or programming language. Keep context factors constant within the scope of estimation.

Output Output refers to products created in the software development project. As discussed in the estimation life cycle (Sect. 2.4), project effort is determined by its volume, which is commonly measured as the size of project deliverables. In other words, the size of project outputs is a proxy of project volume, and as such, it is considered to be a major effort driver.

Tip

▶ Invest proper resources to estimate the size of software in order to determine
  project volume. As software size is a major contributor to project effort, reliable
  size estimates will pay off in more reliable estimates of project effort.

In principle, a software project produces a number of various artifacts for which
a number of different size metrics may be defined. Example project outputs include:
software code, software executables, documentation, test cases, etc. In an industrial
practice, software code has been the most common subject of size measurement.
The most common measure of software size is the program length quantified in
terms of the *lines of source code*—abbreviated as *LOC* or *SLOC*. This metric is as
much loved as hated by the software community. In fact, it has many advantages
and disadvantages, and its concrete usage, as with any other metric, needs to be
considered individually in a concrete application context.

Tip

▶ Use lines of code for estimating software size only when you are able to accurately
  do it. Remember the limitations of simple size metrics.

Alternatively to LOC and other structural metrics of software, a few measures of
software functionality—*functional metrics*—have been proposed. Functional size
metrics are mostly represented by a family of *Function Point Analysis (FPA)*
methods. Many of these have been published as international standards. Although
proposed as an alternative to imperfect LOC metrics, functional size metrics are
also not free from weaknesses. The major criticism regarding functional metrics has
been the subjective character and calculation overhead of functional size measurement. The major points of advantage of functional software size metrics are their
early applicability and technology independence. For example, FPA is applicable
from early requirements specification phases and is independent of any particular
programming language.

In the context of effort prediction, the issue of early applicability plays an
essential role and is a significant advantage of function points over lines of code.
Yet, the issue of technology independence requires certain care. While estimating
effort, the impact of technology—such as programming language—needs to be
considered. This is because technology has a significant impact typically on development productivity and, in consequence, on project effort. In the case of LOC, this
factor is already implicitly "embedded" in the size metric, whereas in the case of
function points, it needs to be explicitly considered in another way; for example, it
is usually regarded as a context factor or effort driver. In Appendix A, we provide a
brief discussion of LOC and FPA, including an overview of the most important
strengths and weaknesses of both approaches.

Tip

▶ Employ functional size metrics for estimating a project in its very early stages, but be aware of the general limitations of functional size measurement and the specific characteristics of particular counting methods.

A common practice for measuring software size is to use a single metric. Yet, single size metrics have numerous drawbacks. In order to avoid drawbacks and exploit benefits of individual size metrics, some researchers have recently proposed combining multiple size metrics for productivity and effort estimation purposes. For example, Kitchenham and Mendes (2004) present an example approach, where several basic size metrics were combined within a single statistical regression model.

2.5.2   Productivity

Productivity represents efficiency of software development. In the context of industrial production processes, productivity has been traditionally measured as the ratio of units of the output delivered by a particular process divided by units of input—resources—provided to the process. This perspective has to a large extent been transferred into the software development context and is usually defined as productivity (in reference to software products) or efficiency (in reference to software services). Our experience shows that in 2006, about 80 % of software organizations adopted this industrial perspective of productivity to the context of software development, where inputs refer to effort expended in the project for producing software deliverables on the project's output (2.1):

$$\text{Productivity} = \frac{\text{Size}}{\text{Effort}} \tag{2.1}$$

The key assumption software organizations make when applying this simple productivity metric is that software development processes are similar to classical manufacturing processes. Yet, software production is typically much more difficult than production processes in other industries. This is mainly because software organizations typically develop new products as opposed to fabricating the same product over and over again. Moreover, software development is a human-based—"soft"—activity, with extreme uncertainties from the outset. Finally, software development takes place in the context of rapid technological changes. In consequence, productivity varies significantly across projects, dependent on a potentially infinite number of associated, mutually interacting, and often unknown factors.

In the context of effort estimation, the productivity of similar already completed projects—analog projects—is employed as a basis for predicting the effort required to complete a new project—target project. The underlying assumption here is that the new project will have, on average, similar productivity to the productivity of baseline projects—*baseline productivity*. Baseline productivity is typically determined based on experience gathered in projects successfully completed in a similar context. In principle, baseline productivity can be computed by analysis of measurement data or, if measurement data are not available, based on human judgment, or using both sources of information.

In the case where little or no information on past productivity is available in a given organization, external project benchmark data repositories, such as ISBSG (2009), can be used to define baseline productivity. But as such repositories typically contain data from multiple organizations that may differ significantly from the one being estimated, great care should be employed in using such data. In practice, it is recommended to use external benchmarks only as a starting point for estimates and then to build up your own organization-specific data repository for more reliable estimates.

Tip

▶ Use external benchmark project repositories, such as ISBSG, for computing rough effort estimates. Use a range of productivities on similar benchmark projects as a baseline for estimating your software project. Focus on the most relevant project context characteristics, such as domain and development type, to identify similar projects for productivity baselining.

In a trivial case, baseline productivity can be computed as a simple average across productivities observed for historical projects. A more desired—yet more complex—approach is to isolate a basic productivity component for each baseline project by extracting specific influences on productivity observed in this project. For example, if a project suffered from exceptionally low capabilities of a development team—which decreased its productivity—we would want to determine baseline productivity, as it would apply to a team having capabilities typical in a given context. An example method that supports isolating specific influences on productivity is CoBRA. We present this method briefly in Chap. 15.

2.5.3 Gross Effort

Gross effort represents a rough estimate of development effort, which is based solely on the size of the project's output and baseline productivity. It does not include any effort drivers, that is, factors that may cause development productivity of the estimated project to differ from the baseline productivity.

2.5.4   Effort Drivers

A gross effort estimate needs to be adjusted using specific characteristics of the current development project, in particular using those characteristics that make the project's productivity differ from the past projects upon which baseline productivity is based. Effort drivers are the most relevant characteristics that account for the difference between the baseline productivity and the actual productivity of a specific development process. Example effort drivers include capabilities of the development team, problem complexity, or customer involvement. In practice, it is difficult to build reliable effort models that would apply to various contexts at the same time. Therefore, effort models that apply to a narrow context—for instance, only to embedded software systems—are built where a few most relevant effort drivers suffice to account for productivity variance observed in this particular context. The rest of the potential factors influencing productivity are either not relevant (have minimal impact on productivity) or are kept constant (part of the estimation context).

Tip

▶ Focus on a few most relevant effort drivers. If there are too many effort drivers,
   limit the context of effort estimation.

2.5.5   Effort

Effort represents the final prediction of project effort. It is the result of adjusting gross effort with respect to identified effort drivers.

2.5.6   Relationships Between Basic Components of Software Development Effort

In principle, the size of the output to deliver (e.g., software product) and baseline development productivity experienced in the past development projects are the two major determinants of development effort. Information on these two factors would be sufficient for accurate effort estimates if past development projects had exactly the same characteristics as the estimated project. In reality, however, each project is unique, and we can at most talk about similar projects. Therefore, for the purpose of estimation, we should always try to take productivity of similar projects as the baseline for estimation. We consider projects similar if they have at least the same characteristics on the most relevant *context factors*, such as application domain or type of development. Still, there are a number of factors that make productivity of similar projects differ significantly. Not considering these factors and simply taking the productivity of similar projects as a baseline would likely lead to unsatisfactory estimates. For this reason, factors that make a project unique should be considered to adjust gross effort estimates derived from baseline productivity. However, we should take into account only the most relevant factors, as considering all possible factors influencing effort would not be reasonable. The cost of considering a huge number of factors—and potential interactions among them—would by far exceed the benefit in terms of gain in estimation quality. Furthermore, practical experience shows that considering a large number of factors influencing effort leads to decreased quality of estimates because of an extensive amount of partially irrelevant and potentially misleading information that many of these factors convey.

In the following chapter, we discuss common factors influencing software development productivity and effort.

Further Reading

- S. Grimstad, M. Jørgensen, and K. Moløkken-Østvold (2006), "Software Effort Estimation Terminology: The tower of Babel," *Information and Software Technology*, vol. 48, no. 4, pp. 302–310.

  This article discusses the negative impact on successful project planning of using imprecise and inconsistent estimation terminology. The authors provide a structured review of typical software effort estimation terminology presented in the software engineering literature and suggests guidelines on how to avoid unclear and inconsistent terminology.

- M. Svahnberg, T. Gorschek, R. Feldt, R. Torkar, S.B. Saleem, and M.U. Shafique (2010), "A systematic review on strategic release planning models," *Information and Software Technology*, vol. 52, no. 3, pp. 237–248.

  The authors provide a comprehensive review of release planning strategies proposed in the context of software engineering. This article can be used as a starting point for detailed investigation of software release planning as a key aspect of software requirements engineering and software project planning.

- Y. Wang (2007a), *Software Engineering Foundations: A Software Science Perspective*, CRC Software Engineering Series, vol. 2, AUERBACH/CRC Press.

  In Sect. 8.5 of his book, the author discusses the basic laws of cooperative work within software projects. The author focuses on the time-effort-staffing trade-offs of software development. He formulates several laws that formally explain empirical observations made by other researchers with respect to associations between project duration, effort, and staffing level.

- P.V. Norden (1958), "Curve Fitting for a Model of Applied Research and Development Scheduling," *IBM Journal of Research and Development*, vol. 2, no. 3.

This is the original article where Norden investigated the Rayleigh curve for modeling the distribution of software development staff across software life cycle phases.

- L.H. Putnam and W. Myers (2003), *Five Core Metrics: The Intelligence Behind Successful Software Management*, Dorset House, New York.

  The book proposes an effort estimation method called Software Life Cycle Management (SLIM) which is based on the Rayleigh distribution of staffing across the software development life cycle.

- K. Pillai and V.S. Sukumaran Nair (1997), "A Model for Software Development Effort and Cost Estimation", *IEEE Transactions on Software Engineering*, vol. 23, no. 8, pp. 485–497.

  This article presents an adjustment of the SLIM estimation method. The distribution of staffing across the software development life cycle is represented by a Gamma curve, instead of Rayleigh.

- S.G. MacDonell and M.J. Shepperd (2007), "Comparing Local and Global Software Effort Estimation Models - Reflections on a Systematic Review," *Proceedings of the 1st International Symposium on Empirical Software Engineering and Measurement*, Madrid, Spain, 20–21 September 2007, IEEE Computer Society Press, pp. 401–409.

  This article discusses utilizing company-specific and cross-company project data for building local (context-specific) and global (cross-context) effort models. The authors provide a number of references to studies where local and global effort models have been developed and validated in a particular application context.

- P. Abrahamsson, R. Moser, W. Pedrycz, A. Sillitti, and G. Succi (2007), "Effort Prediction in Iterative Software Development Processes—Incremental Versus Global Prediction Models," *Proceedings of the 1st International Symposium on Empirical Software Engineering and Measurement*, Madrid, Spain, 20–21 September 2007, pp. 344–353.

  This article discusses the challenges of applying traditional effort estimation methods in the context of agile and iterative software development. The authors propose a detailed development approach and discusses a number of architectures of such estimation models, including regression models and neural networks.

- R. Stutzke (2005), *Estimating Software-Intensive Systems. Projects, Products, and Processes*. The SEI Series in Software engineering, Addison Wesley Professional.

  In Sect. 1.6, the author provides an overview of the estimation process, which he discusses in more detail in the remaining part of the book. Estimation activities are grouped into those performed before, during, and after projects.

- S. L. Pfleeger, F. Wu, and R. Lewis (2005), *Software Cost Estimation and Sizing Methods, Issues, and Guidelines*. RAND Corporation.

  A comprehensive systematic review of software sizing methods is provided including their particular benefits and threats when applied in the context of effort estimation. Moreover, a number of practical guidelines are provided for balancing the use of different sizing methods. Finally, the report provides ready-to-use checklists for considering size-estimation-related risks and for selecting the most appropriate sizing method.

- A.F. Minkiewicz (2009), "The Evolution of Software Size: A Search for Value." CrossTalk—*The Journal of Defense Software Engineering*, vol. 22, no. 3, pp. 23–26.

  This article provides a review of software sizing methodologies employed over the years in the software engineering domain. The review focuses on the uses and misuses of common software size metrics.

- ISO/IEC 20926 (2003), *Software engineering. IFPUG 4.1—Unadjusted functional size measurement method. Counting practices manual*. International Standardization Organization.

  This international standard specifies a method for measuring the functional software size as defined by the International Function Points User Group (IFPUG) in version 4.1. Note that the ISO standard incorporates only the basic method. The complete approach, including guidelines and examples, is published by IFPUG as "Function Point Counting Practices Manual", which can be acquired at IFPUG (http://www.ifpug.org).

- ISO/IEC 24570 (2005), *Software Engineering. NESMA Functional Size Measurement Method Version 2.1. Definitions and Counting Guidelines for the Application of Function Point Analysis*. International Standardization Organization.

  This international standard represents an adjustment of the IFPUG method for functional size measurement, proposed by Netherlands Software Metrics Association (NESMA). Another example of national adjustment has been proposed by the Finnish Software Measurement Association (FiSMA). Similarly to IFPUG, detailed guidelines on measuring NESMA function points are provided in associated documents published by NESMA (http://www.nesma.nl).

- ISO/IEC 19761 (2003), *Software engineering. COSMIC-FFP—A Functional Size Measurement Method*. International Standardization Organization.

  This standard specifies a relatively new method for measuring functional software size proposed as an alternative to the IFPUG method. It addresses the major points of criticism (weaknesses) concerning the IFPUG method, such as limited applicability in the context of embedded software systems.

- E. Mendes and C. Lokan (2008), "Replicating Studies on Cross- vs Single-company Effort Models Using the ISBSG Database," *Empirical Software Engineering*, vol. 13, no. 1, Springer Netherlands, pp. 3–37.

  This article provides an overview of the studies where the ISBSG benchmark repository is used for the purpose of effort estimation. Among the other aspects, the authors discuss the differences in estimation reliability when based on organization-specific vs. multi-organizational project data.

•

Common Factors Influencing Software Project Effort

3

Making mental connections is our most crucial learning tool, the essence of human intelligence; to forge links; to go beyond the given; to see patterns, relationships, context.
—Marilyn Ferguson

The effort required for developing software depends on a number of factors. The major determinant of development effort is the "size" of software, typically approximated in terms of the amount of functionality delivered by the software or the structural size of artifacts delivered by software engineering processes. Still, developing software of comparable size may require significantly different amounts of effort. This variance is related to differences in development productivity, which in turn depends on the environment of the software development project. The ability to reliably estimate software size, knowledge of the most relevant factors influencing development productivity, and an understanding of how they influence productivity are the three pillars of successful prediction of software development effort. The topic of measuring software size is so extensive that it deserves its own book (at least one) and thus is beyond the scope of this work; in Appendix A, we briefly present the most common ways of measuring software size with their most prominent strengths and weaknesses. In this chapter, we discuss common factors that determine software development productivity and thus should be considered when estimating software project effort.

3.1 Context Factors

Context is the invisible environment, the interrelated conditions, the structure of interpretation in which your life occurs. The context of your life is like water to a fish. The fish doesn't see the water, isn't necessarily aware of the water, and doesn't think about the water. And yet, everything in a fish's world is consistent with and generated from the fact the fish exists in water. Similarly, everything that shows up in your life, every word you speak, and every action you take, is naturally consistent with and indicative of your context.
—John Hanley

A. Trendowicz and R. Jeffery, *Software Project Effort Estimation*,
DOI 10.1007/978-3-319-03629-8_3, © Springer International Publishing Switzerland 2014

In practice, it is difficult to build reliable effort models that would be applicable across a variety of project environments. The human-intensive character of software development and rapid changes in software technologies make the software project a highly unstable environment. Depending on the project context, a number of different factors, in different ways, may affect software development productivity and project effort. Even though we have been able to successfully grasp these factors within an estimation method in one context, this success is typically not simply transferable to other situations.

Tip

▶ When modeling software development productivity and project effort, keep in mind that "Past successes, no matter how numerous and universal, are no guarantee of future performance in a new context."—Henry Petroski

Determining and properly documenting the context of estimation is a very important aspect of project effort estimation. At one extreme, an estimation method defined for a wide range of situations must consider a wide range of potential effort drivers and a wide range of their interactions. At the other extreme, an estimation method defined for very specific situations—although being very simple—will apply to very few similar situations; any other situation would require defining individual estimation methods. Building, for instance, an effort model for business applications and embedded real-time software would require covering a large variety of factors that play a significant role in both domains. Alternatively, one may build simpler models for each domain separately. In that case, the factor "application domain" would be constant for each model.

In practice, we must decide on a trade-off between the range of situations covered by an estimation method and the method's complexity—number of effort drivers and their interactions.

The initial estimation context is usually predetermined by the organization in which we estimate effort. For example, it might be a complete software company, a business unit, department, or group. If this initial context still includes a wide range of relevant factors influencing development effort, we need to further reduce the scope. We do this by deciding on which project environment characteristics we keep constant within the scope of estimation; the impact of the remaining ones needs to be covered by the estimation method.

Difference Between Context Factors and Effort Drivers
Factors that describe a project environment—context factors—are actually effort drivers that are kept constant within the scope of effort estimation. Context is typically determined through categorical characteristics of a project environment. Since their quantitative impact on effort is difficult to determine, it is convenient to keep them constant within the scope of effort estimation rather than to consider them as effort drivers.

Table 3.1 summarizes the characteristics of the software development environment that are most commonly applied in the software industry for specifying the context of productivity and effort modeling.

Table 3.1 The most common context factors

Context factor	Description
Programming language	Programming language(s) used to implement software code, e.g., C/C++, Java, or Fortran
Application domain	Application domain of the software, e.g., embedded software systems or management information systems (MIS)
Development type	Type of development, e.g., new development, enhancement, or maintenance
Development life cycle	Applied development life cycle, e.g., waterfall, incremental, or scrum

3.2 Scale Factors

If a software project becomes too large, it will collapse into a black hole. Time and money are absorbed but nothing ever comes out.

—Brian Russell

3.2.1 Effect of Scale

Microeconomics

In microeconomics, O'Sullivan and Sheffrin (2007) define the effect of scale as an economic property of production that affects a producer's average cost per unit as the production scale increases. Typically, two opposite effects of scale are considered, economies and diseconomies of scale.

The term *economy of scale* is defined as the cost advantage that a business obtains due to expansion. In other words, a producer's average cost per unit falls as the scale is increased. The concept of economies of scale refers to reductions in a producer's average cost per unit—increase in production efficiency—as the size of a facility increases. *Diseconomy of scale* refers to the opposite phenomenon, that is, an increase of unit cost as the scale increases. Finally, if per-unit cost behaves proportionately to scale, there is no effect of scale.

Figure 3.1 illustrates the effect of the scale phenomenon. In an ideal scenario, per-unit costs decrease with increasing scale until they reach a certain minimum (*optimal scale*), and then the costs increase as the scale further increases.

Software Engineering

The concept of the scale effect has been adopted in the software engineering domain. It refers to changes in the progression of software development effort as the project scale changes, while other project characteristics remain constant. In other words, the effect of scale refers to changes in software development

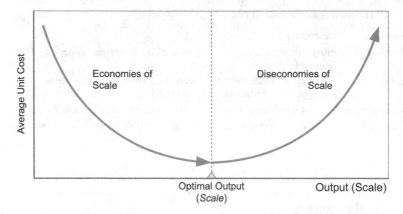

Fig. 3.1 Economies vs. diseconomies of scale in microeconomics

productivity as the project scale changes. These productivity changes are represented by a changing slope of the project effort curve. Consequently, economies and diseconomies of scale refer, respectively, to increases and decreases in development productivity as the project size increases. There is no effect of scale when development productivity remains constant independent of the project size. In the context of software development, the effect of scale is typically regarded as equivalent to returns to scale in microeconomics.

> **Difference Between Effect of Scale and Return to Scale**
> In microeconomics, although the terms economies of scale and returns to scale are related, they refer to different phenomena and should not be confused. Returns to scale is a short run concept referring to changes in production output subsequent to a proportional change in all inputs. Economies of scale refers to a long-run relationship between the average cost of producing a unit of good with increasing level of output.
>
> Other than in manufacturing, project scale in software engineering does not refer to the number of product units—identical or similar copies of a product—manufactured but to the size of the single unique software product developed in the project.
>
> In the context of software engineering, there is principally one major project input—effort—and one major project output—software, from both a short- and long-term perspective; that is, for the software project and software portfolio, respectively. That is why the effect of scale and return to scale are regarded as equivalent phenomena.

Early identification of potential scale effects is a key element of project management. Optimizing the project scale according to scale effects observed in a particular environment may moderate project management stress and save a project from underperforming.

In software engineering, there are several indicators of project scale, which project managers can consider for assessing the scale and the degree of related project risks. Example indicators of software project scale include

- *Software Size*: The size of software deliverables is the most common measure of project scale. This is mostly because the size of deliverables is considered as the major determinant of resources, such as effort, needed to complete the project. Software size can be measured in terms of its structure or functionality.[1] The common structural size metric is lines of code (LOC), while a common functional size metric is function points (FP). Capers Jones (2007, 2009) observed, for instance, that about 80 % of projects up to 100 FP (10 kLOC) are on time, about 70–85 % of projects over 10,000 FP (1,000 kLOC) fail, whereby about 50–65 % of them are cancelled without completion. We need to, however, remember that software size is only one aspect of project scale and that a project might be exposed to the effect of scale even though the size of its deliverables does not change. A typical example of this situation is trading off project effort and duration through manipulating its staffing level as we discussed in Sect. 2.2.2 and illustrated in Fig. 2.3. In this case, the large team implies a negative effect of scale due to increased management stress and, in consequence, productivity loss—although software size does not change.
- *Project Effort*: Sauer et al. (2007) found project effort as the best discriminator of underperforming projects. Their survey among experienced project managers in the UK showed that projects of 24 person-months or less have only a 25 % probability of underperforming. After reaching 500–1,000 person-months, this probability doubles to 50 %. As project scale increases into the 1,000–2,400 person-months category, the risk of underperforming triples to 75 %. Above the 2,400 person-months, no successful project was found.
- *Project Duration*: In their survey, Sauer et al. (2007) observed that projects up to 6 months duration were burdened with little risk (25 %) of underperformance. This risk, however, doubled for projects longer than 18 months.
- *Team Size*: Sauer et al. (2007) also observed that the risk of project underperformance remains at an acceptable level (25–35 %) for teams of up to 20 members. The risk rises dramatically for teams larger than 20 persons.
- *Project Budget*: Sauer et al. (2007) found that budget, in a monetary sense, is a relatively weak indicator of project performance, compared to effort and duration. For companies in the UK, 15 million pounds was found as the barrier for project performance. The risk of underperformance increased dramatically to 50 % for projects exceeding this budget amount.

Software size and the other aforementioned aspects are only indicators of project scale that can be used as proxies for measuring project scale. However, neither the

---

[1] Refer to Appendix A for discussion of common structural and functional measures of software size.

project scale nor its indicators are the root causes of the effects we observe as project scale changes—especially negative effects caused by increasing project scale. We distinguish two types of root causes of the project scale effect:

• *Organizational*: These are personnel- and project-related factors that contribute to what Ross (2008) refers to as project "management stress" and what actually represents organizational overhead as project scale changes. In this category, the level of project work and interpersonal coordination is the major factor responsible for the scale effects. From this perspective, team size seems to be the most useful indicator of project scale. For instance, the larger the project team, the more organizationally complex is coordinative project work and the more management stress and overhead it requires. In consequence, a lower portion of total project effort is spent on delivering a product or service, which results in an overall loss in productivity.

• *Technological*: These are process-, method-, and tool-related factors that contribute to what we can call a project's "technological stress" and what actually represents an overhead for using certain technologies as project scale changes. In this category, the scalability of the employed technologies seems to be the major factor responsible for the scale effects. From this perspective, software size seems to be the most suitable indicator of project scale. Watts Humphrey (2001–2002) gives the following illustration of this issue: "You can't transition from one speed range to the next by merely trying harder. You need progressively more sophisticated vehicles that use progressively more advanced technologies. Unfortunately, we have yet to learn this lesson in software. We attempt to use the same methods and practices for 1,000 lines of code (LOC) programs as for 1,000,000 LOC systems. This is a size increase of 1,000 times, and the commonly used test-based software development strategies simply do not scale up. Organizations that don't anticipate and prepare for scalability problems will someday find that they simply cannot get systems to work safely, reliably, and securely, no matter how much their people test and fix them."

Wang (2007a, b), in his extensive investigation of cooperative work, connects the organizational and technological aspects of the scale effect. He points out work coordination as being directly responsible for performance loss and considers several project and technology factors that influence project coordination overhead and thus, indirectly, project performance. Wang and King (2000) identified ten key factors influencing the level of a project's interpersonal coordination and thus coordination level. Among the most influential factors, the authors list project "scope," "difficulty," and "complexity" as well as the "schedule constraints," "budget constraints," and "need for special processes."

Still, the software effort estimation community tends to consider the effect of scale mainly by means of software size. Consequently, the question of the effect of scale is typically closely related to a more general question about the linearity of the functional dependency between software size and its development effort. In principle, the existence of the effect of scale—economies or diseconomies—implies a nonlinear functional form of the size-effort dependency. Otherwise—no effect of scale—linear size-effort dependency is assumed.

(Dis)Economies of Scale in Parametric Effort Models

Over the years, several basic forms of the size-effort functional dependency established their position in the context of effort estimation:

- *Linear*: Effort $= a + (b \times$ Size$)$
- *Quadratic*: Effort $= a + (b \times$ Size$) + (c \times$ Size$^2)$
- *Log-linear*: Effort $= e^a \times$ Size^b
- *Translog*: Effort $= e^a \times$ Size$^b \times$ Size$^{c \times \text{lnSize}}$
- *Cobb–Douglas*: Effort $= a \times$ Size^b

Parametric effort models use an exponential parameter attached to the software size factor in order to account for effect of scale. For example, the COCOMO II model from Boehm et al. (2000), which basically implements the Cobb–Douglas model, uses an exponent parameter "b" to account for the relative effect of scale of a project in the following way:

- If $b < 1.0$, then the project exhibits an economies-of-scale effect.
- If $b = 1.0$, then neither diseconomies of scale nor economies of scale are displayed by the project. Both effects are in balance, and there is a linear functional dependency between size and effort.
- If $b > 1.0$, then the project exhibits a diseconomies-of-scale effect.

The question about the effect of scale is still the source of much controversy among software practitioners, who argue whether economies of scale effect exist and—if existing—what functional form best reflects it. There has been no consensus achieved in this matter over recent decades. Figure 3.2 illustrates the major alternatives of scale effect considered in the software engineering domain.

The mixed effect of scale seems to be the closest to the industrial reality, where smaller projects are characterized by increasing returns to scale whereas larger projects are characterized by decreasing returns to scale. In small projects, economies of scale effects arise from spreading fixed project costs over a larger development cost and greater utilization of specialized personnel and tools. As a project becomes larger, diseconomies of scale effects arise eventually due to increasing complexity of software, increasing requirements on product and project documentation, and increasing complexity of project communication and coordination caused by the number of inter- and intraproject communication paths.

Summarizing, we recommend as a general rule not to expect a linear functional form for the size-effort dependency over a wide range of project scales. Although it can surely be linear within a limited interval of project scale, it will deviate from a straight line across a wider range of project scales—as illustrated by the example multiple-linear-splines productivity curve in Fig. 3.3.

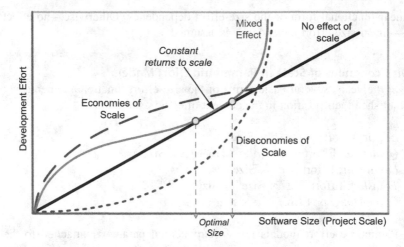

Fig. 3.2 Alternative scale effects considered in software engineering

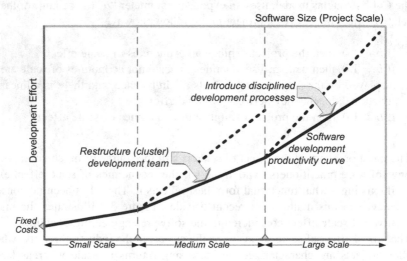

Fig. 3.3 Mixed effect of scale modeled through multiple linear splines

Tip

▶ Do not assume that effort scales up linearly along project size. It is typically
  nonlinear. Remember to consider fixed (e.g., administrative) costs for small projects
  and coordination (e.g., communication) overhead of large projects when
  estimating software development productivity and project effort.

   As illustrated in Fig. 3.3, the negative impact of project scale on development
productivity—and project effort—may be moderated through improved activities

that affect project environment factors directly related to the diseconomies of scale effect. An example initiative to prevent the negative project scale effects can be restructuring the development team in order to decrease the complexity of communication paths and thus reduce project coordination overhead. Another means to decrease organizational project overhead and therefore the diseconomies of scale effect might be to introduce disciplined development processes. In the next section (Sect. 3.2.2), we discuss common factors contributing to the effect of scale and in Sect. 3.5.1, potential ways to reduce this effect.

Numerous polemics on the effect of scale in software engineering prove that just like many other aspects of software development, the effect of scale depends on individual characteristics of a particular software development environment such as the development processes applied or the capabilities of involved personnel. The best thing we can do in this situation is to collect project data and analyze it on a regular basis with respect to the effects of scale. Yet, simply validating and affirming a particular scale effect is not of much benefit from the perspective of project decision-making. Besides knowing about particular effects of scale, project managers would require information on project characteristics that contribute to—amplify or moderate—the observed effects the most. In particular, project managers should focus on the level of project interpersonal coordination and factors influencing coordination overhead. For example, as illustrated in Fig. 3.6 (Sect. 3.5.1), data analysis may indicate to a project manager for what project scale certain team structures and development processes work best; that is, contribute to more effective project coordination and higher development productivity.

Tip

▶ Collect historical project data regarding software size, project effort, and project environmental factors such as those having an impact on project coordination overhead. Analyze them to find out about the effects of scale in a particular context and about the factors that contribute most to these effects.

3.2.2   Factors Influencing Effect of Scale

Similar to microeconomics, in the software engineering domain, the effect of scale is not a spontaneous phenomenon, and the scale alone is not the only determinant of project performance or underperformance. There are particular factors that cause positive or negative effects of scale. It means that, in practice, even a small project can actually be doomed to fail because of its particular characteristics. Project scale typically only magnifies already existing negative effects.

Tip

▶ Project scale alone is not the only determinant of project performance—there are particular project characteristics that cause positive or negative effects of scale.

Factors contributing to the effect of scale are actually much the same as factors influencing development productivity—commonly referred to as effort drivers (Sect. 3.3). In both cases, we consider characteristics of the development environment that have an impact on development productivity. The difference lies de facto in how this impact behaves as project scale changes.

Effort drivers are typically considered across projects of similar size and are assumed to have similar impact on development productivity independent of project scale. For example, it is assumed that the same level of requirements volatility contributes approximately the same extent of development productivity loss independent of project scale.

Other than the impact of effort drivers, the impact of *effect-of-scale factors* on project effort depends on the project's size (i.e., project scale). Even though a particular project characteristic is constant, its impact on development productivity varies as project scale changes. In the extreme case, a particular project characteristic may have the opposite impact on development productivity depending on project scale. For example, sophisticated formal methods may be beneficial for development productivity when applied within a very limited scope—small project or small piece of a larger project—whereas it might impose unacceptable cost if applied to a large-scale project.

There are a few factors for which the impact on project performance can be considered as universally applicable to all software development environments. In Table 3.2, we summarize factors that are most commonly indicated as those mainly responsible for the effect of scale in software engineering.

However, it is always a good idea to find out which factors are actually relevant in a particular environment. For this purpose, we recommend collecting and analyzing context-specific project data.

Unsurprisingly, when it comes to the effect of project scale on performance, it is much—if not all—about people. Even though certain product or process characteristics may contribute to what we call technological project stress, with the right people, we may at least moderate this negative impact. Gerald Weinberg (1986) said it best when he said, "*No matter what the problem is, it's always a people problem.*"

As software development is still largely a human-based process, human factors play an essential role. And since "the basic work unit in innovative software organizations is the team rather than the individual" (Moe et al. 2009), we need to deal with issues that make teams ineffective. It is a long-known fact that simply putting a group of individuals to work together does not automatically guarantee organizational success. There is a long list of issues to be considered before a group of people can work effectively as a team. Yet, the common denominator of all these issues seems to be team interaction, coordination, and communication.

Tip

▶ Since software development is still a human-based activity and since people work on software in teams, the success or failure of a software project depends much on how good or bad are interactions among team members.

Table 3.2 Common factors contributing to the effect of scale in software engineering

Effect-of-scale factor	Description
Team size and structure	The number of communication paths increases exponentially with the number of involved team members—analogous to the increase of edges in a full graph with increasing number of nodes. Moreover, increase in team size potentially contributes to increased number of interpersonal conflicts between team members. Growth of team size is particularly destructive when in the context of poor team structure. Poor team structure not only increases communication overhead but also hinders effective information flow and synchronization of project work. Ebert and De Man (2008) suggest that, in the best-case scenario, one should plan some 5–10 % of overhead for managing distributed teams. In the worst-case—with highly fragmented tasks and loss of escalation mechanisms to resolve conflicts—this overhead can grow to 20–40 %
Complexity of project management activities	Number and complexity of project management activities, such as planning and documenting, increases nonlinearly with increasing project size. As noted by Barry Boehm (1981), "poor management can increase software costs more rapidly than any other factor"; and growth of project scale boosts this effect enormously
Process maturity	Unstable and poorly documented development processes contribute to the diseconomies of scale effect—reduced development productivity—as project size and/or distribution increases
Project novelty	The less knowledge and experience a software organization has regarding a particular project type—domain, product type, and customer—the larger are the diseconomies of scale effect. Project familiarity is particularly important in the context of maintenance projects where overhead to analyze and understand software is relatively large compared to development effort
Complexity of system interfaces and integration	Complexity of interfaces and integration increases as the size of the software system increases

That is why size and structure of the development team is a key success factor as projects grow in size and complexity. And that is why team management activities and disciplined processes need to be recognized as essential means for reducing the negative effects of project scale.

3.3 Effort Drivers

The connection between intention and result, between cause and effect, is not always what it seems.

—Henry Petroski

Effort drivers are factors that are explicitly included in the effort estimation process in order to explain productivity variance within a particular context. In that sense, context factors determine influence factors; that is, they are dependent on the project context. In a different context, different factors may have a different impact on productivity and may interact with each other in a different way. These factors may refer to personnel, product, process, or project characteristics.

Note that success of effort estimation depends as much on considering relevant effort drivers as on not considering—eliminating—irrelevant and redundant factors. As observed by Jørgensen and Grimstad (2008), eliminating irrelevant and misleading information can help avoid inaccurate and overly optimistic software development effort estimates.

Tip

▶ The key to successful estimation is not to consider all factors influencing project effort but to consider only the most relevant and eliminating irrelevant and redundant effort drivers.

Table 3.3 summarizes effort drivers Trendowicz and Münch (2009) found to be the most commonly used in software development practice across various contexts.

Many years after Fred Brooks (1995) formulated his observations, team capabilities, tool support, and specification quality are still the most relevant factors influencing development productivity and effort. And still capable people are much more valuable to the project success than capable tools. As it was nicely concluded by Grady Booch, "*A fool with a tool is still a fool.*"

3.3.1 Personnel Characteristics

Jim McCarthy once said, "You can't have great software without a great team." Dick Fairley, on the other hand, claimed that "Skilled and motivated programmers can overcome inadequate processes but perfect processes can never compensate for inadequate programmers." These two observations conclude how important skills of the software team are to success. Independent of the plethora of great tools and mature processes supporting software development along all phases of the software project, creating software is still a human-intensive process, and—as such—its success depends to a large extent on the capabilities of a project team. Team capability is a composition of the characteristics of individual members as well as the characteristics of a team as a whole.

The most relevant team member characteristics include knowledge, skills, personality, and motivation. Knowledge and skills of individual team members, in particular, comprise two major elements: technical knowledge and domain knowledge. Effective software development requires integration of these two types of knowledge during the development process (Faraj and Sproull 2000; Tiwana and McLean 2003). Such knowledge integration is critical for successful

Table 3.3 The most common effort drivers

Effort driver	Description
Team capabilities and experience	The experience and knowledge of key people in the project team regarding important project-related aspects, such as • Application domain for the project • Process, documentation standards, and common practices to be used in the project • Development platform and environment
• Programming language experience	Team experience regarding the programming language employed in the project at the beginning of the development life cycle
• Application experience and familiarity	The experience and knowledge of people in the project team regarding the customer's business and system characteristics at the start of the project
• Project manager experience and skills	The extent of the project manager's ability and effectiveness in planning, organizing, staffing, leading, coordinating, and controlling the software development project. The project manager's experience may range, for example, from having implemented many prior projects to never having managed a project before
Customer/user involvement	The extent to which the user and/or customer is involved in the project and • Provides necessary—and useful—information and expertise to the project • Performs some of the activities such as reviewing requirements documents • Actively takes part in acceptance testing
Software complexity	The extent to which some aspects of the software product—such as interface, architecture, database, algorithms, or relation to other systems—are expected to be complex or relatively large
• Database size & complexity	The size and complexity of data structures and data management systems
• Architecture complexity	The complexity of the software architecture
• Complexity of interfaces to other systems	The complexity of software-hardware and/or software-user interfaces
Quality of software requirements	Characteristics of the software requirements—both functional and nonfunctional—that determine their usefulness for developing quality software on time and within budget
• Requirements novelty	The extent to which requirements are novel to the development team. Novel requirements refer to functional and nonfunctional software characteristics that have never been faced by a development team before
• Requirements stability	The extent to which requirements change after they have been fixed—typically after the requirements specification phase
Required software quality	The extent to which a particular software product must meet certain nonfunctional requirements. This factor reflects how rigorous are particular quality requirements regarding software products
• Required software reliability	The amount of attention that needs to be given to minimizing failures and ensuring that any failures will not result in safety, economic, security, and/or environmental damage. Required

(continued)

Table 3.3 (continued)

Effort driver	Description
	software reliability can be achieved through actions such as formal validation and testing, fault-tolerant design, and formal specifications
• Required software maintainability	The extent to which the software is expected to be easy to understand and modify. Required software maintainability can be achieved through actions such as information hiding, modularity in design, completeness and traceability of life-cycle documentation, and the recording of design rationale
Project constraints	The additional constraints on the performance of the software development project
• Schedule pressure	The extent to which the planned project schedule is reasonable to attain a software system that meets all of its specified requirements. Schedule pressure is typically measured as the extent to which the schedule is shortened compared to the optimal—reasonable—one
• Project distribution	The extent to which the project team is geographically and organizationally distributed. This means that the members of a software development team can originate from various organizations and are geographically distributed
Tool usage, quality, and effectiveness	The extent to which tools are of high quality and are effectively used throughout the project. Example tool support includes well-suited analysis and design tools, debugging tools, CASE tool integration across the phases, and automated code generation from design
• CASE tools	The extent to which high-quality CASE tools are effectively supporting appropriate software development activities
• Testing tools	The extent to which high-quality tools are effectively supporting software testing activities

software development because it ensures that the design and implementation decisions made on either side of the client-developer organization interface are mutually consistent (Mookerjee and Chiang 2002; Tiwana and Keil 2004). Even if team members miss some capabilities and skills, they still can learn new technical and behavioral skills to improve their work and create a high-performing team. The success of such learning depends on the <u>maturity of team members;</u> that is, the ability to acquire new knowledge and adapt their behavior to social and task structures of a team. Team motivation and satisfaction are special aspects that may depend on other internal or external team characteristics. For example, social behavior or task assignment within the team may greatly impact the motivation of its members. On the other hand, external factors such as reward (or acknowledgment, in general) may improve or diminish personal motivation and satisfaction. As pointed out by David Sirota, *"The main question for management, then, is not, 'How can employees be motivated?', but rather 'How can management be deterred from diminishing—even destroying—employee motivation?'"*

Still, a team of great individuals does not necessarily create a great team. The most relevant characteristics of a team as a whole include team size, diversity, collocation, staff turnover, and shared beliefs. These aspects have an impact on team interaction processes such as coordination, communication, and information sharing, which in turn influences the team's performance (Klein et al. 2009). In Sect. 3.5.1, we discuss in more detail aspects of team structure in particular, as mediators of the influence that project scale has on the project's performance.

Staff turnover is an especially important aspect, because it might at the same time be caused by and have impact on other team characteristics (both internal and external). The turnover of team members may happen for reasons originating within the group, such as personal conflicts, or from outside the team, such as retirement or other job opportunities outside the team. In any case, the team must adapt to this change, which typically results in decreased team performance. Usually, departing staff leads to a loss of knowledge and of expertise and entails an overhead for introducing new staff, unfamiliar with the project. The team may, however, gain in a long-term sense if new staff have higher technical and social skills than the staff leaving the team.

"**Customer/user involvement**" represents an exceptional effort driver in that it connects personnel and process capabilities. For many years, it was broadly believed that user participation had a significant influence on increased performance of software projects. Jon Bentley (1988) summarized that "Great customer relations doubles productivity." Yet, customer involvement is not for free and means an investment, which, however, proves to be a positive return. Capers Jones (2009), for example, claims that "user involvement is time-consuming but valuable" and lists user involvement as one of the software engineering best practices. He observes that although costs of user involvement may range between 5 % and 50 % of project effort (20 % on average), it usually prevents expensive project failures in terms of user dissatisfaction, especially for large and complex software projects.

Yet, as summarized by Bachore and Zhou (2009), the body of existing empirical observation is inconclusive in this matter in that it shows different effects of user involvement—ranging from positive, through no effect, to negative effect on development productivity.

A number of field observations identify negative effects associated with user participation in the software development activities. Example effects include conflicts between users and developers, communication gaps, and frequent changes to requirements. And these lead inevitably to increased development workloads. Moreover, uncooperative behavior results in developers' frustration and stress. These observations imply that there are a number of aspects that influence the successful involvement of users in the development project. The only fact that we may take for granted is that involving users in software development is unavoidable because it is the user's objectives that the development project needs to achieve. Moreover, users possess extensive domain knowledge, which is often missing in developers.

Tip

▶ In a software development project, the developer alone cannot determine the quality of the output. Ultimately, the final outcome must satisfy end user requirements and fit the user's business environment. Therefore, users' objectives and expertise must be elicited and brought into the project.

Now, how <u>user involvement</u> will affect project performance depends on how we implement this involvement. Effective involvement of users in software development requires considering a number of aspects. Some of the most important success factors are

- *Involve the customer prior to and during development*: In practice, user involvement is typically considered and implemented as engaging users in the developmental stages of a software system. Yet, Jiang et al. (2002) observed that successful user involvement during the project depends to a large extent on user–developer partnering in the preproject phases. Their survey among 186 members of Project Management Institute in USA indicated preproject partnering as an effective way to reduce in-project user involvement risks—such as low involvement, negative attitude, or conflicts—and, in consequence, to improve project performance.
- *Ensure that involved users have appropriate knowledge and expertise*: According to Tesch et al. (2009), successful software projects require that developers (besides technical knowledge on how to develop) know what they are supposed to develop (object) and for what domain (context) they are to develop. In this respect, they may face three different situations: (a) designing an unfamiliar object in a familiar context, (b) designing an unfamiliar object in an unfamiliar context, and (c) designing a familiar object in a familiar domain. Only in the latter situation may the project succeed. Involved users should thus bring both object and domain knowledge to the project.
- *Ensure a tied partnership between users and developers*: Successful user involvement requires appropriate team communication and coordination mechanisms so that users and developers can exchange their knowledge and expertise effectively. Three principal aspects of effective team knowledge sharing are (1) when and where particular expertise is needed, (2) who possesses it, and (3) how to apply it. In practice, it requires a shift in the idea of user involvement from solely eliciting requirements to full partnership. We discuss in detail the issue of team knowledge flow in Sect. 3.5.1 ("Facilitate Team Interaction Processes").
- *Ensure that users are fully involved in the project*: Successful user involvement requires that they participate in the project assignments and responsibilities and that they are personally interested in the project outputs.

3.3.2 Process Characteristics

Characteristics of software development processes are traditionally an important factor influencing development productivity and project effort. Knowing the impact of most relevant process characteristics on productivity provides the basis for reliable effort estimates and importantly also indicates potential process improvement opportunities.

"*Tool usage, quality, and effectiveness*" is the process-related effort driver that refers to the usage of tools, methods, and technologies for supporting software project activities—both development and management. Paradoxically, although widely acknowledged, the effect of tool usage on project performance seems still not to be well understood. Empirical observations range from positive, through little or no effect, to negative effects of tool usage on project performance. As for many other effort drivers, this paradox can be explained by the fact that the effect of tool usage on development productivity is coupled with other factors (Tiwana 2008). Successful usage of tools depends on tool maturity and documentation, tool training and experience, appropriate support when selecting and introducing corresponding tools (task-technology fit), and the degree of tool integration.

Although *process maturity* is rarely explicitly mentioned as a factor influencing development productivity and effort, numerous companies use project productivity as the indirect measure of software process maturity and/or use productivity improvement as a synonym of process improvement. Rico (2000) reports, for instance, that 22 % of all metrics applied for the purpose of software process improvement (SPI) are productivity metrics. Another 29 % are development effort, cost, and cycle time metrics, which, in practice, are strongly related to development productivity. A common belief that pushes software organizations toward process improvement is that high-maturity organizations—for example, as measured according to the CMMI (2010)—are characterized by high-productivity processes. For instance, Putnam (2000) analyzed the Quantitative Software Management (QSM) database and showed that there seems to be a strong correlation between an organization's CMM level and its productivity index. Diaz and King (2002) report that moving a certain software organization from CMM level 2 to level 5 in the years 1997–2001 consistently increased project productivity by the factor 2.8. Yet, as observed in many contexts (e.g., Clark 2000; Herbsleb and Mockus 2003), overall organization maturity can probably not be considered as a significant factor influencing productivity. One may say that high maturity entails a certain level of project characteristics (e.g., CMMI key practices) positively influencing productivity; however, which characteristics influence productivity, and to what extent, varies most probably between different maturity levels. In that sense, process maturity should be considered as a context rather than as an influence factor. Influence factors should then refer to single key practices rather than to whole maturity levels. One must be aware that although increasing the maturity of a process will not hurt productivity in the long-term perspective, it may hurt it during the transition to higher maturity levels. It has been commonly observed that the introduction of procedures, new tools, and methods is, in the short term, detrimental to productivity (so-called *learning effect*). This learning effect can be moderated by introducing a so-called *delta team* consisting of very skilled personnel who are able to alleviate the short-term negative effect on productivity of implementing certain key process areas (KPAs). This is, however, nothing more than preventing the productivity decrease caused by investments in implementing certain KPAs by improving factors that have proven to have a significant positive impact on productivity (in this case, team capabilities). Benefits from process improvement and from introducing new technologies can also be gained faster by sharing experiences and offering appropriate training and management support. An alternative way of moderating the short-term negative impact of process improvement on productivity would be to start improvement with KPAs that are relatively inexpensive to implement and have a short-term positive impact on productivity.

Tip

▶ No tool will guarantee project success. Successful usage of tools depends on tool maturity and documentation, tool training and experience, appropriate support when selecting and introducing corresponding tools (task-technology fit), and the degree of tool integration.

For instance, Guinan et al. (1997) observed that when teams receive both tool-specific operational training and more general software development training, the effect of tool usage on development productivity is higher; if tools are additionally used in combination with formal structured methods, the productivity gains may reach up to 50 %.

Introduction of a new tool may—and usually does—have a negative impact on performance. Learning a new tool and integrating it into existing processes requires effort. Transition to new technology requires—as with any change—certain investments. Therefore, we should expect long-term benefits from new tools and technologies rather than short-term benefits.

Tip

▶ Do not overestimate the effect of a new technology in the short run and underestimate its effect in the long run. Remember that new tools and techniques may cause an initial loss of productivity and quality. First, pilot new tools and techniques in less critical projects, and then spread them to other projects.

In the tool introduction phase, usual project management practices need to be adjusted appropriately. Project managers are often blamed as the main source of failed tool application, because they do not institute rudimentary management practices needed before and during the introduction of new tools.

Finally, every tool should fit a particular situation in which it is going to be used. Ambler (2004), for instance, makes an apt remark that each development team works on different things and each individual has different ways of working. Forcing inappropriate tools on people will not only hamper progress but may also destroy team morale. Sean Kenney (2011) gives an example of three criteria for selecting a particular technology, with which nobody would ever identify himself explicitly, but which many are implicitly using in practice. According to him, people often select a certain technology because it is cool, new, or/and complicated. Yet, these are the very last arguments one should consider for selecting a technology, which is supposed to sustain project success.

Tip

▶ Never choose a technology that you don't understand. Never choose a technology that only you understand.—Sean Kenney

3.3.3 Product Characteristics

Characteristics of the software product are traditionally important factors influencing software development productivity and project effort. As we have discussed, size of software is not only the major determinant of project effort, but it also magnifies the effect of other project environmental characteristics on a project in an "effect of size" phenomenon—economies or diseconomies of scale.

Product-related characteristics that most often have an impact on development productivity are software complexity, the level of software quality required, and the quality of software requirements.

"*Software complexity*" is the next most important structural property of software after size. Software complexity starts with the complexity of the problem it solves, through the complexity of architecture, to the complexity of software code and the data it operates upon. The more complex the software, the more mental effort it requires to analyze, understand, and implement. In practice, the complexity of the software product is, at least to some extent, derivative of the communication structure of the team that developed the product. Poor synchronization of the development team would typically result in poorly structured software, for example, in terms of poor interfaces between parts of a product developed by different members of the team. R.E. Fairley noted that "the structure of a software system will reflect the communication structure of the team that built it."

The extent of "*required product quality*" is another aspect of software development that typically affects development productivity. The larger and the more rigid the requirements on software quality,[2] the more effort a software team needs to create the same product. Most commonly considered requirements in the context of effort estimation are software reliability and maintainability. In fact, at a technical level, both requirements often lead to similar product properties. For example, in terms of code structure, both maintainability and reliability promote

---

[2] In software engineering, software product quality requirements are also referred to as nonfunctional requirements. Other than functional requirements, quality requirements specify acceptance criteria with respect to software operation, rather than its specific behaviors or functions.

understandable, well-documented, and well-structured code. From the perspective of maintainability, well-structured code reduces the effort required to analyze, understand, modify, and revalidate it. From the viewpoint of reliability, writing understandable code is less error-prone and thus less likely to contain defects, which, in turn, may lead to software operational failures. Yet, creating highly maintainable and reliable software products requires additional overhead and results in increased project effort.

Finally, "*quality of requirements*" is a relevant aspect of software that we should consider when estimating project effort. Software requirements specifications are the basis for what we should provide in the project's output. With respect to project performance, the most deadly are requirements that change during the project. Volatile requirements drive changes in product and project scope. Additional development and management rework contributes to increased project effort. Novelty of software requirements to the development team is another relevant aspect of software requirements. Project effort is affected by the extent to which requirements are new to a software team; that is, they refer to software functional and nonfunctional characteristics that the team has never faced before. A lack of experience and similar solutions requires the creation of completely new solutions from scratch. On the one hand, dealing with completely new problems may require significant project overhead. On the other hand, planning this overhead is very difficult due to the lack of similar cases from prior projects. In consequence, creating new solutions may take considerably different effort and time to that expected—causing deviation from estimated project effort.

3.3.4 Project Characteristics

Organizational constraints on a software development project have important effects on project performance. Two aspects of project organization are commonly considered as having a particularly strong effect on development productivity: schedule pressure and project distribution.

"*Schedule pressure*" is commonly acknowledged as having a negative effect on the performance of a project team and, in turn, on the project performance in terms of the amount of resources consumed and quality of products delivered. Boehm et al. (2000), for example, observed that schedule compression of 25 %—which is considered a relatively small compression—may, for instance, lead to a 43 % increase in development effort. An interesting observation is that "negative schedule pressure"—referred to as schedule expansion—may also have negative effects on project performance. The most prominent effect, known as Parkinson's Law, is that "Work expands to fill the time available for its completion." Expanding the work to available time can typically be traced to two phenomena. First, when a deadline appears to be far off, people would work more slowly and decrease priority of work tasks for that project, which leads to a delay in the tasks' realization (so-called *Student Syndrome*). Second, when a large amount of time is available, people will do more inessential things on a project than when less time is available

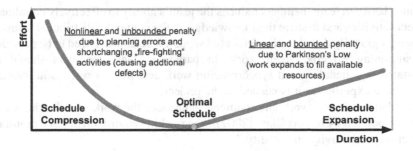

Fig. 3.4 Effects of schedule compression and expansion on effort (based on McConnell 2006)

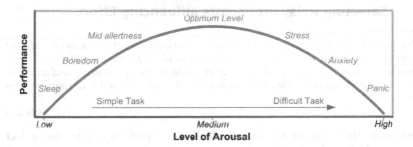

Fig. 3.5 The Yerkes–Dodson law on nonlinear impact of arousal on performance

(so-called *Gold Plating*). This may include performing optional work tasks or spending extra effort on adding unplanned beauty features to the final product.

Schedule compression has a nonlinear effect while schedule expansion has a linear impact on increased project effort (Fig. 3.4).

The negative impact of both schedule compression and expansion has much to do with human behavior. The impact of arousal on human performance has long been researched in psychology. Yerkes and Dodson (1908) observed that performance could increase with intensity of stimuli, but only to a certain point. The optimal performance tends to occur at an intermediate arousal level—if it goes below or above this optimum, the performance decreases (Fig. 3.5).

The main aspect responsible for the loss in performance is a negative effect of stress on human cognitive abilities such as attention, memory, and problem solving. Mediating factors in this relationship are human ego needs such as challenge and pride in one's own work (Frankenhaeuser and Gardell 1976). On the one hand, a low level of task-related pressure often means a lack of challenge and leads to boredom and reduced cognition, which consequently has a negative impact on human performance. On the other hand, extreme pressure often means a challenge humans cannot handle. This leads to anxiety and panic, which also reduces cognitive abilities and consequently performance. The point of optimum performance depends on the particular task, such that different tasks require different levels of arousal for optimal performance.

"*Project distribution*" influences project performance and effort through its impact on project communication and coordination. Geographical and mental distance between team members reduces the team's ability to effectively coordinate project activities and to share their knowledge. In the context of distributed teams—especially globally distributed—dedicated support mechanisms need to be provided for sustaining effective team work. In particular, team members should be facilitated in scheduling and synchronizing work activities as well as in locating appropriate expertise as it is needed in the project.

Last but not least, "work environment" influences the work of individuals in a team. As pointed by Robert Glass (2002), "the working environment has a profound impact on productivity and quality."

3.4   Selecting Relevant Factors Influencing Effort

Even though cost is influenced by a number of factors, knowing those factors exactly will still not enable you to predict cost exactly. Cost depends on far too many factors to study; even the most ambitious cost modelers have limited themselves to collecting and analyzing only a half of dozen or so of the most important cost parameters and have ignored all the rest.

—Tom DeMarco

In principle, there are an almost unlimited number of largely unknown factors potentially influencing software development productivity and project effort. Selecting a minimal set of the most relevant context factors and effort drivers is a critical element in effort estimation, after determining software size. A minimalist set of factors is typically dictated by limited resources for effort estimation. In practice, the fewer factors we consider, the less overhead needs to be spent on collecting, analyzing, and maintaining corresponding project data. On the other hand, the more relevant factors we consider, the better we are able to explain and estimate project effort.

3.4.1   Typical Traps of Selecting Effort Drivers

In practice, there is always a temptation to consider numerous project characteristics. Software practitioners believe that the more effort drivers they consider, the more accurate estimates they obtain. In reality, only very few factors typically have significant impact on development productivity and effort. The benefit of considering additional effort drivers does not compensate for the overhead to collect, analyze, and maintain additional data. Moreover, considering unnecessary and redundant information may mislead estimation analysis and bring a quite opposite effect to improved estimates.

Another trap practitioners get into when selecting effort drivers is to uncritically use fixed effort estimation models that rely on predefined effort drivers. A one-fits-all principle does not work for software effort estimation. Fixed-model approaches are typically founded on information that does not correspond to the situation in which they are later used. By uncritically using such models, we may accept effort drivers that are irrelevant in our situation, while missing effort drivers that actually are relevant. Consequently, we risk failed estimates.

Tip

▶ Be careful with using fixed estimation tools, as they were built in the context that typically may differ much from your particular situation. Make sure that context factors and effort drivers you consider fit your particular estimation environment.

3.4.2 Types of Effort Drivers

A number of different techniques have been proposed over the years to identify effort drivers that are most relevant in a particular estimation situation. In principle, these techniques can be classified into the expert-based, data-driven, and hybrid approaches.

Expert-based factor selection refers to various techniques—ad hoc and structured—that rely solely on human judgment. *Data-driven* factor selection techniques rely on analysis of the available quantitative project data and identifying a subset of already measured factors. Each of these two approaches has its strengths and weaknesses. Expert-based selection, for instance, inherits all the weaknesses of methods based on human judgment, such as subjectivity and dependency on the individual capabilities and preferences of involved human experts. Data-driven selection techniques, on the other hand, are not able to consider potential factors that are beyond those for which measurement data are available. *Hybrid* factor selection techniques integrate elements of the expert-based and data-driven approaches to exploit their strengths and avoid their weaknesses. We discuss the three types of approaches for selecting effort drivers in detail in Sects. 6.3–6.5, where we present basic classes of estimation methods.

Tip

▶ Combine the judgment of human experts with an analysis of project measurement data in order to identify the most relevant effort drivers.

In order to facilitate identification of the most relevant effort drivers, it is often useful to consider four classes of effort drivers:

- *Personnel factors* refer to characteristics of personnel involved in the software development project. These factors usually consider the expertise and capabilities of such project stakeholders as development team members—analysts, designers, programmers, project managers—as well as software users, customers, maintainers, and subcontractors.
- *Process factors* are concerned with the characteristics of software processes as well as methods, tools, and technologies applied during a software development project. They include, for instance, the effectiveness of quality

assurance, testing quality, quality of analysis and documentation methods, tool quality and usage, quality of process management, and the extent of customer participation.

- *Product factors* cover characteristics of software products created throughout all development phases. Example products include software code, requirements, and documentation. Their example characteristics are complexity, size, and volatility.
- *Project factors* regard various qualities of project management and organization, resource management, development constraints, and working conditions.

Tip

▶ When selecting the most relevant effort drivers, consider characteristics of the development project, involved personnel, applied processes, and delivered products.

3.4.3 Deciding on the Most Relevant Effort Drivers

After identifying candidate effort drivers, we may rate their usefulness with respect to the estimation purposes. Traditionally, relevancy of effort drivers has been considered in terms of its impact on project effort. Yet, in the light of typical industrial objectives and capabilities, several other aspects have to be considered. Minimizing project management effort, for instance, requires that a certain effort factor can be measured at reasonable cost. Managing software risks and productivity improvement, on the other hand, requires that a factor's values can be controlled, that is, its values can be affected in order to improve the project's productivity and thus mitigate related risks.

We propose considering the following three aspects for selecting the most relevant effort drivers:

1. *Impact*: The strength of influence an effort driver has on development productivity and project effort.
2. *Quantifiability*: The difficulty of collecting reliable quantitative data regarding an effort driver. This includes the characteristics of a useful metric defined by DeMarco (1982) such as measurability, independency, accountability, and precision.
   - *Measurability* refers to the extent to which the phenomenon represented by an effort driver can be quantified.
   - *Independency* refers to the extent to which values of an effort driver are independent of the conscious influence of the project personnel. An effort driver should be objectively measurable; that is, its values should be difficult to manipulate and not depend on the individual skills and preferences of project personnel.

- *Accountability* refers to the extent to which reliable data on an effort driver can be collected and analyzed. As data collection and analysis are typically error-prone activities, it is required that measurement data and the information on the context of measurement should be easy to collect and store so that they can be analyzed at any time. The information regarding measurement context serves for checking the integrity of the effort driver's data and should cover such aspects as when measurement was performed and who performed it.
- *Precision* refers to the precision and accuracy of data on an effort driver at the time of measurement. In fact, the key point about precision is not that measurement should be maximally precise, but that information regarding measurement precision and accuracy is explicitly documented. Based on this information, an estimator has the ability to account for measurement error while assessing the uncertainty of effort estimates.

3. *Controllability*: It represents the extent to which a software organization can influence/control the factor's value (e.g., a customer's characteristics are seldom controllable).

3.5   Reducing the Negative Impact of Scale and Effort Drivers

For every ailment under the sun
There is a remedy, or there is none;
If there be one, try to find it;
If there be none, never mind it.

—William W. Bartley

Controlling the impact of factors influencing development productivity and effort is one of the keys to successful project management. By affecting appropriate factors, we may increase development productivity and, in consequence, reduce development effort and schedule. The Project Management Body of Knowledge (e.g., PMI 2013) advises putting more resources into the project (*crashing*) and executing simultaneously work activities that were initially planned as subsequent (*fast-tracking*) as two universal approaches to compressing project schedule. Whereas crashing buys shorter schedules at the expense of increased cost, it is applicable only when adding more resources can lead to a faster work completion. Fast-tracking is not always possible and may require additional effort for work coordination. Reducing the negative impact of factors influencing development productivity represents an alternative approach, in which schedule compression activities focus on factors that are relevant in the context of specific projects.

3.5.1   Reducing Negative Effect of Scale

Fools ignore complexity; pragmatists suffer it; experts avoid it; geniuses remove it.

—Alan Perlis

The key to reducing the negative effect of project scale is to remove "complexity" within various project dimensions: complexity of project and team organization, complexity of processes they use, and complexity of products they deliver. In a broad sense, complexity is the main factor responsible for exponential growth of effort as project scale increases.

Traditionally, the "divide and conquer" strategy is recommended for reducing complexity in any art. Yet, we have to keep in mind that thoughtless application of this principle in one dimension of software development, such as product, personnel, project, or process, may easily gain quite the opposite effect in other dimensions. For example, ad hoc decomposition of work items may lead to poor work distribution and, in consequence, to increased complexity of team structure and project management activities.

Tip

▶ Consider multiple dimensions of software development—product, personnel, process, and project—when applying the "divide and conquer" principle. Ad hoc reduction of complexity in one dimension may cause unintended increase of complexity in other dimensions.

In the next few paragraphs, we discuss common ways of dealing with negative effects of project scale through reducing complexity within different project dimensions. In particular, we consider the most relevant project aspects through which we may moderate a project's management and technological stress.

Facilitate Team Interaction Processes

A number of empirical observations confirm that the ability of software project teams to operate effectively as a team arises from who they are—preexisting team characteristics—and how they interact—team communication, coordination, and information sharing (He et al. 2007; Klein et al. 2009; Lee and Yong 2010).

As project size and complexity increase, the role of team interactions in the overall team's performance increases, whereas the role of individual team members' characteristics remains constant. For example, Huckman et al. (2009) found the role experience of an individual team member being associated with better team performance. Yet, in practice, we can rarely and only to a limited extent alter the characteristics of individual team members. Once we select particular individuals for the team, their role experience cannot be changed much.

Therefore, facilitating team interaction and work coordination remain central issues while mitigating any diseconomies of scale.

Tip

▶ The ability of software project stakeholders to operate as a team arises from two aspects: who they are and how they interact. In other words, team performance depends on characteristics of individual team members and team communication and coordination.

In general (Wang 2007a), we may define team coordination as a set of project activities that cannot be done by an individual. Example coordination tasks include communication, meetings, work synchronization, peer reviews of work products, standardization, supervision, and quality assurance. In particular, team coordination comprises two aspects that are related to two distinct information flows within a team:

- *Coordinating work activities (control flow)*: Refers to synchronizing multiple and interrelated work activities and to managing the corresponding inter-dependencies among these activities.
- *Coordinating knowledge and skills (knowledge flow)*: Refers to managing interdependencies between the expertise of individual members of a development team. According to Espinosa et al. (2007), expertise coordination's main objective is to achieve shared team knowledge, which, in turn, contributes to increased team performance. Coordinating expertise includes three central aspects (Faraj and Sproull 2000):
  - Knowing where expertise is located
  - Knowing where expertise is needed
  - Knowing how to apply needed expertise

Mitigating diseconomies of scale can be achieved through (1) applying appropriate activity and expertise coordination mechanisms and (2) mitigating project constraints that have a negative impact on project coordination overhead.

As coordination overhead may, in practice (Wang 2007a), vary from 13 % up to 50 % for an entire project and from 31 % up to 60 % for individual project phases, investing in proper project interpersonal coordination is definitely worthwhile. It is especially important when the number of members in a team (or the number of teams) becomes very large. As Steve McConnell (1996) aptly summarized it, "*Even when you have skilled, motivated, hard-working people, the wrong team structure can undercut their efforts instead of catapulting them to success. A poor team structure can increase development time, reduce quality, damage morale, increase turnover, and ultimately lead to project cancellation.*" Becker and Huber (2008) confirmed this observation in their survey, in which poor team communication and information flows were highlighted as major causes of failed projects. Figure 3.6 illustrates how simple clustering of development teams can vastly reduce complexity of team communication paths and thus reduce the negative impact of larger teams on project performance.

The structure of team coordination is another aspect that should be considered when mitigating the negative effect of scale on project performance. In a vertical coordination pattern, communication between users and developers is realized through project management authorities. In a horizontal coordination pattern, users communicate with team members directly through collaborative work activities.

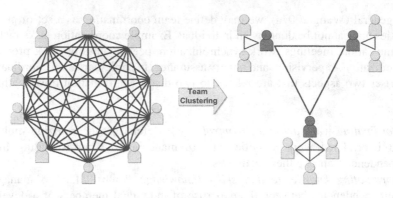

Fig. 3.6 Reducing complexity of team structure

In their survey of 169 project managers, Parolia et al. (2007) observed that *horizontal coordination facilitates team performance* in a number of ways. It enhances a common view of team members on relevant development issues, such as project objectives and organization, team roles and responsibilities, and characteristics of developed software products. Yet, in order to bring a positive effect, *team structure should be aligned with the structure of the whole organization*. Moe et al. (2009) found that misalignment between team structure and organizational structure can be counterproductive.

Another aspect of team structure is the "length" of communication paths in terms of geographical and mental distance between team members. Example aspects of mental distance are cultural differences or conflicting interests of team members.

Therefore, another objective of team building should be to reduce team geographical and mental diversity, that is, to *reduce geographical and mental distance among team members*. In the era of global development, geographically collocating project teams is not always possible. Therefore, team coordination and communication strategies aimed at reducing mental distances between project stakeholders are critical to a successful project (Espinosa et al. 2007; Biehl 2007).

Shared knowledge of team expertise and skills is an important aspect of distributed development. Therefore, in order to offset negative effects of distributed teams, the coordination effort should *focus on increasing shared knowledge of a distributed team's knowledge and skills*. For example, Hsu et al. (2011), in their survey among 194 employees of outsourcing vendors in India, found that continual team-building activities of communication, problem solving, goal setting, and role clarification lead to increased shared teamwork—which in turn leads to increased team performance. At this point, we should mention that *project organization—in terms of development life cycle—is an important factor affecting the knowledge exchange and team communication*. For example, Wang (2007b) observed a significant increase in the level of interpersonal coordination when moving from conventional sequential work flows such as a waterfall life cycle to highly interactive development processes such as extreme programming or agile development. In their investigation of interpersonal coordination rate, the authors observed rates of

30 % in projects organized according to a waterfall model and rates of 50 % in extreme programming and agile projects, whereby the rate of 0 % means no interpersonal cooperation and 100 % means that the whole project time has been spent on interpersonal cooperation.

Awareness of the location of team knowledge and work activities are other important aspects of team performance. An additional aspect of group awareness pointed out by Espinosa et al. (2007) as having an impact on team performance is so-called presence awareness. Typical presence awareness issues include knowing when team members are at their workplace or when their scheduled holidays are. Therefore, team coordination activities should also *increase shared knowledge of team members' presence*.

From the perspective of shared team knowledge, an effective way to facilitate team coordination is to *build the team from people who are already familiar with each other*. For example, in the case of software outsourcing, the extent of both geographical and cultural dispersion can be reduced by preferring nearshoring to farshoring.

Last but not least, we need to *support team communication and work coordination with appropriate media and tools*. Carey and Kacmar (1997) observed that although simple tasks can be accomplished successfully using electronic communication media—such as telephone or e-mail—complex tasks may result in lower productivity and larger dissatisfaction with electronic media used. Kraut and Streeter (1995) suggest that in order to be successful, formal communication methods need to be supplemented by informal interpersonal communication. *Face-to-face project communication is still the most effective way of dealing with project uncertainty and problem solving*. Yet, interpersonal communication, although effective, might not always be efficient—especially in large projects; in such cases, formal coordination methods (e.g., review meetings) and tools (e.g., configuration management) are indispensable. If face-to-face communication is not feasible, for example, due to geographical team distribution, we should *look for simple tools supporting interpersonal communication*. We should keep in mind that the more complex and sophisticated means for communication we provide, the less willing will be the team to use them—and the less communication will take place.

Follow Well-Defined Processes

Even though heavyweight development processes are widely criticized as being an unnecessary burden for small projects, they seem to be inevitable in the context of large software undertakings. Lightweight processes, for example, are based largely on direct interaction among team members. Although they typically work for small teams, they usually do not do the job in the context of large teams. Therefore, well-defined processes, in which comprehensiveness is adjusted to the project size, are an important weapon against any diseconomies of scale effect.

A number of empirical studies—for instance, Agrawal and Chari (2007)—report that high maturity of development processes reduces the negative effect of factors determining project effort, cycle time, and product quality. Mature processes make project effort variance less dependent on factors other than size of deliverables.

Ensure Effective Project Management

Project management is traditionally a key success factor of a software project. If poor project management can still slip unnoticed in the context of small projects, it will typically have fatal consequences as project scale increases. In particular, diseconomies of scale are observed wherever risk management is not a routine part of development.

Systematic project management is therefore one critical activity for preventing diseconomies of scale. Another aspect is skills of the project manager. For example, Stevenson and Starkweather (2010), in their survey among IT managers, identified six critical competencies of a project manager: leadership, the ability to communicate at multiple levels, verbal and written skills, attitude, and the ability to deal with ambiguity and change.

Ensure Efficient Learning

Projects that are completely new to a development team entail much learning overhead, especially in the case of large projects. Although there is not much we can do about project novelty, we may consider some indirect means for moderating the impact of novelty on the diseconomies of scale. On the one hand, efficiency of team learning—*learning curve*—can be improved by providing additional training before projects start. On the other hand, the overall team knowledge and experience can be improved by involving external experts.

Divide Large and Cluster Small Projects

Last but not least, wherever it is possible, project managers should try to ensure that the size of future projects corresponds to sizes for which historical projects achieved best productivity rates. On the one hand, a project manager should seek projects of appropriate scale. On the other hand, if such selection is not possible, a project manager should consider adjusting project size to the most optimal one. For example, too large new development projects should be split into subprojects of reasonable scale, whereas too small maintenance projects—so-called "quick fix" projects—should be clustered into larger maintenance releases.

3.5.2 Reducing Negative Impact of Effort Drivers

> *It's not necessarily the amount of time you spend at practice that counts; it's what you put into the practice.*
>
> —Eric Lindros

Specific ways of reducing the negative impact of effort drivers depend on which particular effort driver they concern, and this, in turn, differs across specific project contexts. Therefore, rather than discussing specific effort factors, we present two general approaches for reducing the negative impact of effort drivers and illustrate them on example effort drivers.

In practice, we can reduce the negative impact of an effort driver by changing its value and/or changing the strength of its influence on effort. These two approaches are similar to basic strategies of handling risk and opportunities in a project: we take actions to change the likelihood of risk/opportunity occurring and/or to change the impact of risk/opportunity when it occurs.

Change the Value of an Effort Driver

This is the most obvious strategy of reducing the negative impact of an effort driver on effort. We change the effort driver's value in a way that leads to a decrease in effort. Using the risk management metaphor, if we perceive the effort driver as having a bad value as a risk, then the approach corresponds to reducing the likelihood of this risky event.

In the case of an effort driver measured on at least an ordinal scale, we need to increase or decrease its value, depending on the exact nature of the dependency between the effort driver and effort. For example, let us consider the effort driver "Requirements volatility" measured on a three-point approximate interval scale "Low," "Medium," "High," where each level refers to a certain percentage of requirements changed after closing the requirements specification phase. For instance, "Requirements volatility" would be "Low" if up to 5 % of requirements will change after closing the requirements specification phase. Requirements volatility has a clear negative impact on effort in that changes to requirements lead to rework in the project—the later in the development the requirements change, the more effort it costs. In the context of a software organization where "Requirements volatility" is typically "High" and significantly increases total development effort, reducing the value of this effort driver would be one of the major strategies for reducing the overall project effort. This could, for example, be achieved by engaging customers in the requirements specification phase and/or creating running prototypes in order to specify requirements that better reflect what the customer really wants and thus are less likely to change. Although reducing "Requirements volatility" will require additional investment in effort and time in early development phases, the resulting savings in later phases will allow for reduction in total project effort and time.

Change the Strength of an Effort Driver's Impact on Effort

In addition to (or instead of) changing the effort driver's value, we may change the strength of its impact on effort in order to reduce the project effort. Using a risk management metaphor, if we perceive the effort driver as having a bad value as a risk, then the approach corresponds to reducing the negative consequences of this risky event in case it will actually occur.

Let us consider the "Requirements volatility" example from the prior paragraph and assume that reducing "Requirements volatility" is not possible, for example, because there is no way we can convince the customer to engage in the requirements specification phase. In this situation, an alternative way to reduce project effort related to volatile requirements would be to reduce their impact on effort. In other words, even though requirements are highly volatile, we would like to reduce the additional effort they entail. One way of achieving this objective can be by introducing short development cycles (as promoted by Agile development) in order to quickly respond to potential requirement changes and to reduce the rework effort required for their realization.

Further Reading

- A. Trendowicz and J. Münch (2009), "Factors Influencing Software Development Productivity - State of the Art and Industrial Experiences." *Advances in Computers*, vol. 77, Elsevier Science Inc., pp. 185–241.

  This article provides a comprehensive overview of the most common context factors and effort drivers. The authors discuss effort drivers that seem to be universally applicable across various project environments and those that seem to apply only within particular project situations.

- B. Kitchenham (1992), "Empirical Studies of the Assumptions That Underline Software Cost-Estimation Models", *Information and Software Technology*, vol. 34 no. 4, pp. 211–218.

  The author examines different software engineering data sets with respect to the existence of economies of scale. The investigation does not provide statistical support for any economies and diseconomies of scale effect.

- B. Kitchenham (2002), "The question of scale economies in software - why cannot researchers agree?" *Information and Software Technology*, vol. 44, no. 1, pp. 13–24.

  The author summarizes results of investigations performed by many researchers regarding the existence of (dis)economies of scale in the software engineering context. Possible sources of significant disagreement on (dis) economies effect in the software community are discussed from the perspective of the potential threats to the validity of empirical investigations that underline contradicting conclusions.

- J. Persson and L. Mathiassen (2010), "A Process for Managing Risks in Distributed Teams," *IEEE Software*, vol. 27, no. 1, pp. 20–29.

  A process for managing risks related to distributed software development teams is defined. They also provide an overview of typical risk factors, and for each factor they describe situations that would result in low, medium, and high risk, respectively. Finally, they propose appropriate risk resolution techniques and guidelines and how to compose them into appropriate risk mitigation plans.

- C. Sauer, A. Gemino, and B.H. Reich (2007), "The impact of size and volatility on IT project performance," *Communications of ACM*, vol. 50, no. 11, pp. 79–84.

  The authors discuss the impact of the size and volatility of a software project on its performance. They investigate several factors that contribute to reduction in project performance as its scale increases.

- J.P. Scott (2000), *Social Network Analysis: A handbook. 2nd Edition*. Sage Publications Ltd.

  This book discusses the characteristics of team work in terms of social relationships among team members. In social network analysis, these relationships are realized as a network. A set of principle metrics is proposed to quantitatively analyze properties of a social network. Aspects such as network density, centrality, or cohesion are considered as useful indicators of potential deficits in team performance.

- Z. Bachore and L. Zhou (2009), "A Critical Review of the Role of User Participation in IS Success," *Proceedings of the 15th Americas Conference on Information Systems*, San Francisco, California, USA.

  The authors provide a comprehensive review of the studies that investigate the influence of user participation on the success of a software development project.

- J. Shim, T.S. Sheu, J.J. Jiang, and G. Klein (2010), "Coproduction in the Successful Software Development Project," *Information and Software Technology*, vol. 52, No. 10, pp. 1062–1068.

  An investigation of key factors for the successful involvement of users in software development projects. They consider "partnership" between developers and users as a crucial driver supporting the expertise exchange. Authors list a number of detailed aspects that need to be considered when assessing the level of partnership between customers and developers as well as when locating and applying expertise required in the project.

- A. Trendowicz, A. Wickankamp, M. Ochs, J. Münch, Y. Ishigai, and T. Kawaguchi (2008), "Integrating Human Judgment and Data Analysis to Identify Factors Influencing software Development Productivity", *e-Informatica Software Engineering Journal*, vol. 2, no. 1, pp. 47–69.

  This article discusses alternative strategies for selecting relevant effort drivers. The authors discuss the strengths and weaknesses of approaches based on human judgment and data analysis. They propose a novel, hybrid approach that combines both strategies in order to exploit their strengths and to avoid their weaknesses. The method elicits relevant factors by integrating data analysis and expert judgment approaches by means of a multicriteria decision analysis

(MCDA) technique. Empirical evaluation of the method in an industrial context indicates that it delivers a different set of factors compared to individual data- and expert-based factor selection methods. Moreover, application of the integrated method significantly improves the performance of effort estimation in terms of accuracy and precision.

Estimation Under Uncertainty

4

> *In the end, an estimate is just an estimate, it is not exact. After all, the process is called estimation, not exactimation.*
>
> —Phillip G. Armour

Uncertainty and inaccuracy are inherent properties of estimation, in particular predictive estimation. Measuring and managing uncertainty and inaccuracy lies at the heart of good estimation. Flyvbjerg (2006) distinguished three categories of reasons for inaccuracies in project forecasts:

- *Technical* reasons for inaccuracy include usage of imperfect estimation methods (and models) and founding estimates on imperfect information.
- *Psychological* causes of estimation inaccuracy include unconscious estimation biases that apply to forecasting involving human judgment. These biases refer to the inability of people to judge future events in an objective way. Psychological biases include the anchoring and planning fallacy, which we briefly define in Sect. 6.4.3 (Table 6.3) when discussing the expert-based estimation approach.
- *Political* reasons include conscious estimation biases and apply to forecasting that involves human judgment. These biases refer to the tendency of people to deliberately and strategically distort estimates for their own gain, for example, overestimate benefits and underestimate costs of a project in order to get it funded and to please the customer. Political biases include wishful thinking and polarization, which we briefly define in Sect. 6.4.3 (Table 6.3) when discussing the expert-based estimation approach.

In this chapter, we focus on technical sources of estimation uncertainty and inaccuracy, in particular imperfect information upon which estimates are based. On the one hand, uncertainty relates to the fact that prediction typically involves information we are unsure of because a corresponding event has not yet happened, and our information about it is missing, incomplete, ambiguous, or imprecise. On the other hand, uncertainty relates to imperfection of methods and models we use for estimation purposes. A number of approaches have been proposed over the

A. Trendowicz and R. Jeffery, *Software Project Effort Estimation*,
DOI 10.1007/978-3-319-03629-8_4, © Springer International Publishing Switzerland 2014

years to cope with estimation uncertainty in the software effort estimation domain. In this chapter, we introduce uncertainty as an inherent element of estimation, and we discuss approaches for representing and reducing uncertainty within the effort estimation process.

4.1   Nature of Estimation Uncertainty

Project effort is not determined by the knowledge we have, it is a function of the knowledge we don't have.

—Phillip G. Armour

In effort estimation, we try to make a well-informed assessment of the effort required to complete a project, based upon past project experiences and actual project information. Goodness of estimates is directly dependent on the quality of information on which the estimate is based. In practice, we must be prepared for imperfect information, that is, information that is incomplete, uncertain, inconsistent, ambiguous, or even contradicting. There are three major aspects of the project and its environment, which contribute to these information deficiencies: (1) random changes, (2) limited cognition, and (3) limited granularity and abstract character. These three constraints lead us to three major types of effort estimation uncertainty: probabilistic, possibilistic, and granulation, respectively.

Tip

▶ Estimation can only be as good—complete, certain, and exact—as the information it is based upon, independent of the quality of the estimation method employed.

Probabilistic uncertainty reflects the random character of changes to the project and its environment (I know something, but it may change unpredictably). In the context of effort estimation, probabilistic uncertainty refers to the variable character of factors influencing software development effort. Uncertainty is considered here in terms of probability, that is, by the unpredictable, nondeterministic character of future software project conditions. For example, a number of aspects of software development may be the subject of unexpected changes over the project lifetime. Particular examples include changes to human-related factors—typically due to staff fluctuations—changes to market situation, or changes to software technologies.

Possibilistic uncertainty—also called epistemological uncertainty—reflects limited cognition, that is, knowledge and/or experience, of the observed phenomena due to subjectivity of the observer's perception (I do not know something). Possibilistic uncertainty may also manifest ambiguity of the observed phenomenon, for example, due to its imprecise or double meaning. Uncertainty is considered here in terms of possibility. This concerns, in particular, phenomena that are measured by qualitative means using linguistic terms such as "low," "moderate," and "high." For example, by saying that a developer's knowledge of a programming language is "high," we are typically not specifying an important aspect, which is the extent to which this capability exists in reality. In other words, we are not specifying the possibility of this capability being actually "high." One typical cause of possibilistic uncertainty is impossibility to collect exact data because it is too expensive to collect, or because the measurement devices have limited precision and burden measurements with an inherent error.

Granulation uncertainty—also called *approximation uncertainty*—reflects limited granularity of the description of the observed phenomena (I know something approximately). In effort estimation, limited granularity of description can, for example, refer to a finite number of individual parameters used to describe project effort. On the one hand, the language humans operate with has limited granularity, because humans can grasp only a limited number of aspects. On the other hand, it is often simply not profitable to consider a large number of possible irrelevant factors due to the relatively high cost of collecting, analyzing, and maintaining corresponding data as compared to the benefits in quality of estimates. For example, it would probably not make much economic sense to consider 20 effort drivers if 5 of them account for 90 % of the observed variability in development productivity. The potential gain in explaining the remaining 10 % of productivity variance would, in most cases, not be worth the cost of collecting, analyzing, and maintaining data on the remaining 15 factors.

Whereas probabilistic uncertainty addresses what is unpredictable in information, possibilistic uncertainty addresses what is incomplete or ambiguous in information, and granulation uncertainty addresses what is imprecise and approximate in information. In other words, probabilistic uncertainty is caused by our limited capability to foresee certain phenomena, possibilistic uncertainty is caused by our limited knowledge of or capability of observing the phenomena, and granulation uncertainty is caused by our limited capability in describing the phenomena. In fact, the term "uncertainty" should actually be used to refer to probabilistic ambiguity of information; in the case of possibilistic and granulation "uncertainty," the term "precision" would better reflect these concepts.

Example 4.1. Probabilistic vs. Possibilistic vs. Granulation Uncertainty

Let us consider a situation where a project manager would like to estimate project effort. He considers "capabilities of development team" as a relevant factor having a significant impact on development productivity and thus on the effort required to complete the project. The project manager decides to consider this factor as the "Capabilities of development team" effort driver and to measure it on an ordinal scale using three values, "high," "moderate," and "low." The effort driver is assigned an appropriate ordinal value based upon the number of years a team member has been working in software development projects.

By making these decisions, the project manager is committing to and must take into account, through appropriate handling, the following types of uncertainty:

- *Probabilistic uncertainty* due to unexpected changes in team capabilities, for example due to stuff turnover or team learning effect.
- *Possibilistic uncertainty* due to the ambiguity of the metrics assigned to the selected effort driver. Uncertainty of estimates is influenced by incompleteness of information—due to the fuzzy character of the ordinal scale using linguistic terms.
- *Granulation uncertainty* due to the generic (abstract) character of the effort driver considered by the project manager. In practice, the capabilities of a development team encompass a whole variety of specific capabilities that should potentially be considered on a lower granulation level as individual effort drivers, e.g., a software architect's domain experience or a developer's knowledge of a programming language. Yet, the project manager decides to consider only one effort driver on a high granulation level.

The project manager may try to reduce these uncertainties or to accept and model them. For example, in order to reduce possibilistic and granulation uncertainty, the project manager may consider refining his estimation model by considering additional relevant team capabilities and defining more precise metrics.∎

Three big theories handle probabilistic, possibilistic, and granulation uncertainty: (1) probability theory and statistics, (2) fuzzy sets, and (3) rough sets. In Sect. 4.4, we provide an overview of selected techniques for handling different types of uncertainty.

4.2 Sources of Uncertainty

There's no sense in being precise when you don't even know what you're talking about.
—John von Neumann

As we postulated in the previous sections, as far as software estimation uncertainty is concerned, it is all about information. Based on information concerning the characteristics of already completed projects—*the past*—and information on the characteristics of a new project—*the present*—we foretell the final characteristics of the new project—*the future*. With all this information, we try always to reflect the reality, that is, the actual state of being. In practice, obtaining complete and correct information is often not feasible and often not reasonable. Not feasible because of limited cognition, limited granulation, and unpredictable change. Not reasonable because of little benefit as compared to the large overhead required to collect, analyze, and maintain all the information. Therefore, effort estimation operates on models that only approximate reality.

Tip

▶ There is no right estimation model. In a sense, all models are wrong because they only approximate reality. Focus on finding the model that is useful, that is, that approximates reality well enough to achieve your estimation objectives.

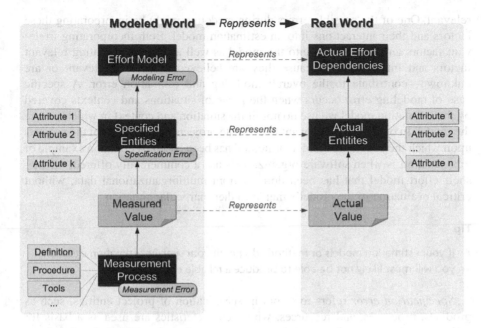

Fig. 4.1 Sources of estimation uncertainty

Estimation uncertainty is connected with the discrepancy between the world that is represented by an effort model and the real world. In practice, estimation models are incomplete and incorrect in that they consider only a small excerpt of reality, and even this excerpt may differ from the actual situation.

Sources of estimation uncertainty are related to particular sources of information used in the estimation. Kitchenham and Linkman (1997) list a few information sources and associated error types that contribute to estimation uncertainty. Figure 4.1 illustrates potential sources of estimation uncertainty and related errors.

An effort model represents effort dependencies in a certain context. In other words, an effort model describes what aspects of the project and its environment influence project effort and how they influence it. *Entities* and their attributes represent relevant elements of a project environment and their characteristics that have impact on project effort. Finally, *measurement process* represents the process of collecting information on the aspects comprised within the effort model. Measurement includes definition of such elements as metrics, measurement procedures, and measurement tools.

Modeling error reflects imperfection in the estimation models as abstractions of reality. In practice, there are an unlimited number of largely unknown and potentially interacting factors that influence development effort. It is thus basically not feasible to construct estimation models that include all these factors and all their interactions. Limited cognition of effort dependencies and limited possibility of considering all of them lead to estimation models that are based upon a very limited number of effort drivers and interactions, which are believed to be the most relevant. One of the possible errors during modeling might be incorporating these factors and their interactions into an estimation model. Both incorporating irrelevant factors and interactions into the model as well as not incorporating relevant factors and interactions—because they are believed to be less relevant or are unknown—contribute to the overall modeling and estimation error. A specific case of modeling error occurs when the range of situations and contexts covered by the estimation model we use do not fit the situation and context in which we use the model. In other words, we want to estimate projects that differ from the projects upon which the estimation model or method has been based. A common example of this situation is when software organizations use a commercially offered, off-the-shelf effort model that has been derived from multiorganizational data, without critical evaluation of the model's match to their particular situation.

Tip

▶ If your estimation models or methods do not fit your specific estimation situation, you will most likely not be able to produce a reliable effort estimate.

Specification error refers to errors in specification of project entities, such as products, processes, and resources, whose characteristics are used as a basis for estimation. For example, we may use software functional size that has been measured on potentially incomplete and/or inconsistent requirements specifications. In this case, errors in size measurement will have significant impact on estimation error because software size is a major determinant of project effort—thus, it is typically the main effort driver in the estimation method or model.

Measurement error reflects the inaccuracy of a measurement process. The measurement error may be inherent in the metric due to its definition or may result from the associated data collection procedures and tools applied to collect measurement data. For instance, measurement error in function point analysis (FPA) can result from imprecise specification of counting rules and the way human experts interpret these rules when counting function points.

These quite generic sources of estimation uncertainty can be used for further identification of exact causes of prediction uncertainty in a particular estimation context. Furthermore, determination of the nature of uncertainty—probabilistic, possibilistic, or granulation—helps to identify appropriate techniques for handling it during estimation. Refer to Sect. 4.4 for a selection of the most common approaches for handling estimation uncertainty.

Example 4.2. Measurement Error of Function Point Analysis

Applying function point analysis (FPA) to measure functional size in early development phases requires consideration of different kinds of uncertainty, which contribute to measurement error:

- *Probabilistic uncertainty*: Software requirements may change unpredictably during the project lifetime as customers learn more about the product and its context. For example, changes in project environment factors, such as IT technologies or legal constraints, may require adjustments in a product's functional and nonfunctional requirements.

- *Possibilistic uncertainty*: Limited cognition of a final software product in early development phases may result in incomplete and incorrect requirements. Moreover, the subjective character of FPA may contribute to measurement error. For example, even though an expert assesses complexity of a certain functional element in FPA as "high," the actual value may differ.
- *Granulation uncertainty*: Function point analysis considers only a very limited number of aspects of software functionality. For example, the function point method (ISO/IEC 20926 2009) distinguishes five basic elements of software functionality, external inputs, external outputs, external inquiries, internal logical files, and external interface files.

In order to moderate or at least model the measurement error of function point analysis, we need to be aware of these uncertainties that affect FPA. ∎

4.3 Representing Uncertainty

False precision is the enemy of accuracy.

—Steve McConnell

In principle, estimation uncertainty is a consequence of limited and uncertain project information upon which estimates are based. There might be different sources of this limited project knowledge. On the one hand, knowledge we have about the project might be incomplete and/or ambiguous, especially at the very beginning of the project. On the other hand, knowledge we have might be imprecise and quite abstract. Finally, knowledge we initially have on the project might not be actual due to project changes. Effective effort estimation requires dealing with uncertainty. We may try to eliminate uncertainty, for example, through preventing project changes. But there will always be a certain level of uncertainty in project estimates—especially because they are about the future, which is typically uncertain. In this case, the best way of dealing with uncertainty is to model it and to represent it within project estimates.

4.3.1 Cone of Uncertainty

The later in the project runtime, the more we know about the project, and the lower the likelihood of potential project changes. An obvious consequence of this fact is that the earlier in the project we estimate, the larger the uncertainty we have to take into account because of fewer and less correct information on actual project

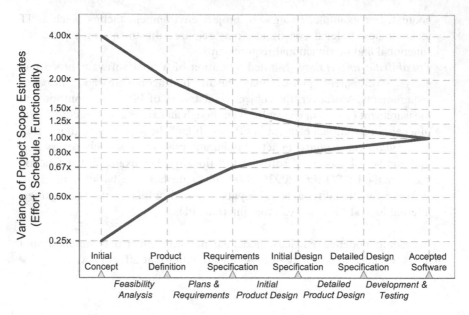

Fig. 4.2 Cone of uncertainty (Boehm 1981)

characteristics. Uncertainty in estimation decreases as the project progresses and more is known about its actual characteristics. Boehm (1981) introduced and McConnell (2006) refined the concept of "the cone of uncertainty" for illustrating estimation uncertainty along phases of a software development project. The cone of uncertainty (Fig. 4.2) represents estimation uncertainty as a function of the level of information we have on the intended software system and the development project.

The level of the project knowledge changes during a project's lifetime. At the beginning, when alternative concepts for a new software product are considered, the relative range of software cost estimates is quite large. Figure 4.2 illustrates example subjective values as provided by Boehm (1981); however, the concrete ranges of estimation uncertainty will differ in various contexts. A wide range of estimation uncertainty reflects high uncertainty regarding the actual characteristics of the software product. The initial uncertainty about a future product is significantly reduced once the feasibility phase is finished and the software operation concept is clarified (*initial concept*). The next large reduction of uncertainty is achieved at the time software requirements are specified. It is assumed here that complete and correct requirements are provided. In practice, poor requirements are one of the major sources of largely uncertain and, in consequence, failed estimates.

Tip

▶ Unstable requirements are the most common source of failed estimates.

During the subsequent phases, as more is known about the actual nature of software products and as fewer unknowns remain to be estimated, estimation uncertainty decreases continuously.

Cone of Uncertainty by Project Management Institute

The Project Management Institute (PMI) proposes an even more conservative approach for addressing uncertainty in that they propose an asymmetric cone of uncertainty, which is shifted toward overestimates. In particular, PMI suggest the creation of an "initial order of magnitude estimate," which ranges from -25% to $+75\%$. Next, the "budgetary estimate" should be created that spans between -10% and $+25\%$, finally followed by "definitive estimate" with a range of 5% to $+10\%$.

The asymmetric cone of uncertainty advocated by PMI may surely preserve project managers from a high risk of exceeding effort and schedule estimates. But increasing estimates—also known as "padding"—only because of the cone of uncertainty may significantly increase the risk of rejecting corresponding project targets and bids by project owners and customers.

Padding estimates without a reasonable rationale behind it may easily turn against a project manager and the project itself—when project owners or customers ask for such a rationale and do not accept the project; saying that this is a recommendation of PMI will surely not suffice.

A good project practice is therefore avoiding commitments in very early stages of development, especially when uncertainty of the project information and of the estimates that had been based upon it has not been thoroughly analyzed. If you have to submit estimates in such cases, you should always accompany the estimates with the constraints that have an impact on the quality of the estimates (e.g., incomplete and uncertain information the estimates were based upon).

Tip

▶ Do not commit to estimates too early in the cone of uncertainty. Always make clear how uncertain estimates are and what are the potential risks related to committing to such estimates.

4.3.2   Measures of Estimation Uncertainty

Another way of representing estimation uncertainty is quantitative metrics. A number of estimation uncertainty metrics have been proposed over the years. In principle, uncertainty metrics represent three basic types of error in predictions: accuracy, precision, and bias. Note that although software engineers often use accuracy and precision as synonyms, these two concepts actually refer to two different phenomena.

Fig. 4.3 Estimation
accuracy, precision, and bias

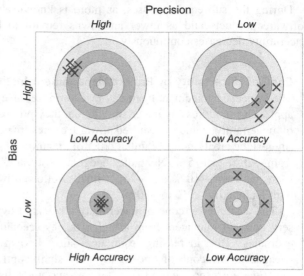

Precision refers to the degree to which several estimates are very close to each other. It is an indicator of the scatter in the data. The less the scatter, the higher is the precision. *Bias* refers to a systematic—constant—error in estimates and is determined as the difference between the average of estimates and the actual, true value. *Accuracy* is a function of bias and precision and describes the nearness of estimates to the true value. Highly accurate prediction methods will provide estimates very close to the actual, true value. Figure 4.3 illustrates differences between concepts of precision, bias, and accuracy.

A common belief that point estimates, as "apparently" more precise, are also more accurate often leads to poor estimates. Driven by this belief, software practitioners make estimates artificially more precise through simple narrowing of the uncertainty range or even taking the middle value as a point estimate. McConnell (2006) warns that in reality, this practice actually leads to lower accuracy of estimates and higher risk of getting into trouble while striving to meet such targets.

Tip

▶ Remember that "false precision is the enemy of accuracy." If your estimates vary within a particular range, do not compress it to a point estimate (e.g., by taking the middle value).

Example 4.3 briefly illustrates actual loss in accuracy due to artificially increased precision.

> **Example 4.3. False Precision Is the Enemy of Accuracy**
>
> Let us consider effort estimates expressed in the form of a range, for example, 50–80 person-days.
>
> This estimate is actually the most accurate and the most precise estimate feasible. On the one hand, there is a high probability that the true effort lies between the range boundaries. On the other hand, a width of the range gives us a notion of the estimation uncertainty and related project risk.
>
> Simplifying this estimate to a middle point of 65 person-hours, although looking more precise, is in reality less accurate. ∎

4.3.3 Estimating Quality Factor

DeMarco (1982), in his book *Controlling Software Projects*, proposed a metric called *Estimating Quality Factor* (*EQF*) for quantifying the goodness of project estimates. It represents a reciprocal of the average discrepancy between estimates and actual value and can, principally, be applied for estimation of any kind, for example, size, effort, or duration estimation.

Figure 4.4 illustrates the concept of the estimating quality factor. At the beginning of a project, the project manager makes an initial effort estimate. Over time, the project manager may revise his estimates up or down. This may result in over- or underestimates, relative to the actual project effort known at project completion. For the actual project end date, the EQM is calculated by dividing the gray dotted area of the actual effort by the slashed area of estimation deviations.

As a result, EQF provides a unitless number between zero and infinity, where high numbers characterize good estimates. For example, DeMarco (1982) reports industry median EQF = 3.8 as not a great achievement. In one of the newer surveys, Little (2006) reported median EQF = 4.8 achieved for 106 software development projects[1] performed from 1999 to 2002 and led by experienced project managers with approximately 20 years of experience.

The EQF measures project estimation accuracy—essentially, the reciprocal of estimation error. Yet, it differs from other measures of estimation quality, such as accuracy, precision, and bias, in that it considers multiple estimates instead of a single estimate. Common estimation uncertainty metrics quantify the difference between single estimates and actual value. A typical way of considering multiple estimates is to compute multiple uncertainty values, for each estimate individually, and combine them either as an uncertainty distribution or as a single value synthesized using one of the common statistics over this distribution, for example, mean or median.

---

[1] Project performed at Langmark Graphics, a vendor of commercial software for the oil and gas exploration and production market.

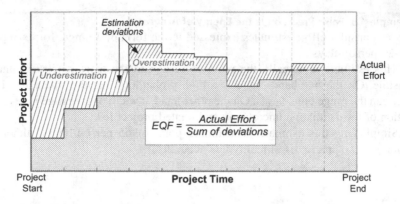

Fig. 4.4 Estimation quality factor (DeMarco 1982)

4.4   Handling Uncertainty

Work with uncertainty, not in defiance of it.
                                               —Lawrence H. Putnam & Ware Myers
True genius resides in the capacity for evaluation of uncertain, hazardous, and conflicting information.
                                                        —Winston Churchill

Predicting future events with incomplete knowledge of the past and of the present makes uncertainty an inherent element of estimation, which we cannot avoid. What we can do is to address uncertainty explicitly and assess its impact on estimates. In industrial practice, estimation uncertainty is often either ignored or addressed using quick and dirty approaches, such as padding estimates. *Padding* refers to adding an extra effort on top of realistic and honest estimates just to be on a safe line when it comes to estimation uncertainty. Padding is analogical to contingency reserves made when planning a project budget in order to account for potential project risks. As long as contingency reserves are a justified risk management best practice, padding is a counterproductive bad practice. On the one hand, padded estimates are very likely not to be accepted by a project owner because they are too high and not supported by reasonable rationale. On the other hand, extra resources planned within padding estimates are often taken away from a project that was honestly estimated and really needs them.

In industrial contexts, a simple and most common way of handling estimation uncertainty is to provide a range of values, instead of a crisp estimate. A simple way to account for the estimation uncertainty is to use the estimation variance ranges observed in similar projects in the past. Note that with respect to uncertainty, estimates should be communicated differently than commitments. Whereas estimates, as inherently uncertain, should be communicated as uncertain, for example, by means of range, commitments should always be crisp values.

Tip

▶ Use value ranges for communicating your estimates but use specific (point) estimates to communicate your commitments. Specify internal and external project risks to communicate factors that may threaten your commitments.

In order to reflect potential uncertainties of project commitments, we may communicate associated risks or directly incorporate them into the communicated commitments. In the first case (communicate risk), we will base commitment on the estimates without uncertainty and inform about likely events that may affect the achievement of commitments, that is, what events, how likely they are, and the magnitude of their effect. In the latter case (incorporate risk), we adjust commitment by a certain contingency margin appropriate for the identified risks. We should, however, be careful not to double count risks. If we already incorporated a negative impact of the same likely events on project effort during estimation, we should not include it again when preparing project commitments.

Tip

▶ Avoid double-counting the effects of uncertainty. If you include it in the model, you should not include it in the risk assessment.

For example, "Capabilities of development team" is an important factor influencing project effort. At the very beginning of the project, it is usually difficult to say exactly which particular people will work on the project. Typically, we would assume "average" capabilities we observe in our organization. Yet, we would also like to account in our plans for the situation where capable staff are not available and we need to run the project with less experienced people. We may consider this issue either in the estimation, through the "team capabilities" effort driver, or during project risk analysis, through an appropriate contingency margin.

In the following sections, we present the most common ways to handle major types of estimation uncertainty.

4.4.1 Handling Probabilistic Uncertainty

Probability theory and statistics provide a number of techniques for handling probabilistic uncertainty. Two types of approaches have become particularly well acknowledged in the context of effort estimation: (1) probability distributions and (2) confidence or prediction intervals.

Probability Distribution

Using probability distributions instead of point values is a common way of handling uncertainty in the context of effort estimation. Representing inputs and outputs of effort estimation as probability distributions contributes—besides handling

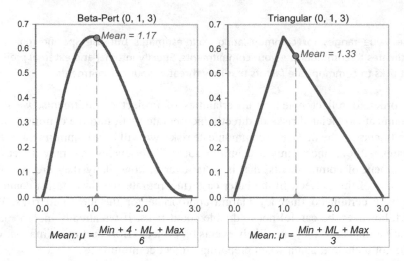

Fig. 4.5 Probability density functions for triangular and beta-PERT probability distributions

uncertainty—to a better understanding of estimation results. Motivated by intuitiveness of probability distributions, a number of estimation methods that operate on mathematical probability have been proposed. Well-known theories and techniques such as Bayes' theorem, Monte Carlo sampling, or Bootstrap sampling are applied to process probabilistic inputs.

A typical context where probability distributions are employed is estimation based on expert opinion reflecting uncertainty in human judgment. Due to their relative simplicity and intuitiveness, two particular distributions are typically preferred for modeling human judgment: triangular and beta-PERT. Figure 4.5 illustrates both probability density functions and formulas for computing their statistical mean (μ).

In contrast to the bell-shaped Gaussian distribution popular in other domains, triangular and beta-PERT[2] distributions do not demand specification of quite unintuitive parameters. They require solely three numbers: the minimal, the maximal, and the most likely value. Minimal and maximal values can also be interpreted as best-case and worst-case estimates. In the context of expert-based estimation, human experts are then simply asked to estimate—based upon their experience and available historical data—the min–max range and the most likely value of the effort drivers specified within the effort estimation model. If experts estimate project effort directly, they then provide their judgment regarding estimated min–max range and most likely project effort—instead of estimating inputs to model-based estimation. For example, the CoBRA method we present in Chap. 15 uses triangular distributions as a means for quantifying uncertainty of expert judgments.

---

[2] Beta-PERT is a version of the Beta distribution and got its name because it uses the same assumption about the mean as PERT networks. It requires the same three parameters as the Triangle distribution. It is considered to better reflect human predictions and as such should be preferred over the triangular distribution in the context of expert-based effort estimation.

A simple way to transform range estimates into a point estimate is to compute the mean over the appropriate probability distribution. However, we advise against using the mean value for project planning purposes. A general deficit of using a point estimate is that we lose valuable information about estimation uncertainty. Specifically, a drawback of using the mean estimate in the context of expert-based estimation is that human experts tend to be overoptimistic in their predictions (we discuss it in Sect. 6.4) and their "most likely" estimates are actually biased toward the "best-case" estimates. Stutzke (2005) proposes a simple way to account for this bias by slightly modifying weights in the mean computation formula (4.1). Still, range values—if available—should be preferred to predict and communicate project effort.

$$\text{Estimate} = \frac{\text{Min} + 3 \ \text{ML} + 2 \ \text{Max}}{6} \tag{4.1}$$

We may and should use point estimates for developing and communicating project commitments. In this case, we should take into consideration that the simple mean theoretically represents an estimate that has a certain chance of being exceeded. For symmetric distributions of estimated effort, taking the mean value as final point estimate would give us 50/50 % likelihood of completing the work within this effort or exceeding it. Note that this does not hold for nonsymmetric distributions where the likelihood of actual effort being greater than or equal to (or lower than or equal to) the mean will vary depending on the exact shape of the distribution (in order to keep the 50/0 % likelihood for nonsymmetric distribution, we would have to take the median value instead of the mean). We need to decide if this is what we want to use as a baseline for project commitment. Typically, we would want to use an estimate that has a lower probability of being exceeded. In order to account for uncertainty in point estimates, confidence intervals and/or the probability of exceeding a certain value X (so-called pX-estimate) might be determined based on the final distribution of estimated effort. The *pX-estimate* addresses the problem we just mentioned, that is, determining a point estimate that has a particular likelihood of being exceeded. In the next paragraphs, we will discuss in more detail prediction and confidence intervals as well as pX-estimates.

Prediction and Confidence Intervals

Another common approach to handling estimation uncertainty is to provide a range into which actual effort is likely to fall. Statistics provide two principal techniques for computing such estimation ranges: prediction intervals and confidence intervals.

The theoretical applicability of confidence intervals is limited by the assumptions made about the nature of the estimation process. For example, it is assumed that the observed phenomenon—in our case, development effort—follows a Gaussian distribution. Yet, software development projects typically do not satisfy this assumption. Prediction intervals, on the other hand, can be determined without any assumptions concerning the underlying population. In the context of software effort estimation, prediction intervals are typically used because they do not make assumptions about effort distribution. For example, a project manager may describe the uncertainty of effort estimates by saying that there is a 90 % probability (which in practice means "very high") that the actual project effort will be in the range between 10 and 20 person-months. It means that the project manager is 90 % confident that the actual project effort will fall between [10, 20] person-months.

In practice, the software engineering community uses a number of alternative terms for referring to prediction intervals. Examples include prediction bounds, prediction limits, interval prediction, and prediction region.

Unfortunately, prediction intervals are often confused with confidence intervals, although they refer to different approaches.

Tip

▶ Do not confuse confidence and prediction intervals—they are not the same.

In statistics, a *confidence interval* (*CI*) provides information on the expected value (mean) of a dependent variable. In other words, a CI provides an interval in which the "true" value—true for the whole population—is expected to lie, with a probability defined by the confidence level. Figure 4.6 illustrates confidence intervals.

Confidence Level and Confidence Limits

Both prediction and confidence intervals are always quantified by a particular *confidence level*—typically expressed in percentages. Therefore, one speaks, for example, of a "90 % confidence interval." Confidence level indicates the likelihood of the interval containing the predicted value of the dependent variable. Predicted value refers to a population mean in the case of confidence interval or value of the next sample in case of prediction interval. By increasing the desired confidence level, we will then widen the confidence or prediction interval. Finally, the endpoints of the confidence or prediction interval are referred to as *confidence limits*.

In statistics, *prediction interval* (*PI*) provides information on individual predictions of the dependent variable. In other words, PI provides an interval in which the additional value—the value of the next sample—is expected to lie, with a probability defined by confidence level. One may say that *prediction interval is confidence interval for the prediction of a single new observation*.

In the context of effort estimation, an interval in which the effort of the next project will fall can be determined on the basis of effort observed across already completed (historical) projects. Prediction intervals are most often used in the context of regression analysis, which we discuss in Chap. 8. Figure 4.7 illustrates the difference between confidence and prediction intervals in the context of regression analysis. In this example, project effort is estimated based upon software size using simple linear regression. One practical consequence of these differences is

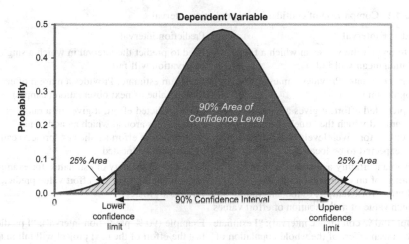

Fig. 4.6 Confidence intervals

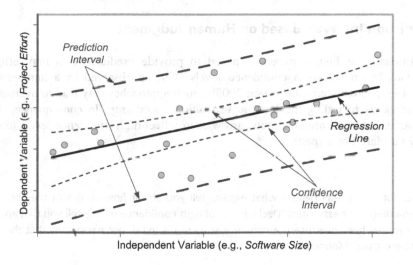

Fig. 4.7 Confidence vs. prediction intervals in regression analysis

that in the same situation, it is more difficult to predict what will happen next than what will happen on average. Therefore, confidence intervals will produce a smaller range of values then prediction intervals. In the context of effort estimation, prediction intervals are the logical choice and are, in fact, most commonly used for quantifying prediction uncertainty. Besides the context of formal estimation methods and models, such as regression analysis, prediction intervals can be computed independently in a particular estimation method. Alternative strategies of computing PI include human judgment and analysis of historical data. Table 4.1 briefly summarizes major differences between confidence and prediction intervals.

Table 4.1 Comparison of confidence vs. prediction interval

Confidence interval	Prediction interval
Used to predict the values in which a future population mean will fall	Used to predict the interval in which a single observation will fall
Long-run estimate: Provides a margin of error for population mean	Short-run estimate: Provides a margin of error for the value of next observation (sample)
For a predicted effort, it gives a range of effort values around which the "true" (population) mean effort (for given levels of effort drivers) can be expected to be located	For a predicted effort, it gives us a range of effort values around which an additional observation of effort (in the next project) can be expected to be located
Refers to uncertainty associated with the parameters of an estimation model or distribution, for example, to the uncertainty of the mean value of a distribution of effort values	Refers to uncertainty of estimates, for example, to the uncertainty of the effort value predicted for a new project
Example (90 % confidence interval): "I estimate that the mean effort of the whole population of projects from which a sample I am considering will fall in this interval 90 % of the time"	Example (90 % prediction interval): "I predict that the effort of the next project will fall in this interval 90 % of the time"

Prediction Intervals Based on Human Judgment

Traditionally, a human expert is asked to provide predicted min–max effort intervals based on given confidence levels. Yet, as observed in a number of industrial contexts (e.g., Jørgensen 2005b), such approaches may lead to overoptimistic views regarding the level of estimation uncertainty. In consequence, the prediction intervals are much too narrow as to reflect high confidence levels (e.g., 90 %) declared by experts.

Tip

▶ Do not necessarily believe what experts tell you about how confident they are regarding their estimates. "Declarations of high confidence mainly tell you that an individual has constructed a coherent story in his mind, not necessarily that the story is true." (Kahneman 2011)

Potential sources of this overoptimism are a lack of analogous data from previously completed projects, low effectiveness of the models used for assessing estimation uncertainty, and overoptimism of human estimators. Unfortunately, over the recent years, no silver-bullet approach for successful uncertainty assessment was found. However, few universally applicable guidelines for assessing estimation uncertainty have been proposed, for example, by Jørgensen (2004c, 2005b). We summarize them in Table 4.2.

Table 4.2 Guidelines for assessing estimation uncertainty

Guideline	Rationale
Do not rely on solely unaided, intuition-based uncertainty evaluation processes	There is strong evidence from industrial studies that unaided, intuition-based uncertainty assessments are on average systematically biased toward overconfidence. In other words, estimators tend to be far less correct in their individual uncertainty assessments than they think they are
Do not replace human (expert) judgment with formal models	Existing formal models are usually not capable of effectively using the available uncertainty information, if such information is available at all. In consequence, the obtained estimation intervals are so wide that they are practically useless
Apply explicit, structured processes based on human judgment	When supported by objective project data and guided by a structured process, human experts are typically capable of providing good assessments of estimation inaccuracy. In particular, a structured process supports review of the quality of assessment outputs, learning and evaluation of reasons for overconfidence, and improvement of the assessment process
Apply top-down strategy to uncertainty assessment	In bottom-up uncertainty assessment, an inside view of the project is taken in that overall uncertainty is composed of individual uncertainties related to elementary project elements, for example, specific activities or tools. Since such a process requires a thorough understanding of the project, it is often not applicable at the time of estimation, that is, early project stages. An alternative, top-down approach takes an outside view of the project, that is, overall uncertainty is based on the uncertainty of the information from previously completed similar projects, so-called project analogs
Use group work for combining multiple uncertainty assessments	In contrast to mechanical/automatic approaches, a group of experts has the potential to improve uncertainty assessments, for instance, due to the possibility of discussing the rationale behind individual assessments. Yet, one needs to be aware of the pitfalls of group work.[a] In the case of a mechanical combination, an appropriate algorithm needs to be defined; a simple average does not perform well
Use motivational mechanisms with care	Additional motivation, such as performance-based rewards, brings positive effects when it is directed at the uncertainty assessment process—more resources for assessment—rather than on the assessment results—less uncertainty. In other words, any motivation should serve the assessors

(continued)

Table 4.2 (continued)

Guideline	Rationale
	about the performance of the assessment, not of the assessment outcomes. Wrong direction of the stimulation mechanisms may easily lead to a "self-fulfilling prophecy," where uncertainty assessments will be biased toward expectations
Fit formulation of the assessment problem to the structure of relevant information and to the assessment process	Relevant information, upon which the uncertainty assessments are based, may be of little or no use if its structure does not fit the formulation of the assessment problem and the assessment process. For example, asking a software developer for 90 % confidence intervals might not be proper, since such information is difficult to extract from the past project data. More effective, in practice, would be to ask the developer to assess the probability of not exceeding the project budget by more than X %. In this case, the developer may easily investigate previous projects and find, for example, what percentage of the projects exceeded the budget by more than X %
Do not reveal the viewpoint of the project sponsors	Communicating the expectations and opinions of project sponsors or other "influential" stakeholders, such as customers or managers, before or at the time of assessments may easily bias assessments toward these expectations
Avoid conflicting goals	Any goals that aim at lowering uncertainty may bias the results of uncertainty assessment. For example, communicating "bidding" objectives may push uncertainty assessments toward overoptimism. Optimally, the only goal of the uncertainty assessment should be realistic assessment outcomes
Motivate human experts to justify their assessments	Instructing experts up-front to explain and defend their assessments typically motivates them to reflect on their judgments and seek realistic rationales during the assessment process. This typically results in more realistic uncertainty assessments

[a]We discuss pitfalls of group estimation in Sect. 6.4.3, Table 6.3

Prediction Intervals Based on Estimation Accuracy

As an alternative to human judgment, Jørgensen and Sjøberg (2003) propose approximating effort prediction intervals for a new project using the information on the estimation accuracy achieved for the past project predictions. The approach is based on well-known statistical principles of prediction intervals and follows five major steps.

Step 1. Select accuracy metric: In this step, we select a measure of prediction accuracy, which enables a separate analysis of bias and precision (spread) of estimates.[3] Example accuracy metrics may include *balanced relative error (BRE)*, proposed by Miyazaki et al. (1991). The mean BRE can be interpreted as the bias of the estimates, and the standard deviation of BRE as their spread.

$$\text{BRE} = \frac{\text{Effort}_{\text{Act}} - \text{Effort}_{\text{Est}}}{\min(\text{Effort}_{\text{Act}}, \text{Effort}_{\text{Est}})} \tag{4.2}$$

Asymmetric probability distribution associated with BRE is more likely in practice than a symmetric distribution assumed by *magnitude of relative effort (MRE)* distributions in situations with large estimation inaccuracies. BRE allows, for example, a three times too high and a three times too low effort estimate to yield the same deviation from the "midpoint" of zero estimation error (BRE = –2 and BRE = 2). This is not the case with the commonly used *MRE* uncertainty metric proposed by Conte et al. (1986).

$$\text{MRE} = \frac{\text{Effort}_{\text{Act}} - \text{Effort}_{\text{Est}}}{\text{Effort}_{\text{Act}}} \tag{4.3}$$

No matter how much the actual effort is underestimated, MRE cannot exceed 1, whereas overestimations lead to BRE values with no lower limits, that is, an asymmetric MRE distribution is likely.

Step 2. Select historical projects of similar estimation uncertainty: In this step, we look for historical projects that had similar estimation uncertainty as we expect for the project being estimated. In a simple case, we may base this selection on human judgment; that is, experts select historical projects based on their experiences regarding estimation uncertainty.

Another way of selecting historical projects of similar estimation uncertainty may be by quantitatively analyzing the association between estimation uncertainty and particular project characteristics. An example analysis might be cluster analysis. In this approach, projects are first grouped regarding their prediction uncertainty, and then factors having a major impact on uncertainty—factors typical for each group—are identified. The new project is then assigned the uncertainty of the group to which it is most similar on the most relevant uncertainty factors. Common factors influencing estimation uncertainty are, for example, the estimation method itself or the stability of software requirements. Note that projects similar with respect to estimation uncertainty are not necessarily of a similar type.

Step 3. Analyze the distribution of historical estimation uncertainty: For the selected group of historical projects, we analyze the distribution of their estimation accuracy in order to select an appropriate approach for computing the min–max interval of accuracy across historical projects. Specific properties of the distribution

---

[3] We discuss the difference between bias and precision in Sect. 4.3.2.

Table 4.3 Computing prediction intervals from parametric distributions

Distribution of accuracy	Equation for prediction interval
Normal distribution, where • μ represents mean value • σ represents standard deviation of accuracy data • n represents number of observations	$\mu \pm t(1\text{-conf}, 1\text{-}n) \cdot \sigma \sqrt{\frac{1}{n} + 1}$ where • $t(1-\text{conf}, n-1)$ is the two-tailed value of the Student's t-distribution for the confidence level $1-\text{conf}$ and $n-1$ degrees of freedom • 1 inside the square root refers to the spread of the estimation accuracy • $1/n$ inside the square root refers to the spread of the mean estimation accuracy
Any distribution, where • Pr represents lower probability limit • y represents any random variable • $k \geq 0$ represents a constant in Chebyshev's inequality	$\Pr[\mu\text{-}k \cdot \sigma < y < \mu + k \cdot \sigma] \geq 1\text{-}\frac{1}{k^2}$ Example: the probability that the actual effort value lies within the prediction interval of $\pm$ two standard deviations (i.e., within $[\mu-2\cdot\sigma, \mu+2\cdot\sigma]$ is at least $1-1/22 = 75\ \%$
Symmetric distribution with only one peak	$\Pr[\mu\text{-}k \cdot \sigma < y < \mu + k \cdot \sigma] \geq 1\text{-}\frac{1}{1.25 \cdot k^2}$

indicate how to calculate this interval. Table 4.3 provides three useful equations for the parametric approach for computing prediction intervals.

If the observed distribution can be approximated with any known probability distribution, such as a normal distribution, a parametric approach should be selected; in other cases, the so-called "empirical" approach is recommended. The empirical approach for computing effort prediction intervals is based on the percentiles of the historical accuracy distribution. For a selected level of confidence level *conf*, we use the percentile $(1-\text{conf})/2$ as the minimum value and the percentile $(1+\text{conf})/2$ as the maximum value of the prediction interval.

If, however, too few empirical observations from the past were available, none of the analytical approaches would perform well. In this case, the accuracy distribution can be based on expert judgment supported by the few quantitative observations available from historical projects.

Step 4. Select confidence level: In order to compute a prediction interval, we must decide on the desired confidence level for which the prediction interval is going to be computed. A confidence level indicates how likely the prediction interval is to comprise the predicted value of effort.

Step 5. Calculate prediction interval: Finally, the prediction interval is computed for the desired confidence level. For that purpose, we first compute a min–max accuracy interval for historical projects, using one of the approaches discussed in Step 3. Next, we put the accuracy interval values and the point effort estimate into the reformulated balanced relative error equation (4.4) for computing the effort prediction interval.

$$\text{Act} = \begin{cases} \dfrac{\text{Est}}{1 - \text{BRE}}, & \text{BRE} \leq 0 \\ \text{Est} \cdot (1 + \text{BRE}), & \text{BRE} > 0 \end{cases} \qquad (4.4)$$

Example 4.4. Computing Prediction Interval Based on Historical Data

Objective: Let us assume that we want to estimate the effort of a new project within the 90 % prediction interval.

Step 1: We select balanced relative error (*BRE*) as the measure of estimation accuracy.

Step 2: We have found several historical projects that were considered as similar to the new one with respect to estimation accuracy, for example, because the same estimation method was applied and a similar level of requirements volatility was observed across projects.

Step 3: The distribution of estimation accuracy across selected historical projects does not resemble any standard probability distribution, thus we select Chebyshev's inequality for computing the prediction interval of BRE. After simple reformulation, the constant k can be computed as

$k \leq \sqrt{\frac{1}{1-\text{Pr}}}$

For the selected 90 % confidence level, k would be lower than or equal to squared root of ten. It means that the BRE's prediction interval is $[\mu - k \cdot \sigma, \mu + k \cdot \sigma]$. We skip detailed computations and assume that after considering mean μ and standard deviation σ, the minimum BRE is equal to -1 and maximum BRE is equal to 2.5.

Step 4: Application of the estimation method, which has been used in similar past projects, returned an effort estimate of 100 person-months. Using (4.4) we compute appropriate effort prediction interval as $[100/(1 - (-1)), 100 \cdot [(1 + 2.5) = [50, 350]$.

The asymmetry of the interval around the point estimate reflects a bias of past project estimates—estimation accuracy—toward underestimation. In order to account for our tendency for overoptimistic estimates, the prediction interval is shifted toward effort values greater than the estimated point value. ∎

Prediction Intervals Based on Bootstrapping

Statistical sampling is another means—after human judgment and analysis of past estimation accuracy data—for assessing prediction intervals. This method is especially useful in the context of data-driven effort estimation where nonparametric estimation models are used. For parametric models, such as statistical regression, prediction intervals can be easily evaluated using appropriate formulas defined within the associated theories of parametric models.

Several researchers (e.g., Stamelos and Angelis 2001; Mittas and Angelis 2009; Port and Korte 2008) proposed using bootstrapping for the purpose of constructing prediction intervals in the context of nonparametric effort estimation models. Bootstrapping is a resampling method introduced by Efron and Tibshirani (1994) for assigning measures of accuracy to sample estimates. In general, the bootstrap technique is used to compute a confidence interval for an unknown population parameter θ. It starts from the available random sample $x = \{x_1, \ldots, x_n\}$ and creates a large number of Z equal-sized samples from it by sampling with replacement. Each bootstrap sample $m = 1, 2, \ldots, Z$ gives an estimate θ^*_m for θ. All these estimates compose an empirical distribution from which the computed values $\theta^*_{\alpha/2}$ and $\theta^*_{1-\alpha/2}$ correspond to its $100(\alpha/2)$-th and $100(1-\alpha/2)$-th percentiles. The prediction interval is then given by $[\theta^*_{1-\alpha/2}, \theta^*_{\alpha/2}]$, where α is the degree of confidence. In order to estimate the actual effort ActEff of an individual project, one must first obtain estimate EstEff*^{m} from each m-th bootstrap sample by applying a certain estimation method, such as, for example, nonparametric case-based reasoning we discuss in Chap. 11. The prediction interval for the individual project is created by finding the appropriate percentiles (4.5).

$$(1 - \alpha)\%\text{PI} = \left[\text{EffEst}^*_{\alpha/2}, \text{EffEst}^*_{1-\alpha/2}\right] \qquad (4.5)$$

Port and Koter (2008) employ Bootstrap for assessing the confidence of the two popular aggregated measures of estimation uncertainty: *mean magnitude of relative error (MMRE)* and *prediction at level m (Pred.m)*.[4] For this purpose, they first apply Bootstrap to a sample set of MMRE and *Pred.m* measurements. Next, they compute Standard Error of the Bootstrapped data in order to assess the confidence of the original sample of MMRE and *Pred.m* measurements.

The "pX-view" on Estimation Uncertainty

Alternatively to a simple X percent prediction interval, Jørgensen (2005a) proposed the so-called pX-estimate approach, where instead of giving a range associated with a particular confidence level, the human estimator gives estimate ranges based on probabilistic distributions.

The pX-view means that there is an X percent probability of not exceeding the estimate. Before specifying pX-estimate, it is often useful to draw cumulative probabilistic distributions of estimated effort, for example, based upon the available probability density function. In case of estimates based upon expert judgments, typical probability density functions are beta-PERT or triangular.

Figure 4.8 illustrates an example cumulative distribution of project effort. In this example, a human expert estimated project effort by providing minimal, maximal,

---

[4] *Pred.m* measures the percentage proportion of estimates that are within a given percentage m of the actual value. The parameter m reflects estimation error and is commonly instantiated with Magnitude of Relative Error (MRE) we present in (4.3); in this case, *Pred.m* measures the percentage portion of estimates that are within a given MRE estimation error.

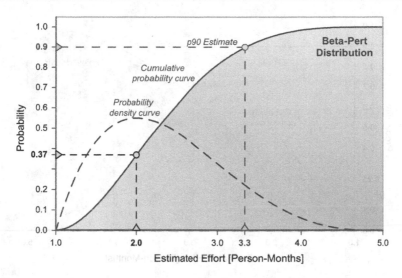

Fig. 4.8 Example application of the pX-view for beta-PERT estimates

and most likely values of expected project effort: one, five, and two person-months, respectively. The triple was next modeled as beta-PERT probability distribution, and the appropriate cumulative curve was drawn to support project decision-making. Based on the cumulative curve, a project manager can find out, for instance, that the probability of not exceeding the effort considered most likely is actually quite low, about 37 %. In other words, we have a 67 % chance that the project actually exceeds estimated effort, which means quite a high risk. In order to increase the probability of remaining within estimated effort up to 90 %, the effort estimate (p90-estimate) needs to be increased from 2.0 up to about 3.3 person-months, which means 65 % on top of what was expected as most likely.

For comparison, Fig. 4.9 illustrates the same situation, only the triangular probability distribution was used to model the expert's estimates instead of beta-PERT distribution.

What we can see is that besides being commonly considered as closer to a human way of estimating, the beta-PERT distribution is at the same time a more liberal approach (less conservative), in terms of pX-view, than the triangular distribution. In our example, the probability of not exceeding the most likely effort expected by a human expert is about 37 % according to beta-PERT distribution and only about 25 % according to the triangular distribution. In other words, the project is more likely to run into trouble according to the triangular distribution than according to the beta-PERT distribution. In order to increase the likelihood of not exceeding estimated effort up to 90 %, the effort estimate (p90-estimate) needs to be increased from 2.0 up to about 3.9 person-months, which means 95 % on top of what was expected as most likely, which is almost twice as much as we initially planned.

We may thus conclude that if one prefers a more conservative estimate, for example, for a very critical project, the use of triangular distributions to model the

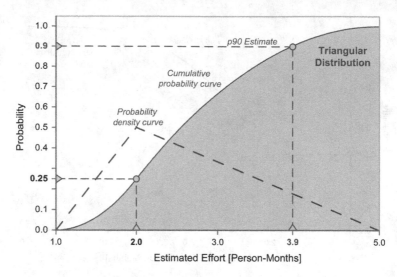

Fig. 4.9 The pX-view on the cumulative triangular probability distribution

uncertainty of estimates provided by human experts should be considered rather than beta-PERT. Although beta-PERT proved to better reflect the way humans estimate, the triangular distribution seems to be more practical for project effort prediction purposes in that it implicitly accounts—at least partially—for overoptimism in human judgment.

Tip

▶ In the pX-view estimation, uncertainty depends on the selected probability distribution. When modeling the uncertainty of human-based estimates, the triangular distribution provides more conservative estimates than the beta-PERT distribution. Therefore, if we expect overoptimism in estimates provided by human experts, then we should use the triangular distribution for representing estimation uncertainty and for planning project targets.

Evaluating Actual Uncertainty of Prediction Intervals

Evaluating the accuracy of the assessed estimation uncertainty is as important as evaluating estimation accuracy. Yet, it is less obvious and much more difficult as there is no actual value to refer to. In the case of estimation accuracy, we simply compare estimated effort against actual effort. In the case of assessed estimation uncertainty, we do not have actual uncertainty to compare to. We may, however, determine (approximately) the actual estimation uncertainty of a series of estimates, for example, after estimating multiple development projects. Jørgensen et al. (2004) propose several metrics for evaluating the uncertainty of prediction intervals. Let us discuss two closely related metrics: Hit Rate and Relative Width. The *hit rate* metric refers to the percentage proportion of correct estimates, that is, estimates that fall within the prediction interval (4.6):

$$\text{Hit Rate} = \frac{1}{n}\sum_{i-1}^{n}h_i$$

$$h_i = \begin{cases} 1, \text{Min}_i \leq \text{Act}_i \leq \text{Max}_i \\ 0, \text{Min}_i > \text{Act}_i > \text{Max}_i \end{cases}$$

(4.6)

where

- Min_i represents optimistic effort estimate of task i
- Max_i represents pessimistic effort estimate of task i

For multiple prediction intervals with associated $X\%$ confidence level, the percentage proportion of correct estimates (Hit Rate) should become close to $X\%$. For instance, given multiple prediction intervals [optimistic, pessimistic] with 90 % confidence level, we would expect that in about 90 % of cases, the prediction interval includes the actual effort. Discrepancy between the assessed confidence level and the Hit Rate would imply that the uncertainty assessments are inaccurate. In particular,

- If the confidence level we assessed is systematically higher than the "Hit Rate," then we were biased toward overconfidence.
- If the confidence level we assessed is systematically lower than the "Hit Rate," then we were biased toward underconfidence.

Yet, even though two estimation approaches or two human experts provide estimates with the same Hit Rate, it does not mean their estimation uncertainty is equal. For example, although both approaches are characterized by the same Hit Rate, one of them may provide a much narrower prediction interval than the other. In such cases, the approach with narrower prediction intervals will always be preferred as more useful for planning software projects. In order to address this issue, Jørgensen et al. (2004) proposed the *relative width* metric (4.7):

$$\text{Relative Width}_i = \frac{\text{Max}_i - \text{Min}_i}{\text{Est}_i}$$

(4.7)

where

- Min_i represents optimistic effort estimate of task i
- Max_i represents pessimistic effort estimate of task i
- Est_i represents most likely effort estimate of task i

Evaluating Risk Exposure

Estimation uncertainty constitutes a risk to the project, among other risks that are in general attributable to uncertainty. Based on this observation, one may want to quantify estimation uncertainty indirectly through a risk exposure introduced by uncertain estimates. Since risk analysis is beyond the scope of this book, we give just a simple example of such an approach. Kitchenham and Linkman (1997) proposed quantifying the impact of project assumptions on the uncertainty of effort estimates by means of risk exposure. In the first step, assumptions taken in the estimation process need to be identified explicitly. In the next step, the impact on effort estimates of an assumption being invalid is investigated using a simple formula (4.8):

$$\text{Risk exposure} = \left(\text{Eff}_{\text{Org}} - \text{Eff}_{\text{Alt}}\right) \cdot P_{\text{Alt}} \tag{4.8}$$

where

- Eff_{Org} represents effort estimate if the original assumption is true,
- Eff_{Alt} represents effort estimate if the alternative assumption is true, and
- P_{Alt} represents the probability that the alternative assumption is true.

4.4.2 Handling Possibilistic Uncertainty

In practice, handling possibilistic uncertainty mainly involves the application of fuzzy set theory defined by Zadeh (1965).

Fuzzy Sets, Fuzzy Logic, and Fuzzy Numbers

The basic principle of fuzzy sets is that elements can belong to a set to a certain degree. For example, let us consider the effort driver "requirements volatility." In classical set theory, we would say that requirements can be definitely volatile or definitely stable, whereas in fuzzy set theory, we can say that requirements are volatile "in 60 percent," that is, the requirements belong to a set of volatile requirements to the degree of truth equal to 0.6.

Each element x of a fuzzy set, representing an observation or an object, is assigned a set with membership values k in the range 0.0–1.0, where

- $k = 0.0$ represents absolute falsity and means that "x is not a member of the set,"
- $k = 1.0$ represents absolute truth and means that "x is a member of the set,"
- $0.0 < k < 1.0$ represents partial truth and means that "x is a member of the set to degree k."

The central assertion underlying fuzzy set theory is that entities in the real world simply do not fit into neat categories. For example, software functional size may, as

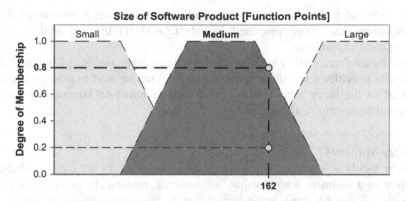

Fig. 4.10 Fuzzy sets—Example membership function

illustrated in Fig. 4.10, be neither small, nor medium, nor large. It could, in fact, be something in-between; perhaps mostly medium-size software but also something like large-size software. This can be represented as a degree of belonging to a particular linguistic category. As shown in Fig. 4.10, a system with 162 function points belongs to the class of medium software to a degree of 0.8 and to the class of large projects to a degree of 0.2.

Fuzzy Sets vs. Probability Theory

Fuzzy set theory should not be confused with probability theory. For example, the medium-size software with 0.8 degree of truth should not be confused with an 80 % probability of being medium. Probability theory supposes that the software is or is not of medium size excluding any "in-between" value. In contrast to probability theory, which addresses likelihood in terms of randomness, fuzzy sets theory addresses "likelihood" (possibility) in terms of subjectivity and lack of exact knowledge.

In the effort estimation domain, fuzzy methods can principally be classified into two categories:

1. *Fuzzification approach (fuzzifying existing crisp models)*: This approach simply adapts existing software effort estimation methods to handle the uncertainty of their inputs and outputs using the theory of fuzzy sets. Inputs and outputs can be either linguistic or numeric. A typical estimation process consists of three steps:
   a) *Fuzzification of inputs*: Finding the membership of input variables with linguistic terms. The membership function can, in principle, be either defined by human experts or analytically extracted from data, whereas fuzzy rules are usually defined by experts.
   b) *Reasoning*: Processing and interpreting imprecise inputs using fuzzy logic.
   c) *Defuzzification of outputs*: Providing crisp numbers from the output fuzzy sets.

Examples of traditional estimation approaches for which a number of fuzzy adaptations have been proposed include COCOMO I/II and analogy-based estimation methods.

2. *Rule-based fuzzy logic (building specific fuzzy logic models)*: This approach directly provides a set of fuzzy rules that can then be used to infer predictions based on the fuzzy inputs. Fuzzy rules may be based on human judgment or learned from empirical data.

Fuzzy Numbers

Fuzzy numbers is a related term derived from the fuzzy set theory, which refers to a quantity whose value is imprecise, rather than exact. In other words, a fuzzy number is just a fuzzy set over the corresponding numeric set. Fuzzy set theory comprises *fuzzy mathematics*, which defines basic operations on fuzzy variables analogous to basic mathematical operations on crisp data. *Fuzzy logic* builds upon fuzzy sets and deals with approximate reasoning using fuzzy variables, analogous to traditional precise reasoning on crisp variables.

Fuzzy estimation methods represent quite a new concept in effort estimation, and it still requires more industrial application and additional research in order to be widely accepted by software practitioners. The major point of critique toward these methods is their complexity, that is, relatively large overhead required to understand and apply these methods in an industrial practice. Example 4.5 illustrates a simple application of the fuzzy-logic ideas for bottom-up estimation of software size.

Example 4.5. Simple Fuzzy-Logic Estimation

Putnam and Myers (1992) proposed a simple way of applying fuzzy logic for bottom-up[5] estimation of software size in terms of lines of code. They propose a hybrid approach that uses human judgments and historical project data.

The expert-based part of the method is based on the authors' observation that human experts are typically capable of consistently classifying software features using linguistic, fuzzy terms, such as "very small," "small," "medium," "large," and "very large."

The data-driven part of the method uses historical project data for computing how many actual lines of code correspond, on average, to each fuzzy size of a feature. In order to obtain LOC sizes, one should go through historical project data and classify features into very small, small, and so on, according to how experts involved in the estimation process understand it. Next, the average LOC per feature is computed by dividing the total LOC over all features in each fuzzy category by the number of features in the category.

---

[5] We discuss top-down and bottom-up estimation strategies in Sects. 5.1 and 5.2, respectively.

The size estimation consists then of two major steps:

- In the first step, human experts estimate the number of software features and the fuzzy size of each feature. Experts may base their estimates, for instance, on the available software requirements specification.
- In the second step, historical data from similar past projects are used to translate the fuzzy size of each feature into a corresponding LOC number. The total size of the software system is then estimated by summing up LOC size estimates over all identified features.

It is important that fuzzy size of features is consistently understood while quantifying features of both past and current projects. One way to achieve that is to simply involve the same experts in both procedures. Another way is to document the specification of different fuzzy values and train experts appropriately.

The same fuzzy logic approach can be applied to directly estimate development effort. In such a case, instead of feature size, it is development effort observed in the past projects that is associated with each class of fuzzy feature size. ∎

4.4.3 Handling Granulation Uncertainty

In practice, handling granulation uncertainty involves mainly the application of the rough set theory defined by Pawlak (1982).

Rough Sets

Rough set theory is used to approximate descriptions of sets which are vague due to a lack of precise knowledge. The basic idea behind rough sets is that while some objects may be clearly labeled as belonging to a particular set (*positive region*) and some objects may be clearly labeled as not belonging to the set (*negative region*), imprecise knowledge on the remaining objects prevents their clear labeling with respect to the set. The remaining objects are neither "in set" nor "not in set" and thus lie in a so-called *boundary region*.

Rough set theory calls the positive region a *lower approximation* of a set, which yields no false positives (objects certainly in set). The positive region plus the boundary region make up an *upper approximation* of the set, which yields no false negatives (objects possibly in set). The lower and upper approximation sets themselves are crisp sets in the standard version of the rough set theory.

Figure 4.11 illustrates the basic concepts of rough set theory. The lack of knowledge (vagueness) about the universe of all objects is represented by indiscernibility relation R. This relation determines elementary portions of knowledge, so-called *granules of knowledge*. If we consider an individual object x in the universe, then the elementary portion of knowledge refers to all objects $R(x)$ that are

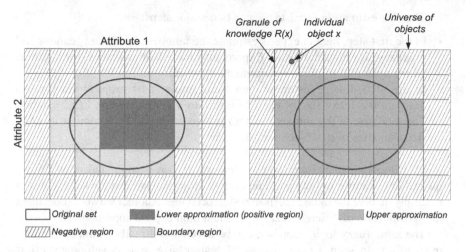

Fig. 4.11 Rough sets—Example membership function

indiscernible from x (indifferent to x). In Fig. 4.11, elementary portions of knowledge are determined by granulation level on Attribute 1 and Attribute 2. Each knowledge granule comprises objects that are indifferent to each other with respect to *Attribute 1* and *Attribute 2*.

The granulation of knowledge means that we are actually unable to observe individual objects but are forced to reason only about accessible granules of knowledge. This demonstrates the practical outcome of rough set theory, which deals with approximating continuous input through discrete bins and deciding which elements of the input should be included in which of various approximations. In terms of knowledge granules, the lower approximation of a set is a union of all granules which are entirely included in the set; the upper approximation is a union of all granules which have nonempty intersection with the set; the boundary region of the set is the difference between the upper and the lower approximation.

Similar to fuzzy sets, rough sets define a membership function. Yet, a rough membership function has slightly different properties from a fuzzy membership function (for details, refer to Pawlak 1991). Rough membership of an object x to set X is defined as the ratio of the number of objects indiscernible from x that belong to X to the total number of objects indiscernible from x. Objects indiscernible from x are objects that belong to the same knowledge granule as x.

Similar to fuzzy sets, application of rough sets in software effort estimation is quite a new subject. In consequence, very few such effort estimation methods have been proposed by researches and exploited in industrial practice. Yet, Pawlak and Skowron (2007) observed a rapid growth in interest for applying rough set theory to handle uncertainty in various domains. We also observe this trend in the software estimation domain, which allows us to believe that new applications of rough sets will be appearing to handle uncertainty in the software effort estimation context.

Classical Sets, Fuzzy Sets, and Rough Sets

A set can very generally be defined as a collection of any objects, which are somehow related to each other and can thus be considered as a whole.

In classical set theory, a notion of set is crisp. It means that a set is uniquely determined by its elements and every element of a set must be uniquely classified as belonging to the set or not. Yet, the concept of set can be vague. That is, our knowledge about the set is not sufficient to define it precisely. In other words, we are not able to definitely say if an element belongs to a set or not.

Two main approaches that deal with vagueness of sets are Fuzzy Set Theory and Rough Set Theory. Both theories represent quite different approaches to vagueness and imprecise knowledge.

Proposed by Zadeh (1965), fuzzy sets address gradualness of knowledge and express vagueness by partial (fuzzy) membership to a set. If the membership of objects to a set is equal either to 1 (belongs to the set) or to 0 (does not belong to the set), then the set is crisp. If, however, there are elements of the set whose membership is between 0 and 1, then the set is fuzzy.

Introduced by Pawlak (1982), rough sets address granularity of knowledge and express vagueness by means of the boundary region of a set. If the boundary region of a set is empty, it means that the set is crisp; otherwise, the set is rough.

Actually, both fuzzy and rough sets define a membership function; yet, fuzzy and rough membership functions have different properties.

4.5   Reducing Uncertainty

Uncertainty is like thermodynamic entropy—it cannot be reduced except through the application of energy.

—Phillip G. Armour

Reducing uncertainty is a critical factor for successful software effort prediction. As already mentioned, in estimation, it is all about the information. Consequently, reducing estimation uncertainty should focus on improving the quality of information on which our predictions are based. Let us briefly discuss alternative approaches for reducing each of the three types of uncertainties discussed in Sect. 4.1.

Tip

▶ Reducing uncertainty of estimates requires (1) removing sources of process, product, and resource variability from the project and (2) founding estimates based upon actual, objective, and complete information.

4.5.1 Reducing Probabilistic Uncertainty

One of the major sources of estimation uncertainty is change in the project and its environment. We may actually say that change is the daily bread of software development projects. This importance of change motivated us to devote a separate Sect. 4.6 to discuss the aspect of change in the context of software projects. The main weapon against probabilistic uncertainty is thus dealing with change. In Sect. 4.6.2, we discuss in detail several common strategies for dealing with change. On the one hand, we may actively avoid change and/or reduce the impact of change on the project. On the other hand, we can accept change and try to anticipate its impact on project estimates. Although we would wish to eliminate uncertainty, in practice it is rather impossible, and we always need to model it to some extent. In this section, we focus on actively reducing probabilistic uncertainty by avoiding project change and mitigating its impact on a project. The basic aim underlying these strategies is to keep information, upon which estimates are based, stable. We can realize change avoidance and mitigation strategies throughout project- and organization-level activities. Figure 4.12 illustrates example activities for reducing probabilistic uncertainty and their effect on the shape of the cone of uncertainty (Sect. 4.3.1).

Organizational Level

At the organizational level, one of the major sources of unpredictable change and nondeterministic consequences of change are chaotic development processes.

Tip

▶ Do not expect reliable predictions for unpredictable processes, even when using best estimation methods. Estimates of chaotic processes will also be chaotic.

Therefore, reducing estimation uncertainty from the probabilistic point of view should focus on ensuring systematic and stable development processes. From the perspective of avoiding changes, mature processes affect stability of human and material resources assigned to the project and quality of product specifications; once they are planned and agreed upon at the project start, they need not to be adjusted during project runtime. From the change mitigation perspective, systematic change management processes support minimizing magnitude and nondeterminism of effects of potential change on the project—and thus the validity of initial estimates. For example, systematic estimation and resource planning processes guide tracking project plans against actual performance, identifying potential sources of deviations in a timely manner, and addressing them properly.

Tip

▶ Track your estimates against actual project performance, and identify sources of deviations for improving your estimates in the future.

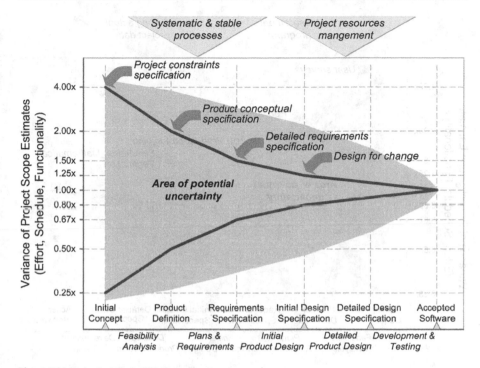

Fig. 4.12 Reducing probabilistic estimation uncertainty

Project Level

At the project level, feasibility of potential project deviations can be limited by early specifications regarding the project and its context. This should, in particular, include agreements on what will and what will not be done in the project and under which conditions. Finally, a project should follow systematic processes defined at the organizational level.

4.5.2   Reducing Possibilistic Uncertainty

Another significant source of estimation uncertainty is subjectivity and sparseness of the information on which effort predictions are based. Potential uncertainty reduction activities should address these two issues. Figure 4.13 illustrates example ways of addressing possibilistic uncertainty at both organizational and project levels. The major weapon against possibilistic uncertainty is to base estimates on actual project information.

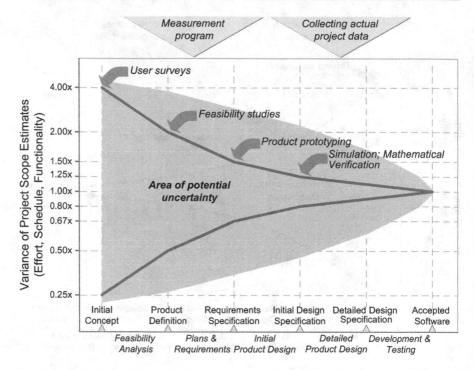

Fig. 4.13 Reducing possibilistic estimation uncertainty

Tip

► Remember to base estimates on actual project values. When reestimating, use current project performance as a basis; avoid using initial targets (planned/wished performance) as inputs for estimation.

Organizational Level

At the organizational level, we may systematically narrow the range of estimation uncertainty by defining appropriate estimation processes where effort is successively reestimated using the actual information gained as the project proceeds and more is known about relevant factors influencing its effort. Moreover, systematic measurement programs should ensure objective and up-to-date inputs for the effort estimation.

Tip

► Initial estimates have typically only a very small chance of being met. Therefore, reestimate regularly based on the most recent, actual quantitative information.

Project Level

At the project level, information constraints can be overcome by involving experienced personnel appropriate to particular development phases, thorough specification of the project scope (work products), and collecting actual measurement data. Moreover, interaction with project stakeholders should be practiced for the purpose of reducing fuzziness of project information flows. For example, we should clearly communicate the status of project stakes and progress to the stakeholders throughout the complete project duration.

Another strategy to defeat the problem of insufficient information is to "buy" necessary information. One of the well-known techniques for buying information, especially at the beginning of a project, is *prototyping*. Although it initially requires additional overhead, it typically pays off with more accurate estimates and less rework due to better project and product specifications. For example, based on a prototype, a customer may better specify the product requirements. Last but not least, a prototype can be reused, at least partially, in a final product. Other useful approaches for buying information include feasibility studies, user surveys, simulation, testing, and mathematical program verification techniques.

4.5.3   Reducing Granulation Uncertainty

Finally, the abstract character of project information is another source of estimation uncertainty. Granulation uncertainty can be reduced by selecting the proper level of detail for analyzing the project scope and context. Figure 4.14 illustrates example approaches for reducing granulation uncertainty. On the one hand, the amount of information considered during estimation should be minimized to the most relevant issues. On the other hand, the level of detail, on which individual issues are considered, should correspond to cost-benefit objectives of the estimation. Potential threats of both extremes are analogous to threats of bottom-up estimation (as we discuss in Sect. 5.4, Table 5.4). Too coarse an analysis of the project and its context may result in omitting relevant factors influencing project effort. Too detailed an analysis may cost much effort to collect, analyze, and maintain data, which are actually irrelevant and/or redundant for the purpose of effort estimation—and thus do not improve estimates.

Organizational Level

On the organizational level, we can learn about the most appropriate granularity level for effort estimation. For example, historical project data, in the form of measurements and expert opinions, can be analyzed for this purpose on a regular basis. We should keep information of the abstraction level for project decomposition—work breakdown—which proved to be most appropriate in the past for estimation purposes. Also, data on the most relevant factors influencing development effort should be maintained. Moreover, top-down and bottom-up

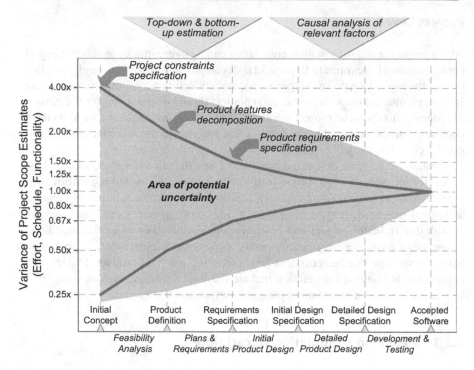

Fig. 4.14 Reducing granulation estimation uncertainty

prediction strategies should be used in tandem for cross-checking the estimates obtained on various levels of granularity.

Project Level

On the project level, experiences gained in past projects should be applied to specify project context and scope at the optimal level of granularity. For example, project constraints and product features should be specified at the level of granularity that, on the one hand, ensures sufficient level of detail in estimates and, on the other hand, does not require too much project overhead to collect, analyze, and maintain.

4.6   Uncertainty and Change

The problem [with software projects] isn't change, per se, because change is going to happen; the problem, rather, is the inability to cope with change when it comes.
                                                                                    —Kent Beck

Paradoxically, one of the very few certain things in effort estimation is uncertainty. Uncertainty is an inherent element of software projects, and handling uncertainty is an essential part of project effort estimation. One of the major sources of uncertainty in software projects is unanticipated change to a project during its lifetime—especially after its scope and budget have been approved.

Tip

▶ A few certain and unchanging things in software are uncertainty and change. Never expect your early estimates to be set in stone. Revise them (reestimate) in order to account for (1) changes to the project and (2) more complete and exact knowledge about the project that is available as it progresses.

4.6.1   Nature of Change

Software projects can be affected by a number of different changes including alterations in technology, project requirements, personnel, and the external environment. After Sauer et al. (2007), we distinguish two types of project change:

- *Target volatility* comprises changes to project targets—such as product scope, project effort, and schedule—while the project is already under way. Empirical observations show a single target change is related to only a small percentage of deviation in project performance. Yet, in reality, projects usually undergo many target changes that entail significant deviations in project performance. For instance, Sauer et al. (2007) observed in their survey that on average, projects undergo three to four changes in schedule, two in budget, and three in product scope. For this amount of change, the example cumulative impact on a target's project duration may be up to 10 %; specifically,
  - A single change in a schedule target is associated with a 1.3 % increase in actual duration, a 1.4 % expansion of budget, and 0.7 % more product scope delivered.
  - A single change in product scope is associated with a 0.6 % increase in project duration and 1.1 % more budget spent on the project.

  In terms of risk, Sauer et al. observed that projects with nine or fewer target changes faced up to a 33 % risk of underperforming, whereas projects with more than nine changes had more than a 50 % chance of underperforming.

- *Governance volatility* comprises changes to project governance, in particular project management and sponsoring. Project management seems to have the greatest impact on project performance. In their industrial survey, Sauer et al. (2007) observed that
  - A single change of project manager entails approximately 8 % increase in project duration, 4 % greater budget expended, and 3.5 % less product delivered.

– Although changes in the project sponsor/client did not show a significant effect on project budget or schedule, it entailed about 5.6 % decrease in the project outcome delivered.

Software practitioners typically still do not know how to properly deal with change. Nor do they know how to adequately handle related uncertainty and risks bound to project predictions—for example, for effective planning and communication of project effort. An example consequence is that they often get trapped by giving or being given point estimates as the accurate and "certain" predictions.

Tip

▶ When you are given a point estimate, ask about its uncertainty.

Neglecting the uncertain nature of estimates—especially initial ones that are based on little qualitative information—is a common cause of project difficulties. As summarized by Daniel Galorath, chief architect of SEER-SEM effort estimation model and associated software application, *"failure to realize the potential imprecise nature of initial estimates and effectively manage and control the risks associated with them certainly is a major contributor to downstream problems, including project failure."*

4.6.2 Dealing with Change

Everyday industrial practice is to accept what seems to be a small change without adjusting initial project plans. Only for apparently large changes are project plans modified. Yet, what developers or—in particular—customers perceive as a small change may in fact, through a ripple effect, require several other changes to the project.

Tip

▶ Remember that what seems to be a small change to product or project scope may in fact, through a ripple effect, entail multiple other changes. Before accepting any change without adjusting project estimates, think about potential ripple effects of the change and about its possible effects on the project. Require adjustment to project plans if necessary.

For any change during the project runtime, possible effects and responses should be considered. We distinguish four principal response strategies to project changes. In order to manage the impact of project creep on the reliability of project estimates, we propose avoiding, transferring, mitigating, or accepting change.

Avoid Change

The first and foremost strategy for managing change is to actually avoid changes to the project during its runtime; that is, reducing the likelihood of change after project estimates have been prepared and approved. Example means for avoiding changes are

- *Product management*: A stable product scope is one of the most essential preconditions of successful estimation. We cannot successfully estimate a moving project target. In particular, volatile requirements are one of the main reasons for missing project outcome, budget, and schedule targets. In order to avoid changes to requirements during project runtime, we should get complete and reliable information regarding the expected product and project scope from the customer before the project start. However, since software development is in most cases an explorative process, it is quite impractical—and unrealistic—to freeze requirements, except for very small projects. Therefore, besides doing our best in the requirements specification phase, we should plan for change in that we mitigate, transfer, and model its impact on estimates.
- *Process management*: Stable and repeatable processes reduce the risk of volatile project targets and scope. First, there must be a process definition that elaborates how projects are to be managed at the level of the whole organization. This includes policies, procedures, templates, roles, responsibilities, and so on. Project management requires formalization because project teams need to follow the same set of policies and procedures to manage risks as well as to reduce variation and improve quality. The more consistently projects are managed, the more opportunities will exist for process improvement, cross-training, automation, effective generation of management information, etc. For example, Wang et al. (2008) suggest regular process reviews as a tool for avoiding project changes. Managers review and audit the behavior of software teams to ensure adherence to the development processes and iteratively perform measurement, assessment, and correction.
- *Resource management*: Proper resource management on an organizational level reduces the risk of project changes driven by conflicts between needed and available resources. For example, disciplined processes for planning and assigning resources help avoid project conflicts on shared resources. Moreover, motivation programs and managing commitment decrease the risk of staff turnover.

Transfer Change

Another strategy to manage change is to shift required project changes to the next project or product release. This strategy concerns mainly changes to product scope, such as modification to required software functionality or quality. Shifting required product changes to the next project leaves the initial product scope unchanged and, thus, does not affect the validity of project estimates. In this situation, effort estimation does not need to actually consider the change.

In practice, transferring change is possible to a limited extent. Small changes to project scope are typically accepted; only large changes that would violate project scope on an unacceptable level are postponed to the next project. If not transferred, changes should be addressed with another strategy. In the best case, consequences of change, such as modified project plan and budget, are shifted to the customer; that is, the customer agrees on adjusted project estimates.

Mitigate Change

Another way of dealing with the uncertainty surrounding project changes is to moderate the negative consequences of change. Wang et al. (2008) refer to approaches for mitigating change as planning for change. Essentially, planning for change improves the ability to react to change, thereby moderating its negative effects, including failed estimates.

- *Change control*: Uncontrolled project changes lead, particularly for large projects, to chaotic reactions, which in turn lead to missed project targets in terms of schedule, budget, and deliverables. Therefore, one element of planning for change should be preparing scenarios and procedures to control change and to make its impact on the project deterministic. Principally, it means that after we establish the project baseline, any change must follow a predefined systematic change procedure.
- *Design for change*: A product-oriented approach to handle change is to invest in developing flexible software; that is, software that can efficiently and rapidly be adapted to potential changes in business needs. For example, object-oriented design traditionally facilitates change by organizing and localizing data processing in an application. Developing flexible software often requires additional investment. Yet, it pays off through decreased rework and inviolate project plans when project change comes.

Accept Change

Finally, we may simply accept potential changes as they are. From the effort estimation perspective, accepting change means anticipating possible changes and considering their impact on projects in the estimates. Incorporating project uncertainty and risks into estimates is the usual way of considering potential project changes. Both probability of change and magnitude of its impact on project targets should be considered through estimation uncertainty.

Further Reading

- S. French (1995), "Uncertainty and imprecision: Modeling and analysis," *Journal of the Operational Research Society*, vol. 46, pp. 70–79.

    The author provides a general discussion of uncertainty and imprecision in the context of statistics and decision making. He identifies potential sources of uncertainty and their impact on analysis. Furthermore, the author discusses possible ways of modeling and methods for analyzing uncertainty.

- B. Kitchenham and S. Linkman (1997), "Estimates, uncertainty, and risk," *IEEE Software*, vol. 14, no. 3, pp. 69–74.

  In this article, the authors discuss in detail the potential sources of uncertainty in the context of software project estimation.

- M. Jørgensen and S. Grimstad (2008), "Avoiding Irrelevant and Misleading Information When Estimating Development Effort," *IEEE Software*, vol. 25, no. 3, pp. 78–83.

  In this article, the authors discuss the sources of uncertainty in the context of expert-based effort estimation. In particular, they discuss the impact on estimates if experts provide irrelevant and misleading information.

- S. Grimstad and M. Jørgensen (2006), "A framework for the analysis of software cost estimation accuracy", *Proceedings of the International Symposium on Empirical Software Engineering*, Rio de Janeiro, Brazil, 2006, pp. 58–65.

  Based upon an analysis of effort estimation studies, the authors propose a framework for analyzing effort estimation effort. Within the framework, they propose a list of typical sources of estimation error.

- T. Little (2006), "Schedule Estimation and Uncertainty Surrounding the Cone of Uncertainty." *IEEE Software*, vol. 23, no. 3, pp. 48–54.

  The author discusses aspects of estimation uncertainty (here schedule estimation) based on example industrial data.

- Z. Xu and T.M. Khoshgoftaar (2004), "Identification of Fuzzy Models of Software Cost Estimation," *Fuzzy Sets and Systems*, vol. 145, no. 1, pp. 141–163.

  Authors describe a fuzzy effort modeling technique that deals with linguistic data and uses historical project data for automatically generating fuzzy membership functions and fuzzy rules.

- J. Li and G. Ruhe (2006), "A Comparative Study of Attribute Weighting Heuristics for Effort Estimation by Analogy," *Proceedings of the International Symposium on Empirical Software Engineering*, Rio de Janeiro, Brazil, pp. 66–74.

  Authors compare in an empirical study several techniques for quantifying the impact of effort drivers on development effort. Investigated techniques are used in the context of an analogy-based estimation method called AQUA+. One of the techniques they employ for modeling the uncertain impact of effort drivers is based on rough sets theory.

- S. McConnell (2006), *Software Estimation: Demystifying the Black Art*, Microsoft Press.

  In Chap. 4 of his book, McConnell considers several ways of addressing estimation uncertainty. He provides several means for narrowing the cone of uncertainty and for considering the remaining uncertainty in project estimates, targets, and commitments.

- A. Stellman and J. Greene (2005), *Applied Software Project Management*, O'Reilly Media.

  In Chap. 9 of their book, the authors discuss project change. They investigate the most common reasons of failed project changes and provide guidelines on how to successfully run projects through change. Additionally, in Sect. 6.4, the authors discuss a change control process for dealing with changes in requirements. They highlight the need for implementing only those changes that are worth pursuing and for preventing unnecessary or overly costly changes. In practice, many changes that apparently look like good ideas ultimately get thrown out once the true cost-benefit ratio of the change is known.

- E.T. Wang, P. Ju, J.J. Jiang, and G. Klein (2008), "The effects of change control and management review on software flexibility and project performance," *Information & Management*, vol. 45, no. 7, pp. 438–443.

  This article discusses the link between project performance, software flexibility, and management interventions. In particular, they investigate software flexibility as a mediator between project performance and two commonly recommended management control mechanisms, management review and change control. In their survey among over 200 project managers from the Project Management Institute, the authors confirmed that the level of control activities during software development is a significant facilitator of software flexibility, which, in turn, improves project performance.

Basic Estimation Strategies

5

At no other time are the estimates so important than at the beginning of a project, yet we are so unsure of them. Go/no-go decisions are made, contracts are won and lost, and jobs appear and fade away based on these estimates. As unconfident and uncomfortable as we may be, we must provide these estimates.

—Robert T. Futrell, Donald F. Shafer, Linda Shafer.

One of the essential decisions during estimation is the abstraction level on which we estimate. At one extreme, we may predict effort for a complete project. At the other extreme, we may predict effort for individual work packages or activities. Dissonance between abstraction levels on which we are able to estimate and the level on which we need estimates is a common problem of effort prediction. We may, for example, have past experiences regarding complete projects and thus be able to predict effort for complete projects; yet, in order to plan work activities, we would need effort per project activity. Two basic estimation "strategies" exist for handling this issue: bottom-up and top-down estimation.

Another important decision during project effort estimation is which particular prediction method we should best employ or whether we should better use multiple alternative methods and find consensus between their outcomes.

In this chapter, we introduce top-down and bottom-up estimation strategies together with their strengths and weaknesses. For bottom-up estimation, we provide approaches for aggregating bottom-up effort estimates into a total project estimate. In addition, we discuss the usage of multiple alternative estimation methods—instead of a single one—and present approaches for combining alternative estimates into a unified final estimate. In Chap. 7, we discuss challenges in selecting the most suitable estimation method and we propose a comprehensive framework for addressing this issue.

5.1 Top-Down Estimation Approach

. . .the purpose of abstraction is not to be vague, but to create a new semantic level in which one can be absolutely precise.

—Edsger W. Dijkstra

A. Trendowicz and R. Jeffery, *Software Project Effort Estimation*,   125
DOI 10.1007/978-3-319-03629-8_5, © Springer International Publishing Switzerland 2014

In top-down estimation, we predict total project effort directly, that is, we estimate summary effort for all project development activities and for all products that the project delivers. We may then break down the total project estimate into the effort portions required for finishing individual work activities and for delivering individual work products. For instance, in analogy-based estimation, a new project as a whole is compared with previously completed similar projects, the so-called project analogs. We adapt the effort we needed in the past for completing project analogs as an effort prediction for the new project. After that we may distribute estimated total effort over individual project activities based on, for example, the percentage effort distribution we observed in historical projects. Another way of determining effort distribution across project work activities is to adapt one of the common project effort distributions other software practitioners have published in the related literature based on their observations across multiple—possibly multiorganizational—software projects. Examples of such distributions include Rayleigh, Gamma, or Parr's distributions, which we illustrated in Fig. 2.2 and briefly discussed in Sect. 2.2.2.

Effective project estimation would thus require the collection of historical data not only regarding the overall development effort but also regarding the effort required for completing major project phases or even individual work activities.

Tip

▶ Collect and maintain experiences regarding effort distribution across development phases and activities in your particular context. Consider project domain, size, and development size when reusing effort distributions observed in already completed projects for allocating effort in a new project.

Knowledge of the project's effort distribution is also useful for purposes other than effort estimation. For example, one of the best practices—reflected by that observed in project effort distributions in practice—is to invest relatively high effort in the early phases of the development, such as requirements specification and design. Such early investment prevents errors in the early stages of the software project and thus avoids major rework in the later phases, where correcting early-project errors might be very expensive. Monitoring the effort distribution across development processes may serve as a quick indicator of improper distribution of project priorities. In this sense, information on effort distribution serves process improvement and project risk analysis purposes.

Tip

▶ Requirements specification and design should take the majority of the project effort. Yet, in practice, testing often takes the major part of project effort. Make sure that you consider all project activities as they occur in the organization with their actual contribution to the overall project effort during project estimation.

5.2   Bottom-Up Estimation Approach

The secret of getting ahead is getting started. The secret of getting started is breaking your complex overwhelming tasks into small manageable tasks, and then starting on the first one.
—Mark Twain

In bottom-up estimation, we typically divide project work into activities (*process-level approach*) or software products into subproducts (*product-level approach*), and then we estimate the effort for completing each project activity or for producing each product component.

At the process level, we determine elementary work activities we want to estimate, size them, and then estimate effort for each of them individually. Total project effort is the aggregate of these bottom-up estimates. The simplest way of aggregating bottom-up estimates is to sum them. In practice, however, we need to consider the form of estimates and their interdependencies when aggregating them into total estimates. Uncritically summing bottom-up estimates may lead to invalid total project prediction. In Sect. 5.3, we discuss common approaches for aggregating bottom-up effort estimates.

5.2.1   Work Breakdown Structure

The *work breakdown structure (WBS)* is a method for identifying work components. It is widely used in the context of effort estimation and relies on hierarchical decomposition of project elements. Figure 5.1 shows an example WBS hierarchy. Three major perspectives of the WBS approach are applied in practice:

- *Deliverable-oriented*: It is a classical approach, defined by PMI (2013), in which decomposition is structured by the physical or functional components of the project. This approach uses major project deliverables as the first level of the work breakdown structure.
- *Activity-oriented*: This approach focuses on the processes and activities in the software project. It uses major life cycle phases as the first level of the work breakdown structure.
- *Organization-oriented*: This approach focuses, similarly to the activity-oriented one, on the project activities, but it groups them according to project organizational structure. This approach uses subprojects or components of the project as the first level of the work breakdown structure. Subprojects can be identified according to aspects of project organization as created subsystems, geographic locations, involved departments or business units, etc. We may consider employing organization-oriented WBS in the context of a distributed development.

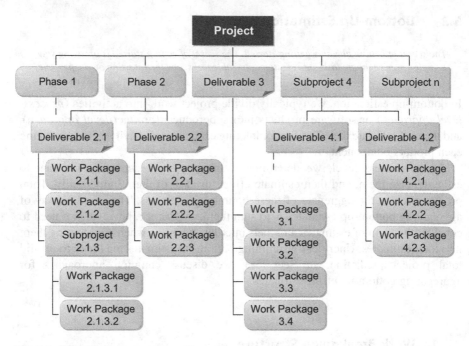

Fig. 5.1 Work breakdown structure hierarchy

In software estimation, a key success factor is to identify all work elements. This aspect is reflected by the most important rule of the WBS, called the 100 % rule. The 100 % rule was defined by Haugan (2002) and states that the work breakdown structure includes 100 % of the work defined by the project scope and captures all deliverables—internal, external, and interim—in terms of work to be completed, including project management. The 100 % rule applies at all levels within the WBS hierarchy. It means that the sum of the work at the subnodes must equal 100 % of the work represented by the node they are connected to. Moreover, the 100 % rule also applies to any perspective of the WBS. For example, for the activity-oriented view, work represented by the activities comprised by a work package must add up to 100 % of the work necessary to complete this work package.

As omitted work may have various sources, such as forgotten features and/or forgotten tasks, software practitioners usually use a mixture of WBS perspectives. Yet, we recommend not mixing too many different perspectives at one level of the WBS hierarchy.

Although WBS may consider project activities, it should always focus on "what" is to be done, not "when" it should be done or "who" should do it—these are the subject of the project plan, which is based on the WBS. In other words, a WBS contains no dependencies, durations, or resource assignments.

PMI's (2006) *Practice Standard for Work Breakdown Structures* proposes strategies for creating the project WBS: top-down and bottom-up.

The top-down WBS creation approach derives a project work breakdown structure by decomposing the overall project work into its subelements. This decomposition continues until work items reach a level where they can be easily and accurately estimated. Example 5.1 presents example steps of the top-down project WBS procedure for the deliverable-oriented perspective. The bottom-up WBS creation approach takes the form of brainstorming, where team members identify all low-level tasks needed to complete the project.

Tips

▶ The 100 % rule: Work breakdown structure includes 100 % of the work defined by the project scope and captures all deliverables: nothing less but also nothing more.
▶ Within one level of WBS hierarchy, try to use one consistent perspective: deliverable-oriented, activity-oriented, or organization-oriented.
▶ Work breakdown structure (WBS) should define "what" is to be accomplished in the project, not "when" it should be done or "who" should do it.

Example 5.1. Top-Down and Bottom-Up Deliverable-Oriented WBS

The PMI's (2006) "Practice Standard for Work Breakdown Structures" defines major steps of the top-down and bottom-up procedures for creating deliverable-oriented project work breakdown structures. In this example, we specify major steps of both WBS creation procedures based upon the PMI's standard.

Top-down WBS creation procedure:

1. *Identify project external deliverables*: Identify products which must be delivered by the project in order to achieve its success. This step is achieved by reviewing specifications of project scope. This includes such documents as "Project statement of work" and "Product requirements specification."
2. *Define project internal deliverables*: Identify and specify all project interim products that are produced during the project but themselves do not satisfy a business need and do not belong to project deliverables.
3. *Decompose project deliverables*: Decompose major project deliverables into lower-level work items that represent stand-alone products. The sum of the elements resulting from such decomposition at each level of the WBS hierarchy should represent 100 % of the work in the element above it. Each work item of the WBS should contain only one deliverable.
4. *Review and refine WBS*: Revise the work breakdown structure until project stakeholders, in particular estimators, agree that project planning can be successfully completed and that project execution and control according to the WBS will result in project success.

Bottom-up WBS creation procedure:

1. *Identify all project deliverables*: Identify all products or work packages comprised by the project. For each work package or activity, exactly one product that it delivers should be identified.
2. *Group deliverables*: Logically group related project deliverables or work packages.
3. *Aggregate deliverables*: Synthesize identified groups of deliverables into the next level in the WBS hierarchy. The sum of the elements at each level should represent 100 % of the work below it, according to the 100 % rule.
4. *Revise deliverables*: Analyze the aggregated WBS element to ensure that you have considered all of the work it encompasses.
5. *Repeat steps 1 to 4*: Repeat identifying, grouping, and aggregating project deliverables until the WBS hierarchy is complete, that is, until a single top node representing the project is reached. Ensure that the completed structure comprises the complete project scope.
6. *Review and refine WBS*: Review the WBS with project stakeholders, and refine it until they agree that the created WBS suffices for successful project planning and completion.

For more details, refer to PMI's (2006) "Practice Standard for Work Breakdown Structures."   ∎

The top-down WBS creation approach is generally more logical and fits better to a typical project planning scenario; thus, it is used in practice more often than the bottom-up approach. The bottom-up approach tends to be rather chaotic, consume much time, and often omit some of the low-level work activities. Therefore, as a general rule, we recommend using top-down estimation in most practical situations. The bottom-up WBS creation approach might be useful when used in combination with a top-down approach for identifying redundant and missing work items. Moreover, a bottom-up approach might be useful for revising existing WBS, for instance, in the context of maintenance and evolution of software systems.

Tip

▶ As a general rule, prefer the top-down approach for creating work breakdown structure (WBS). Consider using bottom-up in combination with the top-down approach for identifying redundant and omitted work items.

Table 5.1 summarizes situations, discussed by PMI (2006), when we should consider top-down and bottom-up WBS development procedures.

Validating Outcomes of WBS

One way of validating WBS is to check its elements (work items) if they fulfill the following requirements:

- *Definable*: Can be described and easily understood by project participants.
- *Manageable*: A meaningful unit of work (responsibility and authority) can be assigned to a responsible individual.
- *Estimable*: Effort and time required to complete the associated work can be easily and reliably estimated.
- *Independent*: There is a minimum interface with or dependence on other elements of the WBS (e.g., elements of WBS are assignable to a single control account and clearly distinguishable from other work packages).
- *Integrable*: Can be integrated with other project work elements and with higher-level cost estimates and schedules to include the entire project.
- *Measurable*: Can be used to measure progress (e.g., have start and completion dates and measurable interim milestones).
- *Adaptable*: Are sufficiently flexible, so the addition/elimination of work scope can be readily accommodated in the WBS.
- *Accountable*: Accountability of each work package can be assigned to a single responsible (human resource).
- *Aligned/compatible*: Can be easily aligned with the organizational and accounting structures.

For a more comprehensive list of aspects to be considered when evaluating the quality of a WBS, refer to PMI's (2006) Practice Standard for Work Breakdown Structures.

Table 5.1 When to use top-down and bottom-up WBS approaches

Top-down	Bottom-up
Project manager and development management team have little or no experience in developing WBS. Top-down procedure allows for progressive understanding and modeling of the project scope	Project manager and development team have large experience in creating WBS. Team members can easily identify a project's bottom-up deliverables and follow the bottom-up WBS procedure
The nature of the software products or services is not well understood. Creating WBS jointly with project stakeholders using the top-down approach supports the achievement of common understanding and consensus with respect to the project's nature and scope—especially when they are initially unclear	The nature of the software products or services is well understood. The project team has past experiences with similar products and services, and has a very good understanding of all interim deliverables required for the project

(continued)

Table 5.1 (continued)

Top-down	Bottom-up
The project life cycle is not clear or well known. Top-down creation of WBS allows for uncovering issues with respect to the software development life cycle, especially in the case of activity-oriented WBS	The project life cycle is clear and well known. Software organization uses a well-defined project life cycle, and all project members are familiar with it. In such cases, the development team can easily identify interim project deliverables and use them to start bottom-up WBS elaboration
No appropriate WBS templates are available. Developing WBS from scratch is far easier in a top-down manner, starting from the overall project deliverable and then iteratively determining its subelements	Appropriate WBS templates are available. The software organization has already developed work breakdown structures for similar projects with similar products or services. These can be easily reused and enhanced within a bottom-up approach

5.2.2 Method of Proportions

The so-called *method of proportions* is (after WBS) another popular instantiation of the bottom-up estimation strategy. This method uses estimates or actual values from one or more development phases of a new project as a basis for extrapolating the total development effort. The extrapolation uses a percentage effort distribution over the development phases observed in historical projects, which, at best, are those that are the most similar to the new project.

Example 5.2. Bottom-Up Estimation Using the Method of Proportions

Let us assume the following situation. A project manager estimates software development effort based on user requirements and needs to predict effort required to maintain the developed software for an a priori assumed operation time.

In the first step, the project manager identifies the most relevant characteristics of the new software, especially those that are critical for maintenance of the software. Next, he looks for already completed projects where similar software has been developed and where the maintenance effort is already known.

After analyzing already completed, historical projects, the project manager selects the one most similar (analog) project and analyzes the distribution of development and maintenance effort. He may also select more than one similar project and use their actual efforts for deriving the estimate. Figure 5.2 illustrates example effort distributions for historical and new projects. The project manager analyzes the percentage distribution of the total life cycle effort among the development and maintenance phases. Assuming that maintenance in the new project will take the same percentage of total effort as in the historical project, he extrapolates the maintenance effort of the new project based on its estimated

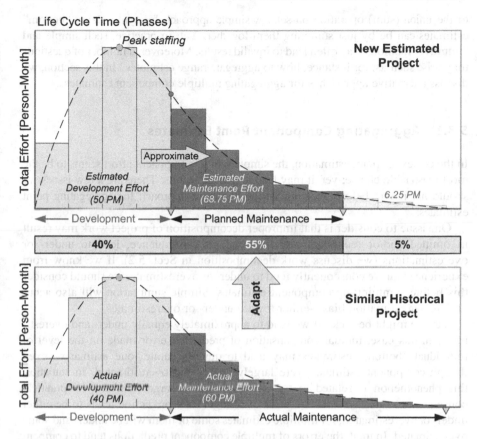

Fig. 5.2 Example bottom-up estimation using the method of proportions

development effort. Since the planned maintenance period of the new project is shorter than the actual maintenance in the historical project, the project manager additionally looks at what portion of the maintenance effort in the historical project was consumed in the planned period and plans the appropriate amount of effort for the new project's maintenance. ∎

5.3 Aggregating Component "Bottom" Estimates

In engineering, as in other creative arts, we must learn to do analysis to support our efforts in synthesis.

—Gerald J. Sussman

In the context of bottom-up estimation, the question of aggregating component "bottom" estimates into the total "upper" prediction arises. In the terminology of set theory, the aggregation operation on component "bottom" estimates would correspond to the union (sum) operation on sets. A simple approach for synthesizing "bottom" estimates can be by just summing them together. Yet, in practice, such simple and "intuitive" methods may often lead to invalid results. Moreover, a number of questions may arise such as, for instance, how to aggregate range estimates? In this section, we discuss alternative approaches for aggregating multiple component estimates.

5.3.1 Aggregating Component Point Estimates

In the context of point estimation, the simple sum of component effort seems to be the most reasonable choice; yet, it may lead to strange results. There are a few issues we should not ignore before deciding on the particular approach for aggregating point estimates.

One issue to consider is that improper decomposition of project work may result in omitted and/or redundant activities and, in consequence, lead to under- or overestimations (we discuss work decomposition in Sect. 5.2). If we know from experience that we consequently tend to under- or overestimate, we should consider this before summing up component estimates. Simple summation will also accumulate our estimation bias—either toward under- or overestimates.

Yet, we might be lucky if we tend to approximately equally under- and overestimate. In this case, mutual compensation of prediction error made on the level of individual "bottom" estimates may lead to quite accurate total estimates—even though component estimates were largely under- and overestimated. In statistics, this phenomenon is related to the so-called law of large numbers. Its practical consequence is that whereas the error of a single total prediction tends to be either under- or overestimated, for multiple estimates some of them will be under- and some overestimated. In total, the errors of multiple component predictions tend to compensate each other to some degree.

So far so good—we may think. Although imperfect decomposition of work items may lead to estimation uncertainties, the law of large numbers works to our advantage. Well, not quite, and as usual, the devil is in the details. There are a few details that need consideration here. First, distribution of estimates is typically consistently skewed toward either under- or overestimates. Moreover, the number of component estimates is quite limited in real situations and restricts applicability of the law of large numbers. Second, bottom-up estimation is typically applied in the context of expert-based prediction where human experts tend to implicitly (unconsciously) assign certain confidence levels to the point estimates they provide. In this case, the probability of completing the whole project within the sum of efforts estimated individually for all its component activities would be the joint probability of each activity completing within its estimated effort. According to probability theory, this would mean not summing up but multiplying probabilities associated to individual estimates of each component activity.

Let us illustrate this issue with a simple example. We estimate the "most likely" effort needed for completing ten project activities, which we identified in the project work breakdown structure. "Most likely" means that each estimate is

50 % likely to come true; that is, we believe each activity will be completed within its estimated effort with 50 % probability. In order to obtain the joint probability of completing all the ten project activities—that is, completing the whole project—we need to multiply probabilities associated to each individual "bottom" estimate. It occurs that the probability of completing the project within estimated summary effort would be merely 0.1 %.

A solution to the problem of summing up component point estimates is to involve estimation uncertainty explicitly into the aggregation process. A simple way of doing this is to collect minimum ("best-case"), most likely, and maximum ("worst-case") estimates for individual work items, aggregate them as probability distributions, and then compute total expected value, for example, as a mean over the resulting distribution. We discuss aggregating range and distribution estimates in the next section (Sect. 5.3.2).

In conclusion, we should avoid simply summing point estimates, especially when we suspect there are certain confidence levels associated with them. In essence, we should actually avoid both point estimates and aggregating them by simple summation. Whenever possible, we should include uncertainty into estimates and combinations of such estimates.

Tip

▶ When applying bottom-up estimation, explicitly consider estimation uncertainty and be aware of statistical subtleties of aggregating such predictions.

5.3.2 Aggregating Component Range Estimates

There are several approaches for aggregating uncertain component estimates. The *exact approach* applies probability theory to formally aggregate probability density functions of the variables represented by uncertain estimates. *The approximate approach* includes applying simulation techniques. In the next paragraphs, we present example aggregation methods for each of these two approaches.

Exact Approach: Sum of Random Variables

One way of aggregating estimates specified in terms of probability distributions is to apply mechanisms provided by probability theory for summing random variables. In probability theory, the distribution of the sum of two or more <u>independent, identically distributed</u> random variables is represented by the so-called convolution of their individual distributions.

Many commonly used probability distributions have quite simple convolutions. For example, the sum of two normal distributions $X \sim (\mu_x, \sigma_x^2)$ and $Y \sim (\mu_Y, \sigma_Y^2)$ is a normal distribution $Z \sim (\mu_x + \mu_Y, \sigma_x^2 + \sigma_Y^2)$, where μ and σ^2 represent the distribution mean and variance, respectively.

Constraints on Summing Multiple Random Variables
Sums of multiple random variables require that

1. They have identical distributions, that is, all aggregated bottom estimates are specified using the same probability distribution, and
2. They are independent, that is, the probability of a particular bottom effort estimate does not depend on the probability of other estimates.

Although the independency of component estimates is a desired property of bottom-up estimation, it may not always be provided. In the case of dependent estimates, dedicated approaches proposed by probability theory should be applied.

Exact discussion of these mechanisms is beyond the scope of our discussion and can be found in a number of publications on probability theory, for example, in Grinstead and Snell (2003).

Example 5.3 illustrates the practical application of the sum of random variables for aggregating bottom estimates provided by human experts. In this example, component estimates represent random variables with beta-PERT distribution.

Example 5.3. Program Evaluation and Review Technique (PERT)

Stutzke (2005) proposes applying the *Program Evaluation and Review Technique (PERT)* for aggregating bottom estimates provided by human experts. In PERT, the estimator provides component ("bottom") estimates in terms of three values: the minimal, the maximal, and the most likely effort. It is assumed that these values are unbiased and that the range between minimal and maximal estimates corresponds to six standard deviation limits of the distribution. In other words, the effort estimate is assumed to be a random variable with associated beta-PERT probability distribution (as we discussed briefly in Sect. 4.4 and illustrated in Fig. 4.5).

As per probability theory, we assume mutual independence of component estimates. Following this assumption, the convolution of individual distributions is computed, in that total expected estimate (mean) is a sum of individual expected estimates (5.1), and total variance is computed as a sum of variances on individual estimates. Total standard deviation is then computed as a root square from the total variance (5.2).

$$\text{Expected}_{\text{Total}} = \sum_{i=1}^{n} \text{Expected}_n, \text{for } n \text{ component estimates} \qquad (5.1)$$

where

$$\text{Expected}_i = \frac{\text{Min}_i + 4\ \text{ML}_i + \text{Max}_i}{6}$$

Table 5.2 Modified divisors for standard deviation of beta-PERT distribution (McConnell 2006)

Percentage of actual estimates within estimated range (historical data)	Divisor
10 %	0.25
20 %	0.51
30 %	0.77
40 %	1.0
50 %	1.4
60 %	1.7
70 %	2.1
80 %	2.6
90 %	3.3
99 %	6.0

$$\sigma_{Total} = \sqrt{\sum_{i=1}^{n} \sigma_i^2} \tag{5.2}$$

where

$$\sigma_i = \frac{Max_i - Min_i}{6}$$

McConnell (2006) noted that the PERT's assumption regarding the standard deviation being equal to the 1/6 range between a minimum and a maximum (5.2) has little to do with the reality of human-based estimation, in which beta-PERT is commonly applied. In order for this assumption to be true, 99.7 % of all true effort outcomes would need to fall into the estimation range. In other words, in 3 cases out of 1,000, actual project effort could fall outside the range between minimal and maximal estimates—which is simply unrealistic!

McConnell suggests a more realistic—in his opinion—approach for computing standard deviation from best and worst cases, in which an individual range is divided by a number closer to 2 rather than to 6. He proposes using a modified divisor (5.3), which is based on individual performance of the estimator:

$$\sigma = \frac{Max - Min}{Modified\ divisor} \tag{5.3}$$

Depending on the percentage cases in which actual project effort fell within estimated ranges in the past, the estimator selects an appropriate divisor. Table 5.2 provides several example percentages with corresponding divisors (McConnell 2006).

In order to determine target effort (budget), we need to consider the predicted effort for a certain confidence level; that is, the percentage confidence that the actual effort will not exceed the estimate. For this purpose, we consider the expected value (statistical mean) and the standard deviation of effort estimates. In

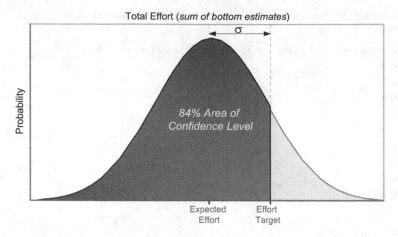

Fig. 5.3 Probability distribution for total effort and percentage confidence

order to simplify calculations, we take advantage of certain laws of probability theory, in particular the central limit theorem, which states that the sum of many independent distributions converges to a normal distribution as the number of component distributions increases.

Assuming Normal Distribution: Exact Approach

In practice, we do not make a significant error by assuming the total estimate is normally distributed. On the one hand, the sum of independent distributions converges to the normal curve very rapidly. Moreover, the error we make by approximating normal distribution is small compared to the typical estimation accuracy objectives, for example, ±20 %.

For a one-tailed normal distribution, the probability that the actual effort value will not exceed a certain target value is illustrated in Fig. 5.3.

We set the target as the expected value μ plus/minus n times the value of the standard deviation σ, where n is associated with target probability (5.4):

$$\text{Expected effort} = \mu \pm t \cdot \sigma \tag{5.4}$$

Table 5.3 provides an example set of calculations for selected percentage confidence levels proposed by McConnell (2006).

One general threat of the simple PERT method proposed by McConnell (2006) is that the expected effort (mean) must truly be 50 % likely. It is thus important to monitor actual effort data and control if they underrun component estimates just as often as they overrun them. If not, the aggregated effort will not be accurate and the estimation error will reflect the disproportion between component under- and overestimates. ∎

Table 5.3 Computing percentage confident effort using standard deviation (McConnell 2006)

Probability of exceeding target effort	Target effort
2 %	ExpectedEffort − (2.00 · StandardDeviation)
10 %	ExpectedEffort − (1.28 · StandardDeviation)
16 %	ExpectedEffort − (1.00 · StandardDeviation)
20 %	ExpectedEffort − (0.84 · StandardDeviation)
25 %	ExpectedEffort − (0.67 · StandardDeviation)
30 %	ExpectedEffort − (0.52 · StandardDeviation)
40 %	ExpectedEffort − (0.25 · StandardDeviation)
50 %	ExpectedEffort
60 %	ExpectedEffort + (0.25 · StandardDeviation)
70 %	ExpectedEffort + (0.52 · StandardDeviation)
75 %	ExpectedEffort + (0.67 · StandardDeviation)
80 %	ExpectedEffort + (0.84 · StandardDeviation)
84 %	ExpectedEffort + (1.00 · StandardDeviation)
90 %	ExpectedEffort + (1.28 · StandardDeviation)
98 %	ExpectedEffort + (2.00 · StandardDeviation)

Approximate Approach: Simulation

The exact method for aggregating uncertain estimates may involve complex mathematical formulas. Therefore, approximate approaches based on simulation techniques have alternatively been proposed.

Total effort estimate can be approximated by applying simulation techniques, such as Monte Carlo, on component estimates. Let us briefly explain how simulation-based aggregation works. Figure 5.4 illustrates the process of aggregating three component effort estimates provided in the form of triangular distributions. In each single simulation run, a crisp effort value is randomly sampled from each one of the component estimates. In our example, a single simulation run results in three discrete effort values. The values sampled in a single run are then summed up to a discrete total effort value on the simulation output. This process is repeated multiple times, for example, 1,000 runs. As a result, a probability distribution of total effort estimate is obtained.

Assuming Normal Distribution: Simulation Approach
Similar to the exact approach, in which we analytically determine sums of probability distributions, in the case of simulation, the central limit theorem also works to our advantage. In consequence, we may assume that the sum of many independent distributions converges to a normal distribution as the number of component distributions increases. In fact, we may already observe this phenomenon for the example sum of three distributions presented in Fig. 5.4. The resulting summary distribution takes the form of a bell-shaped normal distribution.

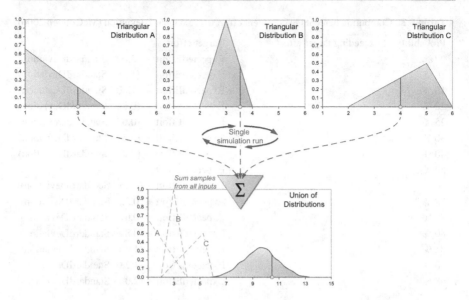

Fig. 5.4 Aggregating component estimates using simulation

An example estimation method that actually uses simulation for integrating multiple uncertain bottom estimates was proposed by Elkjaer (2000) in the context of expert-based estimation. His method, called *Stochastic Budgeting Simulation*, employs random sampling to combine the effort of individual effort items, such as work products or development activities, specified by experts in terms of triangular distributions.

5.4 Selecting Appropriate Estimation Strategy

An intelligent plan is the first step to success. The man who plans knows where he is going, knows what progress he is making and has a pretty good idea when he will arrive.
                                                                                    —Basil S. Walsh

Depending on the particular project application context, both top-down and bottom-up approaches for project effort estimation have various advantages and disadvantages.

> **Estimation Strategy and Estimation Method**
> In the related literature, top-down and bottom-up estimations are often referred to as estimation methods. In our opinion, top-down and bottom-up approaches refer more to an overall estimation strategy rather than to a particular estimation method. In principle, any estimation method, such as regression analysis or expert judgment, can be used within any of these two strategies; although not every estimation method is equally adequate and easy to apply within each of these two strategies.

Table 5.4 Advantages and disadvantages of top-down and bottom-up estimation

Bottom-up	Top-down
Provides detailed estimates for bottom-level project activities and related software subproducts. The more granular the product or activity we want to directly estimate, typically the more accurate are total estimates built upon "bottom" estimates. Yet, the risk of multiplying estimation errors is higher than by top-down estimation	Provides total estimate for all project activities and related software products. It is easier to estimate if only total effort from historical projects is available. If effort per product or activity is needed, additional techniques need to be applied to split total effort
There is a high probability that estimation errors at the bottom level cancel each other (over- and underestimates will balance), resulting in lower error of total estimate than by a top-down approach	In the context of expert-based estimation, the top-down approach avoids accumulation of overoptimistic estimates given by developers at the bottom level
Applicable in later phases of development when detailed information regarding lower-level software components (and process activities) is available	Applicable in early phases of software development where the gross concept of the overall software system is available
There is a significant danger of multiple counts of the same effort. Example reasons include (1) counting effort twice for the same activities provided by different team members, (2) counting effort of overlapping activities twice, or (3) counting additional effort at each bottom-level estimate to account for some common upper-level risks twice	There is significant danger of omitting work that has significant contribution to the overall project effort, e.g., by forgetting relevant project deliverables and/or activities
The development team may expend a significant amount of effort to first prepare project work decomposition, obtain bottom estimates, and aggregate them to total estimate	Overall software estimates are relatively cheap and quick to obtain
In the context of analogy-based estimation, the more granular the individually estimated product component, the more difficult it is to find an analogous historical component to compare it with	In the context of analogy-based estimation, it is easier to find the whole historical project that is an analog to the new one
Bottom-up estimation is more suitable for classical project planning in which elementary work activities are a basis for project scheduling and resource allocation. Estimating effort for individual work activities allows for considering the productivity of particular human resources preallocated to each activity	In order to schedule project work activities and allocate resources, the total project effort needs to be first distributed onto these activities. Moreover, while estimating total project effort, an "average" productivity across all human resources assigned to the project can only be considered

In Table 5.4, we summarize the most relevant strengths and weaknesses of both estimation strategies. Note, however, that particular characteristics should always be considered in a particular context, in which you want to apply them.

In general, top-down estimation lets us obtain estimates for project phases or tasks even though we do not have enough data to perform such estimation for each phase or task separately. The bottom-up approach lets us limit the estimation abstraction level. It is especially useful in the case of expert-based estimation, where it is easier for experts to embrace and estimate smaller pieces of project work. Moreover, the increased level of detail during estimation—for instance, by breaking down software products and processes—implies higher transparency of estimates.

In practice, there is a good chance that the bottom estimates would be mixed below and above the actual effort. As a consequence, estimation errors at the bottom level will cancel each other out, resulting in smaller estimation error than if a top-down approach were used. This phenomenon is related to the mathematical *law of large numbers*.[1] However, the more granular the individual estimates, the more time-consuming the overall estimation process becomes.

In industrial practice, a top-down strategy usually provides reasonably accurate estimates at relatively low overhead and without too much technical expertise. Although bottom-up estimation usually provides more accurate estimates, it requires the estimators involved to have expertise regarding the bottom activities and related product components that they estimate directly.

In principle, applying bottom-up estimation pays off when the decomposed tasks can be estimated more accurately than the whole task. For instance, a bottom-up strategy proved to provide better results when applied to high-uncertainty or complex estimation tasks, which are usually underestimated when considered as a whole. Furthermore, it is often easy to forget activities and/or underestimate the degree of unexpected events, which leads to underestimation of total effort. However, from the mathematical point of view (law of large numbers mentioned), dividing the project into smaller work packages provides better data for estimation and reduces overall estimation error.

Experiences presented by Jørgensen (2004b) suggest that in the context of expert-based estimation, software companies should apply a bottom-up strategy unless the estimators have experience from, or access to, very similar projects. In the context of estimation based on human judgment, typical threats of individual and group estimation should be considered. Refer to Sect. 6.4 for an overview of the strengths and weaknesses of estimation based on human judgment.

Tip

▶ Developers typically tend to be optimistic in their individual estimates (underestimate). As a project manager, do not add more optimism by reducing the
   developers' estimates.

---

[1] In statistics, the law of large numbers says that the average of a large number of independent measurements of a random quantity tends toward the theoretical average of that quantity. In the case of effort estimation, estimation error is assumed to be normally distributed around zero. The consequence of the law of large numbers would thus be that for a large number of estimates, the overall estimation error tends toward zero.

In both strategies, the ability of the software estimation method and/or model to transfer estimation experience from less similar projects leads to equally poor estimates. In other words, lack of quantitative experiences from already completed projects leads to poor predictions independent of whether the data-driven method estimates the whole project or its components.

In summary, although the bottom-up approach intuitively seems to provide better data for estimation, the selection of the proper strategy depends on the task characteristics and the level of the estimators' experience. In principle, one should prefer top-down estimation in the early (conceptual) phases of a project and switch to bottom-up estimation where specific development tasks and assignments are known.

Tip

▶ Prefer top-down estimation in the early (conceptual) phases of a project and switch to bottom-up estimation where specific development tasks and assignments are known. Consider using top-down estimation strategy for cross-checking bottom-up estimates (and vice versa).

Finally, whenever accurate estimates are relatively important and estimation costs are relatively low, compared to overall project effort, we recommend using both estimation strategies for validation purposes.

5.5   Using Multiple Alternative Estimation Methods

In combining the results of these two methods, one can obtain a result whose probability of error will more rapidly decrease.
                                                                    —Pierre Laplace

A number of effort estimation methods have been proposed over the recent decades. Yet, no "silver-bullet" method has been proposed so far, and it is actually hard to imagine that such a "one-size-fits-all" estimation method will ever be created. Each and every estimation method has its own specific strengths and limitations, which depend on the particular situation in which the method is used. The most important consequence of this fact is that a combination of different estimation approaches may substantially improve the reliability of estimates.

In practice, there are two ways of implementing the idea of combining multiple estimation methods or paradigms:

- *Hybrid estimation method*: In this approach, elements of different estimation paradigms, for example, expert-based and data-driven estimation, are integrated within a hybrid estimation method. Hybrid estimation may use alternative information sources and combine multiple elementary techniques into a single estimation method, which typically represents alternative estimation paradigms. We discuss hybrid estimation methods in Sect. 6.5.

- *Multiple alternative methods*: In this approach, multiple alternative methods are applied independently to estimate the same work, and their outcome estimates are combined into a final estimate. Similar to hybrid estimation, multiple alternative methods should preferably represent different estimation paradigms and be based on alternative, yet complementary, information sources.

A major benefit of using multiple estimation methods is the possibility of validating alternative estimates against each other. In the case of significantly inconsistent estimates, we may investigate sources of potential discrepancies between alternative estimates, improve them if possible, and combine them when they start to converge.

Tip

▶ In order to validate and improve prediction accuracy, combine estimates provided by several methods that represent substantially different estimation paradigms and use different sources of information.

A major drawback of using alternative estimation methods is the large overhead required to perform multiple estimations with different methods. We should therefore consider using multiple estimation methods and combining alternative estimates only when

- It is very important to avoid large estimation errors. For example, we know that the cost of potential prediction error is much higher than the cost of applying multiple estimation methods.
- We are uncertain about the situation in which the estimation method is to be applied. For example, the project environment has not been precisely specified yet, and estimation inputs and constraints are not clear.
- We are uncertain about which forecasting method is more accurate. Since, in most cases, we are uncertain about which method is the most accurate, it is always good to consider the use of several methods.
- There is more than one reasonable estimation method available. In practice, we recommend using two alternative methods that differ substantially with respect to the estimation paradigm and to use different sources of information.

5.6   Combining Alternative Estimates

Based on the extensive evidence in favour of combining estimates the question should not be whether we should combine or not, but how?

—Magne Jørgensen

When using multiple estimation methods, we must face the issue of combining multiple effort estimates that these methods provide into a single final prediction. In contrast to combining component estimates in the context of bottom-up estimation

(Sect. 5.3) where we summed up partial estimates, in the context of applying multiple estimation methods, we are interested in finding a consensus between multiple estimates. Using the terminology of set theory, combining multiple alternative estimates would correspond to the intersection operation.

5.6.1 Combining Largely Inconsistent Estimates

In practice, uncritically combining estimates that differ widely may lead to significant errors. We may consider using sophisticated methods for avoiding the impact of outlier estimates. Yet, outlier analysis requires several values, whereas in practice, we will typically have two or three alternative values. Moreover, in the case of outlier analysis, it is not clear if estimates identified as outliers are not the correct ones that should not be excluded from consideration. The simple "majority" rule does not apply to software effort estimation. We need to consider if each individual estimate may be right and then decide on the combined estimate. Therefore, before combining estimates, one should investigate possible sources of discrepancy between outputs of alternative estimation approaches.

At best, estimation should be repeated after potential sources of inconsistencies have been clarified. This process can be repeated until estimates converge and the observed discrepancy is not greater than 5 %. Then, an appropriate aggregation approach should be selected and applied to come up with final effort estimates.

In an extreme case, excluding an estimation method that provides outlier estimates should be considered if the sources of deviation are clear and nothing can be done to improve the convergence of estimates. Yet, this option should be considered very carefully as it may occur that extreme estimates were the most exact ones.

Tip

▶ If estimates provided by alternative methods differ widely, then investigate the reasons for this discrepancy, before combining the estimates. Continue investigating the reasons for discrepancy between estimates provided by alternative methods until the estimates converge to within about 5 %. Exclude individual estimation methods from the prediction process if necessary, for example, if they clearly provide incorrect estimates and nothing can be done to improve them. Combine alternative estimates when they start to converge.

5.6.2 Combining Alternative Point Estimates

Statistical Techniques

Common statistical means for combining multiple point estimates include taking a simple mean or mode value over a number of individual estimates. Yet, individual forecasts may be burdened by large errors, for example, due to miscalculations, errors in data, or misunderstanding of estimation scope and context. In such cases, it is useful to exclude the extremely high and extremely low predictions from the analysis.

Example statistical means that deal with extreme values—so-called outliers—include trimmed means or medians. A less radical approach for handling deviations between individual estimates would be by applying a weighted average, where weights reflect the believed credibility of each estimate. In the case of expert-based estimation, these weights may reflect the experts' level of competence regarding the estimated tasks. When combining predictions provided by data-driven and expert-based methods, higher weight may be assigned to data-driven estimates if a large set of high-quality data is available, or to expert-based methods, otherwise—especially when highly experienced estimators are involved. We recommend, after Armstrong (2001), using equal weights unless strong evidence or belief exists to support unequal weighting.

Tip

▶ When combining multiple estimates by means of weighted average, use equal weights unless you have strong evidence to support unequal weighting of alternative estimates.

Expert Group Consensus

As an alternative to a statistical approach, we may combine multiple alternative effort estimates in a group consensus session. In this approach, alternative estimates are discussed within a group of human experts, where each expert typically represents one individual estimate. As a result of discussion, experts come up with a consensus regarding the final estimate.

Although it can theoretically be applied for any estimation method, the group consensus approach is typically applied in the context of estimation based on human judgment (Sect. 6.4.2). In this context, alternative estimates are provided by individual human experts and then combined in the group discussion.

A group debate might have the form of an unstructured meeting or follow a systematic process, such as one defined by existing group consensus techniques. Examples of the structured group discussion techniques are *Wideband Delphi* (Chap. 12) or, created in the context of agile development, *Planning Poker* (Chap. 13).

The performance of individual group consensus methods typically varies depending on the characteristics of the group, such as motivation of involved experts, their social relations, and communication structure in a group. A common threat is human and situational bias of a group discussion. We address these problems in Sect. 6.4.3, where we discuss effort estimation methods based on group discussion.

Also, characteristics of tasks estimated have an impact on the performance of different group discussion techniques. For example, Haugen (2006) observed that for tasks that experts were familiar with, the planning poker technique delivered more accurate estimates than unstructured combination—the opposite was found for tasks with which experts were unfamiliar.

In the context of expert-based effort estimation, statistical combination of individual experts' estimates was, surprisingly, found less effective than combining them in a group discussion process. Moløkken-Østvold et al. (2004, 2008) observed that group estimates made after an unstructured discussion were more realistic than individual estimates derived prior to the group discussion and combined by statistical means. It is the group discussion that seems to be the key factor reducing the overoptimism in individual estimates. Thus, even taking a simple average, that is, a statistical mean, of individual estimates should often work well under the condition that they were provided after a group discussion. We generally advise conducting an unstructured discussion before experts provide their individual estimates and before we combine these estimates.

Tip

▶ When considering multiple expert estimates, perform a group discussion session before combining individual estimates—independent of the approach used to combine alternative estimates.

5.6.3 Combining Alternative Range Estimates

Statistical Techniques

A simple statistical approach for combining alternative range estimates might be by taking an average, that is, a statistical mean, of the individual minimum and maximum predictions. This approach seems to work well in many practical situations. For example, Armstrong (2001) observed in a number of empirical studies that predictions based on the simple mean across all individual predictions were on average 12.5 % more accurate than the mean of a single randomly selected prediction.

Yet, combining estimates by means of a simple average has been observed ineffective in the context of estimates based on human judgment, where prediction intervals tend to be too narrow and not to correspond to the confidence level believed by the experts. For example, experts believed to provide estimates of 90 % confidence, whereas the actual confidence level represented by intervals they provided was about 70 %. In such situations, applying a simple average over individual minimums and maximums does not improve correspondence between believed and actual confidence levels, that is, it does not deal with overoptimism of the individual estimates.

Jørgensen and Moløkken (2002) observed that in the context of expert-based estimation, taking the maximum and minimum of individual maximum and minimum predictions is much more effective than taking averages. In this approach,

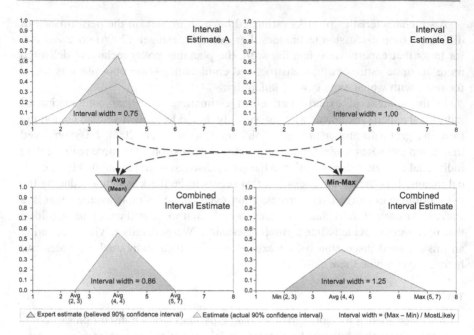

Fig. 5.5 Combining expert estimates using the "average" and "min–max" approaches

overoptimism of individual estimates is reduced by taking the widest interval over all estimates. Figure 5.5 illustrates both average and min-max approaches for combining alternative expert-based estimates. Note that in both cases, most likely estimates are combined by way of simple statistical mean.

Expert Group Consensus

Similarly to combining point estimates, a group consensus approach seems to be again a more effective way of synthesizing expert estimates than "automatic" statistical approaches. In a group consensus approach, final estimates are agreed upon in a group discussion. Although group consensus can be applied to combine any estimates, it is typically applied in the context of expert-based estimation; that is, for synthesizing alternative estimates provided by human experts. A group debate might have the form of an unstructured meeting or follow a systematic process defined by one of the existing group consensus techniques such as *Wideband Delphi* or *Planning Poker*. We present these methods in Chaps. 12 and 13, respectively.

Simulation Techniques

Similar to combining multiple component estimates in the context of bottom-up estimation (Sect. 5.3), alternative estimates provided by different prediction

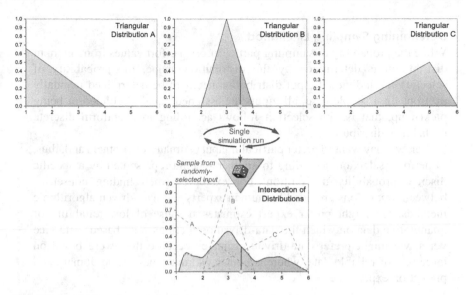

Fig. 5.6 Combining alternative estimates using simulation

methods can also be combined using simulation approaches. However, other than in the case of bottom-up estimation, we are not looking for a sum of partial estimates but for their consensus, that is, their intersection in set terminology.

Figure 5.6 illustrates the process of finding consensus between three alternative effort estimates provided in the form of triangular distributions. Each single simulation run consists of two steps. First, a single effort distribution is selected randomly from among the alternative distributions considered. Next, a single crisp effort value is randomly sampled from the distribution selected in the first step. As a result, the final consensus effort distribution consists of multiple <u>independent effort samples</u> originating from distinct input effort distributions, other than in case of aggregating component "bottom" estimates where the final effort distribution consists of effort values computed as a <u>sum of samples</u> originating from all input effort distributions (Sect. 5.3.2, Fig. 5.4). Based on the outcome effort distribution, a final estimate is determined; for instance, using the cumulative distribution, we select the effort value (or range of values) that has a satisfactorily high probability of not being exceeded in the project. Refer to Sect. 4.4.1 for a discussion on interpreting effort probability distributions.

Determining Sampling Likelihood

While the probability of sampling particular crisp effort values from an input distribution is determined by the distribution shape, the probability of selecting the individual input distribution needs to be determined manually up front. In a simple case, all inputs are assigned equal likelihood of being picked up, that is, the selection follows according to a uniform discrete probability distribution.

Yet, we may want to prefer particular input estimates over others and, thus, to perform selection according to another schema represented by a specific discrete probability distribution. For example, when finding consensus between predictions provided by human experts and data-driven algorithmic methods, we might prefer expert estimates because of low reliability of quantitative data on which the data-driven predictions were based. And vice versa, we might prefer data-driven estimates because they were based on large sets of reliable data, whereas human estimates have little domain and prediction experience.

Further Reading

- R.D. Stutzke (2005), *Estimating Software-Intensive Systems*: *Projects*, *Products*, *and Processes*, Addison-Wesley Professional.

  In Chaps. 11 and 12 of his book, the author discusses bottom-up and top-down estimation strategies, respectively. Example techniques for implementing both estimation strategies are described. The author also discusses threats in making effort-time trade-offs and schedule compression.

- Project Management Institute (2006), *Practice Standard for Works Breakdown Structures. 2nd Edition*. Project Management Institute, Inc. Pennsylvania, USA.

  The practice standard provides a summary of best practices for defining work breakdown structures. It provides an overview of the basic WBS process, criteria for evaluating the quality of WBS, and typical considerations needed when defining WBS. Finally, the standard provides a number of example work breakdown structures from various domains, including software development and process improvement.

- R.T. Futrell, D.F. Shafer, and L. I. Shafer (2002), *Quality Software Project Management*, Prentice Hall.

  In their book, the authors discuss approaches for creating project work breakdown structures and identifying project activities in the context of project management. In Chap. 8, they present top-down and bottom-up strategies for creating project-oriented WBS and show different WBS approaches that implement these strategies. In Chap. 9, the authors show how to populate a WBS to identify project activities and tasks relevant for effective project planning.

- IEEE Std 1074 (2006), *IEEE Standard for Developing a Software Project Life Cycle Process*, New York, NY, USA. IEEE Computer Society.

    This standard provides a process for creating a process for governing software development and maintenance. It lists common software development life cycle phases, activities, and tasks. The standard does not imply or presume any specific life cycle model.

- ISO/IEC 12207 (2008), *International standard for Systems and Software Engineering - Software Life Cycle Processes*, International Organization for Standardization and International Electrotechnical Commission (ISO/IEC), and IEEE Computer Society.

    Similar to the IEEE 1074 standard, this international standard aims at specifying a framework for software life cycle processes. Yet, it comprises a wider range of activities regarding life cycle of software/system product and services. It spans from acquisition, through supply and development, to operation, maintenance, and disposal. Similar to IEEE 1074, this standard also does not prescribe any particular life cycle model within which proposed phases and activities would be sequenced.

- M. Jørgensen (2004), "Top-down and bottom-up expert estimation of software development effort." *Information and Software Technology*, vol. 46, no. 1, pp. 3–16.

    The author investigates strengths and weaknesses of top-down and bottom-up strategies in the context of expert-based effort estimation. In his industrial study, the author asked seven teams of estimators to predict effort for two software projects, where one project was to be estimated using a top-down strategy and the other using a bottom-up strategy. In the conclusion, the author suggests applying a bottom-up strategy unless estimators have experience from, or access to, very similar historical projects.

- S. Fraser, B.W. Boehm, H. Erdogmus, M. Jørgensen, S. Rifkin, and M.A. Ross (2009), "The Role of Judgment in Software Estimation," *Panel of the 31st International Conference on Software Engineering*, Vancouver, Canada, IEEE Computer Society.

    This short article documents a panel discussion regarding the role of expert judgment and data analysis in software effort estimation. Panelists underline the thesis that "there is nothing like judgment-free estimation" but also stress the importance of quantitative historical information for software estimation.

- M. Jørgensen (2007), "Forecasting of software development work effort: Evidence on expert judgment and formal models," *International Journal of Forecasting*, vol. 23, no. 3, pp. 449–462.

This article provides a comprehensive review of published evidence on the use of expert judgment, formal methods, and hybrid methods for the purpose of software project effort estimation. The final conclusion is that combining model- and expert-based approaches works principally better than either one alone.

- M. Jørgensen (2004), "A Review of Studies on Expert Estimation of Software Development Effort," *Journal of Systems and Software*, vol. 70, no. 1–2, pp. 37–60.

  In Sect. 5.2 of his article, the author provides an overview of various approaches for combining multiple estimates provided by human experts. In addition, he discusses typical factors on which benefits of combining multiple expert estimates depend.

- M. Jørgensen and K. J. Moløkken (2002), "Combination of software development effort prediction intervals: why, when and how?" *Proceedings of the 14th International Conference on Software engineering and knowledge Engineering*, Ischia, Italy, pp. 425–428.

  The authors investigate an empirical study of three strategies for combining multiple, interval estimates: (1) average of the individual minimum and maximum estimates, (2) maximum and minimum of the individual maximum and minimum estimates, and (3) group discussion of estimation intervals. Results of the study suggest that a combination of prediction intervals based on group discussion provides better estimates than "mechanical" combinations. Yet, the authors warn that there is no generally best strategy for combining prediction intervals.

Part II

Selecting an Appropriate Estimation Method

It is common sense to take a method and try it. If it fails, admit it frankly and try another. But above all, try something.

—Franklin D. Roosevelt

In this part, we address the basic question of software estimation practitioners: *What estimation should I use?* In order to support selecting the most appropriate estimation method, we first review existing estimation methods and discuss their most relevant characteristics. Next, we refine these characteristics into a set of criteria for selecting the most appropriate method for a specific estimation purpose and specific estimation context.

Chapter 6 provides a classification of effort estimation methods and discussion of the most relevant characteristics.

Chapter 7 presents a systematic approach for selecting the most appropriate estimation method based on particular goals and context of estimation.

Classification of Effort Estimation Methods

6

One of the most difficult concepts to get agreement or even understanding is 'How to estimate software development projects'. The number of techniques and their complexity elevate this discipline almost to a mystical art known only by the chosen few who are adept at reading the tea leaves.

—Robert C. Anderson

In this chapter, we provide a brief overview of the existing software effort estimation methods. First, we identify common characteristics of existing methods and propose a schema for their classification. In the following sections, we provide a brief characterization of each class of methods and provide examples of typical methods belonging to a particular group.

6.1 Classification of Effort Estimation Methods

The purpose of science is not to analyze or describe but to make useful models of the world. A model is useful if it allows us to get use out of it.

—Edward de Bono

Over the years, software researchers have been very productive in providing numerous effort estimation methods. Each newly proposed method is typically more sophisticated and claims to be the one that solves problems that have not been addressed before. Yet, most of the methods we show in Fig. 6.1 have not, until now, gone beyond research and academic applications. Only a few of the methods have been accepted in the software industry, and even fewer can be referred to as widely known and applied in software development practice. We have underlined these methods in Fig. 6.1 and provide short descriptions of their principles in Chaps. 8–15.

In Fig. 6.1, we group effort estimation methods with respect to two basic aspects: (1) the type of data they use as input and (2) the estimation principle they employ. In the following sections, we provide brief characteristics of each group.

A. Trendowicz and R. Jeffery, *Software Project Effort Estimation*,
DOI 10.1007/978-3-319-03629-8_6, © Springer International Publishing Switzerland 2014

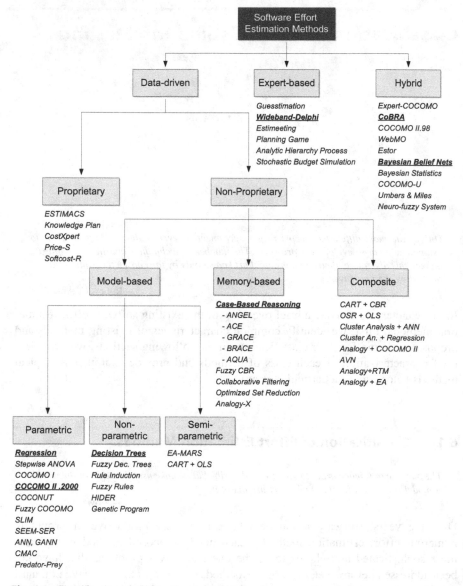

Fig. 6.1 Classification of effort estimation methods

6.2   Proprietary vs. Nonproprietary Methods

> *There are no transportable cost models. If you wait for someone else to develop a set of formulas that you can use for cost forecasting in your shop, you will probably wait forever.*
> —Tom DeMarco

Proprietary effort estimation methods refer to methods that are not fully documented in the public domain. Although basic principles and the estimation algorithm are often publicly available, the details of the estimation procedure are typically not available to the public. Yet, in most cases, it is not the proprietary character of the estimation algorithm that determines the nondisclosure of a particular estimation approach, but rather the proprietary character of the underlying fixed estimation model, or more precisely speaking, of the industrial data upon which the model was developed and/or calibrated. In this case, the benchmark data and the effort model that represents it contain value that is protected, typically by hiding it in an estimation software tool. That is also why proprietary approaches are typically data-driven, fixed-model approaches. The major benefit of such methods is that one can estimate effort without having any historical project data. Project effort is estimated based upon actual effort data (benchmark data) collected across similar projects from external organizations. Typically, all the project data, the estimation model, and procedures to derive it from the data are hidden in a proprietary software tool.

For example, three competing proprietary estimation methods/tools are discussed by Jensen et al. (2006), which include SLIM-Estimate®, SEER-SEM®, and CostXpert®.

The major weakness of proprietary methods is that the goodness of estimates depends on the existence of similar projects in the underlying benchmark data repository. The fewer similar projects available, the weaker the foundation for estimates and the less accurate the estimates are likely to be. That is why it is important that a proprietary effort estimation method/tool is based upon a large number of up-to-date projects that come from a context similar to that in which the method is applied. Moreover, the ability to calibrate the model to new project data is an important feature of a proprietary estimation method. In Sect. 6.6, we discuss the strengths and weaknesses of fixed-model estimation approaches in more detail.

Tip

▶ When using proprietary commercial estimation tools, make sure that (1) the underlying data repository contains a large set of up-to-date projects that are similar to projects you want to estimate and (2) that the tool supports adding your projects to the repository and recalibrating the underlying estimation model appropriately.

6.3 Data-Driven Methods

We're drowning in information and starving for knowledge.
—Rutherford D. Rogers

The goal is to transform data into information, and information into insight.
—Carly Fiorina

Data-driven effort estimation refers to methods that predict effort based solely on the quantitative analysis of historical project data. In the course of estimation, relationships between the actual project effort and project characteristics are explored based on the measurement data collected from already completed projects. The relationships found are then projected onto a new project in order to predict the expected effort.

Tip

▶ Always use actual data from historic projects when estimating a new project with a data-driven method. If the historical project was over/underestimated, basing new project estimates upon it will, most probably, also result in over/underestimates.

6.3.1 Model-Based vs. Memory-Based Estimation

There are two principal ways of exploring and documenting effort relationships from historical project data for the purpose of effort prediction: explicit and implicit. *Explicit analysis* of project effort dependencies is represented by so-called model-based methods. In this approach, an explicit model that relates the development effort (independent variable) to one or more project characteristics (independent variables) is developed based on the analysis of historical project data. *Implicit analysis* of project effort dependencies is represented by so-called memory-based (or analogy-based) methods. In this approach, it is assumed that projects of similar characteristics require similar effort to be completed. In consequence, instead of modeling dependencies between effort and project characteristics, memory-based methods focus on modeling similarity between projects.

> **Role of Software Size in Effort Estimation**
> In both model- and memory-based estimation approaches, software size is considered as the major effort driver. Other effort drivers include characteristics of development products, processes, and resources (including personnel).

Figure 6.2 illustrates the difference between model-based and memory-based effort estimation.

Model-Based Estimation

Model-based methods, such as statistical regression, use data to build a parameterized effort model, where model parameters might be (at least partially) specified a priori (in parametric methods) or might be learned completely from data (in nonparametric methods). After training one or more component *models* with certain *modeling techniques*, an *estimation model* is created. The model is then used

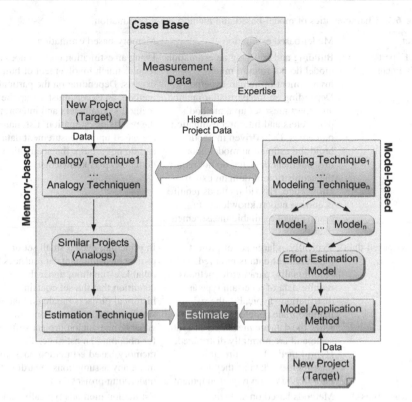

Fig. 6.2 Principles of model- and memory-based effort estimation

for predictions, and the data are generally not needed at the time of prediction. CoBRA (Chap. 15) is an example method that uses an estimation model consisting of multiple component models: effort overhead model and productivity model. They are created using, respectively, causal modeling and statistical regression as modeling techniques.

In statistical regression, for instance, the relationships between development effort (dependent variable) and one or more project characteristics (independent variables) are described by means of a mathematical function that represents lines of mathematical fit in a two- or multidimensional space. In Chap. 8, we provide a brief description of effort estimation based on statistical regression.

Memory-Based Estimation

In contrast to model-based estimation methods, memory-based (analogy-based) methods do not create a model but explicitly retain the available project data and use them each time a prediction of a new project needs to be made. Each time an estimate is to be provided for a new project (*target*), the project data (*case base*) is searched using one or more *analogy techniques* to find the projects that are most similar to the target (*analogs*). Once the most similar projects are found, they are

Table 6.1 Characteristics of model-based and memory-based estimation

Aspect	Model-based estimation	Memory-based estimation
C01. Expert involvement	Building and applying an estimation model do not require much involvement of human experts. Depending on the particular method, an expert must set up a method's parameters and interpret estimation outcomes. Data-driven methods build the estimation model upon measurement data and do not require the acquisition of domain expert knowledge. Hybrid methods require acquiring expert knowledge to complement available measurement data	Using an estimation method does not require much involvement of human experts. Depending on the particular method, an expert must set up the method's parameters and interpret the results of estimation. Estimates are based upon measurement data and do not require the acquisition of domain expert knowledge
C02. Required data	Typically, a large set of project measurement data is required. Additionally, parametric methods require data of a certain type and distribution. Typically, the risk of inappropriate conclusions is removed when the data are measured on a ratio scale and are normally distributed. Hybrid methods require little measurement data as they are partially based on expert judgment	In principle, even a small set of project measurement data suffices for reliable estimation, under the condition that the set contains historical projects (analogs) that are similar to the estimated one. In general, one analog project suffices for obtaining an estimate. Typically, memory-based estimation does not make any assumptions regarding the underlying project data
C03. Robustness	Methods based on statistical techniques typically require high-quality data, meaning data that are complete, consistent, and nonredundant. Methods based on machine-learning techniques usually include mechanisms to handle low-quality, messy data	Estimation methods typically handle imperfect project data. For example, they usually include mechanisms to handle incomplete and redundant data
C04. Flexibility	Limited flexibility, because estimation is bound to a prescribed estimation model. Once built, the model fixes the set of effort drivers and their impact on effort, and it must be rebuilt or at least calibrated each time underlying project data change	Estimation is not bound to any specific estimation model
C05. Complexity	Estimation might be quite complex because developing an estimation model often involves numerous statistical techniques which often go beyond the standard curricula for software engineering	Estimation is based on an intuitive concept of similarity (distance) between projects. Estimation methods based upon this concept typically utilize fairly uncomplicated techniques
C06. Support level	Building and applying estimation models are supported by many free and commercial tools. Especially,	Estimation is supported by fewer tools (compared to model-based estimation). Still, there are several

(continued)

Table 6.1 (continued)

Aspect	Model-based estimation	Memory-based estimation
	methods based on statistics and machine learning are supported by a number of general-purpose data analysis software packages	free and commercial software packages that support basic case-based reasoning techniques
C07. Reusability	Once developed, effort estimation models are seldom reusable in other contexts. In order to estimate effort in different contexts, an estimation model typically needs to be rebuilt from scratch using context-specific measurement data	Hardly any reusable assets available, besides the historical project data used for estimation. The method does not produce any estimation model that could potentially be reused in different estimation contexts. Historical project data can be reused for estimating in different contexts as long as they fit the particular context
C08. Predictive power	Predictive power depends on the particular method and the quality of project data used for estimation. General statements concerning estimation accuracy cannot be made out of context	Predictive power depends on the particular method and the quality of project data used for estimation. General statements concerning estimation accuracy cannot be made out of context
C09. Informative power	Estimation methods deliver an explicit model that documents effort dependencies represented by the project data from which the model has been created. This information may be used to understand and to control projects. While estimating individual projects, this information may support explanation of effort estimates and managing project effort. Yet, the understandability and amount of information conveyed by the estimation model differ for various model-based estimation methods	Estimation methods provide hardly any additional information besides simple effort estimates. Obtaining any additional information typically requires performing additional analysis upon effort estimates and the underlying project data (in particular, characteristics of the project analogs that have been selected for deriving effort estimates)
C10. Handling uncertainty	In its basic form, effort estimation models typically require crisp data on the inputs; a number of methods have however been extended to cope with uncertain inputs (yet, these are mostly limited to the research context and have rarely been used in industry). Except for few methods, most estimation models do not provide information of estimation uncertainty and require additional analysis of estimation outcomes for this purpose; hybrid methods we discuss in Chaps. 14 and 15 are example exceptions	Memory-based estimation includes mechanisms for handling estimation uncertainty. For example, similarity metrics are used to select a certain set of analog projects as the basis for estimates, and then the effort range of the analog projects is used to estimate the new effort range and estimation uncertainty

(continued)

Table 6.1 (continued)

Aspect	Model-based estimation	Memory-based estimation
C11. Comprehensiveness	Principally, effort for any type of project activity and at any granularity level can be estimated. The only prerequisite is that appropriate historical project data are available to build an estimation model	Principally, any type of project activity at any granularity level can be estimated. The only prerequisite is that historical project data used for estimation comprise information for the particular activity measured on the particular granularity level
C12. Availability	Estimation can principally be performed at any time during the project. The only prerequisite is that appropriate historical project data are available to build an effort estimation model prior to estimation and that the appropriate data for the estimated project are available at the time of estimation	Estimation can principally be performed at any time during the project. The only prerequisite is that corresponding historical project data and the data for the estimated project data are available at the time of estimation
C13. Empirical evidence	Data-driven prediction methods are the most intensively investigated group of estimation methods. Among these methods, model-based estimation using statistical regression is supported by the largest empirical evidence. Other model-based estimation methods that were adapted for the purpose of software effort estimation later possess proportionally less evidence. An example is the group of estimation methods based on machine-learning techniques such as decision trees	Memory-based estimation mostly employs machine-learning techniques, usage of which is relatively recent in the software estimation domain (e.g., compared to traditional model-based estimation approaches based on statistical regression). Therefore, empirical evidence behind memory-based estimation is smaller than for model-based estimation; still, it is significant and larger than for hybrid estimation methods we discuss in Sect. 6.5

used as inputs to an *estimation technique* that predicts effort of the target based on actual efforts of analogs.

An example memory-based estimation method is *case-based reasoning (CBR)*, which originates from the machine-learning domain and was successfully adapted for software effort prediction purposes. In CBR, distance metrics defined on the project characteristics are used to determine the historical projects (analogs) that are the most similar to the estimated (target) project. Effort of the analogs is then adopted as an estimate for the target project. In Chap. 11, we provide a brief description of effort estimation based on case-based reasoning techniques.

Table 6.1 presents a comparison between model- and memory-based estimation with respect to several aspects we recommend to be considered when selecting an effort estimation method for a particular application context. In general, model-based and memory-based estimation are similar in that they share many characteristics common to data-driven estimation. Yet, they differ in a number of detailed aspects, which help one decide whether a given approach is, or is not, useful in a particular estimation context.

Composite Methods

Composite methods integrate elements of model- and memory-based methods. They are typically applied to overcome any weakness of individual estimation techniques.

> **Data Outliers**
> A specific issue common in heterogeneous project data is that of data outliers; that is, data points that differ significantly from the main body of the remaining project data. As most of the model-based estimation methods are sensitive to data outliers, the common practice is to exclude them prior to applying an estimation method. Yet, outliers, too, may convey valuable information for the purpose of effort prediction and as such should be considered within the estimation process.

For example, a simple two-step composite approach can be applied to overcome any weakness of a model-based estimation method using heterogeneous project data. In this approach, an analogy-based technique is first applied to identify groups of similar historical projects, and then estimation models are developed on each subset of projects preselected in the first step. In this case, analogy-based techniques are used for clustering historical project data into more homogeneous subsets prior to applying model-based estimation methods that are known to be weak when applied on highly heterogeneous data.

Another set of two-step composite approaches includes extensions of individual memory-based estimation methods that are typically weak against outlier project data. In these approaches, model-based techniques of various levels of sophistication are used to adjust initial estimates provided by memory-based prediction methods. For example, Leung (2002) proposed an *analogy with virtual neighbor* (*AVN*) method, which enhances the classical analogy-based estimation in that the two closest analogs of a target project are identified based on the normalized effort, which is computed from the multiple-regression equation. AVN then adjusts the initial effort estimate provided by the analogy-based method by compensating for the location of the target project relative to the two analogs. Jørgensen et al. (2003) as well as Shepperd and Cartwright (2005) provide a similar approach, in which they cope with an outlier project within memory-based estimation by adjusting the initial estimates toward the productivity values of more average ("typical") projects.

6.3.2 Parametric vs. Nonparametric Estimation

Model-based methods use quantitative project data to build a parameterized effort model, whereby different approaches are required for determining the model's parameters—depending on the type of underlying model. There are two basic types of modeling methods with respect to the way the model's parameters are determined: parametric and nonparametric. In the software effort estimation context, methods that are a combination of parametric and nonparametric methods have been proposed. We refer to them as semiparametric methods.

Parametric Estimation

Parametric methods require specifying a priori the parameters of the estimation model. Statistical regression methods, for instance, require a priori specification of the model's functional form and assume that estimation errors follow a certain parametric distribution. Table 8.2 provides an overview of typical functional forms of the regression models employed for the purpose of software effort estimation.

Nonparametric Estimation

Nonparametric methods differ from parametric methods in that the model structure is not specified a priori but instead is determined from quantitative (project) data. In other words, nonparametric estimators produce their inferences free from any particular underlying functional form. The term nonparametric is not meant to imply that such methods completely lack parameters, but rather that the number and nature of the parameters are flexible and not fixed in advance.

The most trivial parameter-free, data-driven approach commonly used in the software industry is the so-called *Proxy-based Estimation* (*PROBE*). It was first proposed by Humphrey (1995) for the purpose of software size estimation. In principle, the term proxy is used since it is an approximation or indirect measure of something else. In the context of effort estimation, the term proxy refers to a software characteristic that best approximates the development effort. In practice, the effort proxy used most often is software size, measured, for example, in terms of *function points* (*FP*) or *lines of code* (*LOC*).

Typical nonparametric methods, however, nowadays originate from the machine-learning domain. Examples include *Classification and Regression Trees* (*CART*) and *case-based reasoning* (*CBR*), which we discuss in Chaps. 10 and 11, respectively.

Semiparametric Estimation

Semiparametric methods represent methods that contain both parametric and nonparametric components. In the context of effort estimation, this typically encompasses methods that are the result of combining several techniques, where some are parametric and some nonparametric.

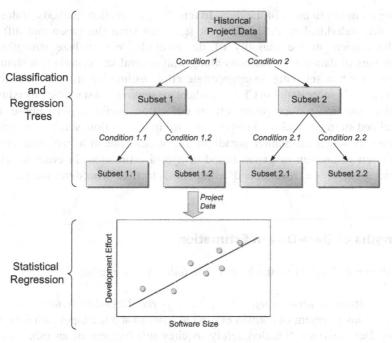

Fig. 6.3 Example semiparametric estimation method: CART+Regression

Semiparametric Estimation in Statistics

In statistics, a semiparametric method produces its inferences free from a particular functional form but within a particular class of functional forms; for example, it might handle any functional form within the class of additive models.

A typical example of the semiparametric method where parametric and nonparametric elements were combined is the integration of decision trees and statistical regression (*CART+Regression*) proposed by Briand et al. (2000). The method generates a CART tree to group similar historical projects in the terminal nodes of the tree model and then applies regression analysis to interpret projects at each terminal node to obtain final effort estimates. Figure 6.3 illustrates the idea of combining CART and regression methods; yet, we will not further elaborate this method due to its marginal applicability in industrial contexts.

6.3.3 Strengths and Weaknesses of Data-Driven Estimation

In this section, we briefly summarize major strengths and weaknesses of data-driven estimation. Thereby, we will try to generalize in that we focus on aspects that are common to most of the data-driven effort estimation methods. It does not mean that individual methods may not stand out from the group and differ on specific aspects to the majority of the methods. We analyze strengths and weaknesses of data-driven methods along with several key criteria that should be considered when selecting an appropriate effort estimation method. We discuss these criteria in more detail in Chap. 7, where we present a systematic procedure for selecting the most appropriate effort estimation method. We advise using generalized strengths and weaknesses, as listed in this section, solely as an orientation toward which estimation paradigm one should use in a particular context: data-driven estimation or expert-based or hybrid estimation. In order to select a specific method, we recommend using the selection procedure we present in Chap. 7.

Strengths of Data-Driven Estimation

Data-driven estimation methods share the following strengths:

- *(C01) Minimal involvement of human experts*: Data-driven methods do not require involvement of domain experts in order to acquire input data for estimation. Data-driven estimation solely requires involvement of an estimator who applies the estimation method using appropriate quantitative project data and then interprets the outcomes of estimation.
- *(C04) High flexibility of estimation method*: Data-driven estimation does not impose any specific estimation model. Memory-based estimation methods, such as case-based reasoning, do not make any assumption regarding the structure of the project effort relationships. Model-based approaches, such as statistical regression or decision trees, predefine a certain structure of the effort model; yet, they do not force any specific instantiation of the model in terms of particular effort drivers. Estimation method exceptions are the so-called fixed-model approaches, such as COCOMO (Boehm et al. 2000). They offer an off-the-shelf fixed estimation model, in which all effort relationships are already predefined. Consequently, fixed-model estimation requires very specific input data, for example, a particular software size metric and a particular set of effort factors.
- *(C06) Large documentation and tool support*: Data-driven methods typically use well-established data analysis techniques that have been investigated in statistics and/or machine-learning domains for many years. Therefore, these methods—at least their core—are usually well documented and supported by a number of software packages, both free-of-charge and commercial.
- *(C11) Applicability for any project activities*: Data-driven estimation methods can be principally used for estimating any kind of project activities at any level of granularity. The only prerequisite is the availability of corresponding measurement data for already completed projects on which to base estimation.

For example, if we wanted to estimate effort required to complete a specific development activity, we would need past project data regarding this activity (e.g., size of outcomes delivered from this activity, the effort it actually consumed, and aspects of the activity's context that may influence effort).

- *(C12) Availability at any stage of software development*: Data-driven estimation principally can be used at any stage of the software development life cycle. The only prerequisite is that appropriate project data are available on which to base estimates. Collecting appropriate data from past projects is usually easy because actual information regarding any project stage is known after project completion. However, it might be difficult to obtain appropriate input information for the new (estimated) project because actual information is usually not available at the time of estimation. This issue arises especially when estimation is performed in the very early stages of a software project. This problem is typically addressed by using approximate information, for example, judged by domain experts. Of course, effort estimates based on approximate information will be burdened by additional error, but they can (and should) be refined by repeating the estimation procedure as the project progresses and more actual information becomes available.

- *(C13) Significant amount of empirical evidence*: Data-driven estimation methods have been investigated in a number of empirical studies, although the amount of evidence available varies for particular methods. For example, the more recent the method, the less evidence for it. Moreover, typical evaluation of data-driven methods is performed in a laboratory context where one or more alternative methods are applied on publicly available project data sets (usually containing multiorganizational data). Using the laboratory context and multiorganizational data significantly limits the applicability of evaluation results to the context of a specific software development organization and thus should be utilized with care. We discuss the threats of laboratory evaluation, especially concerning estimation accuracy, in Sects. 7.1.1 and 7.1.3.

- *(Cost) Relatively low application cost*: Once properly introduced, data-driven estimation costs much less than estimation based on expert judgment. Properly introducing data-driven estimation requires initial investment into collecting historical project data, developing effort estimation models, and training users on the method (Jørgensen et al. 2009; Yang et al. 2008). After that, estimating projects is limited to collecting data, feeding the estimation model with the data, and interpreting estimation outputs. With appropriate tool support, the costs of measurement and estimation are minimal.

Weaknesses of Data-Driven Estimation

Data-driven estimation methods share the following weaknesses:

- *(C02) Extensive requirements regarding quantitative data*: Data-driven estimation usually requires large sets of high-quality project data. Large amounts of data include multiple project characteristics measured over a number of already completed projects. The wider the range of different project situations to be covered by estimation, the more data required. Moreover, many data-driven estimation methods state specific requirements regarding the quality of data. For example, methods based on statistical techniques state restrictive requirements with respect to the functional form of underlying regression models and distribution of underlying data. Finally, few data-driven estimation methods can cope with messy project data. Most of them require data preparation prior to estimation, requiring additional data preprocessing techniques.

- *(C05) Relatively high complexity of estimation methods*: In most cases, data-driven estimation methods use sophisticated techniques and theories, which go beyond standard curricula of software engineering. There are few estimation methods based on simple statistical regression with which most engineers are familiar. Yet, recently, popular machine-learning methods such as decision trees or artificial neural networks require knowledge from beyond computer science and software engineering in order to be understood and properly applied for project estimation.

- *(C07) Limited reusability of estimation outputs*: Once developed in one context, the outcomes of data-driven estimation are rarely reusable—entirely or partially—in other estimation contexts. In particular, effort models developed within model-based estimation methods are very rarely reusable. In order to use an effort model in a context other than the one for which it has been developed, the complete model typically needs to be redeveloped using project data that corresponds to the new estimation context. Reusability of estimation approaches based on fixed "off-the-shelf" effort models depends on the comprehensibility of the project data set upon which the model has been developed. If the underlying data set encompasses a wide range of various contexts, then the resulting model will be quite generic and applicable across a corresponding wide range of estimation situations. Other than custom-tailored effort models, adjusting an off-the-shelf effort model is usually limited to merely minor calibration of the predefined model.

- *(C03) Inconsistent robustness against messy data*: Various data-driven estimation methods offer different levels for handling messy input data; that is, if incomplete, inconsistent, or redundant. Estimation methods originating from statistics typically do not handle any of these data issues and require extensive data "cleaning" using independent preprocessing techniques. Estimation methods based upon machine-learning techniques are often already equipped with internal mechanisms to cope with selected aspects of messy data.

- *(C10) Little support for handling information uncertainty*: Hardly any data-driven estimation method "as-is" handles uncertainty of input data. They typically require exact (crisp) data on the input. Moreover, data-driven estimation methods provide rather little support for assessing the uncertainty of output estimates. If such uncertainty assessment is possible, it often requires additional analyses. For example, analogy-based estimation requires analyzing the range of effort across analogous projects in order to determine the final estimates and assess their uncertainty. For the regression models, uncertainty of estimates can be assessed using prediction and confidence intervals, which require additional analysis of the project data used for estimation.

- *(C09) Moderate informative power*: Besides simple effort estimates, data-driven methods provide rather little additional information for supporting project management tasks such as negotiating project scope, managing project risks, or improving development processes. Model-based methods typically provide a transparent estimation model that captures effort dependencies represented by the project data upon which the model has been developed. Yet, estimation models differ widely with respect to their understandability and the amount of useful information project decision makers may extract. For example, interpreting regression models requires a basic knowledge of mathematics. Yet, the amount of useful information they offer is rather small and reduces in the usual case to the relative impact of considered effort factors on effort. On the other hand, interpreting an *artificial neural network (ANN)* is extremely difficult for nonexperts. In consequence, for an average project manager, ANN represents rather a black-box estimation tool. Memory-based estimation methods provide hardly any insight into project effort dependencies represented by the underlying project data. Unlike model-based estimation, memory-based estimation does not explore project data for patterns regarding project effort dependencies, which are then documented in a form of estimation model. Memory-based methods merely look for project analogs from the past in order to adapt their actual effort to estimate the unknown effort of a new project.
- *(C08) Inconsistent predictive power*: The predictive power of data-driven estimation methods depends on (1) the project data the estimates are based on and (2) the ability of the estimation method to deal with deficits of the data (see C02). Predictive power results published in the literature differ vastly even for (apparently) the same estimation method. For example, the estimation error for the same method evaluated on different project data sets varies between several and several hundred percent. This makes empirical evaluations presented in the related literature of rather little use in practice.

6.4 Expert-Based Methods

We surrounded ourselves with some really experienced professionals who helped us along. The development team had some really great knowledge and insight.

—Brian Averill

Estimation based on expert judgment is still the most popular estimation method in the software industry. Typically, 70–80 % of industrial estimates are made by experts without using formal estimation models. Expert-based methods involve consulting with one or more experts, who use their domain experience as well as understanding of the organization context for estimating project cost.

6.4.1 Single-Expert Approaches

The simplest instance of expert-based estimation is the so-called *guesstimation* approach, where a single expert provides final estimates. An expert could guess the predicted effort directly ("rule-of-thumb" method) or estimate on the basis of more structured reasoning. An example of such structured reasoning is breaking the project down into tasks (e.g., using work breakdown structures technique), estimating them separately, and summing these predictions into a total estimate. This simple procedure adapts the bottom-up estimation strategy, which we discussed in Sect. 5.2. In order to sum up "bottom" estimates, a number of potential techniques can be applied as presented in Sect. 5.3.

Example 6.1. Structured Single-Expert Estimation Based on the Analytic Hierarchy Process Technique

A more sophisticated approach for structured expert reasoning was proposed by Shepperd and Cartwright (2001), who adapted the *analytic hierarchy process* (*AHP*) method for structuring expert-based effort estimation. AHP is widely used for multicriteria decision making and supports decomposing the given decision problem (goal) into a hierarchy of subproblems, which are easier to comprehend and thus to evaluate independently by means of subjective human judgment. Elements of a problem hierarchy are then systematically evaluated in a pairwise comparison process (i.e., by comparing them to one another two at a time). Based on these evaluations, AHP derives numerical weights that are assigned to elements of a problem hierarchy and reflect their relative importance in a decision-making process. Finally, numerical weights are derived for each of the decision alternatives, where the weight assigned to an alternative represents the alternative's relative ability to achieve the decision goal.

For example, the decision problem/goal "Select car" is decomposed into a hierarchy of criteria (i.e., aspects) that need to be considered for achieving the goal (i.e., selecting car) from a set of alternatives (cars). Numerical weights assigned to criteria reflect relative importance of a certain car aspect to the decision maker when selecting a car.

In the effort estimation problem, effort becomes the topmost node (goal) in the problem and development projects become alternatives. The set of development projects (alternatives) include at least one historical project for which effort is known, and new projects whose effort we would like to estimate. In a simple case, human experts perform pairwise comparisons between projects in that for every two projects, they are asked to subjectively judge which of the two requires more effort and how much more (e.g., twice as much, three times as much, etc.). Using the known effort value of the historical project (reference project), the unknown effort of the remaining projects in the set can be computed. In a simple case, where effort is the only criterion in the decision hierarchy, i.e., where the effort becomes the topmost node in the hierarchy and the alternatives are projects between which pairwise comparisons are performed, the unknown effort can be computed using equation 6.1. For details of determining effort in more sophisticated cases (as

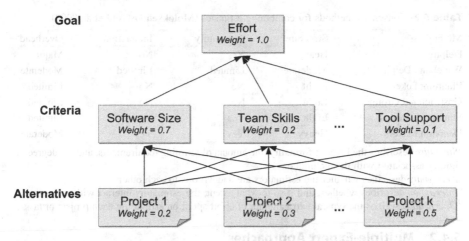

Fig. 6.4 Example analytic hierarchy process tree for single-expert effort estimation

presented in Fig. 6.4), where the decision hierarchy contains other criteria (effort factors), please refer to Shepperd and Cartwright (2001) and/or the specification of the AHP method (Saaty 1980).

$$\text{EstEffort}_i = \frac{w_i}{w_k} \cdot \text{ActEffort}_k \qquad (6.1)$$

where

- EstEffort$_i$ is the estimated effort for the ith project
- ActEffort$_k$ is the known effort for the kth project
- w_i is the weight of the project to be estimated
- w_k is the weight of the project with known effort

In principle, the effort estimation problem can be defined at any granularity level, beginning from the complete project down to a simple task (in the latter case, the "bottom-up" strategy needs to be employed for computing total project effort).

In a more sophisticated case, the effort estimation problem will be decomposed into a hierarchy of multiple project attributes, which contribute to actual effort (see example hierarchy in Fig. 6.4).

Numerical weights assigned to these attributes (through pairwise comparisons) reflect their relative impact on the effort. Alternatives (e.g., projects) are then evaluated with respect to the extent to which each of them possesses these attributes. Again, the effort of at least one alternative needs to be known in order to estimate the effort of the other alternatives. ∎

Still, even though supported by a systematic procedure, estimates provided by a single expert are subject to a number of potential biases (optimism, pessimism, desire to win, desire to please, political preferences, etc.). Therefore, in practice, it is preferable to obtain estimates from more than one expert.

Table 6.2 Consensus methods for combining estimates (Moløkken-Østvold et al. 2008)

Method	Structure[a]	Anonymity[b]	Interaction[c]	Overhead[d]
Delphi	Heavy	Yes	No	Major
Wideband Delphi	Moderate	Limited	Limited	Moderate
Planning Poker	Light	No	No	Limited
Unstructured Groups	Light	No	No	Limited
Statistical Groups	Light	Yes	Yes	Limited
Decision Makers	Heavy	Yes	Yes	Moderate

[a]*Structure* describes the level of formality, the amount of learning requirements, and the degree of rigidity associated with the technique
[b]*Anonymity* describes whether the estimators are anonymous to each other
[c]*Interaction* describes whether, and if so to what extent, the estimators interact with each other
[d]*Overhead* describes the typical extra amount of effort spent on estimating each project or task

6.4.2 Multiple-Expert Approaches

Estimating in a group has some advantages as the enthusiasm of some can be balanced by the caution of others. Moreover, group estimation may exclude the most common obstacle of individual estimates which are forgotten tasks, especially in the case of bottom-up estimation.

There are a number of possible ways to combine estimates obtained from numerous experts into a single estimate. In principle, estimates provided by multiple experts can be combined mechanically (without involving experts) or by means of group discussion.

Combining Estimates Mechanically

In principle, any of the methods for combining multiple alternative estimates discussed in Sect. 5.6 can be applied here. An example of simple mechanical integration applied commonly in the context of expert-based estimation is to compute the mean or median estimate of all individual estimates. This is quick and proven to be typically sufficient in practice (often even outperforming other, more sophisticated mathematical integration methods).

Combining Estimates in Group Discussion

Mechanical integration of multiple-expert estimates may, however, be subject to adverse bias by individual extreme estimates. This issue can be handled easily by holding a group discussion in order to come up with final estimates. For this purpose, we may consider using a number of alternative methods. Table 6.2 presents an overview of a few popular group discussion methods used in software effort estimation.

Let us briefly discuss some important aspects of group discussion methods to be considered from the perspective of their structure, that is, level of formality.

Unstructured Group Estimation

In unstructured group estimation, a group meeting is held where experts obtain consensus with regard to a single estimate in a less formal way. These techniques span from informal conversation to group estimation guided by a lightweight process as is the case in *Planning Poker* (refer to Chap. 13 for a brief description of the latter technique).

Moløkken and Jørgensen (2004) found that group estimates made after an unstructured discussion were less optimistic and more realistic than individual estimates derived prior to the group discussion and combined in a statistical manner. The main sources of this decrease in optimism seemed to be the identification of additional activities and an awareness that activities may be more complicated than was initially thought. Yet, informal group discussion has several threats we should be aware of before applying these techniques. Common negative effects of unstructured group decision making include (Table 6.3) *groupthink*, *risky shift*, and *polarization*.

The occurrence and strength of unwanted effects in group estimation depend largely on the selection of group members. Moløkken and Jørgensen (2004) propose two principal strategies for selecting the group of estimators:

1. Selecting a designated group of experts whose only objective is to estimate the project and who do not participate in the development process
2. Selecting people who are likely to develop the project as those responsible for the estimates

A dedicated estimation group may be much less prone to personal or political biases and more likely to improve their estimation skill over time. It would, however, require additional investment (typically feasible only in large organizations) and good internal communication. Development teams, on the other hand, may probably get to know the project better than anyone else and may have a higher motivation for a thorough project analysis (before they commit to any estimates). Yet, this is not always the case; surprisingly, people with technical competence often tend to be too optimistic regarding their own capabilities and, in consequence, provide less realistic project effort estimates than those with less technical competence. These issues need to be considered before applying unstructured group estimation.

Structured Group Estimation

Drawbacks of unstructured group estimation can be avoided by applying formal group discussion techniques, also called *group consensus techniques*, where besides

Table 6.3 Common threats of group discussion estimation

Threat	Description
Wishful thinking	This effect refers to the tendency of humans to make estimates according to what might please the receiver of the estimates (e.g., customer) or even themselves (overoptimism about own performance) instead of based on evidence or rationality. In result, estimates are biased toward expectations of certain project stakeholders instead of reflecting the realism of the project situation (project scope and environment). In practice, wishful thinking typically leads to underestimation of effort required for task completion
Groupthink	This effect is close to wishful thinking and refers to the situation where people with stronger personalities dominate the deliberations and some group members are influenced by others. In practice, senior and management project members have much influence on the young technical staff. Since senior staff are typically affected by wishful thinking (e.g., to please the customer) and less realistic about the project (e.g., lacking technical perspective), they influence other estimators toward underestimations
Polarization	This effect is close to the groupthink effect and refers to the situation where a majority of the group creates the behavior of the whole group. For example, groups in which members are prone to make risky judgments become more prone to making such judgments, while groups with a majority of members who are averse to making risky judgments become more risk averse
Anchoring	This effect (also known as *focalism*) refers to the common human tendency to rely too heavily (to place too much importance) on one aspect or piece of information when making estimates. As a result, estimates are biased toward a specific aspect without accounting for other important elements influencing estimated values. Tversky and Kahneman (1974) in their research on humans' cognitive biases define anchoring as follows: "*In many situations, people make estimates by starting from an initial value that is adjusted to yield the final answer. The initial value, or starting point, may be suggested by the formulation of the problem, or it may be the result of a partial computation. In either case, adjustments are typically insufficient. That is, different starting points yield different estimates, which are biased toward the initial values*"
Planning fallacy	This effect refers to the common human tendency to be overoptimistic when predicting complex matters. In consequence, the more complex the work task, the less realistic (underestimated) is the effort for completing the task. Tversky and Kahneman (1974) in their research on humans' cognitive biases define planning fallacy as follows: "*Biases in the evaluation of compound events are particularly significant in the context of planning. The successful completion of an undertaking, such as the development of a new product, typically has a conjunctive character: for the undertaking to succeed, each of a series of events must occur. Even when each of these events is very likely, the overall probability of success can be quite low if the number of events is large. The general tendency to overestimate the probability of conjunctive events leads to unwarranted optimism in the evaluation of the likelihood that a plan will succeed or that a project will be completed on time*"
Risky shift	This effect refers to the tendency of people in a group, where individual responsibility is diminished, to adopt riskier courses of action than they would take on a personal basis. This effect typically leads to unrealistic underestimations

following a formal process, group discussion is additionally supported by systematic processes and additional tools, such as checklists. Typical estimation checklists have the form of a standard work breakdown structure that decomposes relevant software products and processes contributing to development effort and thus prevents their omission in the estimation process. Using checklists to support group estimation improves accuracy, transparency, and confidence of estimates as well as supporting learning for the involved domain experts—particularly when they are inexperienced. In Chap. 12, we provide a brief description of the *Wideband Delphi* technique, which is the most popular group consensus technique used in practice.

6.4.3 Biases in Group Discussion Approaches

Success of estimation with a group discussion technique depends to a great extent on the humans involved in the estimation. Although group consensus techniques provide ways to minimize the impact of human and situational biases on the quality of estimates, there are still a number of unwanted effects that may occur. Table 6.3 summarizes the most common threats of group discussion estimation. For a more comprehensive list of biases in human judgment under uncertainty, refer to Tversky and Kahneman (1974) and related literature.

How to Avoid or Reduce Situational and Human Biases

Experience gained over decades of estimation based on human judgment has shown several issues that have particular impact on bias in human-based estimates. Arkes (2001) and Jørgensen (2004a) summarize these experiences:

- *Evaluate estimation accuracy, but avoid high evaluation pressure*: A high motivation for accuracy (e.g., when people feel personally responsible, perceive that the estimation task is very important, or receive monetary rewards for accurate estimates) actually decreases estimation accuracy, for example, due to a "self-fulfilling-prophecy" effect.
- *Avoid conflicting estimation goals*: The estimation process is impacted by goals other than prediction accuracy. The most common conflicts relate to
  - Mixing "bid," "target," and "estimate," which, by definition, have different goals. Typically, a bid should (optimally) be low enough to get the job and high enough to maximize profit, the target should enable a successful project and motivate efficient work, and the estimate should represent the most likely effort needed to complete the project work.
  - "Wishful thinking" and lack of "realism" while estimating, which typically lead to overoptimistic estimates.
- *Ask the estimators to justify and criticize their estimates*: During estimation, experts often run through expected project activities. In practice, such a process often leads the estimator into the mode of confirming his theories on how to complete the project, rather than critically identifying and rejecting incorrect

elements of these theories. In consequence, confidence in estimates depends more on the amount of effort human experts invest in the process of estimation than on the actual accuracy of the estimate. One of the approaches to reduce expectation effects on predictions is to ask experts to list explicitly the reasons why their predictions might go wrong. Another way is to ask experts for a detailed justification of their estimates. Finally, occasional involvement of an external expert—so-called devil's advocate—who criticizes estimations in an objective and nonemotional manner has proved to be an effective way to decrease the overconfidence effect in group estimation.

- *Avoid irrelevant and unreliable estimation information*: Human experts are often not able to distinguish irrelevant and unreliable information. Therefore, such information should not be presented to experts at all.
- *Use documented data from previous development tasks*: Supporting human estimators with objective data from already completed, similar work tasks can moderate the impact of subjectivity and bias in human judgments in the final estimate.
- *Find estimation experts with highly relevant domain background and a good estimation record*: Human estimators should possess expertise in both areas: the task being estimated and the estimation process itself.
- *Provide estimation and/or domain training opportunities*: If human estimators do not possess expertise in either the task being estimated or the estimation process itself, then they should be provided with appropriate training opportunities.
- *Use estimation checklists based on work breakdown structures*: A bottom-up strategy is used typically in expert-based estimation since it is easier for human experts to estimate simple work activities than the overall project work. As noted in Chap. 5, using checklists improves accuracy, transparency, and confidence of estimates as well as supporting learning of the involved domain experts—particularly when they are inexperienced.
- *Estimate top-down and bottom-up strategies independently of each other*: If possible, top-down estimation and bottom-up estimation should be employed independently, and their results should be compared for verification purposes.
- *Assess the uncertainty of the estimate, and provide feedback on estimation accuracy*: In order to learn, human estimators should be aware of the accuracy of their estimates. Therefore, estimates should be verified against actual effort measured at project completion and communicated to estimators together with the actual project's scope of work (e.g., in a form of a breakdown structure). This supports human estimators to reflect on the facts and assumptions they took at the time of estimation.

6.4.4   Strengths and Weaknesses of Expert-Based Estimation

In this section, we briefly summarize major strengths and weaknesses of effort estimation based on judgment by human experts. Thereby, we generalize and focus on aspects that are common to most of the expert-based effort estimation methods. Still, individual methods may stand out and differ on specific aspects from the majority of the methods. We analyze strengths and weaknesses of expert-based methods along several key criteria that we recommend be considered when selecting a suitable effort estimation method. We define these criteria in more detail in Chap. 7, where we present a systematic procedure for selecting the most appropriate effort estimation method for a particular estimation context. We advise using generalized strengths and weaknesses we list in this section solely as an orientation point, toward which estimation paradigm one should go in a specific estimation context: toward expert-based estimation or toward data-driven or hybrid estimation. In order to select a particular method, we recommend using the selection procedure we present in Chap. 7.

Strengths of Expert-Based Estimation

In general, estimation based on expert judgment has the great advantage of being applicable in the context where appropriate quantitative data are not available and thus data-driven estimation cannot be used.

One common situation where expert-based estimation is the only alternative is where a software organization starts building up its estimation process and does not yet possess appropriate quantitative data to employ data-driven or hybrid estimation. In this case, expert-based estimation can be used while the organization is building up the base of historical project data. After collecting the necessary quantitative project data, the organization can move from estimation based solely on human judgment toward hybrid and data-driven approaches.

Another common scenario for applying expert-based estimation involves highly specific projects for which historical project data are missing (because a similar project has never occurred before or quantitative inputs to estimation are difficult to acquire. For example, the project is very specific and is distinguished from all other projects in that there is a serious conflict of interest between developers and project management. Quantifying this factor and collecting appropriate project data might be quite difficult because of the lack of comparable situations in the past. In this case, effort can be estimated using structured expert judgment. At the same time, if the project is expected to reoccur in the future, it should be quantified, and appropriate measurement data should be stored in the historical project base with the intention of transferring toward estimation based on quantitative data (that is data-driven or hybrid estimation).

Expert-based estimation methods typically share the following strengths:

- *(C02) Few requirements regarding quantitative data*: An inherent advantage of expert-based estimation is that it does not need any explicit quantitative project data. Although quantitative data are not necessary, the estimation would typically benefit, for example, with respect to credibility, when expert judgment is supported by quantitative information.

- *(C04) High flexibility of estimation methods*: Estimation based on human experts is applicable in any situation and does not impose any specific model of project effort dependencies. While estimating effort, the involved human experts are encouraged to consider those project aspects that they personally perceive as important. The only prerequisite for estimation is that involved human experts have experience in the context of the estimation.
- *(C05) Simplicity (low complexity) of estimation method*: Expert-based estimation methods are very simple compared to other estimation approaches. Even systematic estimation with group consensus techniques such as *Wideband Delphi* (Chap. 12) or *Planning Poker* (Chap. 13) is still very simple and intuitive.

Weaknesses of Expert-Based Estimation

In principle, all major weaknesses of expert-based estimation are associated with extensive involvement of humans in the estimation process. The human factor contributes to the relatively large overhead needed for estimation and the relatively high risk of estimates being biased by individual experiences and preferences of the involved humans. In particular, expert-based estimation methods share the following weaknesses:

- *(C01) Extensive involvement of human experts*: An inherent disadvantage of expert-based estimation is, in fact, the involvement of human experts. On the one hand, estimation requires involving one or more human experts each time estimates are needed. For a single project, this would typically mean several estimation rounds to initially estimate the project at its very beginning and then to revise estimates as the project proceeds and more is known about it. In the case of systematic group consensus approaches such as Wideband Delphi (Chap. 12), this makes up a significant part of the total project management effort. Even though single-expert estimation is used, when performed systematically, it also requires noticeable effort to break down work activities, estimate their effort, and integrate estimates. On the other hand, estimation requires that involved human experts are experienced in the estimation context, thus being capable of providing credible estimates for the projects within the context. In practice, this means senior developers and project managers, who are time-bound and whose involvement in estimation is very expensive.
- (C03) Relatively low robustness against messy inputs: Although expert-based estimation usually does not involve quantitative project data, the robustness against messy inputs also plays an important role here. Estimates based on human judgment are often biased due to misleading information the experts are exposed to prior or during estimation. Human experts are vulnerable to misleading information, which can be represented by the expert's own experiences and preferences or by opinions of other experts involved in the estimation process. Table 6.3 in Sect. 6.4.3 summarizes typical sources of bias in expert-based estimation.

- *(C06) Relatively little support*: Surprisingly, estimation methods based on human judgment are rather poorly supported, both in terms of documentation and automation of the estimation procedure. Despite the apparent simplicity of expert-based estimation, it is not easy to find a complete and detailed description of estimation procedures based on human judgment. Often, several sources are needed to get a complete picture of a given estimation method. The most prominent example is the Delphi group consensus method. Over the years, the method has become a standard approach for systematic estimation with multiple human experts. Yet, the method's individual descriptions found in the literature were incomplete and/or partially inconsistent with each other. In Chap. 12, we present the Wideband Delphi method based on a synthesis of descriptions found in multiple sources. Regarding tool support, automation of the estimation procedure is not as critical as for data-driven estimation. It might, however, reduce estimation overhead, especially for group consensus methods where one must coordinate, analyze, and synthesize individual estimates of multiple human experts. Appropriate tool support is not really available and typically must be developed in-house.
- *(C07) Limited reusability of estimation outputs*: Outcomes of expert-based estimation are seldom reusable across different projects. Typically, the only outcome of expert-based estimation is the predicted project effort, which is specific to the particular project situation. As with any other estimation method, simple effort estimates cannot be reused for estimating other projects without prior adjustment—at least not if source and target projects are not very similar to each other. Since it is typically not clear what project aspects experts considered to develop their estimates, it is also difficult to adapt these estimates to the context of other projects. Explicit consideration of factors influencing project effort would require acquiring this knowledge from experts, thus increasing estimation overhead.
- *(C08) Inconsistent predictive power*: The predictive power of expert-based estimation depends to a large extent on the expertise of the human experts involved. Therefore, it is difficult to make general statements regarding the predictive power of expert-based estimation methods. Of course, expert-based estimation is more powerful than methods based on data in the context where appropriate data are not available or messy and unreliable. One thing that we can conclude from previous studies on expert-based estimation is that if one satisfies a few prerequisites, then there is a good chance of getting good estimates. Example prerequisites include appropriate breakdown of estimated work tasks, involving highly experienced multiple human experts, and applying systematic estimation procedures in order to avoid bias in group decision making (as we list in Sect. 6.4.3, Table 6.3).
- *(C09) Little informative power*: In its basic form, expert-based estimation focuses on acquiring direct effort estimates from one or more human experts, without any additional information that may support project decision making such as the most relevant factors influencing project effort. In the case of group estimation, a moderator may document and analyze arguments raised by experts to support their individual estimates in order to infer relevant factors influencing

project effort. However, getting insight into the project effort cause and effect dependencies would usually require the application of additional knowledge acquisition techniques.

- *(C10) Moderate support for handling information uncertainty*: Subjective human judgment is inherently burdened with uncertainty. Therefore, handling uncertainty is one of the key issues in expert-based estimation. In order to address this issue, several approaches for handling uncertainty can be adapted in the context of expert-based estimation. We discuss example approaches in Sect. 4.4. However, using a particular approach requires that the estimator have appropriate theoretical background and that the involved human experts have a basic understanding of the approach. Otherwise, handling uncertainty will lead to wrong conclusions and, in consequence, failed project decisions.

6.5   Hybrid Methods

The best forecasting approach is one that takes advantage of the strengths of both [quantitative and judgmental] forecasting approaches.

—Sanders and Ritzman

A number of effort estimation methods have been proposed over the recent decades. Yet, no "silver-bullet" method has been proposed so far. Each and every estimation method has its strengths and limitations, and its goodness largely depends on the context in which it is applied. Jørgensen et al. (2009) aptly noted that "Making a one-size-fits-all decision on using models versus experts in all situations doesn't appear to be a good idea."

The most important consequence of this finding is that a combination of estimation approaches can substantially improve the accuracy of estimates (Hughes 1996; MacDonell and Shepperd 2003; Jørgensen 2007). Two most important strategies for implementing this idea are (1) combining multiple estimation paradigms, such as expert-based and data-driven methods, into a hybrid method and (2) combining multiple estimates provided by independent estimation methods, preferably representing different estimation paradigms (we discuss this topic in Sect. 5.6).

In the light of a lack of consensus on which expert-based or data-driven approaches are "better" (e.g., as discussed by Jørgensen et al. 2009), the hybrid methods offer the combination of strengths of both strategies while avoiding their weaknesses.

6.5.1   Methods Based on Bayes' Theorem

Recently, the software community has given much attention to Bayes' theorem as a potential technique for handling estimation uncertainty and integrating measurement data with subjective human judgment. Several estimation methods arose from this interest. In this section, we briefly discuss two of them: application of basic Bayes' theorem for adjusting COCOMO cost multipliers and application of *Bayesian belief networks (BBN)* for estimating effort.

Bayes' Theorem

Bayes' theorem is a theorem of probability, which can be perceived as a way of representing the probability that a certain hypothesis is affected by a new piece of evidence. Bayes' theorem (6.2) expresses the posterior probability (i.e., after evidence E is observed) of a hypothesis H in terms of the prior probabilities of H and E and the probability of E given H.

$$P(H|E) = \frac{P(H) \cdot P(E|H)}{P(E)} \tag{6.2}$$

where

- $P(H \mid E)$ represents the posterior probability of H given E
- $P(H)$ represents the prior probability that H is a correct hypothesis in the absence of evidence E
- $P(E \mid H)$ represents the conditional probability of the evidence E occurring if the hypothesis H is true; it is also called a likelihood function of H for fixed E
- $P(E)$ represents the marginal probability of E, that is, the a priori probability of witnessing the new evidence E (under all possible hypotheses)

In other words, Bayes' theorem provides a mathematical rule that explains how we should adjust our existing beliefs in the light of new evidence and previous experiences.

> **Context as Implicit Condition within Bayes' Theorem**
> In the real world, all events are conditioned by some context c. The simple Bayes' equation as illustrated in (6.2) implicitly assumes the existence of a background context (past experience). Considering the context explicitly, as factor c, would lead us to the following equation:
>
> $$P(H|E, c) = \frac{P(H|c) \cdot P(E|H, c)}{P(E|c)}$$
>
> where each probability in (6.2) is explicitly conditioned given prior experience c.

Bayes' theorem is well suited for software effort estimation. On the one hand, it allows for integrating subjective experiences (beliefs) with actual project data (evidence) for the purpose of effort prediction. On the other hand, it supports updating initial effort estimates (belief) as a project progresses and actual project information (evidence) becomes available. The later application scenario might be particularly useful when dealing with the "cone of uncertainty" phenomenon, as we discussed in Sect. 4.3.1.

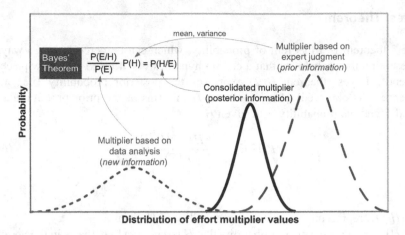

Fig. 6.5 Hybrid calibration of COCOMO II.2000 Model (Chulani et al. 1999)

Applying Bayes' Theorem for Adjusting COCOMO II Cost Multipliers

In the late 1990s, Chulani et al. (1999) proposed applying *Bayesian inference* statistics to determine COCOMO cost multipliers by combining expert judgment and data analysis. As we discuss later in Chap. 9, the COCOMO model is actually a regression model whose parameters have been fixed on a set of multiorganizational project data. In his first COCOMO model, Boehm (1981) applied statistical regression to determine multipliers associated with cost drivers. However, later it was observed that certain domain experts disagreed with the results of the regression analysis used to derive cost drivers and associated multipliers with regard to their effects on overall project cost.

In order to address both quantitative data and human expertise in the COCOMO cost multipliers, Chulani et al. (1999) combined expert knowledge (*prior information*) with sample measurement data (*new information*) to derive final estimates of effort multipliers (*posterior information*). Figure 6.5 illustrates this idea, where multiplier information is obtained in the form of probability distributions.

In the example presented in Fig. 6.5, the variance of an a priori (expert) probability distribution for a certain multiplier is smaller than the corresponding sample data variance. In consequence, the a posteriori distribution will be closer to the a priori distribution.

Bayesian Belief Networks (BBN)

Bayesian belief network (*BBN*) or *belief network* is a probabilistic graph model in which each node in the graph represents a random variable, while the edges between the nodes represent probabilistic dependencies among the corresponding

Fig. 6.6 Example Bayesian
Belief Network

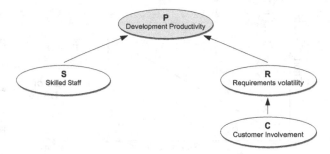

random variables (Fig. 6.6). Note that although BBNs are typically used to represent causal relationships, this need not be the case.

BBNs combine principles from graph theory, probability theory, computer science, and statistics. The recent interest in BBNs originates from the fact that BBNs are both mathematically rigorous and intuitively understandable.

BBNs represent knowledge about an uncertain domain and are mainly used in situations that require statistical inference, that is, situations where beliefs regarding the likelihood of the events that have not been yet observed (i.e., hypotheses) need to be updated in the light of other events that have actually been observed (evidence). BBNs use probability calculus and Bayes' theorem (6.2) for propagating the evidence throughout the belief network, thereby updating the strength of beliefs regarding the likelihood of the events, which have not yet been observed.

One of the very useful properties of BBNs is that it allows inference in any direction on the path between related nodes, thus supporting two basic purposes of estimation:

- *Predictive reasoning* (predictive inference): a hypothesis regarding the value of node X is updated based on evidence for nodes influencing X, directly or indirectly through its parent. This kind of reasoning is called top-down or forward inference.
- *Diagnostic reasoning* (predictive inference): a hypothesis regarding the value of node X is verified in the light of evidence for nodes that X directly influences (X's children nodes). This kind of reasoning is called bottom-up or backward inference.

For detailed discussion of BBNs, refer to Chap. 14.

6.5.2 The CoBRA Method

The CoBRA method developed by Briand et al. (1998) is based on the idea that project effort consists of two basic components (Fig. 6.7):

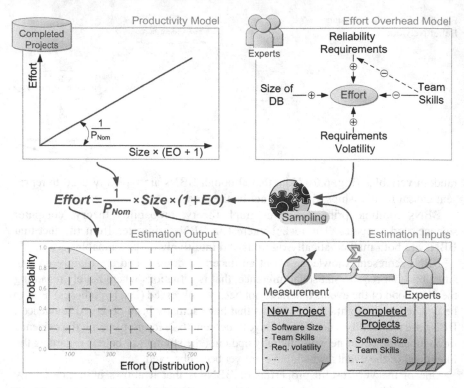

Fig. 6.7 Overview of the CoBRA Method

- *Nominal project effort* (represented by quotient $1/P_{Nom} \times$ Size) is the effort spent solely on developing a software product of a certain size in the context of a nominal project. A nominal project is a hypothetical "ideal" project in a certain environment of an organization (or business unit). It is a project that runs under optimal conditions, that is, all project characteristics are the best possible ones ("perfect") at the start of the project, and there is no loss in productivity (P_{Nom}) caused by activities required for overcoming imperfections in the project environment.
- *Effort overhead* (*EO*) is an additional portion of effort (overhead) spent on overcoming the imperfections of a real project environment, such as insufficient skills of the project team. In such a case, a certain effort is required to compensate for such a situation; for example, team training has to be conducted.

In CoBRA (Fig. 6.7), the actual effort of project X is estimated based on nominal productivity determined from already completed projects (P_{Nom}), effort overhead resulting from X's environment (*EO*), and size of software products that are to be delivered on the output of X.

The CoBRA method combines data-driven and expert-based paradigms by its two main elements (Fig. 6.7): causal effort model and regression model.

Causal Effort Model

The first component is a causal effort model that produces an estimate of effort overhead (EO), that is, the additional effort that needs to be spent on overcoming "imperfections" of a real project environment such as insufficient skills of the project team. The causal model consists of factors (so-called *effort drivers*) affecting the project effort within a certain context.

The causal model is typically obtained through expert knowledge acquisition (e.g., involving experienced project managers). Recently, Trendowicz (2008) proposed an integrated approach where causal analysis of measurement data is combined with expert judgment.

An example causal effort model is presented in Fig. 6.8. The arrows indicate direct relationships. The "+" indicates a positive relationship, and "−" indicates a negative relationship. One arrow pointing to another indicates an interaction effect. For example, an interaction exists between "Disciplined requirements management" and "Requirements volatility." In this case, a decreased level of disciplined requirements management magnifies the negative influence of volatile requirements on cost (increased development effort).

The qualitative information is quantified through expert opinion elicitation, and its inherent uncertainty is explicitly captured for all relationships in the causal model. The quantification is the percentage of effort overhead above that of nominal effort and is referred to as an *effort multiplier*. *Nominal effort* is the effort spent only on developing a software product of a certain size in the context of a nominal project since a nominal project is one that runs under optimal conditions; that is, all project characteristics are the best possible ones ("perfect") at the start of the project. In that sense, achieving productivity higher than nominal is theoretically not possible, as illustrated in Fig. 6.9.

For instance, the project objectives are well defined and understood by all staff members and the customer and all key people in the project have appropriate skills to successfully conduct the project. *Effort overhead (EO)* is then the additional effort spent on overcoming imperfections of a real project environment such as insufficient skills of the project team. For example, if an expert gave a value of 20 % overhead for a certain value of an effort driver (e.g., "high" if the effort driver was measured on an ordinal scale), that would mean that the project effort would be 120 % that of the nominal project.

The multipliers for the effort drivers are modeled as distributions to capture the uncertainty inherent in expert opinion. Triangular or beta-PERT distributions can be used to reflect the experts' opinion about each effort driver's impact on cost by giving three values: minimum, most likely, and maximum value of a multiplier.

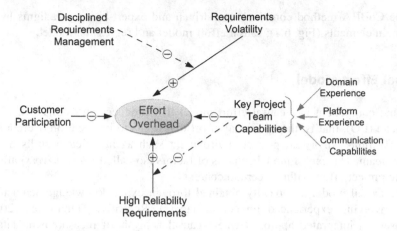

Fig. 6.8 Example of effort overhead model

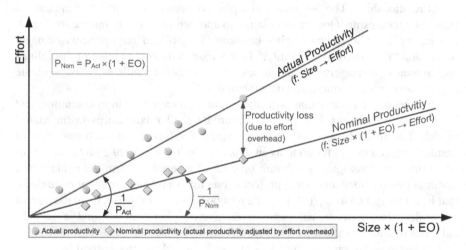

Fig. 6.9 Nominal productivity and actual productivity

Regression Model

The second component of CoBRA is a *regression model* that produces an estimate of nominal productivity (P_{Nom}). The regression model uses data from past similar projects to identify a relationship between effort overhead and actual effort (Fig. 6.9). Note that this is a simple bivariate relationship that does not require a large data set. This is important, as it explains why CoBRA does not have demanding data requirements, as opposed to data-driven estimation techniques. The baseline, nominal productivity (P_{Nom}), can be computed based on the linear relationship between actual effort and size multiplied by effort overhead, which can be obtained from past project data.

In principle, the higher the effort overhead, the higher the actual effort (the lower the actual productivity). Yet, this is true when we consider projects of the same size. In reality, the CoBRA model is built upon data from numerous past projects that usually differ with respect to size. Therefore, we consider a project's size by multiplying effort overhead (EO) by size (regression line f: Size $\times$ $(1 + EO)$ $\rightarrow$ Effort in Fig. 6.9). This represents the basic idea of the CoBRA method that nominal effort is linearly dependent on size and that actual nonlinearity is caused by environmental characteristics represented by effort drivers. The slope of the line represents nominal productivity (P_{Nom}), which is constant across all projects in a given context. The effort estimate for a new project is then based on the nominal productivity computed from already completed (historical) projects and the effort overhead on the new project. The project's effort overhead is determined based on its actual characteristics. Since not all of them are known at the time of estimation (typically at the very beginning of the development process), value distributions (e.g., triangular) instead of exact values are given to cover the uncertainty. Using Monte Carlo simulation, sampling is performed from each of the distributions, and each sampled value is summed to obtain an effort overhead estimate. This is repeated many times (e.g., 1,000 times), resulting in a distribution of effort overhead and ultimately effort.

For a more detailed discussion of the CoBRA method, refer to Chap. 15.

6.5.3 Strengths and Weaknesses of Hybrid Estimation

In this section, we generalize and focus on aspects that are common to most of the hybrid effort estimation methods. It does not mean that individual methods may not differ on specific aspects from the majority of the methods. We analyze strengths and weaknesses of hybrid methods using several key criteria that should be considered when selecting an appropriate effort estimation method. We define these criteria in more detail in Chap. 7, where we present a systematic procedure for selecting the most appropriate effort estimation method. We advise using generalized strengths and weaknesses we list in this section solely as an orientation point toward which an estimation paradigm should go in a particular context: toward hybrid estimation or better toward data-driven or expert-based estimation. In order to select a specific method, we recommend using the selection procedure we present in Chap. 7.

Strengths of Hybrid Estimation

Hybrid estimation methods share the following strengths:

- *(C01) Moderate expert involvement*: Using a combination of expert judgment and quantitative data allows hybrid methods to reduce human expert involvement compared to estimation methods based solely on human judgment. Typically, involvement of very few experts with appropriate expertise suffices for building a reliable estimation model. Potentially inconsistent or incomplete expert inputs can then be complemented by quantitative data. For example, in estimation methods that use causal models, some parts of a causal model can be inferred using expert judgment, whereas other parts make use of analysis of quantitative data. After building a model, even when it is not satisfactory straight away, experts can easily find improvement points based on the results of the quantitative analysis. Finally, other than in expert-based estimation, a hybrid approach does not require involving experts each time estimates are needed. Experts are required only once, for developing an effort estimation model, which then can be used for estimation purposes.

- *(C2) Moderate data requirements*: Hybrid estimation methods do not require much quantitative data. For example, the CoBRA method requires software size and project effort data from about ten completed projects. Optionally, hybrid methods can utilize whatever additional quantitative data are available in order to infer parts of the estimation model instead of, or in addition to, using expert judgment. For example, individual elements of a causal model in the CoBRA or BBN method can be created using expert judgment, or they can be inferred from quantitative data using appropriate analysis techniques. Depending on the particular method and analysis techniques it employs, specific constraints might be put upon the type and distribution of quantitative data. For example, CoBRA requires size and effort data to be measured on at least a ratio scale, while the BBN approach does not require input data to be measured on a particular measurement scale. Building BBN models for more sophisticated (interval or ratio) or mixed measurement scales requires employing complex causal modeling techniques.

- *(C4) High flexibility*: Hybrid estimation methods such as CoBRA or BBN support tailoring estimation models to a specific application context. The resulting effort estimation model reflects effort drivers, their interactions, and their impact on effort that are characteristic for the specific estimation context for which the model has been developed.

- *(C6) Moderate support level*: Hybrid methods are relatively new and therefore not as well documented and supported by tools as are, for example, long-established methods such as statistical regression. BBN as a generic approach is supported by a number of commercial software packages. CoBRA is supported by few freely available software tools. Yet, since CoBRA is relatively simple to implement, the availability of ready-to-use tool support for CoBRA is not as critical as for the more complex BBN approach.

- *(C7) High reusability*: Hybrid estimation methods, such as CoBRA or BBN, are typically used to deliver custom-tailored effort models. This property of hybrid methods allows for better estimation within specific contexts, which limits the use of such models outside the context for which they have been developed. Yet, the transparent and easily understood structure of effort models created in hybrid estimation facilitates adapting these effort models and/or reusing its parts across different estimation contexts. For example, if causal relationships among some effort factors are common for several estimation contexts, then the part of effort model representing these relationships can be reused "as is" within a different effort model developed for these contexts.

- *(C8) Predictive power*: As with any other estimation method, it is hard to draw general conclusions regarding predictive power of hybrid estimation methods. Any source that offers such across-the-board statements should principally be carefully considered. Similar to other estimation approaches, predictive performances of hybrid methods depend on the quality of information upon which estimates are based. The advantage of hybrid estimation is the ability to utilize alternative information sources. In this way, hybrid estimation ensures optimal quality of information for the purpose of predictions. Once developed, an estimation model provides repeatable outputs. In this respect, hybrid estimation methods avoid nonrepeatable and expensive estimates using expert-based methods. Industrial applications of hybrid methods showed an estimation error within the range of 5–30 %. Yet, since hybrid methods are relatively new, the empirical evidence regarding their performance is relatively small compared to long-established data-driven and expert-based methods.
- *(C9) Informative power*: Combining quantitative and judgmental data facilitates their comprehensibility. Human estimators can follow the process of creating an effort model relatively easily and use it for the purpose of understanding and controlling software development projects.
- *(C10) Handling uncertainty*: An essential advantage of hybrid estimation over alternative approaches lies in how estimation uncertainty is handled. Hybrid estimation methods provide support for explicitly addressing uncertainty in both estimation inputs and estimation outputs. On the one hand, existing hybrid methods provide relatively simple mechanisms to account for uncertainty of information upon which estimates are based. On the other hand, effort estimates are presented together with information about their uncertainty. Project decision makers thus get a basis for assessing project risks with respect to budget and schedule.
- *(C11) Estimation scope*: Existing hybrid estimation methods are not bound to any particular type of project activities. An estimation model can be developed for any type of project activity and at any level of granularity. With respect to the type of activity, in addition to predicting complete project effort, hybrid estimation can be used to predict engineering or management effort alone or a project's work tasks or activities. The only prerequisite to estimating the effort of particular project activities is that the input information upon which the estimation model is based refers to the same project activities.
- *(C12) Availability*: Existing hybrid estimation methods are applicable at any point of time during the software development project. The only limitation on the method's use is the availability of inputs for estimation, which typically include the size of the software to be delivered and the values of the relevant effort drivers. However, since hybrid approaches handle estimation uncertainty, they can be reliably applied in the very early project stages using inaccurate inputs and then reapplied as a project proceeds and more accurate inputs become available.
- *(C13) Empirical evidence*: Hybrid estimation methods are relatively new, and the amount of empirical evidence for them is relatively small compared to

long-established data-driven or expert-based estimation approaches. Yet, the high consistency of positive experiences made with hybrid estimation in various industrial contexts suggests large potential for this estimation approach for managing software projects.

Weaknesses of Hybrid Estimation

Despite numerous advantages, a hybrid estimation method should not be selected blindly as the best estimation approach. Decisions about using a particular estimation method in a specific context should be based on thorough consideration of the advantages and disadvantages in this very context. On the one hand, the contribution of the method's strengths to the achievement of the estimation objectives should be evaluated. On the other hand, the impact of a method's weaknesses on its feasibility in a given context should be considered. Hybrid estimation has a few weaknesses that should be considered before it is selected as the suitable estimation paradigm. The two major weaknesses hybrid methods share are

- *(C3) Little robustness*: Robustness of existing hybrid estimation methods against messy information is rather limited. Through combining measurement data and expert judgment, hybrid methods offer effective support for identifying potential information inconsistencies and for complementing incomplete information. Besides that, hybrid methods provide hardly any dedicated mechanisms for coping with redundant, inconsistent, or incomplete information. For this purpose, external data preprocessing techniques need to be used on the input information prior to using an estimation method.
- *(C5) Moderate to high complexity of estimation method*: Existing hybrid estimation methods employ techniques and theories that partially go beyond the standard curricula of computer science and software engineering. In consequence, mastering these methods may require additional training. For example, deciding on proper parameters of estimation will require understanding basic theories upon which an estimation method is based. In particular, usage of estimation based on Bayesian belief networks (BBNs) might require up-front learning overhead because BBN utilizes advanced elements of probability and causation theories, which might be difficult to understand for beginners in this area. The CoBRA method, on the other hand, is based on basic principles of probability theory, which are typically part of any engineering education.

6.6   Fixed-Model vs. Define-Your-Own-Model Estimation

Many models have been proposed over the last several years, but, because of difference in the data collected, types of projects and environmental factors among software development sites, these models are not transportable and are only valid within the organization where they were developed.

—John W. Bailey and Victor R. Basili

Among the data-intensive effort estimation methods, some require past project data in order to build customized models, whereas others provide a "ready-to-use" defined model in which effort factors and their relationships are already fixed. The first group of estimation approaches is commonly referred to as define-your-own-model approaches, whereas the second group are fixed-model approaches. Figure 6.10 illustrates the difference between employing fixed-model and define-your-own model estimation approaches.

In the *fixed-model approach*, the providers of the off-the-shelf effort estimation method (*model owner*) use multiorganizational data to develop the model. For this purpose, a provider may use one of the publicly available modeling techniques or their own proprietary modeling technique. The provider offers the model to software organizations (*software organization*). The effort estimation and the associated calibration technique are often hidden within a proprietary software tool. The calibration technique allows the software organization to adjust the predefined estimation model to their particular estimation context using its own project data. A software organization may acquire the fixed model and use it for estimating its software development projects. Optionally, it can calibrate the model using its own project data and the calibration method provided by the owner of the estimation model (*estimation tool provider*).

In the early 1980s, Bailey and Basili (1981) noted that "it is not generally possible for one software development environment to use the algorithms developed at another environment to predict resource consumptions." As a solution to this challenge, they proposed that "each environment consider its own past productivity in order to estimate its future productivities." Thus, each organization should consider building its own model, based upon its own data. Alternatively, a software organization may utilize the *define-your-own-model approach*. In this approach, a software organization uses one of the publicly available effort modeling techniques upon its own project data in order to develop a custom-tailored effort estimation model. The software organization then uses the model to estimate the effort of future software development projects. Note that a provider of the off-the-shelf model and the software organization developing its own model may potentially use the same effort modeling technique.

The popular (Boehm's 1981; Boehm's et al. 2000) COCOMO model or Putnam's and Myers' (2003) SLIM model are examples of fixed-model approaches, which offer off-the-shelf effort estimation models. The major advantage of fixed-model approaches is that they, theoretically, do not require any data from already completed projects. Those methods are especially attractive to organizations that have not started collecting quantitative data. However, in practice, fixed estimation models are developed for a specific context and are, by definition, only suited for estimating the types of projects for which the fixed model was built. The applicability of such models for different contexts is usually quite limited. In order to improve their performance, organization-specific project data are required anyway to calibrate the generic model to a specific application context.

Moreover, applying a fixed estimation model requires feeding the model with a specific set of measurement data that are predefined by the model. This often includes a specific size metric (e.g., source lines of code) and a specific set of

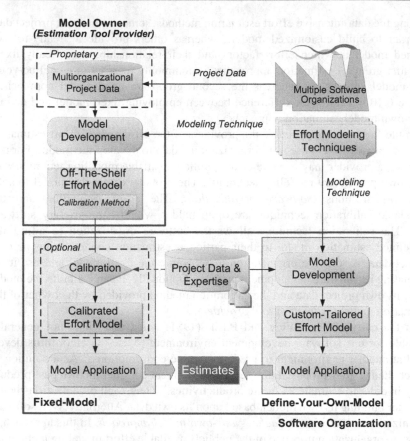

Fig. 6.10 Define-your-own-model vs. fixed-model estimation

additional effort factors. A significant threat to the reliability of estimation based upon off-the-shelf models is that they may include factors that are irrelevant in the context of a particular organization, while possibly missing factors that actually have a significant impact on project effort and thus should be considered to get reliable effort estimates. Table 6.4 summarizes the differences (benefits and threats) of fixed-model and define-your-own-model estimation approaches.

6.7   Comparison of Estimation Paradigms

No matter how well developed a thing or system becomes, however, it will never be without limitations.

—Henry Petroski

Table 6.4 Characteristics of fixed-model and define-your-own-model estimation

Aspect	Fixed-model estimation	Define-your-own-model estimation
C01. Expert involvement	No expert involvement is required to develop an estimation model. A human expert is needed only to apply an already created model and to interpret its outcomes	A human is needed to run the model development technique upon historical project data in order to create a custom-tailored model. A human expert is then needed to apply the model and to interpret its outcomes
C02. Required data	No context-specific data are required, unless the off-the-shelf estimation model is to be calibrated in a specific context	Context-specific data are required to develop a custom-tailored estimation model
C03. Robustness	Off-the-shelf estimation models require a fixed set of inputs when estimating effort. For example, data on a specific size metric and a specific set of effort factors must be provided	Developing a custom-tailored model does not require any specific project data. The type of data used for developing a model depends on the purpose and context of the model's future application. The quantity and quality of required data depend on the model development techniques employed
C04. Flexibility	A predefined fixed estimation model determines the type and granularity of project activities that can be estimated using the model. Adaptability of an off-the-shelf model is limited to model calibration (typically only to a limited extent)	A custom-tailored model can be developed for estimating project tasks of any type and granularity. The only prerequisite is that appropriate historical project data are available for developing the model
C05. Complexity	Use of fixed-model estimation approaches is quite straightforward. It consists solely of feeding the model with project data and interpreting its outcomes	Complexity of the define-your-own model approaches depends mainly on the complexity of techniques and theories used for the purpose of developing the model. Complexity may range from very simple methods based on linear regression to complex machine-learning methods such as artificial neural networks
C06. Support level	Fixed-model approaches are typically associated with a comprehensive software package, which supports applying the estimation model and interpreting estimation outcomes. Tool support often includes calibrating the fixed model using custom-specific project data. Fixed-model approaches are often rather poorly documented. For so-called nonproprietary methods, such as SLIM or COCOMO, basic principles have been published. Yet, detailed description of these methods	Define-your-own model approaches represent nonproprietary methods and are typically well documented. Tool support for these methods varies widely. Estimation methods based on well established, generic theories, such as statistical regression, are supported by a number of commercial and free software packages. Estimation methods based on relatively new and/or dedicated effort estimation theories, such as causal modeling,

(continued)

Table 6.4 (continued)

Aspect	Fixed-model estimation	Define-your-own-model estimation
	is not available (e.g., model calibration procedures). For so-called proprietary approaches, the estimation method documentation is typically not available; the only way to use the method is to acquire the associated software package	are supported by fewer software packages
C07. Reusability	Reusability of an off-the-shelf estimation model depends on the range of project situations it covers. The wider range of software project situations covered by the data upon which the model was fixed, the more generic the model (thus reusable for a wider range of estimation contexts). However, reusability of a fixed effort model depends on the extent to which it can be calibrated to the specific software project context. Existing off-the-shelf estimation models provide rather limited calibration support and often require much project data for calibration. The amount of data needed for reliable calibration would often suffice for developing custom-tailored estimation model	Reusability of custom-tailored effort models is typically limited to the project context similar to that for which a given model has been developed. Though define-your-own models are not generic enough to be applied in a wide range of project situations they can typically be easily redeveloped for different project contexts using context-specific project data
C08. Predictive power	Published industrial case studies and our personal experiences indicate that the fixed-model approach generally performs worse than define-your own-model. We must, however, consider that the blame for this situation is shared between the estimation approach itself and the organization that utilizes it. Software organizations often expect that off-the-shelf estimation models and associated tool support relieve them from investing in thorough evaluation and improvement of effort estimation technology. A consequence of this is a quick-and-dirty use of the estimation model, which typically results in poor estimates. Disappointed organizations abandon the estimation and are typically discouraged from any further attempts to improve their effort estimation practices	Published industrial case studies and our personal experiences regarding the performance of data-driven estimation methods favor define-your-own-model approaches. The prominent reason is that the necessity of developing a customized effort estimation model motivates organizations to thoroughly think about their development processes, factors influencing effort, and quality of data used for developing the effort model. In consequence, organizations benefit while developing an effort model by learning about their processes and by identifying improvement potential. In the end, they get a custom-tailored model, which typically performs better than uncalibrated off-the-shelf-models developed upon external project data

(continued)

Table 6.4 (continued)

Aspect	Fixed-model estimation	Define-your-own-model estimation
C09. Informative power	Informative power of the fixed-model approaches depends on the project data upon which the model has been developed, the comprehensibility of the model, and information provided by the associated estimation tool. Even though the effort model and analyses in the associated tool provide insight into project effort dependencies, these are a generalization over different organizations. In the best case, part of these dependencies are relevant in the context of model application whereas another part is not relevant and may confuse interpretation of estimation results. For example, the COCOMO model considers a number of effort factors and quantifies their impact on project effort. Yet, in the context of specific organizations, only some of these effort factors will typically be relevant, whereas some will be completely irrelevant; moreover, some relevant factors will be missing in the model. Even calibrating a model to a specific estimation context does not usually improve informative power of the fixed effort model because typical calibration does not allow for adjusting the set of considered effort factors but only for adjusting numerical parameters assigned to the fixed set of factors	Informative power of a define-your-own-model approach depends on how well the project data, upon which customized effort is developed, are reflecting true effort dependencies in the context that the data are used. Critical aspects are completeness and correctness of the project data. One must have in mind that model development techniques extract relevant information from quantitative data. For example, if some relevant effort factors are not covered by project measurement data, then they cannot be identified through the analysis of the data. Hybrid estimation methods offer a solution to this problem by using measurement data and expertise of human experts. Still, the risk of getting much irrelevant information while using custom-tailored estimation models is lower than while using off-the-shelf models
C10. Handling uncertainty	In principle, the support for handling uncertainty does not depend on the origin of the estimation model (whether it is an off-the-shelf or custom-tailored model) but on the structure of the model and the underlying estimation method. If the model allows for handling uncertain inputs and supports assessing uncertainty of resulting estimates, then it does not matter if it has been	The extent to which develop-your-own-model approaches support handling estimation uncertainty depends on the model development and application techniques employed. In the best case, the effort estimation model accepts and can process uncertain estimation inputs (such as size measurements) and indicates uncertainty of output estimates. For example, the model

(continued)

Table 6.4 (continued)

Aspect	Fixed-model estimation	Define-your-own-model estimation
	developed on external or organization-specific data Handling uncertainty is, however, more critical for off-the-shelf models as they are based on external data and the risk of uncertain estimates is principally higher than for custom-tailored models developed on context-specific data. Software tools associated with off-the-shelf estimation models typically offer a number of analyses that support assessing uncertainty of estimates	accepts inputs in a form of probability distribution and provides an output distribution of effort estimates. Yet, there are few such methods. Typically, handling estimation uncertainty requires employing additional analysis techniques, which makes estimation more complex and more expensive
C11. Comprehensiveness	Fixed-model estimation approaches typically offer a limited range of software project activities that can be estimated. Off-the-shelf estimation models usually allow for estimating the total effort of a complete project and effort per major development phase, such as requirements specification, design, or coding	Define-your-own-model approaches allow for estimating effort of any type of software development activity. The only prerequisite is that appropriate project data be available. It means that historical project data (including actual effort and relevant effort factors) for the particular activity are available to develop such an estimation model
C12. Availability	Availability of estimates depends on the availability of input data required by the off-the-shelf estimation model. Off-the-shelf models usually require a fixed set of specific inputs such as a particular size metric and a specific set of project environment characteristics. For example, fixed estimation models that require software size in terms of lines of source code are actually applicable only after software coding when the actual size of software is known. One may circumvent the problem by using estimated inputs. In the aforementioned example, one may estimate effort before the coding phase by using estimated lines of code. Yet, estimation using estimated inputs is typically burdened by large uncertainty because uncertainties across multiple inputs accumulate in	Availability of estimates depends on the availability of inputs required by the custom-tailored effort model. For example, if one wants to estimate effort in the requirements specification phase, then the estimation model should be developed on the data that are available in this phase. For example, one should consider using software size that is measurable for requirement specifications (such as function point analysis). Since an estimation model is customized to a specific context and needs, the availability of estimates is typically high

(continued)

Table 6.4   (continued)

Aspect	Fixed-model estimation	Define-your-own-model estimation
	a multiplicative way (not additive as commonly assumed)	
C13. Empirical evidence	Empirical evidence on the performance of fixed-model estimation approaches is rather scarce, especially for proprietary models where availability to research is limited due to license costs. An exception is Boehm's et al. (2000) COCOMO model. The basic version of the model is publicly available and has been subject to many studies. Yet, the results of these studies do not seem to be helpful since reported estimation error varies between several dozen to several hundred percent	Empirical evidence for the develop-your-own-model approaches varies widely depending on the particular effort modeling method and context. In principle, much evidence exists for the well-established and simple effort modeling techniques such as regression analysis. However, little evidence exists for relatively new and complex techniques such as artificial neural networks. As far as hybrid estimation models are concerned, increasing evidence has been recently published

There is no universally good estimation method. Each and every estimation method has its strengths and limitations. Estimation methods that are useful in one situation might be completely useless in another situation. Therefore, selecting the most suitable effort estimation method requires considering the context in which the method is to be applied—in particular, requirements and constraints with respect to effort estimation. In Chap. 7, we propose a complete procedure for selecting the most suitable estimation method. In this section, we summarize general characteristics that are common for major classes of effort estimation methods discussed in this chapter.

Table 6.5 briefly summarizes the most prominent characteristics of each group of estimation methods we synthesized based on our experiences as well as experiences that other software estimation practitioners have presented in the literature. The overview we present in the remainder of this chapter should be used for orientation purposes. Refer to Sect. 7.2 for a detailed explanation of the characteristics (aspect) we consider for comparing the estimation methods in Table 6.5.

Table 6.6 synthesizes the evaluation of major estimation paradigms we present in Table 6.5. For this purpose, we define a list of requirements toward effort estimation. We assess the extent to which each of the considered estimation paradigms meets each requirement using a simple four-point ordinal scale:

- "++": estimation methods fully meet requirement
- "+": estimation methods partially meet requirement
- "–": estimation methods minimally meet requirement
- "– –": estimation methods do not meet requirement at all

Table 6.5 Common characteristics of estimation method classes

Aspect	Expert-based	Data-driven	Hybrid
C01. Expert involvement	Requires one or more domain experts knowledgeable in the estimation method and project domain. Significant time needed for estimation	Requires an analyst to operationalize the estimation method: develop or calibrate the estimation model in model-driven estimation, preparing project data and setting estimation parameters for memory-based estimation. Reusing the method requires one expert to run the method and interpret estimation outcomes	Requires one analyst for building a model. Domain experts are needed to provide information missing in project measurement data. Reusing the model requires one expert to simply feed the model with project data and interpret estimation outcomes
C02. Required data	Project measurement data are not required but can be used to support human experts in estimating project effort	Large amounts of data from similar projects are required to perform estimation. In the case of model-based methods, the data are needed for building and/or calibrating the estimation model	Few project measurement data are required for estimation. Remaining inputs to estimation are provided by domain experts
C03. Robustness	Expert-based estimation is independent of the measurement data. Using messy measurement data (or messy information, in general) to support experts may mislead experts and lead to wrong estimates	Robustness against complex and messy data depends strongly on the data analysis techniques used. Various methods are robust against different types of data deficiencies	Robustness against complex and messy data depends on the analysis techniques used. Existing hybrid methods are not robust against typical data deficits such as incompleteness or inconsistency. Yet, these deficits are (at least partially) managed through human involvement
C04. Flexibility	Estimation based on expert judgment is very flexible. Neither a specific set of effort factors nor any particular effort model is imposed	Define-your-own-model approaches are very flexible because they do not impose any specific effort model. Fixed-model approaches are rather inflexible because they impose a particular effort model and a specific set of project measurement data for	Existing hybrid methods are very flexible because they do not impose any particular effort model. They may at most require that software size and effort be considered in estimation

(continued)

Table 6.5 (continued)

Aspect	Expert-based	Data-driven	Hybrid
		effort estimation. Memory-based methods do not require any specific set of effort factors or any specific effort model	
C05. Complexity	Expert-based estimation does not involve any complex techniques or theories. It requires basic skills in project effort estimation	The analyst responsible for introducing and maintaining the effort estimation method must comprehend the theoretical foundations of the method. This often comprises multiple theories that often go (at least partially) beyond standard curricula of computer science and software engineering. Estimators who use the method in projects must have a basic understanding of the estimation method in order to understand and interpret estimation outcomes	The analyst responsible for introducing and maintaining the effort estimation method must comprehend the theoretical foundations of the method. This may comprise theories that go beyond standard curricula of computer science and software engineering. Those who use the method in projects must have a basic understanding of the estimation method in order to understand and interpret estimation outcomes
C06. Support level	Expert-based estimation is well documented and basically does not require any tool support. Estimation procedures are simple and can easily be supported using basic software tools such as MS Office	Most of the data-driven estimation methods are based on theories from other knowledge areas where these theories are long-established, well-documented, and supported by software tools. For example, statistical regression and machine-learning techniques are supported by a number of free and commercial tools. Off-the-shelf estimation models are often embedded in relatively expensive commercial estimation software packages and thus of limited availability to small and	Existing hybrid estimation methods are well documented. Estimation based on Bayesian Belief Networks is supported by a number of free and commercial software packages. The CoBRA method is supported by a few software tools[a]

(continued)

Table 6.5 (continued)

Aspect	Expert-based	Data-driven	Hybrid
		medium software organizations	
C07. Reusability	Estimates based on human judgment are not reusable and are hardly adaptable in new project situations. Costly estimation procedure must be repeated each time estimates are needed	In model-based estimation, effort models are reusable for estimating projects that are similar to those upon which the model has been developed. Outcomes of memory-based estimation are not reusable; yet, estimation can be easily (at minimal cost) repeated each time estimates are needed. In general, the range of project situations for which the estimation model or memory-based estimation can be reused depends on the range of situations represented by the historical project data upon which estimation is based	Similar to data-driven estimation, hybrid estimation models are reusable for estimating projects that are similar to those upon which the model has been developed. Moreover, the transparent and intuitive structure of the model supports reusing its parts for developing effort models for other (yet similar) project situations. Similar to data-driven methods, the range of project situations for which the hybrid estimation model can be reused depends on the range of situations represented by the historical project data (measurements and judgments) upon which the model was based
C08. Predictive power	Estimates built upon human judgment are not repeatable and may be biased by individual skills and preferences of estimators. Typically, human estimators tend to be overoptimistic and underestimate	The data-driven estimation method provides repeatable outcomes when applied on the same measurement data.[b] Accuracy of data-driven estimation depends on the particular method and quality of underlying data. In practice, accuracy in terms of relative estimation error varies even for the same method from several to several hundred percent	Once developed, a hybrid estimation model delivers repeatable estimates. Yet, due to involvement of human judgment, the estimation model may vary when developed under the same conditions, that is, upon the same measurement data and involving the same domain experts. Like data-driven estimation, accuracy of hybrid estimation depends on the particular estimation method and the quality of historical project data. Yet, on average, existing hybrid

(continued)

Table 6.5   (continued)

Aspect	Expert-based	Data-driven	Hybrid
			estimation methods seem to perform better than estimation based solely on measurement data
C09. Informative power	Expert-based estimation typically does not provide any explicit information in addition to effort forecasts. Experts estimate using an "implicit effort model" hidden in their heads and based on their individual expertise. Obtaining any further information regarding effort dependencies in a project requires applying additional knowledge acquisition techniques to extract this implicit effort model (or its pieces) from experts	The extent of the information data-driven methods provide, in addition to simple effort forecasts, differs for various estimation methods. If such information is provided, then its reliability largely depends on the comprehensiveness and quality of measurement data upon which estimates have been based. For example, information on the most relevant effort drivers cannot go beyond factors for which measurement data are available	Hybrid methods provide many different outputs in addition to simple effort forecasts. For example, most relevant effort drivers, their impact on effort, and their mutual dependencies are presented. Moreover, effort forecasts are associated with information about the probability of exceeding them. An important aspect of hybrid estimation is that the knowledge presented in its output is based on two alternative, usually complementary, sources of knowledge: expertise of human experts and quantitative measurement data
C10. Handling uncertainty	In order to handle estimation uncertainty, the confidence of human judgment can be considered in a systematic manner. Yet, experts must provide information regarding their confidence and these data have to be analyzed using extra analysis techniques. In the context of group estimation, the range or distribution of estimates across multiple experts can be analyzed to indicate uncertainty of estimates	Model-based estimation methods do not typically support handling estimation uncertainty, especially when information on which estimates are based is largely missing. Handling estimation uncertainty is often limited to determining the range of estimates related to the heterogeneity of historical project data upon which estimates are based. Memory-based methods typically do not handle	Handling estimation uncertainty is an integral part of hybrid estimation. It is realized in a number of ways and considers multiple uncertainty aspects. Estimation based on Bayesian Belief Networks involves quite complex theories, which might be difficult to understand for nonstatisticians. Another hybrid method, CoBRA, employs quite simple and intuitive techniques for handling estimation

(continued)

Table 6.5 (continued)

Aspect	Expert-based	Data-driven	Hybrid
		estimation uncertainty. For this purpose, extra analysis techniques have to be used	
C11. Comprehensiveness	Expert-based estimation is very flexible and can be applied to any type of project activity at any granularity level. The only prerequisite is that human estimators have expertise regarding the estimated activity. For example, experts may estimate effort required for managing software tests, under the condition that they have experience in managing software tests	Memory-based and define-you-own-model estimation methods are principally applicable to any type of project activities and at any granularity level. The only prerequisite is that historical project data used for estimation correspond to the estimated activity. The scope of estimation based on off-the-shelf models is quite limited because these models are typically fixed for certain project activities (most commonly, complete project effort and effort per development life cycle phase)	As hybrid methods actually represent a define-your-own-model estimation paradigm, they can be principally applied for estimating any type of project activities at any granularity level. The only prerequisite is that historical project data (quantitative measurements and expert judgments) used for estimation correspond to the estimated activity. The advantage of hybrid estimation over the data-driven methods is that even if appropriate measurement data are not available, the method can still be applied because the missing quantitative data can be complemented by expert judgment
C12. Availability	Estimation via expert judgment can be applied at any time throughout the software development life cycle starting from very early project stages	Availability of data-driven estimation methods depends largely on the availability of the measurement data needed for estimation. The method can reliably be applied when actual project information is known. Before that, the effort prediction can at most be based on estimated information. In this case, however, estimation error associated with each	Similar to data-driven methods, availability of hybrid methods depends on the availability of project information that is needed for estimation. Yet, since hybrid methods typically require fewer quantitative data than data-driven methods and use expert judgment, they have higher availability than data-driven estimation. In case actual project

(continued)

Table 6.5   (continued)

Aspect	Expert-based	Data-driven	Hybrid
		input will propagate into total error of effort estimation. In the define-your-own-model methods, an estimation model can be constructed on data that are available from the very beginning of the project	information is not available and expected values need to be used instead, hybrid estimation methods typically provide mechanisms to account for the uncertainties associated with such estimation
C13. Empirical evidence	There are a number of published empirical studies that investigate many relevant aspects of expert-based software effort estimation	Simple data-driven methods such as regression or analogy-based estimation have been widely investigated and the results have been published in the related literature. Relatively little empirical evidence exists with respect to recent estimation methods, for example, methods that employ techniques from the machine-learning domain. Very little or no empirical evidence exists for the estimation based on proprietary off-the-shelf models	Relatively little empirical evidence exists on relatively recent hybrid methods. Yet, recently increasing interest in these methods results in an increasing number of empirical studies and related publications

[a]Free license of the CoBRIX tool can be acquired from the http://www.cobrix.org page. A free tool based on MS Excel can be acquired in Japanese from http://sec.ipa.go.jp/tool/cobra/(in order to enter the page, a free-of-charge sign in on the page is required)
[b]Estimates that involve simulation techniques, like in the CoBRA method, may vary. In practice, relative variations in estimates across multiple simulation runs are so small that they have actually no impact on the overall predictive power

Notice that Table 6.6 represents our subjective assessments of the major estimation paradigms. It is a generalization of detailed characteristics of these paradigms we discussed above based on our own expertise and the expertise of the software engineering community presented in the related literature.

Table 6.6 Summary of strengths and weaknesses of major estimation paradigms

Characteristic		Single expert	Group consensus	Model-based	Memory-based	BBN	CoBRA
Cost— Necessary acceptance criteria	*Expert involvement*: The method requires involving one or more experts whose only responsibility is to run the method and to interpret its outputs	–	– –	++	++	+	+
	Required data: The method does not require any measurement data or very few data (very few measures) and does not impose any requirements on its type and distribution. Moreover, the method is robust against typical data quality problems such as missing data	++	++	– –	–	+	+
	Robustness: The method handles—to a large extent –low-quality data. In other words, it can handle different imperfections of quantitative data such as incomplete, redundant, inconsistent, or collinear measurements. In consequence, it does not require much overhead for preparing data prior to estimation	+	++	–	+	+	++
	Flexibility: The method does not impose any specific estimation model. For example, in the case of model-based estimation methods, it would refer to the so-called define-your-own-model approaches	++	++	–	++	++	++
	Complexity: The method is simple and intuitive, and it requires basic skills that do not go beyond standard curricula of software science and software engineering	++	+	–	+	–	+
	Support level: The method is well supported by	+	+	++	+	+	+

(continued)

Table 6.6 (continued)

	Characteristic	Single expert	Group consensus	Model-based	Memory-based	BBN	CoBRA
	accompanying documentation and tools						
	Reusability: The estimation method and its outputs can be easily reused in similar situations and adapted—partially or entirely—in new situations	– –	– –	+	–	++	++
Benefit—sufficient acceptance criteria	*Predictive power*: The estimation method provides accurate, precise, and repeatable output	–	+	+	+	–	+
	Informative power: The method provides complete and well-understandable information that contributes to full achievement of the organizational objectives	– –	– –	–	– –	+	++
	Handling uncertainty: The method accepts uncertain inputs and provides an intuitive mechanism for covering uncertainties (e.g., triangular distribution) The method supports uncertainty evaluation of the estimation output	– –	–	–	–	++	++
	Comprehensiveness: The method may be applied to estimate the effort of project activities of any type and at any granularity level	+	+	+	+	+	+
	Availability: The method can be applied at any stage of the project's life cycle; specifically, it is already applicable in early project phases (e.g., proposal phase). It could then be used at any point in time to revise the initial estimates	++	++	+	+	+	+

(continued)

Table 6.6 (continued)

Characteristic	Single expert	Group consensus	Model- based	Memory- based	BBN	CoBRA
Empirical evidence: There are numerous published studies on the method's empirical applications in the industrial context	–	+	++	+	–	+

Further Reading

- L.C. Briand and I. Wieczorek (2002), "Resource Modeling in Software Engineering," in J.J. Marciniak (ed.) *Encyclopedia of Software Engineering, 2nd Edition*. Wiley & Sons.

  In their chapter, the authors provide a brief classification of effort estimation methods followed by a brief overview and comparative evaluation of selected methods.

- M. Jørgensen, B. Boehm, and S. Rifkin (2009), "Software Development Effort Estimation: Formal Models or Expert Judgment?" *IEEE Software*, vol. 26, no. 2, pp. 14–19.

  This publication presents a polemic on expert-based and data-driven effort estimation methods. The most prominent strengths and weaknesses of both approaches are presented by "gurus" of both approaches, Magne Jørgensen and Barry Boehm.

- R.W. Jensen, L.H. Putnam, and W. Roetzheim (2006), "Software Estimating Models: Three Viewpoints," *Cross-Talk: The Journal of Defense Software Engineering*, vol. 19, no. 2, pp. 23–29.

  Authors discuss three different perspectives on software development effort and its estimation represented by three leading effort estimation tools: SEEM-SER, SLIM, and Cost-Xpert (where the latter one implements the COCOMO model). The article provides a brief overview of the origins, basic principles, and core equations implemented by the three tools.

- C. Schofield (1998), *Non-Algorithmic Effort Estimation Techniques*. Technical Report TR98-01, Department of Computing, Bournemouth University, UK.

  Author provides a brief overview of software effort approaches based on the techniques from the artificial intelligence domain, such as rule induction, fuzzy systems, regression trees, neural networks, and case-based reasoning. For each approach, the author summarizes its basic principles.

- J. Wen, S. Li, Z. Lin, Y. Hu, and C. Huang (2012), "Systematic literature review of machine learning based software development effort estimation models," *Information and Software Technology*, vol. 54, no. 1, pp. 41–59.

  This article presents a comprehensive review of effort estimation methods based on machine-learning techniques such as Case-Based Reasoning (CBR), Artificial Neural Networks (ANN), Decision Trees (DT), Bayesian Networks (BN), Support Vector Regression (SVR), Genetic Algorithms (GA), Genetic Programming (GP), and Association Rules (AR). Authors look at the estimation accuracy of the considered methods (as reported in the related literature) and compare the performance of machine-learning methods against "conventional" non-machine-learning estimation models. Finally, the authors investigate particular project situations in which effort estimation based on machine-learning techniques should be favorable over other data-driven methods.

- M. Jørgensen (2004), "A review of studies on expert estimation of software development effort," *Journal of Systems and Software*, vol. 70, no. 1–2, pp. 37–60.

  This article provides an extensive review of studies on expert estimation of software development effort. Based on the review, the author formulates 12 "best practice" guidelines for expert-based software effort estimation.

- J. S. Armstrong (2001), *Principles of Forecasting: A Handbook for Researchers and Practitioners, 2nd Edition.* Kluwer Academic Publishers, Dordrecht, The Netherlands.

  In Chap. 4, the authors discuss the most relevant aspects of estimation based on human judgment. The section "Improving Judgmental Forecasts" discusses procedures for improving experts' forecasts. The section "Improving Reliability of Judgmental Forecasts" explains how the accuracy of expert forecasts is reduced when people use unreliable procedures to collect and analyze information. The section "Decomposition for Judgmental Forecasting and Estimation" describes how to decompose problems so that experts can make better estimates and forecasts. Finally, the section "Expert Opinions in Forecasting: Role of the Delphi Technique" provides an overview of forecasting with expert opinions (the authors use the Delphi procedure as a framework to integrate principles for improving expert forecasts).

- I. Ben-Gal (2007), "Bayesian Networks", in F. Ruggeri, F. Faltin, and R. Kenett (eds.), *Encyclopedia of Statistics in Quality & Reliability*, Wiley & Sons.

  This short chapter of the Encyclopedia of Statistics and Reliability provides a well-written compact introduction to Bayes' Theorem and Bayesian Belief Networks. It presents all relevant concepts in a concise and clear way and supports them with intuitive examples.

- Trendowicz (2013), Software Cost Estimation, Benchmarking, and Risk Assessment. Software Decision Makers' Guide for Predictable Software Development. Springer Verlag.

This book presents Cost Estimation, Benchmarking, and Risk Assessment (CoBRA), which combines human judgment and measurement data to systematically create custom-specific effort estimation models. Author provides a comprehensive specification of processes for developing a CoBRA effort model and for applying the model in a number of different project management scenarios. Moreover, the book provides a number of practical guidelines on applying these processes, based on industrial experiences regarding project effort estimation in general, and using the CoBRA method, in particular. Several real-world cases of applying the CoBRA method illustrate the practical use of the method.

Finding the Most Suitable Estimation Method

7

All models are wrong, but some are useful.

—George Box

A number of effort estimation methods have been developed over the recent decades. The key question software practitioners ask is "Which method is the best one for me?" The bad news is that there is no "best" estimation method. The good news is that there are many useful estimation methods; yet, in order to be useful, an estimation method must be selected with a particular estimation context in mind.

The choice of estimation method depends on the particular use situation; we refer to this as estimation context. Estimation context comprises many aspects such as software application domain (e.g., information systems, embedded systems), project size (e.g., small, medium, large), the point in time when the estimation is to be performed (e.g., concept, requirements specification, coding), development type (e.g., new development, enhancement, maintenance), and so on. There are a very large number of aspects that influence the performance of a particular effort estimation method—yet, not all of them are necessarily worth considering in practice.

In this chapter, we provide a systematic and structured way to identify the estimation methods that best suit a particular estimation context. For this purpose, we construct a simple decision tree upon a set of simple decision criteria. These criteria encompass aspects of estimation context that have proved in practice to determine the feasibility and usefulness of estimation methods. In other words, we consider criteria that refer to (1) the capability of a software organization to fulfill the prerequisites for applying a particular estimation method and (2) the capabilities of the estimation method to support the achievement of estimation objectives of the organization.

After reading this chapter, you should be able to assess one or more effort estimation methods with respect to their suitability to the needs and capabilities of your specific organization, that is, of your specific estimation context. Notice that we suggest selecting multiple estimation methods that fit the context of a specific

A. Trendowicz and R. Jeffery, *Software Project Effort Estimation*,
DOI 10.1007/978-3-319-03629-8_7, © Springer International Publishing Switzerland 2014

software organization. That is simply because none of the existing estimation methods will fit perfectly to a particular context—instead, multiple methods will likely fit different aspects of the estimation context.

7.1 Pitfalls of Selecting "the Best" Estimation Method

The fact that the juxtaposition of the words "accurate" and "estimate" produces an oxymoron does not seem to deter people from the quest for what is clearly a contradiction in terms.

—Phillip G. Armour

Reading dozens of empirical studies that compare multiple estimation methods and looking at how software organizations decide between alternative estimation methods in their everyday practice, we get an impression that prediction accuracy is the holy grail of software effort estimation. In practice, however, such an attitude leads very quickly to disappointment, in consequence often abandoning any further endeavors to improve effort estimation practices. In this section, we look closer at the typical threats related to accuracy-driven selection of "the best" software effort estimation method.

In Chap. 12 of his book, Scott Armstrong (2001) summarizes different ways of reasoning taken when selecting forecasting methods in various application domains. In fact, these general approaches reflect our observation regarding the ways software engineering research and industry decide on "the best" effort estimation method. Let us briefly discuss these ways and related threats:

- *Convenience* ("what is easy"): This strategy prefers methods that are convenient to apply, independent of their other characteristics. Estimation methods are assumed to offer similar predictive performance because effort does not vary much across projects and any method can actually yield similar estimates. It thus makes little sense to invest much effort in applying sophisticated effort estimation methods, and the easiest to apply is typically selected.

  Threat: In reference to estimation methods, "easy" does not necessarily mean simple. For example, estimators may prefer a very sophisticated method to a simple one only because they are knowledgeable in the method, are used to it, and thus feel comfortable in using it. Although quite inexpensive, this way of selecting an estimation method might be risky. If a new project differs much from those experienced in the past, an easy-to-use estimation method may provide misleading forecasts.

- *Market popularity* ("what others do"): This strategy favors methods that are preferred in other organizations; that is, methods that are commonly used within organizations and organizations are satisfied with them.

  Threat: Armstrong identifies two basic assumptions underlying this selection strategy: (1) over time, organizations find out which estimation methods work best; (2) what is best for others will be also best for me. Yet, these assumptions might be very misleading, first of all because what is used does not necessarily equal what should be used. Software organizations do not typically compare multiple methods and do not measure the method's success—or measure it only to a very limited extent. Besides informal beliefs and people's satisfaction, there is little evidence that the method that is used is actually the one that should be used. Even if success is measured and a method is the one that should be used, its success depends on a number of factors. Yet, these factors differ across software organizations and are typically not known. In consequence, it is quite risky to uncritically adopt an industrial practice as "best practice" based solely on its common usage.

- *Structured judgment* ("what experts advise"): This strategy involves structured judgment of human experts who evaluate alternative methods against specified criteria. Armstrong notes this approach as the most promising one for selecting the most suitable forecasting method. Structured judgment proceeds in two steps. First, experts define criteria against which candidate estimation methods will be evaluated, and they rate these criteria with respect to their importance. Next, candidate estimation methods are evaluated with respect to the predefined set of criteria.

    Threat: Important prerequisites in this selection approach are that (1) experts consider all relevant criteria for evaluating candidate estimation methods, (2) they do not miss any relevant estimation method in their evaluation, and (3) their ratings are unbiased. It means that experts have good knowledge of aspects that determine the usefulness of an estimation method, they have an overview of existing estimation methods, and they are not biased toward any particular method.

- *Statistical criteria* ("what should work"): This strategy involves rating estimation methods on statistical criteria such as distribution of estimation error or significance of effort relationships provided by an estimation approach.

    Threat: This strategy might be very valuable if a proper set of selection criteria is considered for selecting the appropriate estimation method. Using statistical criteria might, however, not be appropriate for choosing between substantially different methods such as expert judgment and quantitative analysis. This selection strategy might be also very risky if applied on a narrow set of criteria. It happens, for example, in the software engineering domain, where estimation methods are selected using solely the prediction accuracy criterion. We discuss threats of accuracy-driven method selection later in this chapter (Sect. 7.1.3).

- *Relative track records* ("what has worked in this situation"): This strategy involves selecting between alternative methods in a systematic empirical evaluation study. Although expensive, this strategy should be preferred as the most reliable way for choosing the estimation method that is suitable for a particular situation.

    Threat: In practice, empirically comparing alternative estimation methods in a software organization would probably be unacceptable because of the high cost of such "in-house" evaluation. Alternatively, software organizations rely upon the results of empirical evaluations performed by researchers in laboratory environments and published in the literature. This corresponds to the

"Guidelines from prior research" selection strategy, which we discuss in the next bullet, and inherits threats of this strategy.

- *Guidelines from prior research* ("what works in this type of situation"): This strategy relies on published research. In practice, it is often not possible to evaluate an estimation method in the situation for which it will be used. In such cases, the most suitable method might be chosen using the estimation results achieved in similar situations, published in related literature.

    Threat: This strategy offers a low-cost approach to selecting between alternative methods. Yet, its effectiveness and reliability depends on how well the available research was conducted and documented. Before using published studies as a basis for selecting an estimation method, such aspects as study validity, repeatability, and comparability should also be considered. The threat is that study conditions typically differ significantly from the environment of a particular software organization. It is not so bad if study conditions are fully and clearly reported. In such a case, the software organization can reliably assess the discrepancy between the method evaluation environment and their estimation environment. The problem is that many empirical studies omit a clear description of the study conditions which impose significant risks in relying on study results even though its conditions apparently correspond to the organizational context of estimation. We discuss this issue in more detail in the next section (Sect. 7.1.1).

7.1.1 Academic Perspective

The literature on software effort estimation methods is rich with studies that evaluate several alternative estimation methods. Still, they do not provide a clear answer to the fundamental question "which method is the most suitable in a particular estimation context?" There are two reasons for the inconclusive nature of published studies:

- *Unclear and incomparable evaluation context*: Research studies often provide neither a clear description of the environment in which they evaluated the estimation methods nor a clear description of the evaluation procedure. This makes it rather hard to assess the extent to which presented evaluation results apply in other contexts, for example, the context of a software organization that wants to use these results for selecting an appropriate estimation method. In practice, there are a large number of factors that may potentially influence the performance of estimation methods. In order to ensure comparability between empirical studies, the impact of these factors on the performance of evaluated estimation methods needs to be either isolated or explicitly considered—in any case, not ignored as often happens. For instance, results of evaluation are sensitive to the experimental design, which includes such aspects as characteristics of the employed data set, norms for preprocessing the data, test statistics used, and characteristics of involved human experts. Example discussions of particular aspects that lead to inconsistent results of empirical evaluations of effort estimation methods are presented by Jørgensen (2004c), Jørgensen and Moløkken (2004), and Myrtveit et al. (2005).

- *Oversimplified, incomparable, and wrong evaluation*: Research studies typically narrow evaluation criteria to a single statistical aspect, namely estimation accuracy. In practice, however, estimation accuracy is only one of many aspects that count. For example, what good is even the most accurate estimation method when it is not applicable in our particular context, for example, because it requires inputs that we are not able to provide; or what good is the most accurate estimate when it comes out of a "black box" and we are not able to justify it to our customer or management? Research studies employ a variety of accuracy metrics that—besides being simply not comparable—are often used inappropriately, leading to wrong conclusions. For example, Foss et al. (2003) conclude from their simulation experiment that reliability of accuracy metrics depends on the situation they are used in and that no metric should be uncritically applied to compare competing estimation methods of different types, for example, for comparing data-driven estimation methods against expert judgment.

In consequence, instead of converging results for similar methods applied in similar situations, empirical investigations often provide significantly inconsistent outcomes. This might be the reason why over the years, the software industry has not really cared about empirical evaluations presented by researchers and worked their own ways of selecting "the best" estimation methods.

7.1.2   Industrial Perspective

When selecting the most suitable estimation method, the software industry typically focuses on a combination of several criteria. At first, practitioners look at what others do regarding effort estimation and what has actually worked in similar situations. For judging a situation's similarity, software organizations typically consider a few basic aspects such as business sector or software domain. For example, an original equipment manufacturer (OEM) that produces embedded software-system components for cars would probably look for what estimation approaches other automotive OEMs dealing with embedded software have successfully applied. In assessing how well an estimation method worked for others, software organizations often uncritically adopt the academia's view on the goodness of an effort estimation method in that they select estimation accuracy as the only relevant criterion. After preselecting the most accurate candidate estimation methods, they are then assessed with respect to how convenient they are to use. Here, software organizations typically rely on opinions of human experts who judge potential costs of adopting particular methods. The expenses considered include acquiring and introducing an estimation method into the software organization, using it in projects, as well as maintaining related project data and outcomes of the estimation.

Costs of Effort Estimation

Similar to any other technology, effort estimation requires certain investments related to acquiring, introducing, applying, and continuously improving it in the context of a specific software organization. In particular, the following elements typically contribute to the overall cost of using an effort estimation method:

- *Acquisition* includes searching for an appropriate method and acquiring it and/or an appropriate tool support. For example, in the case of proprietary methods, where an estimation model and often the underlying project data are integrated into a commercial software tool, the acquisition makes up a significant part of the overall method's cost.
- *Introduction and application* includes mainly staff training and preparing an infrastructure needed to apply an estimation method. In individual projects, method application costs encompass collecting necessary input data, running the estimation method, and interpreting its outcomes.
- *Maintenance* includes maintaining the method, related processes, and artifacts they produce. For example, the performance of an estimation method and related processes should be continuously monitored with respect to their performance, and appropriate improvement actions should be undertaken where necessary.

At first glance, the combination of estimation accuracy and cost criteria used by the software industry for selecting the most suitable estimation method seems to be reasonable. Yet, in practice, it leads to many disappointments because selected methods turn out not to work as expected. First of all, methods that are popular among others might not include the very method that is actually the most suitable for a specific software organization. Moreover, successful estimation depends on many more factors than solely the estimation method.

Tip

▶ Selecting an estimation method based on its popularity may be misleading due to two reasons: (1) it overlooks methods that, although unpopular, may work best for you and (2) successful estimation depends on many more factors than the estimation method alone.

Now, let us assume that the proper estimation method is a key aspect of successful estimation and that one of the methods others use is the most suitable for our situation. Still, there are two threats to this selection approach commonly used:

- Assessment of an application situation is reduced to considering just a few general environmental factors. In practice, there are a number of factors that need to be considered before transferring estimation performance results obtained in one context to other contexts. On the one hand, all relevant characteristics of the environment, in which a particular method was applied, need to be known. On the other hand, exact parameters of the procedure used to evaluate the method need to be fully and clearly documented. Only when a method's application environment and procedure are similar can the method's performance results be reliably considered for adopting in another context.

- Evaluation of a method's performance is reduced to a single accuracy criterion. Accurate estimates are important, but software organizations need more than simple effort numbers to support their estimation objectives. For example, customers often require clear justification of the bids. In that situation, a transparent rationale behind the estimates is needed. Depending on the particular needs and objectives, a number of evaluation criteria—other than solely estimation accuracy—need to be considered.

In the next section, we discuss the threats of selecting "the best" estimation method based upon accuracy results published in related literature.

7.1.3 Threats to Accuracy-Driven Selection of Estimation Method

One of the major threats of deciding upon "the best" method based upon both software research and industry is using estimation accuracy as the primary—and often the only—relevant decision criterion. However, accuracy does not support many estimation objectives defined within software organizations, and also, estimation accuracy presented in various studies usually cannot be used due to unclear or missing descriptions of the conditions under which particular methods were evaluated.

Published empirical studies differ with respect to their design. The accuracy results presented are sensitive to such aspects of study design as: the characteristics of the data set, the criteria for removing outliers and other data points from the original data set, the accuracy metric, statistical significance tests and significance levels, and the use of human subjects and their level of expertise.

In this section, we briefly discuss typical issues that threaten the use of published accuracy results for selecting the most suitable method for a particular situation. The threats we include are

- *Terminology*: Wording used across various estimation studies is inconsistent. Authors either use different terms for referring to the same concepts or use the same terms for referring to different concepts.
- *Isolation*: The impact of nonobservable environmental factors (context of estimation) on the performance of the effort estimation method is not considered and/or not reported.
- *Source of Data*: Characteristics of the project data used in different studies to evaluate the same estimation methods are not consistent and/or not reported.
- *Data Quality and Preparation*: Quality of the data used for evaluating the same estimation method differs significantly across different studies. Quality refers to

a number of aspects such as reliability of the underlying data collection procedures and techniques used for processing the data prior to estimation.

- *Method Configuration*: The parameter settings of compared estimation methods differ across different studies. Reported evaluation results suggest that exactly the same method in the same configuration was evaluated, whereas factually different parameter settings were applied.

- *Evaluation Strategy*: Settings of the evaluation studies for comparing estimation methods differ. For example, the way project data have been split in a set for building the estimation model and a set for validating the model differs across studies evaluating the same methods, although reported information suggests exactly the same evaluation procedures.

- *Performance Indicators*: Analysis techniques and statistics used for evaluating the predictive performance of estimation methods are often not appropriate for the particular estimation and validation context and thus may lead to wrong conclusions.

- *Fitness of Evaluation Function*: Metrics and functions used for guiding the process of developing an effort estimation model are not independent of the metrics used later for evaluating the accuracy of the estimation model. In consequence, accuracy evaluations will be biased and favor the estimation models in which development was guided by particular fitness metrics.

In the following paragraphs, we will discuss in more detail the threats to accuracy-driven estimation. Thereby, we will take a critical look at the practical usefulness of empirical evaluations of effort estimation methods.

Terminology

Inconsistent terminology is one of the most important reasons for incomparable estimations and, in consequence, limited usefulness of estimation performance results provided by different empirical studies (Grimstad et al. 2006). For instance, the definition of effort may vary across studies; experts may interpret estimated effort as "most likely effort," "planned effort," or "best-case effort." In consequence, comparisons of effort estimation accuracy presented by studies that use different definitions of effort will not be comparable.

Tip

▶ Before adopting estimation results provided by an external study, make sure that the terminology used there is consistent with yours.

Isolation

Comparable estimation results require assurance that estimation is not influenced by any factors that vary across different studies (Grimstad and Jørgensen 2006). The impact of such "nonobservable" factors may make adopting these results in a particular situation quite risky. It may happen that some unobserved characteristics of the study environment differ significantly from the situation in which the evaluated method is supposed to be applied—in this case, the accuracy results of the empirical study will likely not be applicable to the target situation.

Isolation of the impact of nonobserved factors, therefore, should be considered as an important aspect when evaluating estimation accuracy and when using accuracy evaluation results for selecting the most suitable effort estimation method—especially when inconsistent results come from various studies. Before uncritically adopting such results, we should ensure that the impacts of factors that may make them nonapplicable to our situation have either been explicitly considered or isolated. Grimstad and Jørgensen (2006) provide an example framework for the evaluation of estimation error where they propose randomization, grouping, adjustment, and exclusion as example isolation approaches.

Tip

▶ Before adopting estimation results provided by an external study, make sure that any factors that differ for your organization from the study context have either been explicitly considered or their impact on evaluation results isolated.

Source of Data

Another important factor that influences the results of empirical studies is project data upon which estimation accuracy has been evaluated. It is rather unlikely that an estimation method will perform exactly the same when applied to different project data.[1] Therefore, a search for "the best" estimation method should be based on estimation performance results obtained on project data similar to those on which the method is intended to be used.

Different studies typically use different project data for evaluating the performance of estimation methods. Such results should not be compared—not only because of different contents of data sets but also due to their different quality. Data sets may, for instance, exhibit different characteristics in terms of the functional form of the relationship between size and effort, the size and completeness of the data set, type and number of variables, etc. For instance, quite different conclusions regarding the performance of different estimation methods when applied to company-specific versus multicompany data were reported depending on the particular data repository used.[2]

---

[1] See, for example, Pickard et al. (1999), Shepperd and Kadoda (2001), and Mendes et al. (2003a).

[2] Systematic reviews of the studies comparing cross- versus within-company effort estimation are presented by Mendes et al. (2005), Kitchenham et al. (2007), MacDonell and Shepperd (2007), and Mendes and Lokan (2008).

Tip

▶ Before adopting estimation results provided by an external study, make sure that
the data used there have similar characteristics to data you will use for estimation.

Data Quality and Preparation

The quality of project data, on which an estimation method is evaluated, has
significant impact on the method's performance. One way to ensure proper quality
of data is by employing proper measurement processes for collecting estimation
inputs; another is to apply appropriate data preprocessing techniques for preparing
the data prior to estimation.

Consequently, depending on the particular preprocessing applied prior to the
estimation, the performance of the estimation method may differ. Therefore, before
adopting a particular method to a specific situation, we should make sure that we
are about to use the same preprocessing as in the studies used as a reference for
selecting the method. In cases where the preprocessing techniques applied in the
reference study differ, or are not clearly and fully documented, we must accept the
risk that the method will perform other than in the reference study.

For some empirical studies, for example, it is known that instead of the whole
data set, only some subset of the original data was used; however, little is known
about the criteria for selecting the data subset. A critical element of the estimation
procedure—an approach for filtering the input data—is thus unknown. In this case,
you have to be aware that using none or different preprocessing may result in
completely different performance of the estimation method than that provided by
the reference study.

One example might be handling data outliers. Some authors excluded data
outliers before performing the estimation method; yet, only few of them state
explicitly the exact criteria and procedure used and which data points were
excluded. This example might be behind conflicting performance results presented
by different studies for the same estimation method, although all studies used the
same set of data.[3]

Myrtveit and Stensrud (1999) suggest considering the following aspects of data
quality and preparation as having significant impact on the performance of effort
estimation:

- The norms for cleaning the data, that is, for removing outliers and data points
  with missing values
- The number of data points, that is, projects in the data set

---

[3] Examples of such conflicting results can be found in Briand et al. (2000), Wieczorek and Ruhe
(2002), and Mendes and Kitchenham (2004). The two former studies simply excluded from the
data set the projects with missing values, whereas the latter study replaced missing values with
values sampled randomly from the other projects in the set (thus preserving projects that were
excluded by the two former studies).

- The number of independent variables, that is, project characteristics measured in the data set
- The interval between the smallest and largest projects
- The homogeneity of the data set with respect to nonobservable project environmental characteristics such as application domain, development type, etc.
- The general data quality, that is, the reliability of the measurement procedures used for collecting the data
- Representativeness of data samples, that is, the extent to which the set of projects considered represents the estimation context and thus future projects

Tip

▶ Before adopting estimation results provided by an external study, make sure that you apply the same data preparation procedures prior to estimation.

Method Configuration

Estimation methods—in particular, data-driven ones—are sensitive to the configuration choices made by their users. For example, analogy-based methods may provide various results depending on the kind of similarity metrics employed or the number of analogs used for estimation or the rules for selecting analogs for deriving final effort estimates.

There are a number of examples in which studies provide significantly different performance results for apparently the same estimation method only because they used different method configurations. For instance, Srinivasan and Fisher (1995) report a great variation of classification and regression trees (CART) using different error thresholds for building the tree; mean magnitude of relative error (MMRE) thresholds ranged from 3.64 to 8.35. Estimation accuracy of genetic programming (GP) methods evaluated on Boehm's COCOMO data set by Dolado in two studies (Dolado 1999, 2001) vary between 323 % and 178 %, respectively. Yet, no detailed information regarding the configuration of the GP used was provided.

Therefore, before adopting a particular method based upon its published accuracy results, we should ensure that (1) all details on the method's configuration have been published and (2) we use the method using the same configuration. Otherwise, we should accept the risk of significantly different performance when applied in different configurations.

Tip

▶ Before adopting estimation results provided by an external study, make sure that you use the same method configuration in your estimation.

Evaluation Strategy

The performance of estimation methods in empirical studies depends on the applied evaluation approach. For example, Menzies and Hihn (2006), in their review of 17 cost estimation experiments, found numerous examples where minor details regarding performance of the experiments confused the authors' conclusions. They observed, for instance, that the way project data are split into the set on which estimation is built—training set—and the set on which the model's accuracy is assessed—testing set—might significantly differentiate between evaluation results obtained. A concrete outcome could be inconsistent performance results provided for the same estimation methods by Briand et al. (2000), Wieczorek and Ruhe (2002), and Mendes and Kitchenham (2004). One reason might be different percentage of projects used for model building purposes. While Mendes and Kitchenham used the complete data set, Briand et al. used 15 %, and Wieczorek and Ruhe used 22 % of data.

Indicators of Predictive Performance

An obvious but surprisingly often forgotten fact is that the performance of estimation methods depends on the performance metrics used (e.g., estimation accuracy metrics) and their interpretation. On the one hand, different metrics focus on different aspects of a method's performance—even though they all are commonly referred to as "accuracy metrics." On the other hand, not all metrics are appropriate and valid for all situations.

Proposed by Conte et al. (1986), *Magnitude of Relative Error* (*MRE*) and *Prediction of level* (*Pred.m*) metrics have been widely used over decades with little consideration of their practical limitations. Yet, as pointed out by several authors,[4] these metrics cannot be uncritically used for comparing different estimation methods. In their simulation experiments, Foss et al. (2003) and Myrtveit et al. (2005) observed that employing MMRE can lead—in certain experimental settings—to counterintuitive results and concluded that it is quite unsafe to use MMRE as an accuracy metric.

Kitchenham et al. (2001) generally criticize summary statistics and propose an analysis of the whole distribution of accuracy obtained when evaluating a method's performance on multiple projects. The authors suggest additionally analyzing residuals and box plots of z *statistic*[5] because they can help explain summary statistics. The mean z statistic, for instance, alone is asymmetric and as such favors models that minimize overestimates. It could be a problem since overestimates are

---

[4] For example, Briand et al. (1999), Shepperd et al. (2000), Shepperd (2005), Kitchenham et al. (2001), Foss et al. (2003), and Myrtveit et al. (2005).

[5] "z" statistic represents the ratio of estimated to actual effort.

usually less serious than underestimates. Therefore, the whole distribution of z should be always considered.

Inconsistent Definition of Accuracy Metrics

Definitions of the accuracy metrics are sometimes not consistent across various studies, although their authors claim to use the same metric. For instance, Conte et al. (1986) originally defined *prediction at level m* (*Pred.m*) as the percentage of estimates for which *magnitude of relative error* (*MRE*) is lower than or equal to m. In practice, the greater the *Pred.m*, the better is the estimation performance. Ohsugi et al. (2004) define Pred.25 as "the ratio of operations whose relative errors are under 25 %," whereby they actually use absolute errors as a basis for computation instead of relative errors as in the original *Pred.m* metric. Moreover, they claim that estimation is considered accurate when Pred.25 is small—which is counterintuitive.

Finally, we should strictly avoid using the same metric to fit and, later on, to evaluate an estimation model. Using the same metric for fitting and then for evaluating a particular estimation model will most probably prefer this very model as compared to other models where the metric was not used as a fit criterion.

Tip

▶ Before adopting estimation accuracy presented by an external study, make sure that valid metrics have been applied and that they are meaningful for your particular situation.

Fitness Evaluation Function

Many data-driven estimation methods use measures of a model's fit to project data for guiding the modeling procedure. Accuracy of the estimation model depends not only on the use of a particular fitness function but also on how it relates to accuracy metrics used later on for evaluating the estimation model.

For example, estimation models developed by minimizing squared deviations between estimated and actual effort naturally grant more importance to large projects, in which the scope for large estimation errors is the greatest (Lokan 2005). On the contrary, models that are developed by minimizing relative estimation errors naturally grant more importance to the most common types of projects. In consequence, these two strategies would coincide only if large projects were also the most common in the data upon which the models were built. Since software engineering data are generally tending toward smaller projects, the models based on minimizing the sum of absolute deviations seem to be a better choice. Still, we need to be aware of the high sensitivity of the magnitude of relative error (MRE) metric to the weights that a regression model grants to the projects of different size.

One consequence would be that, when used for comparing linear and log-linear regression models, MRE would always prefer the log-linear model, because it actually grants more weight to small projects (Briand et al. 1999). Due to its log-linear transformations, the MRE values for the log-linear model become smaller than for the linear model. Yet, this does not mean that a log-linear model is the better alternative.

Regarding particular performance metrics, the magnitude of relative error (MRE) and magnitude of error relative to the estimate (MER) perform well as accuracy statistics, but not as fitness functions (Lokan 2005). Instead, fitness functions based on mean squared error (MSE), least absolute deviation (LAD), and z statistic perform better across a wide range of accuracy metrics.

Independently of particular metrics, using the same metric to fit and, later on, to evaluate the estimation model will most probably prefer this very model as compared to other models where the metric was not used as a fit criterion.

Tip

▶ Before adopting estimation accuracy presented by an external study, check if any fitness metrics have been used to guide estimation model building and, if yes, how they relate to the presented accuracy statistics.

7.2   Criteria for Selecting the Best Estimation Methods

Things work because they work in a particular configuration, at a particular scale, and in a particular context and culture.
—Henry Petroski

Most people don't know what they want unless they see it in context.
—Dan Ariely

In this section, we define a set of criteria for evaluating alternative effort estimation methods and selecting those that are the most suitable for a particular estimation situation.

7.2.1   Necessary and Sufficient Acceptance Criteria

While defining selection criteria, we take, in principle, a cost-benefit view on candidate effort estimation methods. Thus, we suggest considering cost—in an extreme case, feasibility—of using a particular estimation method, and we suggest considering the benefits a particular method will provide us, for example, with respect to our estimation and project management objectives. In that sense, cost aspects refer to necessary conditions, whereas benefit aspects refer to sufficient conditions for accepting a particular estimation method as suitable in particular estimation context.

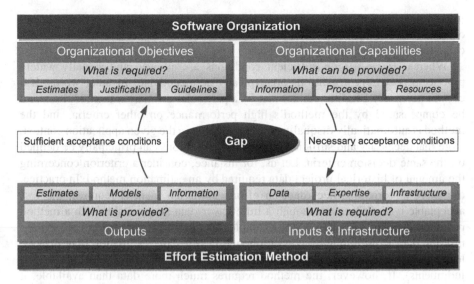

Fig. 7.1 Approach for selecting suitable estimation methods

The gap between costs and benefits of using a particular effort estimation method creates a basis for accepting or rejecting candidate methods as suitable or not suitable for a particular context. Figure 7.1 briefly illustrates this idea.

Necessary acceptance conditions refer to *"What is required by an estimation method vs. what can be provided by the organization in which the method is to be used?"* In order to check whether an estimation method fulfills necessary acceptance conditions, we need to assess our capabilities of fulfilling the requirements imposed by the method. In other words, we need to look at whether we can provide the needs of a particular method in order to be properly applied and how much it will cost. It may, for instance, be the case that we are not capable of meeting the requirements of a particular estimation method. On the other hand, it may happen that although we would be able to provide what is needed for applying a particular method, the associated cost is unacceptably high. In both cases, the candidate estimation method will be rejected as not appropriate in our situation. If two or more methods meet the necessary criteria, then the decision regarding which one to use should be based on the extent to which the methods fulfill sufficient acceptance conditions.

Sufficient acceptance conditions refer to *"What is provided by the method vs. what is required by the organization in which the method is to be applied?"* Estimation methods need to be assessed from the viewpoint of the purposes and objectives of estimation defined in the organization. Thereby, we assess alternative estimation methods by the extent to which they contribute to the achievement of our effort estimation goals. Objectives of effort estimation are usually related to project management activities. For example, we may need effort estimation to support justifying and negotiating project costs. In this case, we would prefer methods that offer us information that is useful for these purposes and reject methods that do not offer such support.

Whereas trade-offs on sufficient conditions are allowed and actually widely practiced, necessary conditions are typically nonnegotiable. In other words, if a certain necessary condition is not met by a particular estimation method, it cannot be compensated by the method's high performance on other criteria, and the method is automatically disqualified as not feasible in the given application context. Note that necessary and sufficient acceptance conditions can principally be defined on the same decision criteria. Let us, for instance, consider a criterion concerning the amount of historical project data required by an estimation method. In practice, the more historical project data an effort estimation method requires, the less acceptable it is. Still, even though a little fewer data are available than a method requires, it could be applied, for example, because an organization can acquire missing data from human experts (although in this case, estimation may provide less reliable outputs because it was partially based on uncertain, subjective expert judgments). If, however, the method requires much more data than available, it would most likely not be acceptable at all. The amount of the data required by the method beyond which it is definitely no longer acceptable would define the necessary acceptance conditions for the method.

A simple technique for selecting suitable estimation methods might be defining a triage-like "must," "should," and "could" requirements upon relevant decision criteria and using them for selecting a suitable estimation method. Fulfilling "must" requirements would correspond to necessary conditions, whereas fulfilling "should" and "could" requirements would correspond to sufficient conditions for accepting an estimation method as suitable in a given application context.

Triage

The term triage originates from emergency medicine and refers (Webster Dictionary) to "sorting of, and allocation of, treatment to patients according to a system of priorities designed to maximize the number of survivors."

The notion of triage has been widely adapted to software engineering and project management for quick prioritizing, for example, of product requirements, project objectives, and process activities. For example, in software development, we prioritize software requirements into "must do," "should do," and "could do," according to their importance to the customer. In order to maximize the development value delivered to a customer (benefit) within limited project resources, we focus on the "must-do" requirements first; next, if there are resources left, we move to the "should-do" requirements; and, at the end, if we still have resources left, we work on the "could-do" requirements.

7.2.2 Decision Criteria

In this section, we define a set of 13 decision criteria for selecting suitable effort estimation methods from a set of alternative methods. We synthesized the criteria based on experiences we and other practitioners gained during selecting and applying various effort estimation methods in different industrial contexts.

(C1) Expert Involvement

This criterion refers to the extent of human expert involvement required by the effort estimation method. The expert involvement criterion encompasses several aspects:

1. *Number of experts*: The number of experts involved in the estimation process. For example, group estimation methods such as Wideband Delphi, Planning Poker, or CoBRA require involving more than one human expert in the estimation process.
2. *Intensity of involvement*: The effort a single human expert needs to spend when involved in the estimation process. For example, data-driven effort estimation methods such as COCOMO require a human expert solely to feed the estimation tool with appropriate data and interpret its outputs. Expert-based methods, on the contrary, require experts to derive estimates, often in a multistep, iterative estimation procedure.
3. *Level of expertise*: The level and area of expertise required by involved human experts, in particular, practical experience and theoretical knowledge in applying an estimation method. For example, familiarity with theoretical principles of classification and regression trees (CART) is required in order to properly set up its parameters and interpret its outcomes. CART uses machine learning techniques, which go beyond standard curricula of software engineering education. In consequence, it requires significant skills and overhead to learn for somebody who is new in this area.

(C2) Required Data

This criterion refers to the requirements of an effort estimation method regarding project measurement data. The data requirements criterion encompasses several aspects:

1. *Data quantity*: The amount of measurement data—variables and data points—required by the estimation method. For example, it is said that building multivariate regression requires as many as 30 data points for each independent variable. Even if we have already developed an off-the-shelf COCOMO

model, its usage requires providing measurement data on 24 specific attributes (including software size, 17 effort multipliers, and 5 scale factors).

2. *Data type*: The extent to which an effort estimation method requires/accepts input information on a particular measurement scale. The most common data types include
   - Qualitative: natural language description; data may be measured on categorical or ordinal scale
   - Quantitative: numerical measurement; data may be measured on interval or ratio scale
   - Mixed: data cover any combination of measurement scales

3. *Data distribution*: The extent to which an effort estimation method assumes and requires input data to originate from a particular statistical distribution. Simple regression analysis, for example, assumes that the error term originates from a normal distribution (in Sect. 8.1, we discuss key assumptions of regression analysis).

(C3) Robustness

This criterion refers to the extent to which the method is robust against low-quality inputs. This criterion may also be interpreted as the level of data quality required by an estimation method. If a method cannot handle low-quality data, this may require applying appropriate preprocessing techniques for preparing input data prior to estimation—which implies additional overhead. The robustness criterion encompasses several different aspects, which actually refer to particular attributes of data quality:

1. *Incompleteness*: The extent to which an effort estimation method is sensitive to incomplete inputs or, in other words, the extent to which an estimation method can handle incomplete data provided as input. In particular, data-driven methods are sensitive to missing data. While some methods handle missing data, others cannot be applied directly to incomplete input and require appropriate data cleaning prior to using the data for estimation.

2. *Redundancy*: The extent to which the method is sensitive to redundant information. A particular form of data redundancy is data dependency. In this case, the data conveys redundant information in that one factor is functionally dependent on one or more other factors. For example, in the case of data collinearity, a factor is a linear combination of other factors. In this case, the factor is redundant.

3. *Inconsistency*: The extent to which an effort estimation method is sensitive to inconsistent inputs. Example inconsistencies include data outliers. For example, effort estimation based on ordinary least-squares regression is highly sensitive to data outliers.

4. *Nonlinearity*: The extent to which effort estimation methods can handle a nonlinear effect of the input information, for example, nonlinear impact of a particular effort driver on effort.

(C4) Flexibility

This criterion refers to the extent to which an effort estimation method imposes a fixed estimation model and/or requires a specific set of inputs. The specificity of estimation inputs includes such aspects as

- A fixed set of specific effort drivers (which implies that specific information is required on the method's input)
- Fixed functional dependencies between effort drivers
- Fixed impact of effort drivers on effort

(C5) Complexity

This criterion refers to the sophistication level of the estimation method, and it encompasses such aspects as

1. *Employed techniques*: The number and complexity of techniques and processes used within the estimation method. For example, the classification and regression trees (CART) method employs quite complex algorithms and several data analysis techniques to derive the effort estimation model.
2. *Underlying theory*: The complexity of the underlying theory that is required to understand and use the estimation method. Estimation methods typically use such theories as information theory, mathematics, statistics, and probability theory. For example, effort estimation methods that originate from the artificial intelligence domain typically involve a mixture of all these theories. Consequently, using such methods for those who are new in this knowledge domain might be difficult and require large overhead to master the method.
3. *Parameterization*: The number and complexity of parameters that must be set up before applying the estimation method. This aspect includes the support the method provides for setting up its parameters (e.g., mechanisms for automatic or semiautomatic parameter learning). Example parameters may be the functional form of a regression model or the number of hidden layers of an artificial neural network.

(C6) Support Level

This criterion refers to the extent of support available for using the effort estimation method. The support level criterion encompasses two aspects:

1. *Documentation level*: The level and quality of the method's documentation. This includes accessibility of the documentation, its completeness (coverage of all relevant aspects of the method), and its understandability. The method's documentation should cover such aspects as underlying theory, estimation procedure,

setting up the method's parameters, interpreting its outcomes, and practical guidelines for using the method.

2. *Tool support*: The extent to which a method's application is supported by automatic tools. This includes such aspects as
   - Availability of tools: acquisition process, license cost, support, etc.
   - Quality of tools: failure-free operation, documentation, etc.
   - Functionality of tools: user-friendliness, method's coverage, support for setting up the method's parameters, etc.

(C7) Reusability

This criterion refers to the extent to which an estimation method and its outputs can be reused in (partially) or ported to (entirely) estimation contexts other than those for which it has been developed. For example, significant overhead can be saved if, once developed, an estimation model can be reused—possibly with small adjustments—for estimation in multiple projects. Another example of reusability is an estimation model that covers a wide variety of situations and thus is sufficiently generic to be used in different contexts with minor or no adjustments. The reusability criterion encompasses two aspects:

1. *Genericness*: The extent to which estimation outputs, such as an estimation model, are universally applicable across various contexts. For example, high genericness of an estimation model implies that it can be reliably used (with minimal or no adjustments) in a variety of project situations.
2. *Adaptability*: The extent and difficulty of adjustments that are potentially needed before reusing an estimation method and/or its outputs in contexts other than those for which the method was intended. An example of common adjustment before use is calibration of the effort estimation model.

(C8) Predictive Power

This criterion refers to the extent to which an effort estimation method provides credible outputs; that is, how close are the estimation results to the factual situation. Credibility of estimation outcomes comprises three major aspects:

1. *Accuracy*: The extent to which estimates are near to the true value.
2. *Precision*: The extent to which estimates provided are close to each other for different projects in a similar situation. When applied over multiple projects, a precise estimation method provides outcomes that are close to each other (not scattered), although the outcomes do not have to be close to the true value.
3. *Bias*: The extent to which estimates are burdened by a systematic error. For example, if human estimators are exposed to particular information that increases their optimism, estimates they provide will probably consistently turn toward underestimates.

4. *Repeatability*: The extent to which the estimation method provides repeatable outputs when applied multiple times in the same context and upon the same input information. The repeatability of estimates can be evaluated using similar techniques as for assessing estimation precision.

The difference between accuracy, precision, and bias is discussed in Sect. 4.3.2.

(C9) Informative Power

This criterion refers to the extent to which an effort estimation method provides additional information beyond effort estimates alone. Such additional information comprises any knowledge that may support the achievement of the effort estimation objectives. For example, if we want to use effort estimation for the purpose of improving development productivity or justifying project effort, such information as relevant effort drivers, their mutual interactions, and the magnitude of their impact on effort will be indispensable. The informative power criterion encompasses two aspects:

1. *Comprehensiveness*: The extent to which the estimation method provides any useful information in addition to simple effort estimates.
2. *Comprehensibility*: The extent to which the method provides the additional information in a transparent, intuitive, and understandable way.

(C10) Handling Uncertainty

This criterion refers to the extent to which the method supports the handling of uncertain information. It encompasses two aspects:

1. *Handling uncertain inputs*: The extent to which the effort estimation accepts and can properly process uncertain information provided as its input. For example, estimation can use uncertain input data provided in the form of probability distributions.
2. *Handling uncertain outputs*: The extent to which the estimation method supports presenting and interpreting uncertainty of outputs provided. For example, effort estimates are presented in the form of probability distributions with associated confidence intervals.

(C11) Comprehensiveness

This criterion refers to the extent to which an effort estimation method can be used in estimating different kinds of project activities at various levels of abstraction (granularity). The estimation scope criterion encompasses two aspects:

1. *Versatility*: The extent to which the estimation method can be applied for estimating different types of project activities (e.g., engineering, management, or administrative) within different types of projects (e.g., new development, enhancement, or outsourcing).
2. *Granularity*: The extent to which the estimation method supports estimating project activities, artifacts, and resources on different granularity levels. Example activities on various granularity levels include project phase, activity, and task. Example artifacts include complete software, individual component, or feature. Finally, example resources include complete development team, group of similar roles (e.g., coders or testers), or individual team member.

(C12) Availability

This criterion refers to the extent to which the estimation method can be applied to various stages of the software development life cycle. In practice, estimates are expected in early phases of software development such as requirements specification or software design. The time in the development cycle that a method is applicable depends largely on the availability of the appropriate information required for the method's input. In this sense, the availability criterion is related to the "flexibility" criterion. At best, an estimation method should be available throughout the whole software development life cycle in order to revise estimates whenever new information relevant to project effort becomes available.

(C13) Empirical Evidence

This criterion refers to the amount and quality of evidence when using the method in practical situations. The empirical evidence criterion encompasses such aspects as

1. *Context of evaluation*: The type of environment in which the method was evaluated. Example questions we should consider in this respect include: Was it industrial organizations or academia? Were situations in which the method was applied similar to the situation in which we would like to apply it?
2. *Type of evaluation*: The type of empirical evaluation and evidence it provides. Basic types of empirical study, from the informal to the formal, include: experience surveys, case studies, and laboratory experiments. One of the basic questions to consider regarding the type of evaluation is whether the evidence it provides represents informal experiences or quantitative proof.
3. *Credibility of evaluation*: The reliability of the in-field method's evaluation. With this respect, we should take a careful look at the way the method was evaluated

and the way evaluation outcomes were documented. Credible evaluation should fulfill principles of empirical evaluation[6] and completely document the evaluation procedure and outcomes, including potential threats to their validity.

7.3   Procedure for Selecting the Best Estimation Method

The most important goal of decision analysis is insight, not numerical treatment.
—Ward Edwards and F. Hutton Barron

In this section, we propose a simple systematic procedure for deciding on the suitable effort estimation methods for a specific estimation context. In the procedure, candidate estimation methods are evaluated with respect to the multiple criteria we defined in the previous section (Sect. 7.2). For the purpose of evaluation, we adapt techniques of *multicriteria decision analysis* (*MCDA*). We illustrate the procedure with an example, in which we evaluate the most common estimation methods presented in Chaps. 8–15. In the example evaluation, we abstract from any particular estimation context and consider general properties of alternative estimation methods. We use our individual experiences to evaluate methods from the perspective of typical characteristics of software companies nowadays. For example, we consider the most common estimation objectives, capabilities, and constraints we gathered in a systematic literature review and industrial surveys.

Note that the presented examples should not be used "as is" for accepting or rejecting particular estimation methods in a specific context. They can, at most, give an overview of general characteristics of common effort estimation methods considered. The selection approach needs to be adjusted appropriately before it can be used reliably in a specific estimation context. For instance, in the example, if an estimation method requires particular measurement data on its input, we would rather consider the method feasibility as generally limited. Yet, if in a concrete situation, the particular measurement data the method requires are actually easily available, then the method should be evaluated as perfectly feasible.

As we will show in the next sections, there is no universally "best" effort estimation method. Every method has its strengths and weaknesses that depend strongly on the specific context in which they are considered. Consequently, the most suitable method can only be selected for a particular estimation situation.

Tip

▶ Every effort estimation method has its strengths and weaknesses that depend strongly on the context in which they are considered. Consequently, the most suitable method can only be selected for a particular situation.

---

[6] For an example overview of principles of empirical evaluation, refer to C. Wohlin et al., *Experimentation in Software Engineering: An Introduction*, Kluwer Academic Publishers, 2000.

7.3.1   Requirements on Selection Method

In order to support practitioners in selecting the most suitable effort estimation method, we aim at a selection procedure which is theoretically sound and practically useful. As selecting an effort estimation method requires considering multiple criteria, the multicriteria decision analysis (MCDA) technique was chosen to base our selection procedure on. MCDA techniques are well founded and have been successfully applied in many domains, from medical diagnostics through software quality assessment to planning the location of power plants. MCDA techniques can be very sophisticated, so in order to keep the selection procedure applicable in software engineering practice, we fit it to four basic requirements (Ozernoy 1992):

- *Comprehensible*: Selection procedure is able to request the required information from the user, recommend the most appropriate estimation method for a given situation, and then justify its recommendations by displaying its line of reasoning. The system will enable the user to determine the genuine assumptions under which she or he selects a particular effort estimation method.
- *Intuitive*: Selection procedure considers closely the expert's behavioral constraints. That is, the selection procedure explicitly takes into account the expert's ability to provide particular types of preference information, such as the user's ability to answer specific questions.
- *Credible*: In terms of accuracy, reliability, and consistency of its conclusions, the performance of a selection procedure is comparable to that of a human expert. Moreover, the selection procedure has the potential to achieve results which may otherwise be unobtainable. This is because the system does not mimic any one expert in selecting the most appropriate estimation method. Instead, it can capture the knowledge of many experts.
- *Informative*: The selection procedure will make implicit knowledge regarding effort estimation methods more widely available in explicit form. This knowledge is easy to update and expand. The knowledge regarding effort estimation methods can then be used effectively by analysts and nonexpert decision makers with no technical training.

7.3.2   Theoretical Background

We propose adapting simple techniques of the *multicriteria decision analysis (MCDA)* for the purpose of assessing alternative effort estimation methods and for selecting the most suitable ones. We use MCDA techniques that fit the problem of making a decision (selecting suitable methods) from among multiple options (candidate estimation methods), based upon multiple decision criteria (relevant characteristics of an estimation method).

Terminology

The objective of MCDA (Vincke 1992) is to support a decision maker in obtaining objective information regarding the preference among a set of decision variants— alternatives—based on multiple decision viewpoints—criteria. A preference among m alternatives $a \in A$, $|A| = m$, defined upon a family of n decision criteria $g \in G$, $|G| = n$, where the i-th criterion g_i represents typically the alternative's attribute that is relevant from the perspective of a decision maker for deciding about the preference among the alternatives.

The evaluation of an alternative a on criterion g is referred to as the *performance score*—or *score,* for short—of a on g and is denoted as $g(a)$. The value $g(a)$ is assigned according to a metric associated with the criterion and an appropriate measurement procedure (usually expert judgment). Typically, $g(a)$ represents a real number, but it is not always the case. It is thus necessary to define explicitly the set X_g of all possible evaluations to which criterion g may lead. In order to allow for comparisons among alternatives, it should be possible to define a complete order $<_g$ on X_g, such that $(<_g, X_g)$ is called the scale of criterion g.

In the simplest case, the preference relation among alternatives $a \in A$ is defined using the performance score $g(a)$. We say that alternative a is strictly preferred to alternative b on criterion g if and only if the value of a on criterion g is greater than the value of b on this criterion: $a > b \Leftrightarrow g(a) > g(b)$. If $g(a) = g(b)$, then alternatives a and b are *indifferent.*

In practice, decision criteria are not often equally important to a decision maker. One way MCDA addresses this issue is to associate each criterion g_i with a numerical weight w_i, which corresponds to the criterion's importance (*priority*) to the decision maker in the context of his/her particular needs and capabilities. In context of MCDA, weights w_i on n criteria g must typically fulfill two constraints:

1. $w_i \in [0, 1]$
2. $\sum_{i=1}^{n} w_i = 1$, for all $i = 1, 2, \ldots n$

In this case, preference among alternatives needs to consider both their performances on multiple criteria and their weights. One convenient way of doing this is using a so-called value function.

Utility function represents indirectly the preference among alternatives throughout a function of their utilities. Utility function $U: A \rightarrow \Re$ rationalizes preference relation *Pref* on a set of alternatives A in that for each pair of alternatives a and b, alternative a is strictly preferred to alternative b on criterion g if and only if the utility of a on criterion g is greater than the value of b on g: $a > b \Leftrightarrow u(a) > u(b)$. If $u(a) = u(b)$, then alternatives a and b are *indifferent.*

The utility function u upon a criterion g may, in principle, be defined almost in an arbitrary way. It allows for mapping values of criterion g measured on any scale onto continuous utility u. In this sense, utility $u(a)$ of an alternative a corresponds to performance score $g(a)$ on the alternative, and the utility function is an example implementation of the scoring function.

Preference on an alternative estimation method a is based on the utility u (a) the method has to a decision maker with respect to a set G of n decision criteria g. The total utility $u(a)$ of an alternative estimation method a is an aggregation of the alternative utilities $u_i(a)$ on all n criteria and the criteria weights w_i, $i = 1, \ldots, n$. One of the simplest and most intuitive aggregations is weighted sum. A more reliable, although less intuitive, aggregation is weighted product (7.1).

$$u(a) = \prod_{i=1}^{n} u_i(a)^{w_i} \qquad (7.1)$$

Two major advantages of weighted product aggregation against weighted sum include

- *Support for veto*: Weighted product aggregation supports realizing the idea of a necessary acceptance condition in that the utility of 0 on any decision criteria automatically leads to total utility of 0. In order to implement a necessary condition on a certain decision criterion, we need to define its utility function in such a way that an unacceptable criterion's value will lead to utility equal to 0.
- *Robustness against dependent decision criteria*: A weighted product aggregation is not sensitive to potential dependencies among decision criteria when utilities are aggregated. Criteria for selecting suitable estimation methods might be partially related. Using a simple weighted sum for aggregation purposes may lead to misleading outcomes and wrong decisions regarding the most suitable estimation method.

Hierarchical Multicriteria Decision Problem

In a hierarchy-based decision problem, a criterion g_i can be further decomposed into k subcriteria that may further be decomposed into their subcriteria, and so on, eventually creating a tree structure of criteria (Fig. 7.2).

In this case, an additive utility function (7.1) may be applied for each node in the tree to compute its total utility of the root node over the hierarchy of all its subnodes (7.2).

$$u_i(a) = \prod_{j \in \text{subnodes}(i)} u_j(a)^{w_j} \qquad (7.2)$$

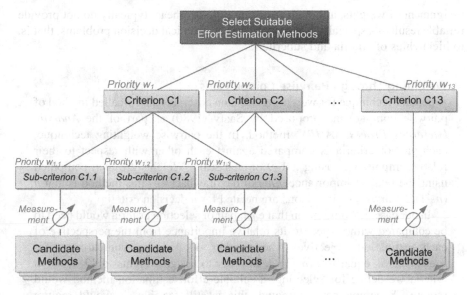

Fig. 7.2 Hierarchical multicriteria decision making

where

- i represents a criterion (node) in the hierarchy tree,
- a represents the alternative under analysis,
- subnodes(i) represents the set of subcriteria (subnodes) of criterion i,
- $u_j \in [0, 1]$ represents the utility of alternative a on the subcriterion j,
- $w_j \in [0, 1]$ represents the weight assigned to the subcriterion j, and
- $u_i \in [0, 1]$ represents the total utility of alternative a on the root criterion i.

In principle, MCDA offers many more and less sophisticated techniques that support any decision-making process, including deciding on the set of best alternatives. The weighted product technique represents a simple model for combining an alternative's utilities on multiple criteria into one overall utility. We suggest using this aggregation technique as a straightforward and sound approach for the purpose of identifying the most suitable effort estimation methods.

Weighting Relative Importance of Decision Criteria

MCDA proposes a number of techniques for prioritizing decision criteria with respect to their relative importance to a decision maker in the context of estimation goals and capabilities of the particular organization. Simple ones, such as direct assignment of weights, although requiring little overhead, typically do not provide reliable results—especially when applied to hierarchical decision problems, that is, to hierarchies of criteria and subcriteria.

> **Weighting Through Pairwise Comparisons**
> A popular technique for weighting decision criteria is the so-called method of pairwise comparisons proposed by Saaty (1980) as part of the *Analytic Hierarchy Process* (*AHP*) method. In the pairwise weighting technique, each pair of criteria is compared against each other with respect to their relative importance, using a 1–9 ordinal scale. Weights are then computed using the relative importance. One of the drawbacks of this method is that n $(n-1)/2$ pairwise comparisons are needed for n decision criteria.
>
> In our case, it would mean that each pair of selection criteria would need to be compared with respect to its relative importance from the perspective of each estimation objective. The number of pairwise comparisons for n elements is equal to $n(n-1)/2$. In order to assign weights to 13 decision criteria we define for selecting, a suitable effort estimation method would require 78 comparisons; although this is still feasible, it would require significant overhead from the decision maker.

Major points against the method of pairwise comparison are that (1) the number of comparisons increases exponentially for large sets of decision criteria and (2) resulting weights do not consider ranges in the decision criteria.[7] The latter drawback is, however, important in case criteria are measured on different scales and different ranges—which is not the case in the approach for selecting suitable effort estimation methods we propose in this book.

In the following two paragraphs, we propose two simple weighting procedures. A weighting procedure is used in each criterion (node) in a hierarchical structure of decision criteria for assigning numerical weights to its subcriteria (subnodes). For the purpose of selecting suitable effort estimation methods, we would generally weight the criteria on which we allow trade-offs. We would start with weighting the relative importance of major criteria (e.g., criteria C9–C13 we defined in Sect. 7.2.2). For each criterion, we may also weight the relative importance of its detailed aspects (subcriteria). For example, for the predictive power criterion (C8), we may weight the relative importance of its four aspects: estimation accuracy, precision, bias, and repeatability.

---

[7] Weight on a criterion should reflect two aspects: (1) range of the criterion being weighted and (2) relative importance of the criterion to a decision-maker. For example, when buying a car, the price of the car is usually important. But it would not be important if the prices of alternative cars being considered ranged from 15,000€ and 15,100€. In this example, the importance of price criterion depends obviously on the spread of the values on this criterion.

Weighting Criteria with Rank Order Centroid Technique

One of the weighting techniques that addresses the two weaknesses of the pairwise comparisons approach and is, at the same time, quite simple is the rank order centroid (ROC) technique proposed by Barron and Barrett (1996). ROC is motivated by the fact that it is often easier for human experts to rank order criteria than directly assign weights between 0 and 1, which then sum up to 1. Moreover, in the case of group decision making, it may be much easier for multiple decision makers to agree on criteria rank order than on direct numerical weights. ROC uses rank order criteria for computing their numerical weights. The ROC procedure consists of the two following steps:

Step 1. Ranking with Swing: In the first step, criteria are rank ordered using a "swing" approach. In this approach, the word "swing" refers to the operation of changing the score of alternative estimation methods on a single criterion from the worst to the best possible value, for example, from 0 % to 100 % fulfillment of the criterion.

Ranking with swing consists of asking decision makers the following type of questions: "Imagine an effort estimation method that performs the worst possible (0 %) on all relevant acceptance criteria. It is the worst possible estimation method. Yet, you are allowed to improve it on exactly one criterion by changing its score from 0 % (worst possible) to 100 % (best possible). Which characteristic would it be?" The selected criterion is then the highest one in ranking. Next, the decision maker is asked, "Next, imagine that you have the same worst possible estimation method and that you are allowed to improve (from 0 % to 100 %) any of its characteristics except the one(s) you already selected in the previous question(s). Which characteristic would it be?" The next selected characteristic (criterion) is then the next highest in the ranking. These questions are asked until all criteria considered are fully ranked.

Step 2. Compute Numerical Weights: In this step, ordinal ranks on criteria are translated into numerical weights. For a total number of n criteria considered (in ranking), the weight on the *k*th criterion is computed according to the following formula 7.3):

$$w_k = \sum_{i=k}^{n} \frac{1}{i}$$ (7.3)

where
- w_k represents the numerical weight on the kth highest criterion in ranking.
   If $w_1 \geq w_2 \geq \ldots \geq w_k$, then
$$w_1 = (1 + 1/2 + 1/3 + \ldots + 1/n)/n$$
$$w_2 = (0 + 1/2 + 1/3 + \ldots + 1/n)/n$$
$$w_3 = (0 + 0 + 1/3 + \ldots + 1/n)/n$$
$$\ldots$$
$$w_k = (0 + 0 + 0 + \ldots + 1/n)/n$$

In the case of *partial order* (*tied ranks* on criteria), a simple approach is to compute weights for the complete order and then distribute the weights equally for each tied rank. In other words, we sum the weights across the tied ranks, divide it by the number of tied ranks, and assign the resulting average weight equally to each rank.

Weighting Decision Criteria Using Simple Point Scores

Alternatively to ROC, the relative importance of decision criteria may be determined by assigning them simple point scores. This approach can be used when decision makers prefer scoring criteria importance with points rather than rank ordering them. The score-based weighting approach consists of the following two steps:

Step 1. Assigning Point Scores: In the first step, the decision maker assigns point scores to the criteria. In principle, any number of points can be assigned to criteria as long as the ratios between scores associated with different criteria reflect their relative importance. A decision maker may, for example, begin with the least important criterion and assign a small baseline score, say 10 points. Next, the decision maker continues scoring for more important factors and assigns them appropriate multiplications of the baseline score, depending on their relative importance to already scored criteria. Vice versa, the decision maker may begin with the most important criterion and assign it a large baseline score, say 1,000 points. Then, the decision maker continues scoring less important criteria and assigns them a portion of the points assigned to the more important criteria, starting from the most important criterion.

For example, a decision maker selects criterion C1 as most important for accepting or rejecting an estimation method and assigns it 100 points. Next, he considers criterion C2 and assigns it 30 points, which would mean that C1 is about three times as important as C2. Then, the decision maker considers criterion C3 and assesses its importance compared to C2 for 10 points, which would mean that C3 is three times less important than C2 and ten times less important than C1.

Step 2. Eliciting Weights: In the second step, point scores assigned to criteria are converted into numerical weights such that each weight is between 0 and 1 and that all weights on adjacent criteria sum up to 1.

Point scores assigned to n adjacent criteria g_i ($i = 1, \ldots, n$) can easily be converted into numerical weights w_i that meet the aforementioned two conditions. First, we sort n criteria with respect to their point scores such that g1 refers to the criterion with the highest and g_n to the criterion with the lowest score. The weights w_1 to w_n for the criteria g_1 to g_n are computed by solving the following set of equations:

$$w_1 + w_2 + \ldots + w_n = 1$$
$$w_2 = w_1 \times [\text{score } (g_2)/\text{score } (g_1)]$$
$$w_3 = w_1 \times [\text{score } (g_3)/\text{score } (g_1)]$$
$$\ldots$$
$$w_n = w_1 \times [\text{score } (g_n)/\text{score } (g_1)]$$

7.3.3   Overview of the Selection Procedure

In this section, we propose a systematic procedure for assessing alternative effort estimation methods with respect to their suitability for a particular estimation context. Though the procedure uses well-defined assessment criteria and techniques, it is still based on the judgment of human experts. Therefore, in order to ensure reliable assessments, involved experts (at best multiple) should have no personal preference regarding any estimation method and also have knowledge of the context in which the method is intended to be used. Figure 7.3 presents the assessment procedure, followed by a brief explanation of each step. Section 7.4 illustrates the procedure through an example application.

Specify Context and Goals of Effort Estimation

In the first step, we characterize the context and goals for which we are selecting an effort estimation method.

Context of effort estimation refers mainly to those aspects of the estimation environment that may boost or constrain applicability of considered candidate effort estimation methods. Context aspects typically determine feasibility of an estimation method and thus define necessary conditions for accepting or rejecting the method. We consider estimation context to filter out candidate methods that are definitely not applicable (feasible) in a specific estimation context. Example context constraints on the feasibility of an estimation method are the availability of human experts who need to be involved in the effort estimation and the availability of project measurement data required as input to the effort estimation method. If expert or data availability does not fulfill minimal requirements of an estimation method, then the method is not feasible in this context.

Goals of effort estimation refer to the objectives, the achievement of which the effort estimation should support. Estimation goals typically determine the usefulness of an estimation method and thus define sufficient conditions for accepting or rejecting the method. We consider the estimation goals for assessing the usefulness of the feasible estimation methods (that is, the methods which already fulfilled necessary acceptance conditions).

Prioritize Goals of Effort Estimation

In the next step, we prioritize goals of effort estimation according to their relative importance to intended users of the estimation method and of its outcomes. We will be referring to them as *decision makers*. Prioritizing estimation goals allows for

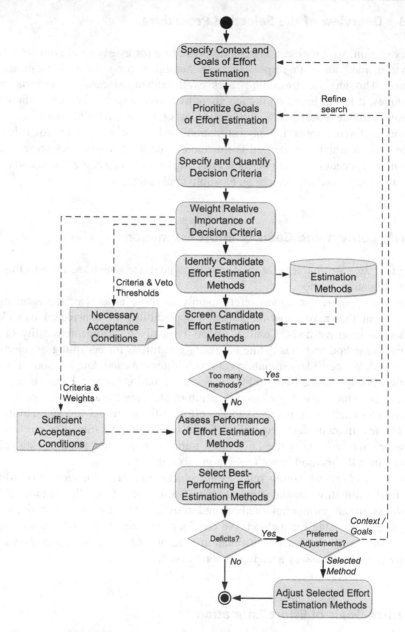

Fig. 7.3 Basic steps of selecting suitable effort estimation method

focusing assessment procedures on the effort estimation methods that best address the most important estimation goals. We propose using one of the two simple prioritization approaches:

- *Ranking*: We rank order estimation goals from most to least relevant.
- *Scoring*: We assign numerical scores to estimation goals, whereby the ratio between scores assigned to two goals reflects their relative importance. For example, if one goal is assigned 100 points and another 50 points, then it would mean that achieving the first goal is twice as important to the decision maker as achieving the second goal.

In the example assessment procedure (Sect. 7.4), we systematically utilize goal priorities for deriving quantitative weights on the decision criteria we then use for assessing the suitability of candidate effort estimation methods. This way, we relieve the decision maker from assigning importance weights to each decision criterion individually, which typically costs significant overhead.

Specify and Quantify Decision Criteria

Systematically assessing suitability of an effort estimation method requires explicitly specifying quantitative suitability criteria (decision criteria). These criteria should refer to the most relevant cost and benefits of using an effort estimation method. From the cost perspective, suitability criteria would refer to what the method requires to be applied (e.g., what kind of inputs it needs). From the benefit perspective, decision criteria would refer to what the method provides in its output, in particular in light of fulfilling the estimation goals.

Decision criteria can be further refined into more detailed subcriteria and organized into a hierarchical structure of decision criteria. Figure 7.4 illustrates an example hierarchy of decision criteria we use in the example method selection in Sect. 7.4.

For a hierarchy of decision criteria, the assessment procedure follows a bottom-up manner. It starts with assessing candidate estimation methods on the criteria located in the leaf nodes of the hierarchy and continues by aggregating these assessments in the higher-level nodes up to the root node, which represents the overall assessment of a method's suitability.

For each decision criterion, we must define how to measure it and what are the preferences of decision makers regarding its measurement values (i.e., values preferred or not).

Defining metric: In order to make a decision criterion measurable, we define an appropriate metric for the aspect to which the estimation method criterion refers. For this purpose, we may use the *Goal-Question-Metric* (*GQM*) approach (Basili and Weiss 1984; Basili et al. 1994b).

Defining preference: In order to define a decision maker's preferences on a criterion, we propose using the idea of utility function defined in the context of multicriteria decision analysis (MCDA), introduced in Sect. 7.3.2. For each decision criterion, we map its measurement values onto the utility values. This mapping is called a utility function and returns real-number utility values that range between 0 and 1 (or 0–100 %). Utility function quantifies the preferences of a decision maker

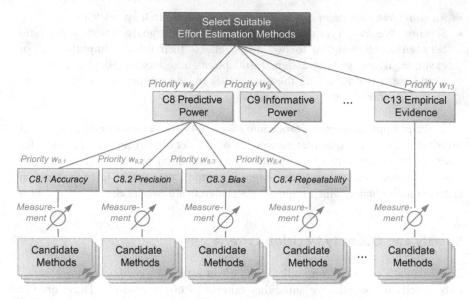

Fig. 7.4 Example decision model for selecting a suitable estimation method

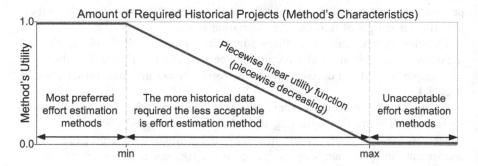

Fig. 7.5 Example utility function for selecting suitable effort estimation method

regarding the measurement values of a criterion, where higher utility means higher preference. In principle, a utility function may have any form. Figure 7.5 illustrates an example utility function defined upon the criterion "The amount of historical measurement data required by an effort estimation method." The utility is represented by a piecewise linear function defined upon two thresholds. The "Min" threshold corresponds to the number of historical projects up to which an estimation method is highly preferable (utility = 1), say because we already have this amount of data available. The "Max" threshold corresponds to the amount of historical projects beyond which an estimation method is definitely unacceptable (utility = 0), for example, because there is no way we can provide such a number of historical project data. Between "Min" and "Max," the utility decreases (say linearly for the sake of simplicity), meaning that the utility of methods that require more historical data than "Min" decreases, for example, because the amount of data is not available but can be collected postmortem, yet at the expense of significant extra overhead.

If we consider the criterion "Type of data required by estimation method," then utility might be represented by a simple dichotomous function according to which utility equals zero if the data of the required type are not available or utility equals one otherwise.

Method's Characteristic vs. Decision Criterion

In the MCDA area, existence of preference information is the element that distinguishes a simple characteristic of an object (in our case, an effort estimation method) from a decision criterion. Let us consider "predictive power" characteristics of an effort estimation method. It can be measured in many different ways, for example, by mean of percentage deviation between estimated and actual value of effort. As such, predictive power is free from preference. Intuitively, we would say that the lower the estimation error, the more preferred is the estimation method. Yet, the exact mapping between values of an estimation error and preference level may differ across various estimation contexts. Defining a decision criterion upon "predictive power" characteristics requires defining the preference relation.

Weight Relative Importance of Decision Criteria

In practice, not all decision criteria are equally important. Depending on estimation goals and capabilities, decision makers typically prefer an estimation method to fulfill some criteria more than others. In this step, we weight relative importance of decision criteria we defined for assessing suitability of alternative effort estimation methods. For this purpose, we propose an MCDA weighting approach as presented in Sect. 7.3.2.

During criteria weighting, we consider priorities of estimation goals, in that we grant higher importance to those criteria that contribute more to the achievement of higher-priority estimation goals. While weighting decision criteria, we may consider goal priorities informally or use them within a systematic weighting procedure. In Sect. 7.4.4, we present an example approach for systematically deriving criteria weights from quantitative priorities assigned to goals of effort estimation. The procedure we propose makes use of our domain experience and can be adapted to a specific effort estimation context at relatively little expense.

Identify Candidate Effort Estimation Methods

In this step, we identify candidate effort estimation methods, which we will investigate with respect to their suitability to a particular estimation context and goals. We should ensure that the selected candidate methods do actually include the most suitable method (although we do not know yet which one is it). Therefore, the set of candidate methods should be relatively broad, yet not with respect to the number of methods but with respect to the estimation paradigms they represent. We recommend looking through the related literature, in particular recent publications from the software project management and effort estimation area, which present overviews of most common estimation approaches. The methods of overview and classification we present in Chap. 6 and more detailed description of most common estimation methods in Chaps. 8–15 may be of help.

Screen Candidate Effort Estimation Methods

We propose dividing the actual assessment of candidate effort estimation methods into two stages. In the first stage, we look for and exclude methods that are not feasible in the considered estimation context because they do not fulfill its basic constraints (necessary acceptance conditions). We then assess suitability of the remaining candidate methods. The underlying rationale is that even the potentially most beneficial method is worth nothing if it is not applicable. The two-stage approach saves effort spent on assessing methods that are not feasible.

In order to screen candidate effort estimation methods, we first define the necessary acceptance conditions upon the set of identified decision criteria. We focus on those decision criteria that may alone decide rejection of candidate estimation methods (as inapplicable) independently of how well the method performs on other criteria. Necessary conditions can be defined by setting up a *veto threshold* on the criteria values or by defining an *unacceptable situation*. For example, let us consider decision criterion "*C2. Required data.*" An example veto threshold can be set on the amount of historical project data required by an estimation method. If a candidate method requires more data than defined by the veto threshold, then it should be excluded from further consideration as simply not feasible. Another example unacceptable situation might be the candidate method's requirements for particular metrics on its input (e.g., software size in function points). If this specific measurement data cannot be collected in the considered estimation context, then the method cannot be used.

Assess Performance of Effort Estimation Methods

The candidate estimation methods that remain after this screening step are then assessed against sufficient acceptance conditions defined on the identified decision criteria. For this purpose, we compute each candidate method's total utility as a weighted product of its utilities on individual decision criteria. We presented the utility computation procedure in Sect. 7.3.2. For each decision criterion, we first characterize the candidate effort estimation method on this criterion. Next, we assess the method utility on this criterion using the utility function we defined in the "Specify and quantify decision criteria" step. Finally, we aggregate utilities on all decision criteria as a weighted product using the numerical weights assigned to decision criteria in the "Prioritize decision criteria" step. The total utility of each candidate effort estimation method will then serve as a basis for selecting the most suitable method.

Select Best-Performing Effort Estimation Methods

We use utilities of candidate effort estimation methods for selecting the most suitable methods. The higher the utility of a method, the more suitable it is, meaning, the more useful it is from the perspective of estimation needs and capabilities defined in the form of decision criteria. Based on the methods' utility, we make a decision on which one to select as the most suitable. Let us consider several situations:

1. One method clearly outperforms other candidates and reaches a satisfactory utility level. In this case, the decision is easy. We select the method with the highest utility. Still, we may decide to consider using one of the next best methods—if they performed well enough—in combination with the best one in order to increase reliability of estimates (see Sect. 5.5 for the discussion on using multiple alternative estimation methods).
2. None of the candidate methods achieves satisfactory utility. In such cases, we need to either adjust our requirements with respect to effort estimation and/or adjust one of the candidate estimation methods with the highest utility.
   - *Adjust estimation requirements*: We decrease our goals with respect to effort estimation and/or increase our estimation capabilities. For example, we might need to reconcile the higher cost of estimating and allow for higher involve-ment of human experts. On the one hand, we should look at the context characteristics and estimation goals that we can adjust at low cost. We can review context and goal adjustment on a particular method. For example, a certain method actually performs satisfactorily on a majority of criteria but fails on "expert involvement" because we did not want to involve our experts in estimation and therefore assessed the method poorly on this criterion. In this case, one way to get a useful estimation method would be to accept (at least temporarily) the higher cost of estimation and reconcile the higher involvement of experts in estimation.
   - *Adjust estimation method*: In this case, we could adjust one of the best-performing estimation methods in order to bring it onto a satisfactory utility level. Yet, it does not have to be the method with the highest utility. We should look for the method with the lowest cost and the highest gain regarding necessary adjustments. For example, if the cost-benefit ratio of adjusting the

highest-utility estimation method regarding one decision criterion is worse than adjusting another method on two criteria, then we would adjust the latter method.

3. Several candidate effort estimation methods have the same (and acceptable) utility. In such cases, we can consider the following options:

   - *Consider utility profile*: We can look at the utilities of the top-performing methods obtained on individual decision criteria. We can then decide on the method that performs best on the most important criteria.
   - *Select multiple methods*: We can select multiple methods that represent different estimation approaches (e.g., data-driven and expert-based) and use them in tandem in order to get more credible estimates. In Sect. 5.5, we discuss the estimation strategy based on a combination of multiple estimation methods.
   - *Adjust estimation method*: We can select one of the highest-utility methods, which can easily be adjusted and outperform other candidate methods. In order to decide on which method to adjust, we should look at the method utilities on individual decision criteria and at the potential cost-benefit ratio of adjusting it. The selected method should show the lowest cost and the highest gain from adjustment.

Adjust Selected Effort Estimation Methods

Optionally, we may adjust the effort estimation method we selected in the previous step. It may, for instance, happen that the selected method does not meet our needs and capabilities, although it is the best one out of the candidate methods we considered. In that case, we would probably consider adjusting the method. If, however, the selected method fully meets our acceptance criteria, then there is probably no need to invest in adjusting the method. In the previous step, we discuss a few other situations that may require adjusting a candidate effort estimation method.

Before we decide on adjusting particular effort estimation methods, we need to consider potential constraints. First of all, the method must allow adjustments, that is, it must be sufficiently transparent and flexible. Moreover, we need to have appropriate expertise to correctly adjust the method. Messing up an estimation method may have much more severe consequences than using it "as is" even though it is not perfect.

7.4   Example Selection Procedure

In this section, we describe an example instantiation of the procedure for selecting the most suitable effort estimation method we sketched in the previous section. The exact parameters we use within the procedure are based on effort estimation experiences we and other software practitioners gained in software development contexts. Instead of considering a specific estimation context, we consider an estimation situation by considering estimation goals and constraints which we found most common in software industrial organizations.

7.4.1 Specify Context and Goals of Effort Estimation

The objective of this step is to identify relevant aspects of the effort estimation context and the most important goals of effort estimation.

Context of Estimation

Regarding estimation context, we consider three aspects of the estimation environment that may boost or constrain applicability of an effort estimation method. Industrial experiences show that key context characteristics to consider when selecting suitable effort estimation methods include

- *Availability of domain experts*: The number of experts who need to be involved in the effort estimation and the required expertise they need to have in the environment in which effort estimation is performed.
- *Availability of project measurement data*: The amount of required project data (number of historical projects), the quality of data (completeness, consistency, and reliability), the particular metrics that are required (software size, project effort, effort factors), and the original environment of the data (embedded vs. information systems, new software development vs. software enhancement).
- *Cost of effort estimation*: The organizational overhead needed for using an effort estimation method. Although closely related to the previous two constraints, the cost of effort estimation is most often an explicitly expressed constraint in industrial contexts. Moreover, as we will see below, the cost aspect is also expressed in the form of an estimation goal.

Goals of Estimation

Regarding goals of effort estimation, we consider common industrial goals (Sect. 2.4 presents a detailed discussion):

- *G1. Managing and reducing project risks*: An effort estimation method is expected to support project risk management. On the one hand, it should support explicit consideration of known project risks when estimating project effort. On the other hand, it should also provide insight into effort-related project risks and the means to manage them.
- *G2. Process improvement and organizational learning*: An effort estimation method is expected to support identification of weak points in the development processes. Improving these weaknesses would lead to improved process

performance, for example, in terms of increased development productivity and reduced project effort.

- **G3.** *Baselining and benchmarking productivity*: An effort estimation method is expected to support reliable benchmarking of software development productivity. For this purpose, the method should allow determining productivity baselines and provide insight into the factors that make baseline productivity differ across individual development projects.
- **G4.** *Negotiating project resources and scope*: An effort estimation method is expected to support justifying and negotiating project scope and resources. For this purpose, estimation is supposed to explicitly provide information that may be used as argumentation for rationalizing a project to project sponsors and customers.
- **G5.** *Managing project changes*: An effort estimation method is expected to support changes to project context and scope. In other words, it is supposed to facilitate project agility in that it can adjust and quickly provide revised estimates after changes to the project.
- **G6.** *Reducing management overhead*: An effort estimation method is expected to reduce overhead for managing software projects. In particular, it is supposed to be cost-effective and to provide information that improves efficiency of the related project management and decision-making activities such as planning, bidding, and controlling projects.

7.4.2 Prioritize Goals of Effort Estimation

In practice, no single effort estimation method would equally well support achieving multiple estimation goals. Therefore, in order to select the most suitable effort estimation method, we need to allow trade-offs between attained estimation goals. Fortunately, in industrial contexts, estimation goals are typically not equally important and can be prioritized. We propose prioritizing relative relevancy of estimation goals by assigning them numerical weights. For this purpose, we used results of a literature review and a small industrial survey in which we looked for the estimation goals considered by software practitioners (Trendowicz 2008, Chap. 2). We assigned to each goal a score based on the number of publications in the literature review and votes of respondents in the industrial survey that referred to this goal. Finally, we transformed scores into numerical weights using the "Simple Point Scores" approach we presented in Sect. 7.3.2.

7.4.3 Specify and Quantify Decision Criteria

In order to decide on a suitable effort estimation method, we need to consider alternative methods with respect to multiple criteria. In Sect. 7.2, we specified a set of such decision criteria based upon our industrial experiences with respect to the most important determinants of practical feasibility and usefulness of an effort estimation method.

For the purpose of selecting a suitable effort estimation method, we propose using a multicriteria decision support approach. In this approach, each alternative effort estimation method is assessed on each decision criterion. For each method, assessments on individual decision criteria are then aggregated into an overall assessment. The method that gains the highest assessment is then considered as the most suitable one among the considered alternatives.

In order to ensure reliable and consistent evaluations, we must quantify decision criteria by assigning them valid measurement scales. We propose quantifying each decision criterion using a simple 0–100 % scale. We assign 100 % to an effort estimation method on a given decision criterion if it completely fulfills the desired value of the criterion and 0 % if the method does not fulfill the criterion at all. In order to ensure consistent evaluations, we need to define when a particular percentage amount is assigned. For example, let us consider the "Informative power" criterion. We would assign a 100 % score to an effort estimation method on this criterion if, in addition to simple effort estimates, the method provides information in a transparent and understandable form. On the other hand, we would assign 0 % if the method represented a black-box approach that does not provide any information besides a simple effort number.

Table 7.1 provides example quantification of the method selection criteria we defined in Sect. 7.2. For the sake of simplicity, we specify the evaluation scale on each criterion by defining only the two extreme ends, 0 % and 100 %. In practice, equal intervals between these two extremes—for example, every 20 %—might additionally be defined in order to ensure consistent measurements on the intermediate levels.

7.4.4 Prioritize Decision Criteria

Depending on the estimation situation, different decision criteria may be of different importance and thus should be prioritized. Importance of a decision criterion depends firstly on the goals and context of effort estimation. For example, in the context of limited availability of measurement data, the decision criteria "C2. Required data" and "C1. Expert involvement" would be of high importance in order to discard methods that require much data and prefer methods that use experts' judgment instead of quantitative inputs.

Tip

▶ List and prioritize potential criteria before evaluating candidate estimation methods and selecting the most suitable one. Note that preference regarding various evaluation criteria may differ depending on goals and context of effort estimation.

Readers who feel confident in directly assessing the relative importance of decision criteria may do it using the rank-order technique, for example, presented

Table 7.1 Example: Quantification of decision criteria

Criterion	Rating scale
C1. Expert involvement	*Best (100 %):* The method requires involving one expert whose only responsibility is to run the method and to interpret its outputs *Worst (0 %):* The method requires extensive involvement of numerous experts with extensive skills and experiences
C1.1. Number of experiences	*Best (100 %):* The method requires involving at most one expert *Worst (0 %):* The method requires involving numerous experts, for example, more than three
C1.2. Intensity of involvement	*Best (100 %):* The method requires minimal effort from the involved expert(s). Involvement reduces to solely running the method and interpreting its outcomes *Worst (0 %):* The estimation method is a human-intensive process that requires excessive involvement of human experts throughout all estimation steps. Involved experts need to provide inputs for estimation, analyze these inputs, and come up with estimates "manually"
C1.3. Level of expertise	*Best (100 %):* The method does not require involved human expert to possess particular skills or expertise in any specific area. The method is easy to run and provides very intuitive outputs *Worst (0 %):* The method requires extensive expertise in several areas. For instance, both software domain and effort estimation expertise are required—including knowledge of the theories that underlie the method. The reliability of the estimation output depends to a large extent on the skills of involved human experts
C2. Required data	*Best (100 %):* The method does not require any measurement data or very few data (very few measures) and does not impose any requirements on its type and distribution. Moreover, the method is robust against typical data quality problems such as missing data *Worst (0 %):* The method requires a large amount of data. The method requires a specific type of data and makes a number of assumptions regarding data distribution
C2.1. Data quantity	*Best (100 %):* The method does not require any or requires few quantitative data on its input, e.g., less than 10 data points for 2 or less effort drivers. For example, a data-driven method may require size and effort data measured for 10 historical projects *Worst (0 %):* The method requires a large amount of quantitative project data, for example, data on more than 25 factors and from more than 50 projects need to be provided
C2.2. Data type	*Best (100 %):* The estimation method does not require any specific type of data and can handle measurements on different scales at the same time, that is, the method can handle mixed-scale data *Worst (0 %):* The estimation method requires input data to be consistently measured on a particular scale
C2.3. Data distribution	*Best (100 %):* The estimation method does not require any particular distribution of the input data *Worst (0 %):* The estimation method requires a certain distribution of the input data. For example, some data-driven methods require quantitative project data to be normally distributed

(continued)

Table 7.1 (continued)

Criterion	Rating scale
C3. Robustness	*Best (100 %):* The method handles—to a large extent –low-quality data. In other words, it can handle different imperfections of quantitative data such as incomplete, redundant, inconsistent, or collinear measurements. In consequence, it does not require much overhead to prepare data prior to estimation *Worst (0 %):* The estimation method requires high-quality data. In particular, it requires complete, consistent, and nonredundant data. Significant data preparation overhead—using independent data processing techniques—is required to prepare the data prior to estimation
C3.1. Incompleteness	*Best (100 %):* The estimation method handles largely incomplete inputs. In practice, it should handle up to 25 % of missing data without simply ignoring the complete historical projects or complete effort drivers on which at least one measurement is missing; such a simple approach is known to lead to loss of much information *Worst (0 %):* The estimation method requires complete inputs
C3.2. Redundancy	*Best (100 %):* The estimation method handles redundant and dependent data, that is, situations in which different measurements convey the same information. For example, the method contains internal mechanisms to exclude the impact of redundant inputs on the quality of the estimation outputs *Worst (0 %):* The estimation method does not identify redundant and dependent inputs. For example, running regression-based estimation on collinear data may lead to invalid estimates
C3.3. Inconsistency	*Best (100 %):* The estimation method handles inconsistent data, for example, through internal mechanisms that minimize the impact of inconsistent inputs on the quality of the estimation outputs *Worst (0 %):* The estimation method is very sensitive to inconsistent inputs. Running estimation on inconsistent inputs may lead to invalid estimates
C3.4. Nonlinearity	*Best (100 %):* The method handles multiple nonlinear effects in the input information, for example, nonlinear impact of particular effort drivers on effort *Worst (0 %):* The method can only deal with simple linear effects between effort drivers and effort
C4. Flexibility	*Best (100 %):* The method does not impose any specific estimation model. For example, in the case of model-based estimation methods, it would refer to so-called define-your-own-model approaches *Worst (0 %):* The method provides a fixed estimation model. In the case of model-based estimation methods, it would refer to the so-called fixed-model approach
C5. Complexity	*Best (100 %):* The method is simple and intuitive and requires basic skills that do not go beyond standard curricula of software science and software engineering *Worst (0 %):* The method is very complex and requires advanced knowledge that, for example, goes far beyond typical academic courses
C5.1. Employed techniques	*Best (100 %):* The method employs a limited amount of simple and easy-to-understand techniques *Worst (0 %):* The method employs numerous sophisticated and interrelated techniques

(continued)

Table 7.1 (continued)

Criterion	Rating scale
C5.2. *Underlying theory*	*Best (100 %):* The theoretical foundations of the method are simple and do not go beyond basic academic courses, such as basic mathematics *Worst (0 %):* The method is based on multiple theories and requires advanced knowledge in order to be properly applied
C5.3. *Parameterization*	*Best (100 %):* The method does not require setting up any parameters. In other words, it does not specify any parameters or provide ready-to-use parameter setups, or contain an embedded mechanism for automatically learning the parameters *Worst (0 %):* The method includes a number of parameters that are difficult to understand and set up. Usually the only way to find out a reasonable setup of parameters is to perform multiple experiments in a specific context where the method is to be applied later
C6. Support level	*Best (100 %):* The method is well supported by accompanying documentation and tools *Worst (0 %):* There is hardly any support—neither in documentation nor in tools—provided for the method
C6.1. *Documentation level*	*Best (100 %):* There is sound, complete, and easy-to-understand documentation for the method. Documentation includes practical examples and guidelines that support applying the method in practical situations *Worst (0 %):* There is either hardly any documentation available for the method or existing documentation is sparse, incomplete, and/or difficult to understand
C6.2. *Tool support*	*Best (100 %):* There is fully automated support for the method, in the form of a high-quality software tool. The tool is easily available at a reasonable cost and supports all possible method application scenarios. It provides a user-friendly interface and supports the estimator in potential decisions, such as setting the method's parameters. Finally, the tool provides a robust reporting facility and output interpretation support *Worst (0 %):* There is no automated support for the method
C7. Reusability	*Best (100 %):* The estimation method and its outputs can be easily reused in similar situations and adapted—partially or entirely—in new situations *Worst (0 %):* The estimation outputs are hardly reusable. They are not portable across multiple projects and cannot be easily adapted for new situations. In practice, the estimation method has to be reapplied each time the estimation situation changes
C7.1. *Genericness*	*Best (100 %):* The method and its outputs cover a variety of situations, and thus are portable without any or with minor adjustments across different contexts *Worst (0 %):* The method or its outputs are bound to a narrow context and are hardly portable to dissimilar situations without substantial modifications. For example, the estimation model must be calibrated or rebuilt from scratch

(continued)

Table 7.1   (continued)

Criterion	Rating scale
C7.2. Adaptability	*Best (100 %):* The method and/or its outputs can easily be adapted to different situations, for example, by means of simple calibration of a few parameters *Worst (0 %):* The estimation method cannot be adapted across different contexts at all, that is, without significant loss of reliability. The method needs to be reapplied and its outputs created from scratch each time estimates are needed in different situations
C8. Predictive power	*Best (100 %):* The estimation method provides accurate, precise, and repeatable output *Worst (0 %):* The estimation method provides highly inaccurate, imprecise, and not repeatable output
C8.1. Accuracy	*Best (100 %):* The estimation method provides accurate output. For instance, the estimates are characterized by mean magnitude of relative error MMRE < 0.2 *Worst (0 %):* The estimation method provides highly inaccurate outputs. For instance, the estimates are characterized by mean magnitude of relative error MMRE > 1.0
C8.2. Precision	*Best (100 %):* The estimation method provides precise outputs. In particular, the estimates do not vary across projects in similar context, e.g., by means of the standard deviation statistic *Worst (0 %):* The estimation method provides highly imprecise outputs. In particular, estimates that the method provides across similar situations vary widely
C8.3. Bias	*Best (100 %):* The method provides precise output. For instance, the output estimates should be characterized by Pred(.25) > 0.75 *Worst (0 %):* The method provides highly imprecise output. For instance, the output estimates are characterized by Pred(.25) < 0.25
C8.4. Repeatability	*Best (100 %):* The method provides repeatable output when applied in the same context and with the same input data *Worst (0 %):* The estimation method provides highly nondeterministic output, i.e., the outputs vary widely when the method is applied in the same context and with the same input data
C9. Informative power	*Best (100 %):* The method provides complete and well-understandable information that contributes to full achievement of the organizational objectives *Worst (0 %):* The output of the estimation method is not visible at all (so-called black-box method) or is difficult to interpret and understand (so-called gray-box method)
C9.1. Comprehensiveness	*Best (100 %):* The method provides additional information in a transparent and complete way *Worst (0 %):* The method does not provide any additional information besides the estimates
C9.2. Comprehensibility	*Best (100 %):* The method provides transparent, complete, relevant, and understandable information regarding the interactions between effort factors *Worst (0 %):* The method does not provide any information regarding the interactions between the considered effort factors

(continued)

Table 7.1 (continued)

Criterion	Rating scale
C10. Handling uncertainty	*Best (100 %):* The method accepts uncertain inputs and provides an intuitive mechanism for covering uncertainties (e.g., triangular distribution). The method supports uncertainty evaluation of the estimation output *Worst (0 %):* The estimation method requires exact (point) inputs and provides in its output point estimates without any support for uncertainty evaluation
C10.1. Handling uncertain inputs	*Best (100 %):* The method accepts uncertain inputs and explicitly copes with different types of uncertainty (probabilistic, possibilities, and granulation). Moreover, the method can consider any number of risk factors (effort drivers) of any type *Worst (0 %):* The method accepts only crisp (certain) inputs and considers a fixed set of very few risk factors (effort drivers)
C10.2. Handling uncertain outputs	*Best (100 %):* The method indicates explicitly and quantitatively the uncertainty of effort forecasts. Moreover, it provides a lot of additional information that is useful for managing project risks. For example, it identifies effort drivers that have the greatest impact on project effort *Worst (0 %):* The method provides crisp estimates and does not provide any information useful for analyzing effort-related project risks
C11. Comprehensiveness	*Best (100 %):* The method may be applied to estimate the effort of project activities of any type and at any granularity level *Worst (0 %):* The method's applicability is limited to activities of a certain type (e.g., engineering) and granularity level (e.g., entire project)
C11.1. Versatility	*Best (100 %):* The method is applicable to projects and activities of any type *Worst (0 %):* The method is applicable to only one selected type of project activities
C11.2. Granularity	*Best (100 %):* The method provides outputs on any level of process-/project- and product-granularity *Worst (0 %):* The method provides estimates on a specific level of granularity. For instance, it uses the characteristics of software code as input and provides estimates for the whole project (development life cycle)
C12. Availability	*Best (100 %):* The method can be applied at any stage of the project's life cycle; specifically, it is applicable in early project phases (e.g., proposal phase). It could then be used at any point in time to revise the initial estimates *Worst (0 %):* The method's availability is limited to a specific, later development phase (e.g., early design or coding)
C13. Empirical evidence	Best (100 %): There are numerous published studies on the method's empirical applications in the industrial context Worst (0 %): The estimation method has not yet been applied in an industrial context (not applied at all or applied in an academic or laboratory context)

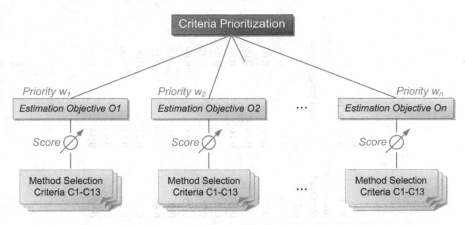

Fig. 7.6 Example: Decision tree for weighting decision selection criteria

in Sect. 7.3.2. For those who would prefer a more intuitive approach, we propose deriving relative importance of decision criteria from priorities on goals of effort estimation as defined in Sect. 7.4.2. For this purpose, we quantify the contribution of each decision criterion (its fulfillment) to the achievement of each estimation goal. Based upon our expertise, we predefine the contribution of each decision criterion to common effort estimation goals. The relevance of an objective and the contribution of a criterion to a certain goal are both quantified on a 0–100 % scale. Notice that relevancies of all considered goals have to sum up to 100 % while criteria contributions do not have to. For example, fulfilling the criterion "*C9. Informative power*" contributes significantly to the achievement of the goal "*G4. Negotiating project resources and scope.*" An effort estimation method that provides a rationale for delivered estimates in a transparent and understandable way would be very useful for justifying and negotiating effort estimates. Vice versa, an estimation method that delivers solely crisp effort would be useless for the purpose of justifying and negotiating project scope as it does not give any rationale for its estimates.

In order to prioritize decision criteria, you must assign relevancy weights (priorities) to the goals of effort estimation and compute corresponding criteria weights. The total priority of each decision criterion is computed as the weighted product of the criterion's contributions to each goal, multiplied by the goal's relative importance weight. Figure 7.6 illustrates this idea.

In Table 7.2, we weight the relative importance of popular effort estimation goals and score contribution of method selection criteria to each of these goals. These numbers are based on our experience and are rather independent of the particular estimation context. You may adapt Table 7.2 to a particular estimation context by preserving the contribution scores, assigning your priority weights to estimation goals, and recomputing the criteria weights accordingly. Appropriate computations can easily be implemented using any spreadsheet calculation software package.

Table 7.2 Example: Computing weights for decision criteria

Estimation goal	G1. Managing and reducing project risks	G2. Process improvement and organizational learning	G3. Baselining and benchmarking productivity	G4. Negotiating project resources and scope	G5. Managing project changes	G6. Reducing management overhead	Criterion's priority: point scores (weighted sum)	Criterion's weight
Goal's importance (weight)	0.19	0.23	0.08	0.19	0.06	0.25	–	–
C01. Expert involvement	0.00	0.00	0.00	0.00	0.25	0.75	0.20	0.05
C02. Required data	0.00	0.00	0.25	0.25	0.25	0.75	0.27	0.07
C03. Robustness	0.50	0.25	0.25	0.25	0.00	0.50	0.34	0.09
C04. Flexibility	0.00	0.00	0.00	0.00	0.50	0.50	0.16	0.04
C05. Complexity	0.00	0.00	0.00	0.00	0.00	0.50	0.13	0.03
C06. Support level	0.50	0.50	0.00	0.25	0.50	0.75	0.47	0.12
C07. Reusability	0.25	0.00	0.75	0.25	0.50	0.75	0.38	0.09
C08. Predictive power	0.50	0.50	0.50	0.25	0.25	0.00	0.31	0.08
C09. Informative power	0.75	0.75	0.00	0.75	0.00	0.00	0.45	0.11
C10. Handling uncertainty	0.75	0.00	0.25	0.00	0.00	0.25	0.22	0.06
C11. Estimation scope	0.25	0.00	0.50	0.50	0.00	0.25	0.24	0.06
C12. Availability	0.75	0.25	0.00	0.50	0.25	0.50	0.43	0.11
C13. Empirical evidence	0.50	0.50	0.50	0.50	0.00	0.00	0.34	0.09

7.4.5 Identify Candidate Effort Estimation Methods

For the purpose of example method selection, we consider several popular effort estimation methods, which represent expert-based, data-driven, and hybrid estimation:

- *Regression*: Data-driven effort estimation based on multivariate statistical regression. We present principles of regression-based estimation in Chap. 8.
- *COCOMO*: The Constructive Cost Model (COCOMO) is probably the most well-known effort estimation method. It implements a data-driven estimation approach based on a fixed effort model. We present principles of the COCOMO II method in Chap. 9.
- *SLIM*: Data-driven estimation approach based on a fixed effort model proposed by Putnam and Myers (1992, 2003).
- *CART*: Classification and Regression Trees (CART) represents a data-driven approach, in which a decision-tree technique originating from the machine learning domain is used to create an effort estimation model (define-our-own-model strategy). We present principles of the CART method in Chap. 10.
- *CBR*: Case-based Reasoning (CBR) represents a model-free estimation approach, in which a machine learning technique is used to search for project analogs from the past and to adapt their actual effort for effort estimation of a new project. We present principles of the CBR method in Chap. 11.
- *CoBRA*: Cost estimation, Benchmarking, and Risk Assessment (CoBRA) method represents a hybrid approach, in which judgment of domain experts and few project measurement data are combined into an effort estimation model. We present principles of the CoBRA method in Chap. 15.
- *BBN*: Hybrid estimation method based on the Bayesian Belief Networks (BBN). We present principles of the BBN method in Chap. 14.
- *Expert*: Effort estimation based on the judgment of a single human expert. In this approach, also referred to as Guesstimation, a human expert estimates effort using her/his expertise and experience. The expert may, but does not have to, be supported by additional information such as historical project data.
- *Delphi*: Group consensus effort estimation method, in which multiple human experts follow a structured estimation procedure in order to come up with an agreement regarding the effort estimate. We present principles of the Wideband Delphi method in Chap. 12.

7.4.6 Screen Candidate Effort Estimation Methods

The example assessment procedure we present here is very generic and does not consider any particular estimation context with its specific capabilities and constraints. In consequence, it is rather difficult to define any concrete necessary acceptance conditions in order to screen candidate estimation methods that are not feasible in this context. Therefore, we skip this step of the assessment procedure and continue the assessment procedure on the complete set of candidate effort estimation methods.

Table 7.3 Example: Utilities for candidate effort estimation methods

Decision criterion	Weight	Estimation method								
		Regression	COCOMO	SLIM	CART	CBR	CoBRA	BBN	Expert	Delphi
C01. Expert involvement	0.05	0.75	1.00	1.00	0.75	0.75	0.50	0.50	0.25	0.10
C02. Required data	0.07	0.10	0.50	0.50	0.25	0.25	0.50	0.50	1.00	1.00
C03. Robustness	0.09	0.10	0.25	0.25	0.50	0.50	0.75	0.50	0.50	0.75
C04. Flexibility	0.04	0.50	0.10	0.10	0.75	0.75	0.75	0.75	0.75	0.75
C05. Complexity	0.03	0.50	0.50	0.25	0.25	0.50	0.50	0.10	0.75	0.75
C06. Support level	0.12	1.00	0.75	0.75	0.50	0.75	0.75	0.50	0.10	0.75
C07. Reusability	0.09	0.10	0.50	0.50	0.50	0.25	0.75	0.75	0.25	0.25
C08. Predictive power	0.08	0.50	0.25	0.50	0.50	0.50	0.50	0.25	0.25	0.25
C09. Informative power	0.11	0.25	0.25	0.25	0.50	0.10	0.75	0.50	0.10	0.10
C10. Handling uncertainty	0.06	0.25	0.25	0.25	0.25	0.10	0.75	0.75	0.25	0.25
C11. Estimation scope	0.06	0.75	0.10	0.25	0.75	0.75	0.75	0.75	0.50	0.50
C12. Availability	0.11	0.75	0.25	0.50	0.75	0.75	0.75	0.75	0.25	0.50
C13. Empirical evidence	0.09	0.75	0.75	0.10	0.50	0.75	0.50	0.25	0.50	0.25
Total utility	–	0.37	0.35	0.35	0.50	0.41	0.63	0.49	0.26	0.36

7.4.7   Assess Performance of Effort Estimation Methods

We assess the suitability of candidate effort estimation methods by computing their utility on the set of 13 decision criteria. For a given method, we first assess its utility on each individual decision criterion using the criteria's quantifications we defined in Table 7.1 (Sect. 7.4.3). Next, we aggregate these elementary utilities by means of weighted product under consideration of the criteria's weights we specified in Sect. 7.4.4. Table 7.3 presents elementary and total utilities for each candidate estimation method.

7.4.8   Select Best-Performing Effort Estimation Methods

Finally, we select as the most suitable those effort estimation methods that performed best based on all decision criteria, that is, methods that obtained the highest value of total utility. In our example, the top-performing effort estimation methods are: CoBRA, BBN, and CART. Recall that we used the most common effort estimation goals and constraints for defining example estimation context. The first two places in the rank suggest that hybrid methods seem to be generally most suitable for estimating software development projects. However, they are not free from weaknesses and thus might need appropriate adjustments before fully supporting estimation goals.

7.4.9   Adjust Selected Effort Estimation Methods

Optionally, we may consider adjusting selected effort estimation methods in order to resolve their remaining deficits and thus make them better at addressing our estimation goals and constraints. For example, all three methods we selected in the previous step suffer from relatively high complexity. Simplifying any of these methods would require expertise in the method and effort estimation techniques in general and thus may not be feasible for typical users of effort estimation methods. The CART method suffers additionally from little support for handling estimation uncertainty. It can be relatively simply improved on this aspect by, for example, applying CART on data intervals or distributions instead of crisp data.

Further Reading

- B.A. Kitchenham, L.M. Pickard, S.G. MacDonell, and M.J. Shepperd (2001), "What accuracy statistics really measure," *IEE Proceedings Software*, vol. 148, no. 3, pp. 81–85.

    This article investigates two common aggregated measures of estimation performance: the mean magnitude relative estimation error (MMRE) and the number of estimates within 25 % of the actuals (Pred.25). Authors analyze what exact aspect of estimation these metrics quantify and their relationships to the elementary metric z of estimation uncertainty, computed as $z = estimate/actual$. Based on these example measures of accuracy, the authors discuss the benefits of using elementary and aggregated metrics.

- T. Foss, E. Stensrud, B. Kitchenham, and I. Myrtveit (2003), "A Simulation Study of the Model Evaluation Criterion MMRE," *IEEE Transactions on Software Engineering*, vol. 29, no. 11, pp. 985–995.

  The article investigates the mean magnitude of estimation error (MMRE) which is the most widely used measure of estimation uncertainty. Authors perform a simulation study in order to investigate the limitations of MMRE. As a result, they cast some doubts on the reliability of assessing performance of effort estimation methods using the MMRE metric. Finally, the authors propose alternative measures of estimation error.

- J. S. Armstrong (2001), *Principles of forecasting: A handbook for researchers and practitioners*. Kluwer Academic Publishers, Dordrecht, The Netherlands.

  In Chap. 12, the book considers common ways of selecting appropriate forecasting methods and discusses their threats and opportunities. Moreover, best-practice guidelines for selecting forecasting methods in specific contexts are formulated. The author summarizes recommendations in the form of a tree graph for selecting an appropriate forecasting method depending on several characteristics of the estimation context.

- J. R. Figueira, S. Greco, and M. Ehrgott (2005), *Multiple Criteria Decision Analysis: State of the Art Surveys*. vol. 78. Springer Verlag.

  The book presents the state of the art in multicriteria decision analysis (MCDA). It motivates MCDA and introduces its basic concepts. Furthermore, it provides an overview of the basic MCDA approaches, including multiattribute utility theory employed in this book for assessing the suitability of effort estimation methods for specific estimation contexts. Finally, the book presents in detail the most popular MCDA methods.

- K. P. Yoon and Ch.-L. Hwang (1995), *Multiple Attribute Decision Making. An Introduction. Quantitative Applications in the Social Sciences*, vol. 104, Sage Publications, Thousand Oaks, California, USA.

  The book provides an easy-to-understand introduction to multicriteria decision analysis (MCDA). They introduce the basic concepts of MCDA, such as weighting relative importance of decision criteria. Moreover, they overview the basic types of MCDA approaches and illustrate them by discussing concrete MCDA methods that represent each approach.

Part III

Popular Effort Estimation Methods

Methods and means cannot be separated from the ultimate aim.

—Emma Goldman

In this part, we present in some more detail the most common effort estimation methods. For each method, we discuss its basic principles, usage scenarios, as well as strengths and weaknesses of the method concerning the set of criteria we specified in Sect. 7.2. The strengths and weaknesses are based on the related literature and the authors' practical experiences.

Chapter 8 presents effort estimation based on *statistical regression*, which represents a data-driven, model-based, define-your-own-model estimation approach.

Chapter 9 presents the *Constructive Cost Model* (*COCOMO*) method, which represents a data driven, model-based, fixed-model estimation approach.

Chapter 10 presents the *Classification and Regression Trees* (*CART*) method, which represents a data driven, model-based, define-your-own-model, estimation method.

Chapter 11 presents the *Case-Based Reasoning* (*CBR*) method, which represents a data-driven, memory-based estimation method.

Chapter 12 presents the *Wideband Delphi* method, which represents an expert-based estimation approach based on group consensus.

Chapter 13 presents the *Planning Poker* method, which represents an expert-based estimation approach based on group consensus.

Chapter 14 presents Bayesian Belief Networks (BBN), which represents a hybrid estimation approach.

Chapter 15 presents Cost Estimation, Benchmarking, and Risk Assessment (CoBRA) method, which represents a hybrid effort estimation approach.

Statistical Regression Analysis

8

A judicious man uses statistics, not to get knowledge, but to save himself from having ignorance foisted upon him.

—Thomas Carlyle

In this chapter, we briefly introduce effort estimation based on statistical regression analysis. Regression analysis represents a data-driven, model-based, parametric estimation method that implements the define-your-own-model approach. In other words, in this approach an effort estimation model is created "from scratch" using quantitative project data.

When presenting the approach, we focus on those aspects of statistical regression that are important from the perspective of its application for the purpose of software project effort estimation. Regression analysis has a long history in statistics, and there are a plethora of publications presenting the method. At the end of this chapter, in the Further Reading section, we point out just a few example publications you may read in order to better understand and master regression analysis.

8.1 Principles

Regression analysis is a statistical method for investigating relationships between a dependent variable and one or more independent variables based upon the analysis of data collected for these variables.

In the context of effort estimation, the dependent variable is effort and independent variables are effort factors[1]; that is, the characteristics of the software project environment having an impact on the effort. Example effort factors include software size and complexity, capabilities of the development team, or requirement volatility. The dependent variable is also commonly referred to as a response or

---

[1] Chapter 3 provides an overview of the most common effort factors used in the context of software effort estimation.

A. Trendowicz and R. Jeffery, *Software Project Effort Estimation*,
DOI 10.1007/978-3-319-03629-8_8, © Springer International Publishing Switzerland 2014

endogenous variable, whereas independent variables are also referred to as explanatory or exogenous variables.

8.1.1 Basic Regression Model

In general, a regression model has a form of an equation, as presented below:

$$Y = \alpha + \beta \times X + \varepsilon \tag{8.1}$$

The Y stands for the dependent variable and the X represents the independent variable. The coefficient β is called the regression coefficient, while α is the intercept or constant. Finally, the term ε is a random variable with mean zero that represents the error reflecting random effects caused by unobserved factors and not explained by the explanatory variable considered in the regression model. The term ε is also commonly referred to as a "noise" term and is assumed to follow a normal distribution with mean 0 and variance σ^2. The actual values of Y (the observed project effort) are assumed to be the sum of the mean value $\mu(Y)$ and the error term ε.

Graphically, if we ignore the error term ε, the regression model represents a line with an "intercept" of α on the vertical axis and a "slope" of β. Figure 8.1 illustrates an example of a true regression line. The figure shows bell-shaped curves representing normal distributions of the dependent variable Y for two values x_1 and x_2 of the independent variable X and corresponding error terms ε. Such a true regression line is not known in practice and is approximated by estimating regression coefficients upon a sample of observational data using one of many existing regression analysis techniques. In Sect. 8.2.1, we discuss one of the simple techniques for estimating regression parameters called ordinary least-squares (OLS).

8.1.2 Univariate vs. Multivariate Regression

With respect to the number of explanatory variables that are considered in regression analysis, we distinguish between univariate and multivariate regression. *Univariate regression* considers the relationship that exists between just one response variable and one or more explanatory variables. Regression with one independent variable is referred to as *simple regression*, whereas regression with multiple independent variables is referred to as *multiple regression*. *Multivariate regression*, by extension, is an analysis of the relationship between more than one response variable and one or more explanatory variables.

In general, in a multivariate multiple regression, Y represents an $[n \times p]$ matrix containing p dependent variables, X represents an $[n \times q]$ matrix containing q independent variables, β represents a $[q \times p]$ matrix containing regression coefficients, and ε represents an $[n \times p]$ matrix containing noise terms. Table 8.1

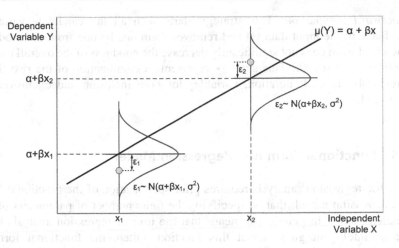

Fig. 8.1 Example regression model

Table 8.1 Types of regression with respect to the number of variables

Type of regression	Dependent variables Y	Independent variables X	Regression coefficients β	Error terms ε
Simple univariate	$[1 \times 1]$	$[1 \times 1]$	$[1 \times 1]$	$[1 \times 1]$
Multiple univariate	$[n \times 1]$	$[n \times q]$	$[q \times 1]$	$[n \times 1]$
Multiple multivariate	$[n \times p]$	$[n \times q]$	$[q \times p]$	$[n \times p]$

summarizes the typical cases of regression analysis with respect to the number of dependent and independent variables considered.

8.1.3 Stepwise Regression

In the context of multivariate regression, explanatory variables can be selected from the initial set of the variables by means of an automatic procedure. This kind of procedure is called *stepwise regression*, and it is commonly used in the multivariate regression analysis approach. The number of independent variables in the final regression model is not known beforehand and can vary in practice between one and all of the variables provided with the data set on which regression analysis is run. Three major strategies for selecting predictor variables are

- *Forward selection*: This strategy starts with no variables in the model and iterates by trying out the variables available in the input data set one by one, and including them if their inclusion contributes to a significant increase in the goodness of the overall model.

- *Backward elimination*: This strategy starts with all the candidate variables available in the input data set and removes them one by one from the model if their exclusion does not significantly decrease the goodness of the overall model.
- *Bidirectional search*: This strategy represents a combination of the two listed previously. In each iteration, variables for both inclusion and exclusion are analyzed.

8.1.4 Functional Form of a Regression Model

Parametric regression[2] analysis requires prior specification of the functional form of the regression model; that is, specifying the finite number of parameters of the regression model. In practice, it means that the user of regression analysis must make an intelligent guess about this function. Often, the functional form is unknown and must be found by a trial-and-error process. The regression analysis domain offers a number of approaches to iteratively search for parameters of a regression model, including functional form and regression coefficients, using a sample of data. Each candidate functional form is tested statistically with respect to how well it explains the variance in the population represented by the sample data. Note, however, that this approach may lead to overfitting the model—that is, selecting a model that fits exactly the sample data, yet does not fit the complete population this sample represents. In consequence, an "overfitted" model would be useless for prediction purposes. Therefore, regression analysis builds appropriate "penalty" mechanisms into model building algorithms in order to prevent overfitting.

In the domain of software effort estimation, several functional forms of the regression model have established their position over the recent years. Table 8.2 summarizes these basic functions with "Size" as the only independent variable. Since the size of the software delivered is the major determinant of the software development effort, basic regression models always consider this factor.

Table 8.2 Typical functional forms of effort models based on statistical regression

Name	Functional form
Linear	$\text{Effort} = a + (b \times \text{Size})$
Quadratic	$\text{Effort} = a + (b \times \text{Size}) + (c \times \text{Size}^2)$
Log-Linear	$\text{Effort} = e^a \times \text{Size}^b$
Translog	$\text{Effort} = e^a \times \text{Size}^b \times \text{Size}^{c \times \ln\text{Size}}$
Cobb-Douglas	$\text{Effort} = a \times \text{Size}^b$

---

[2] If the functional form is not known and cannot be parameterized in terms of any "basis" function, then methods known as nonparametric regression should be applied. Nonparametric regression constructs regression models according to information derived from the data. Please refer to work of Green and Silverman (1994) for more information on available nonparametric regression analysis techniques.

8.1.5 Model's Fit

To assess the percentage of variance explained by the regression model, the coefficient of determination R-squared—or R^2—is typically used. Its value ranges from 0 to 1 and denotes the amount of variability in the data that is explained by the regression model. In the context of software effort estimation, using R^2 as an indicator of the predictive performance of the regression model should rather be avoided. The R^2 indicates merely how well the model fits the observed data, but it does not say anything about how well the model can predict unobserved data in new situations. Moreover, R^2 is a measure of the *linear* association between dependent and independent variables and should not be used for comparing different regression models; for instance, it has a different meaning for linear and log-linear regression models (Greene 2011, Chap. 3). R^2 can be reliably used for comparing only nested models, meaning models that belong to the same family (Pesaran and Deaton 1978, Pesaran and Weeks 1999). Two models are nested if both contain the same parameters and one has at least one additional term; nested models can be derived from a complex model by restricting one or more of its parameters to be zero. For comparing non-nested regression models, dedicated statistics should be used. MacKinnon (1983) provides an overview of statistical tests for comparing non-nested regression models.

Tip

▶ There is no guarantee that a model that provides a good fit will also produce good predictions. When building a predictive model, validate its performance on data different from those the model was built upon. For example, split the available data into a learning set—on which the model is built—and a testing set on which the model's predictive performance is validated.

Using R^2 as a criterion for building a regression model may lead to overfitting of the model, which means that the model is actually representing the relationships specific to the sample data the model was built on and not the relationships in the whole population the sample data represents. In statistics, a model is said to be overfitted when it describes a random error or noise instead of the underlying relationship.

8.1.6 Key Assumptions of Regression Analysis

Classical regression analysis is known for making a number of assumptions that, in practice, limit its applicability in the context of software engineering, where most of these assumptions do not hold. Yet, many of these assumptions refer to simple linear regression and may be relaxed through more advanced treatments. For example, some of the assumptions of the ordinary least-squares regression can be handled by applying robust regression.

Traditionally, the following assumptions should be considered before applying classic statistical regression:

- *No Specification Error*: The functional form of the regression model is correctly specified; in particular, the following assumptions are met:
  - *Correct Functional Form*: The functional form of the relationship between dependent and independent variables specified in the regression model is correct. For example, if the underlying relationship between variables is nonlinear but a linear function was assumed, then the estimated regression coefficients will be biased.
  - *No Omitted Variables*: All relevant independent variables that have an influence on the dependent variable are included in the model and covered by the data sample. The omitted variables result in the bias of a regression model because the effect of omitted variables on the independent variable becomes a part of (1) the error term biasing it toward a nonzero mean, (2) regression coefficients associated with the included variables (except that the omitted variables are correlated with the included ones).
  - *No Irrelevant Variables*: Irrelevant independent variables are not included in the model. Including irrelevant variables into regression analysis increases the risk of their correlation with actually relevant variables. In such a case, the magnitude of standard errors associated with the regression coefficients of relevant variables will increase, making them look irrelevant (the null hypothesis that there is no association with the dependent variable cannot be rejected).
- *No Measurement Error*: Dependent and independent variables are accurately measured; that is, the corresponding sample data are not burdened by the measurement error. Inaccurate data imply inaccurate estimates of regression parameters and thus an inaccurate regression model.
- *Representative Sample*: The data sample upon which a regression model is built is representative of the population for the inference prediction.
  - *Sufficient Sample Size*: In order to apply regression analysis, the number of observations in the sample should be greater than the number of independent variables. Yet, meeting this minimum requirement does not guarantee a reliable output of regression analysis. In the related literature, a practical rule of thumb of 5–30 data cases per independent variable is used as the minimum amount of data that is reasonable for performing regression analysis. Yet, this way of determining the number of cases for regression is criticized by many researchers (e.g., Green 1991). In order to determine the number of cases required for reliable regression modeling, power analysis techniques should be used (Fitzmaurice 2002; Maxwell 2000).
  - *No Selection Bias*: Even though there are enough cases in the sample and the measurements are accurate, the sample may still not be representative of the underlying population. Typically, biased data result from incorrectly designed studies where there is a bias in selecting measurement objects.

- *Error Term* needs to meet several assumptions:
  - *Zero Mean*: The error term ε is a random variable with zero mean and constant variance. In practice, the normal distribution is applied to the error term.
  - *No Autocorrelation*: The error term associated with one observation is not correlated with any of the errors associated with other observations. In other words, error terms are independently distributed so that their covariance is equal to zero. In a time series, where repeated observations of the same unit over time are considered, no autocorrelation means that error terms for subsequent observations are not correlated—what is commonly referred to as serial independence.
  - *No Correlation*: Error terms are uncorrelated to independent variables. If the observed independent variables are correlated to error terms, then the estimates of regression parameters will be biased.
  - *Homoscedasticity (No Heteroscedasticity)*: The variance of the error terms is constant across observations; that is, it does not change with different data samples.
  - *Normality*: A useful implication of this assumption is that error terms are independent and uncorrelated (Greene 2011).
- *No Multicollinearity*: Independent variables are linearly independent; that is, none of the independent variables can be expressed as a linear combination of the other independent variables. The multicollinearity problem does not result in biased coefficient estimates, but does increase the standard error of the estimates and thus reduces the degree of confidence that one can place in them. The difficulty arises when two independent variables are closely correlated, creating a situation in which their effects are difficult to separate.

Moreover, simple regression analysis does not, generally, handle noisy and incomplete data. Typical problems that must be considered before applying regression analysis are:

- *Missing Data*: Regression analysis requires complete data sets. Run on incomplete data, regression analysis will typically exclude from the analysis all variables for which data are missing. In consequence, much data can be excluded from the analysis; in an extreme case, regression analysis may not run at all. Therefore, incomplete data need to be preprocessed prior to regression analysis. Simple approaches for dealing with missing data include removing from the data set cases and variables for which a significant number of data are missing. As this approach typically leads to loss of much data, imputation techniques are recommended, in which missing data are replaced with other values.[3]

---

[3] There are a number of imputation techniques available. Please refer to Rubin and Little (1983) for brief introduction to the problem of missing data and to Schafer (1997) for an overview of techniques for dealing with missing data.

- *Data Outliers*: Data outliers are the data that differ much (e.g., by 3 standard deviations) from the main body of data. Unless they are invalid data, they may belong to a population other than the main body of data. Simple regression analysis does not handle outliers and results in a regression model biased toward outliers. In order to prevent this, outliers should be investigated with respect to their causes and then handled appropriately prior to regression analysis. Alternatively, robust regression analysis can be applied, in which the impact of outliers on the overall analysis is moderated or completely excluded.

8.2   Usage Scenarios

8.2.1   Building a Regression Model

There are a number of techniques to build a regression model (i.e., an approximate true regression line using a sample of observational data). The most straightforward *Ordinary Least-Squares* (*OLS*) linear regression approach attempts to find the line that minimizes the squared error in the relationship between predictive and dependent variables and parameters, for example, between development effort and potential effort drivers. With least-squares regression, one first needs to specify a model, that is, the functional form of the relationship between dependent and independent variables. The least-squares regression method then fits the data to the specified model trying to minimize the overall sum of squared errors, as illustrated in Fig. 8.2.

OLS regression is particularly sensitive to data outliers. Figure 8.3 illustrates the extent of the influence that an outlier value may have on the least-squares-derived regression model.

Prediction of a new data point, such as the one shown using the OLS approach, would clearly be ineffective in this case. To alleviate this problem, it is useful to identify and possibly remove outliers from the data before building an OLS regression model. Standard techniques also exist for outlier analysis. However, despite the fact that many of the difficulties discussed earlier are addressed in the literature on OLS regression, these techniques remain difficult to use for most engineers and managers and require extensive training and experience.

In order to remedy the sensitivity to outlying observations, so-called *Robust-Regression* (*RR*) techniques have been developed, within which alternative minimizing methods are proposed. Instead of minimizing the sum of squares of absolute error, like in OLS regression, other methods are applied in robust regression. For example, *least median of squares regression* (*LMS*) minimizes the median of squares of absolute error (Rousseeuw and Leroy 2003). Robust regression aims to be robust against outlying observations, thus addressing an important issue in software engineering data. In contrast to OLS regression, there is no closed-form formula that can be applied to some of the alternative algorithms. Therefore, RR methods are typically computational intensive and cannot be performed without appropriate tool support.

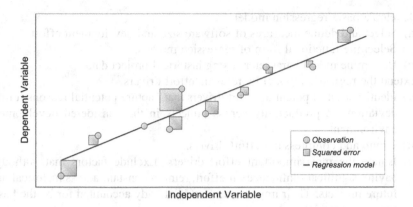

Fig. 8.2 Least-squares regression

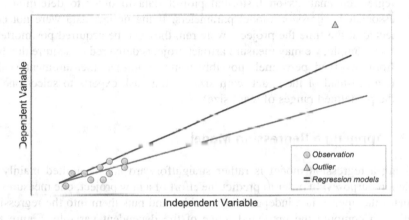

Fig. 8.3 Regression model: influence of a data outlier

The examples we used so far for illustrating regression models use the size of software as the only independent variable. This reflects the common observation of software size being the single major determinant of the software development effort. Consequently, a regression model for project effort should always include size as independent variable. Yet, software size alone does not typically explain well enough the difference between the predicted and actual project effort. In order to account for this difference, the regression equation must consider additional independent variables—effort drivers (see Chap. 3)—that make effort deviate across various software development environments. Bailey and Basili (1981) proposed a general stepwise procedure for building a regression model that fits a specific software development environment. The procedure consists of the following steps:

1. Develop a basic regression model
   (a) Select and define measures of software size and development effort.
   (b) Select the functional form of regression models.
   (c) Determine model parameters using historical project data.
2. Extend the regression model by relevant effort drivers
   (a) Identify a set of potential effort drivers that capture potential reasons for the deviations in productivity across projects in the considered development environment.
   (b) Group and compress the effort drivers.
   (c) Isolate the most important effort drivers. Exclude factors that, although having significant influence on effort, remain constant across historical and future projects. Their impact on effort is already accounted for by the basic regression model.
   (d) Incorporate the effort drivers into the regression model and run a multiple regression analysis on historical project data in order to determine the associated regression model parameters. If the project data were not collected at the time the projects were run, they can be acquired postmortem. For example, we may measure artifact projects delivered or acquire the data from involved personnel, possibly using simplified measurement scales (e.g., instead of the exact team size we may ask experts to select one of the predefined ranges of team size).

8.2.2 Applying a Regression Model

Applying a regression model is rather straightforward and is limited mainly to prediction purposes. In order to predict the effort of a new project, one measures or estimates the appropriate independent variables and puts them into the regression equation to compute the predicted value of the dependent variable. Figure 8.4 provides a graphical interpretation of this process.

The values of independent variables are mapped onto the regression line from which the expected value of the dependent variable is read. Additionally, the

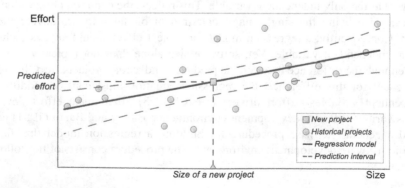

Fig. 8.4 Applying a regression model for the purpose of prediction

prediction interval can be computed during regression analysis and used when applying the regression model as an indicator of prediction uncertainty.

If stepwise regression has been applied, then the output regression model can be used as an indicator of the most relevant factors influencing development effort. Factors that have been included in the model can be considered as the most relevant from among the variables covered by the data set used to build the regression model. In addition, regression coefficients can be used as indicators of the strength of an independent variable's impact on the predicted variable.

8.3 Strengths and Weaknesses of Regression

In principle, regression-based methods share, to a large extent, general characteristics with other data-driven, model-based estimation methods. Table 8.3 summarizes the strengths and weaknesses of statistical regression, including characteristics that distinguish this estimation method from other data-driven methods.

Table 8.3 Strengths and weaknesses of statistical regression

Aspect	Strengths (+) and weaknesses (−)
Expert involvement	• (+) Statistical regression does not require much expert involvement. An expert knowledgeable in using statistical regression is solely needed to apply regression analysis (using the appropriate tool) and interpret the results
Required data	• (+) Statistical regression models perform well for continuous effort functions • (−) Statistical regression requires (similar to other data-driven methods) relatively large data sets; it requires approximately 10–20 data points for each effort driver considered • (−) Applying statistical regression on discrete or mixed-type data requires using specific types of regression or employing additional analysis techniques
Robustness	• (−) Statistical regression makes quite restrictive assumptions with regard to the input data • (−) It requires a particular distribution of underlying data (typically normal) • (−) It requires independence (non-collinearity) of effort drivers • (−) It does not cope with missing data; data preprocessing is needed prior to using regression on incomplete data sets • (−) It is susceptible to the effect of outliers
Flexibility	• (+) Statistical regression allows for using any set of effort drivers to build the effort model • (+) Once developed, a regression model can be used for estimating multiple times without the necessity of accessing the base of historical projects • (−) Regression parameters such as the functional form of the regression model need to be fixed prior to modeling • (−) The variety of function shapes that regression can deal with is limited • (−) Statistical regression models are not, in general, capable of capturing complex nonlinear relationships between effort drivers and effort
Complexity	• (+) Statistical regression has a sound and relatively simple mathematical basis

(continued)

Table 8.3 (continued)

Aspect	Strengths (+) and weaknesses (–)
	• (–) Robust regression techniques might be quite complex (yet they are typically supported by widely available statistical tools)
Support level	• (+) Statistical regression is extensively documented in a variety of publications • (+) Statistical regression belongs to the standard curriculum of higher education • (+) Statistical regression is supported by a plethora of statistical tools, both free and commercial
Reusability	• (+) Estimation models created with statistical regression are reusable for similar situations • (+) Regression models can be easily rebuilt for a new situation using appropriate project data—under the condition that appropriate tool support is available
Predictive power	• (+) Statistical regression provides accurate estimates within homogenous contexts, e.g., stable development processes • (+) Statistical regression has proved to often work better than other, much more complex, data-driven methods (e.g., Mendes and Mosley 2008) • (+) Statistical regression produces the same outputs when provided with the same inputs • (–) Statistical regression does not provide accurate estimates for the context in which development productivity varies widely and depends nonlinearly on numerous types of effort drivers
Informative power	• (+) Statistical regression is helpful for explaining effort relationships • (–) Only those factors for which historical data are available can be considered as effort drivers. In other words, project characteristics that are not covered by the historical data set used for building a regression model cannot be considered during estimation, even though they are relevant
Handling uncertainty	• (+) Statistical regression provides relatively good support for handling the uncertainty of output estimates • (+) It allows for estimating a full probability distribution for the effort, instead of obtaining just a single point estimate • (+) Additional statistics such as variance, standard deviation, and confidence/prediction levels can be used for assessing the uncertainty of effort estimates • (–) Statistical regression provides rather little support for handling uncertain inputs
Estimation scope	• (+) Statistical regression is, principally, applicable to any type of project activities at any granularity level. The only requirements for estimating the effort associated with particular project activities is that historical data regarding these very activities are available for building the regression model
Availability	• (+) Availability of the estimates provided by statistical regression depends on the availability of information on effort drivers covered by the regression model. For example, if a regression model requires the number of lines of code on its input, then it is applicable only after the code is available for size measurement; i.e., at the end of the coding phase. Earlier estimation requires estimating software size. Yet, as regression poorly supports uncertain inputs, using estimates on its input may lead to highly unreliable effort estimates
Empirical evidence	• (+) Related literature documents a large number of field studies where statistical regression—in its various forms—has been applied for the purpose of software effort estimation and compared to other estimation methods

Further Reading

- L. Schroeder, D. L. Sjoquist, and P. E. Setphan (1996), *Understanding Regression Analysis: An Introductory Guide.* Sage Publications, Inc.

  The book provides a basic introduction to regression analysis. It aims at beginners in this topic and provides background knowledge for understanding regression analysis methods and application results presented in the literature.

- N. R. Draper and H. Smith (1998), *Applied Regression Analysis. 3rd Edition.* John Wiley & Sons, New York, NY, USA.

  This book provides a comprehensive view on applied regression analysis. It covers linear and parametric regression in detail and provides many other useful references.

- P.J. Green and B.W. Silverman (1994), *Nonparametric Regression and Generalized Linear Models: A roughness penalty approach. 1st Edition.* Monographs on Statistics and Applied Probability, Chapman & Hall/CRC.

  This book describes nonparametric regression and Generalized Linear Models.

- J. Miller, J. Daly, M. Wood, M. Roper, and A. Brooks (1997), "Statistical Power and Its Subcomponents—Missing and Misunderstood Concepts in Empirical Software Engineering Research," *Information and Software Technology*, vol. 39, no. 4, pp. 285–295.

  Authors discuss typical misconceptions of power analysis in the context of empirical software engineering.

- Y. Miyazaki, M. Terakado, K. Ozaki, and H. Nozaki (1994), "Robust Regression for Developing Software Estimation Models," *Journal of Systems and Software*, vol. 27, pp. 3–16.

  Authors discuss different types of robust regression analysis for the purpose of developing software effort estimation models. Example analyses include the least-squares of balanced relative errors (LBRS) method that minimizes the sum of squares of balanced relative error or least-squares of inverted balanced relative errors (LIRS) that minimizes the sum of squares of inverted balanced relative error.

Constructive Cost Model—COCOMO 9

Parametric models contain a good deal of information about which factors cause software costs to go up or down, and by how much. This information is based on extensive analyses of real-project data and feedback from real-project users.

—Barry Boehm

The COCOMO method represents a data-driven, model-based, parametric estimation method that implements a fixed-model approach. In other words, COCOMO provides a fixed estimation model that has been built on multi organizational project data using statistical regression, which represents a data-driven, parametric method.

Boehm (1981) developed the first COCOMO model using a multiple regression analysis. The most recent COCOMO II results from calibrating the original model, which Boehm et al. (2000) conducted using measurement data and expert judgment. For this purpose, they used a hybrid approach of model parameters learned from measurement data using statistical regression and provided directly by human experts, which have been integrated using Bayes' Theorem.

Major additional capabilities of the COCOMO II model compared to the original model include the following (Boehm et al. 2000):

- Size measurement is custom tailorable involving lines of source code (LOC), Function Points, or Object Points metrics.
- The model accounts for reuse and reengineering.
- Five exponential factors are used for modeling diseconomies of scale.
- Several additions, deletions, and updates with respect to effort drivers and their impact on effort as compared to the previous COCOMO model.

In this chapter, we briefly present basic concepts of COCOMO II. For more detailed specification, refer to Boehm et al. (2000).

A. Trendowicz and R. Jeffery, *Software Project Effort Estimation*,   277
DOI 10.1007/978-3-319-03629-8_9, © Springer International Publishing Switzerland 2014

9.1   Principles

9.1.1   COCOMO II Model

The basic COCOMO model (9.1) is represented by a statistical regression model that has been created based upon a set of multi organizational project data:

$$\text{Effort} = A \times \text{Size}^E \times \prod_{i=1}^{n} \text{EM}_i \tag{9.1}$$

where

- Effort represents total project effort
- A represents development productivity and is initially set up to $A = 2.94$
- EM represents effort drivers
- E represents effect of scale and is computed as follows:

$$E = B + 0.01 \times \sum_{j=1}^{5} \text{SF}_j$$

where

- B represents a constant and is initially set up to $B = 0.91$
- SF represent scaling factors

Effort is measured in person-months and is a function of development baseline productivity, software size, and several effort drivers. Size represents volume of software product and is measured in terms of thousands of lines of source code (kLOC). COCOMO II also offers other sizing options, such as function points or object points. Yet, these are internally converted to kLOC prior to estimation. *Effort drivers (EM)* represent characteristics of the development environment that have been found to have a significant impact on baseline development productivity, and thus on project effort. Constant A approximates baseline development productivity observed in the projects on which the model has been developed. The exponential element E assigned to size accounts for the effect of scale. In COCOMO II, diseconomies of scale are assumed to occur due to two main factors: (1) growth of interpersonal communications and (2) growth of integration overhead for large software systems. The model considers five *scale factors (SF)* that are assumed to have a significant impact on exponential variation in software development productivity and effort (see Table 9.1).

Table 9.1 COCOMO II scale factors

Abbr.	Name	Definition
PREC	Precedentedness	The extent to which a software product is similar to products developed in already completed projects. This factor encompasses such aspects as: • Organizational understanding of product objectives • Experience in working with related software systems • Concurrent development of associated new hardware and operational procedures • Need for innovative data processing architectures and algorithms
FLEX	Development flexibility	The extent to which a software product is free from the need of being conformant to preestablished requirements or external interface specifications
RESL	Architecture/risk resolution	This factor represents a weighted average of several project characteristics: • The extent to which a risk management plan identifies all critical project risks • The extent to which a risk management plan establishes schedule, budget, and internal milestones for resolving them by means of product design review (PDR) • Percent of development schedule devoted to establishing architecture • Percent of required top software architects available to the project • The extent of tool support available for resolving risks as well as for developing and verifying architectural specifications • Level of uncertainty with respect to key architecture drivers such as mission, user interfaces, COTS, hardware, technology, and performance • Number and criticality of project risks
TEAM	Team cohesion	The level of difficulty in synchronizing the project's stakeholders such as users, customers, developers, maintainers, interface designers, and others. Such team synchronization issues may, for instance, arise when project stakeholders: • Differ significantly with respect to the vision, objectives, and cultures • Show limited ability and/or willingness to accommodate other stakeholders' objectives • Are lacking experience and familiarity in operating as a team
PMAT	Process maturity	Maturity of software development processes determined in terms of Capability Maturity Model (CMMI 2010). The assessment of PMAT is organized around CMMI's key process areas (KPAs) and takes place at the beginning of the project. During the assessment, the percentage of compliance for each individual KPA within the project is evaluated

Modeling Effect of Scale in COCOMO II

In COCOMO II, the effect of scale is implemented through scaling factor E, which is a function of scaling factors. The model distinguishes three types of scale effect, depending on the resulting value of factor E:

- If $E < 1.0$, then the project exhibits economies of scale effect.
- If $E = 1.0$, then neither diseconomies of scale nor economies of scale are displayed by the project. That is, both effects are in balance, and there is a linear functional dependency between software size and project effort.
- If $E > 1.0$, then the project exhibits diseconomies of scale effect.

Productivity and scale constants, A and B, have been initially set up respectively to 2.94 and 0.91 using the project data upon which the COCOMO II model was based. However, they can—and should—be tailored to a particular situation using context-specific project data. Such tailoring is the simplest way of calibrating the COCOMO II model to the context of a particular organization.

9.1.2 Early-Design and Post-Architecture Model

In order to cope with the different availability of information across the development life cycle, COCOMO II defines two sub models: early-design model and post-architecture model. These models offer different effort drivers, effort equations, and different rules for measuring software size, depending on the project phase in which estimation takes place.

The *early-design model* is intended for use in the early stages of a software project when very little is known about the nature of the project and the software products to be delivered. Such aspects as the size of the product to be developed, the target platform, the personnel to be involved in the project, or the detailed specifics of the processes to be employed are typically not known in very early phases of the project. In order to cope with sparse information, the early-design model requires less data than the post-architecture model, yet provides less accurate estimates. The model is used to make rough estimates of a project's effort before the entire software architecture is determined; that is, while alternative software architectures and concepts of operation are still explored.

The *post-architecture model* represents a detailed estimation model, and it is intended to be used after an overall software architecture has been developed; that is, during actual development and maintenance of a software product. In order to produce more detailed estimates, the post-architecture model requires appropriately more input information, which should, however, be available by the time of the intended model's use.

9.1.3 Size Parameter

In the COCOMO II model, software size is treated as a special effort driver that reflects the amount of intellectual work put into software development. In order to account for the effect of scale, the size is additionally assigned an exponent parameter E, which is computed using the five scale factors we discussed earlier in this section.

Backfiring Size Metrics

The base size metrics in COCOMO II are thousands of lines of source code (kLOC), wherein a standard line of code is defined as a logical source statement. In addition to structural size, the model accepts software functional size in terms of IFPUG[1] Unadjusted Function Points or Object Points (Banker et al. 1992). However, before COCOMO computes effort estimates, it converts functional size into lines of code for a specific programming language according to so-called *backfiring* conversion coefficients provided by Jones (1996, 2007). However, we discourage use of functional size and recommend using lines of code directly when estimating software for the COCOMO II model. We base our recommendation on two observations:

The reliability of backfiring is quite controversial and widely criticized in software engineering. A major claim involves limited applicability of the conversion rules beyond the data from which these rules have been derived, for example, because of the unclear definition of the LOC metric used when defining backfiring rules. As Jones (2007) says: "the accuracy of backfiring is not great."

The backfiring coefficients are based on industrial data that differ from the data upon which the COCOMO II model has been developed. In consequence, two parts of the same model possibly refer to two different application contexts.

If, however, functional size is the only available metric, then context-specific or other reliable conversion rules should be applied to transform function points into lines of code before providing it as an input to the COCOMO II model. For example, the Function Point Language Gearing Factors provided by Quantitative Software Management (QSM 2013) can be used for converting function points into LOC.

Tip

▶ Avoid using function points in the input to the COCOMO II model. Instead, provide size in terms of lines of code directly. If function point size is available, use custom-tailored rules for converting the size into kLOC before using it within the COCOMO II model.

---

[1] The IFPUG Counting Practices Manual has been published as ISO 20926 standard (2009).

Converting the Size of New, Adapted, and Reused Software

COCOMO II provides an opportunity to account for new, adapted, and reused software when estimating effort in the context of enhancement projects. Unfortunately, instead of using these size metrics directly for estimation, the effective size of the reused and adapted software code is converted to its equivalent in terms of new lines of code. The conversion coefficient is based on the additional effort it takes to modify the code before including it into a software product, and it accounts for nonlinear effects of software reuse. In COCOMO II, the same conversion rules are used for function points and lines of code metrics as well as for early-design and post-architecture models. For more details regarding the conversion procedures, refer to Boehm et al. (2000).

Notice that similar to converting functional size into lines of code, rules for adapting reused software are based on observations made in a very limited context, which might not correspond to the actual situation in a particular organization. Again, developing your own custom-tailored rules for converting the size of reused code into new code equivalent should be considered.

Tip

▶ Be careful when applying the COCOMO II for enhancement projects. Remember that COCOMO II converts the size of reused code into new code equivalent using rules that have been fixed on data that might not correspond to your actual project environment. Therefore, consider developing custom-tailored conversion rules for adjusting the size of reused code before providing it on the input of COCOMO II.

9.1.4 Scale Factors

Scale factors represent project characteristics that have an impact on relative (dis) economies of scale observed across projects of different size. All scale factors are assigned qualitative rating levels that range from "Very Low" to "Extra High." Each rating level of each scale factor is associated with a specific value that is then aggregated to overall scale parameter E (9.1). The same set of scale factors is applied in both early-design and post-architecture models. Table 9.1 provides brief definitions of the COCOMO II scale factors (Boehm et al. 2000).

9.1.5 Effort Drivers

Effort drivers represent characteristics of the software development environment that are believed to have a significant influence on the effort required to complete the project. Similar to scale factors, all effort drivers in the COCOMO II model are assigned qualitative rating levels, such as "Low," "Nominal," or "High." Each rating level of each effort driver is associated with a specific value—so-called *effort multiplier*—which reflects the effort driver's impact on effort.

Effort drivers have a multiplicative character; that is, effort is multiplied by the value of the multiplier associated with the certain effort driver. For example, "Nominal" rating means that a factor has neither a positive nor a negative impact on effort, and thus an associated multiplier has the value of 1.00. Except for "Nominal" rating, for which a multiplier value is always equal to 1.00, multipliers differ across effort drivers. If the rating of a particular effort driver is believed to cause extra development effort, then the corresponding multiplier is greater than 1.00. Conversely, if the rating of a particular effort driver is believed to reduce development effort, then the corresponding multiplier is lower than 1.00.

> **Project- and Component-Level Estimation**
> Scale factors and Required Development Schedule (SCED) effort drivers are used only on the project level—all other effort drivers and sizes apply to individual project components.

Early-Design vs. Post-Architecture Effort Drivers

In order to account for the different amount and uncertainty of information that is available along the project lifetime, COCOMO II defines individual sets of factors for each early-design and post-architecture model. In early project stages, only a few general characteristics of development are known, whereas in the post-architecture phases, a lot more information is available. Therefore, the post-architecture model uses a full set of 17 effort drivers, whereas the early-design model uses only seven effort drivers. The full set of post-architecture effort drivers (Table 9.2) is additionally divided into four groups: product factors, platform factors, personnel factors, and project factors.

The seven effort drivers defined for the early-design model (Table 9.3) are obtained by combining the effort post-architecture model cost drivers. In that sense, the early-design model uses a reduced set of effort drivers relative to the full set of effort drivers defined within the post-architecture model.

Mapping the full set of post-architecture effort drivers onto the early-design ones involves combining numerical equivalents of the effort drivers' rating levels. For a combined early-design effort driver, the numerical values of the contributing post-architecture effort drivers are summed, and the resulting total is mapped onto an expanded early-design model rating scale. Note that in the early-design model's rating scale, the "Nominal" value is always equal to the total sum of the "Nominal" ratings of the corresponding post-architecture effort drivers. Refer to Boehm et al. (2000) for a detailed procedure for mapping the full set of post-architecture effort drivers and rating scales onto their early-design model counterparts.

Table 9.2 COCOMO II post-architecture effort drivers

Abbr.	Name	Definition
RELY	Required software reliability	The extent to which the software must perform its intended functions over a certain period of time. If the effect of a software failure is only of slight inconvenience, then RELY is low. If a failure would risk human life, then RELY is very high
DATA	Database size	The size of database (in bytes) relative to the size of software measured in terms of LOC. This factor covers the impact of a large database on the effort required for generating the sample data used for testing the software
CPLX	Product complexity	Complexity of software, with respect to five major aspects: • Control operations • Computational operations • Device-dependent operations • Data management operations • User interface management operations In order to assess the complexity of a product, a combination of the aspects that best characterize it is selected, rated subjectively, and combined into a total evaluation by means of weighted average
RUSE	Developed for reusability	The extent to which constructed software components are intended for reuse on the current or future projects. This factor is motivated by the observation that significant extra effort is needed for creating more generic design of software, for more elaborate documentation, and for more extensive testing of components in order to ensure their reusability
DOCU	Documentation match to life cycle needs	The extent to which a project's documentation is suited to its life cycle needs. It is rated with respect to what part of life cycle needs is covered by project documentation
TIME	Execution time constraint	The extent of execution time constraints imposed upon a software system—expressed in terms of the percentage of the available execution time resource to be consumed by the software system
STOR	Main storage constraint	The extent of main storage constraints imposed upon a software system—expressed in terms of the percentage of the available main storage resource to be consumed by the software system
PVOL	Platform volatility	The volatility of the platform, where "platform" refers to the combination of hardware and software (OS, DBMS, etc.) the software product calls on to perform its tasks. For example, if the software to be developed is an operating system, then the platform is the computer hardware; if it is a database management system, then the platform is the hardware and the operating system
ACAP	Analyst capability	Capabilities of personnel who work on requirements, high-level design, and detailed design. The major capabilities include: • The ability for analysis and design • Efficiency and thoroughness of the work • The ability to communicate and cooperate in a team

(continued)

Table 9.2 (continued)

Abbr.	Name	Definition
PCAP	Programmer capability	Capability of the programmers as a team rather than as individuals. These capabilities include: • Programming abilities • Efficiency and thoroughness of the work • The ability to communicate and cooperate as a team
PCON	Personnel continuity	The level of a project's annual personnel turnover in terms of percentage of team change
AEXP	Applications experience	The level of a project team's experience with the type of the application being developed in the project. The experience is rated in terms of years of experience with the particular type of application
PEXP	Platform experience	The capability of understanding the use of more powerful platforms such as graphic user interface, database, networking, and distributed middleware
LTEX	Language and tool experience	The level of programming language and software tool experience of the project team developing the software system. In addition to experience in programming with a specific language supported by a particular tool set, this factor includes experience with tools supporting such software development activities as: • Requirements and design • Representation and analysis • Configuration management • Document extraction • Library management • Program style and formatting • Consistency checking
TOOL	Use of software tools	The extent of tool support in the project, ranging from simple editing and coding tools to integrated life cycle management tools
SITE	Multisite development	The extent of project distribution and communication between multiple development sites. This factor covers two major aspects: • Site collocation: ranging from fully collocated to international distribution • Communication support: ranging from surface mail and some phone access to fully interactive multimedia support
SCED	Required development schedule	The level of schedule constraint imposed on the project team developing the software system. Schedule constraint is defined as the percentage of schedule stretch-out or acceleration relative to a nominal (reasonable) schedule for a project that requires a given amount of effort

In addition to restriction on the amount of information available in the early stages of software development, the information is typically burdened with high uncertainty. In order to account for this fact, early-design effort drivers employ expanded rating scales relative to the ones used by the post-architecture model. Whereas ratings of the post-architecture effort drivers range between "Very Low"

Table 9.3 COCOMO II early-design effort drivers

Abbr.	Name	Post-architecture effort drivers
PERS	Personnel capability	ACAP, PCAP, PCON
RCPX	Product reliability and complexity	RELY, DATA, CPLX, DOCU
PDIF	Platform difficulty	TIME, STOR, PVOL
PREX	Personnel experience	AEXP, PEXP, LTEX
FCIL	Facilities	TOOL, SITE
RUSE	Developed for reusability	RUSE
SCED	Required development schedule	SCED

and "Very High," the ratings of the early-design factors go from "Extra Low" to "Extra High."

9.2   Usage Scenarios

9.2.1   Applying the COCOMO Model

As a regression model, COCOMO II is used mainly for prediction purposes. In order to predict the effort of a new project, one measures or estimates project parameters required as input to COCOMO and uses these data for computing effort according to the COCOMO II equation.

Moreover, a trade-off analysis can be performed, in which the impact of different levels of particular effort drivers on total project effort is investigated. Changing an effort driver's level implies a change in the associated effort multiplier and, in consequence, changes the total effort predicted. In practice, such analysis can be used to mitigate project risks. For example, one may compensate for increased project effort due to high reliability requirements by affecting other effort drivers, for example, improving the experience of the key members of the project team.

9.2.2   Calibrating the COCOMO Model

The major critique of the COCOMO II model is that it has been fixed on multi-organizational, heterogeneous project data that typically do not correspond to characteristics of the particular organization in which the model is to be employed. Potential reasons of this discrepancy include the following:

- Definitions of effort drivers and scale factors used in COCOMO II may differ from those used in a particular organization—or at least may be understood and interpreted differently across different organizations—leading to inconsistent project data across different organizations.

- The rating scales of effort drivers defined within COCOMO II have a subjective character and thus are vulnerable to inconsistent ratings across different organizations.
- The life cycle activities as covered by COCOMO II may differ from the life cycle activities in a particular organization.
- The relevancy of factors influencing project effort and factor dependencies may differ from those observed in the data from which the COCOMO II model has been created.

Consequently, using the COCOMO II model "as-is" in the context of a particular organization may lead to largely inaccurate estimates. In order to mitigate this risk, COCOMO II should be calibrated/tailored to local characteristics of the specific organization in which it is to be employed. The need for calibration applies particularly to the post-architecture model that is intended to provide accurate estimates. Boehm et al. (2000) list three basic ways for calibrating the post-architecture COCOMO II model:

- Calibrating the model's multiplicative constants to local, organization-specific project data
- Consolidating or eliminating redundant or irrelevant model parameters
- Adding relevant effort drivers that have not yet been explicitly modeled

Calibrating Multiplicative Constants

Calibrating to local project data involves either adjusting multiplicative constant A alone or adjusting both multiplicative constants A and B. For that purpose, Boehm et al. (2000) recommend having at least 5 data points per calibrated factor; that is, 5 data points for calibrating constant A and 10 data points for calibrating both constants A and B. The calibration procedure involves transforming the COCOMO II equation into a logarithmic form (9.2) and employing multiple linear regression analysis in order to fit equation coefficients to the local project data.

$$\ln \ (\text{Effort}) = \beta_0 + \beta_1 \times \ln \ (\text{Size}) + \beta_2 \times \text{SF}_1 \times \ln \ (\text{Size}) + \ldots + \beta_6$$
$$\times \text{SF}_5 \times \ln \ (\text{Size}) + \beta_7 \times \ln \ (\text{EM}_1) + \ldots + \beta_{23}$$
$$\times \ln \ (\text{EM}_{17}) \tag{9.2}$$

The corresponding COCOMO II coefficients are as follows: $A = e^{\beta_0}$ and $B = \beta_1$. Dillibabu and Krishnaiah (2005) propose an analogical approach. Instead of transforming the COCOMO into a linear curve first and then fitting it to local data, they propose fitting the parameters A and E of the COCOMO power equation (9.1) directly. In the curve fitting approach, both effort drivers and scale factors remain unchanged.

Consolidating Effort Drivers

Consolidating effort drivers takes place when ratings for closely related factors should be the same, that is, when factors should be considered as one. The most common situation is when COCOMO factors correspond to detailed aspects of a major effort driver. For example, a particular organization may not distinguish between detailed aspects of resource constraints such as execution time constraints (TIME) and main storage constraints (STOR) in the COCOMO model. In this case, the organization may want to aggregate these two resource constraint factors into one factor, say RESR. For each factor rating, the multiplier value of a new factor is computed as a product of the multiplier values associated to its component factors for the same rating. For example, the multiplier assigned to "Very High" rating of a new RESR effort driver will be computed by multiplying multiplier values assigned to "Very High" rating of effort factors TIME and STOR:

$$RESR \ (VH) = TIME \ (VH) \times STOR \ (VH) = 1.29 \times 1.17 = 1.51$$

Eliminating Effort Drivers

Eliminating effort drivers takes place when an effort driver obtains the same rating across all projects within an organization. In this case, such an effort driver does not actually introduce any variance in development productivity across projects and can be removed from the model. After removing this effort driver from the model, the constant parameters A and B should be calibrated in order to account for the removed effort driver.

Adding Effort Drivers

Adding effort drivers takes place in the situation when an effort driver that is relevant in a particular context is missing in the COCOMO II model. Boehm et al. (2000) give an example of an organization within which software development projects differ widely with respect to the level of security constraints. In other words, since fulfilling security constraints requires additional project overhead, development productivity of projects differs depending on this factor. In this situation, the organization might want to account for the effect of security constraints on project effort by including a new factor—say SCON—into the COCOMO II model. In that case, a suitable rating scale needs to be developed for SCON, and the new parameter needs to be calibrated to the particular context using measurement project data or expert opinion in a hybrid approach as described in the next ("Adjusting values of effort multipliers") paragraph.

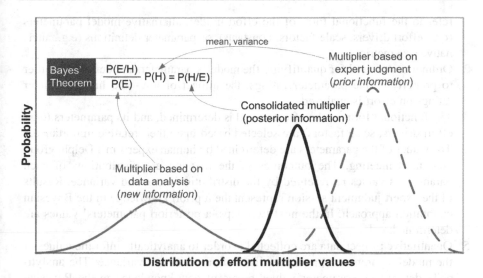

Fig. 9.1 Adjusting values of COCOMO II effort multiplier

Adjusting Values of Effort Multipliers

Adjusting values of effort multipliers represents an advanced calibration approach. It has been proposed by Chulani et al. (1999), and it employs Bayes' statistics for combining expert knowledge with project measurement data for deriving final estimates of effort multipliers. Figure 9.1 illustrates the basic idea of the Bayesian calibration.

Bayesian calibration considers mean and variance for each model parameter, that is, effort driver or scale factor. The advantage of Bayesian consolidation is that it grants a higher weight to this input (prior knowledge or sample information), which has lower variance. In other words, the posterior mean of a parameter will be closer to the mean of this input—prior or sample—which has lower variance. If the prior variance of a parameter is equal to zero, then the posterior mean of the parameter will be completely determined by the mean of prior information. Yet, we should not be too concerned about such a situation because perfect consensus is rather rare in the software engineering context. For example, if model parameters obtained from regression have much larger variance than parameters judged by the domain expert, for example, due to sparse and noisy measurement data used in regression, then consolidated parameter values will be closer to those judged by experts.

For detailed procedures of Bayesian calibration, refer to Boehm et al. (2000, Sect. 4.5.2) or to Chulani et al. (1999). They propose a seven-step procedure for Bayesian calibration of the COCOMO model's parameters.

1. Available software effort modeling literature is investigated for potential improvement to the calibrated COCOMO model. Such improvements may

refer to the functional form of the effort model, alternative model parameters (e.g., effort drivers, scale factors, constants), or parameter definitions (e.g., alternative size metrics).

2. Ordinal scales used for quantifying the model's parameters are defined. In order to properly define parameter ratings, the impact of low- and high-parameter ratings on effort is analyzed.

3. The functional form of the effort model is determined, and its parameters (e.g., effort drivers, scale factors) are selected based upon their relative importance.

4. The values of the parameters are determined by human experts in a Delphi group consensus meeting. The outcomes of the meeting are distributions of each parameter's values represented by the distribution mean and variance. Results of the expert judgment session represent the a priori knowledge in the Bayesian calibration approach. In the next two steps, a posteriori parameters' values are determined.

5. Quantitative project data are collected in order to analytically infer the values of the model's parameters, again as distribution mean and variance. The analytically determined parameter values represent new knowledge in the Bayesian calibration.

6. The Bayes' Theorem is applied on the parameter values obtained through expert judgment (Step 4) and data analysis (Step 5) in order to determine calibrated parameter values (a posteriori knowledge).

7. This step represents iterative refinement of the effort model though collecting further data and repeating calibration Steps 1–6.

The calibration may lead to such comprehensive model adjustments that they actually correspond to rebuilding the complete model.

Threats of Model Calibration

One of the common threats of calibrating and using the COCOMO model is that the model's parameters might be interpreted differently from their original meaning. In consequence, local data used to calibrate the model and to estimate effort do not correspond to data upon which the model was created. In consequence, the calibrated model and estimates it produces are not correct. With respect to key measures of size and effort, the following aspects need to be considered:

• *Software size*: Different organizations use different rules for counting lines of code. Example differences include counting logical and physical lines of code, counting non executable statements, counting reused code as new, and counting the source code of supporting software such as testing modules.

• *Project effort*: Different organizations use different effort units and different effort measurement rules. For example, COCOMO uses person-months as a base unit of effort, which is equivalent to 152 person-hours. Yet, this equivalence factor may differ from organization to organization. Much more critical aspects

Table 9.4 Strengths and weaknesses of COCOMO II

Aspect	Strengths (+) and weaknesses (−)
Expert involvement	• (+) COCOMO II does not require much expert involvement. An expert knowledgeable in using the model and interpreting its outputs is solely required • (−) For calibrating the COCOMO II model, a substantial amount of expert effort is required
Required data	• (+) COCOMO II does not require any historical data to be used for estimation • (−) Yet, it typically requires calibration to a specific context and thus can be difficult to adapt and use where there are limited or incomplete data
Robustness	• (−) COCOMO II does not handle incomplete data—all required information needs to be provided on the model's input
Flexibility	• (+) COCOMO II provides capabilities and guidelines for an organization to add new effort drivers and calibrate major model parameters • (−) COCOMO II can be difficult to adapt and use where there are limited or incomplete data and limited expertise in statistical techniques • (−) COCOMO II requires specific information on its input, i.e., a set of particular metrics
Complexity	• (+) COCOMO II is represented by a quite simple and intuitive mathematical formula • (−) Calibrating the COCOMO II model requires expertise in particular statistical techniques—unless the calibration process is fully supported by an appropriate software tool
Support level	• (+) COCOMO II is comprehensively documented by the book of Boehm et al. (2000). Moreover, several additional articles deal with selected aspects of COCOMO II • (+) Estimation with COCOMO II and model calibration is supported by several software tools, including free and commercial ones
Reusability	• (−) Because of its fixed character, COCOMO II is not simple to reuse across various contexts. It requires calibration prior to application in the context different from that in which it was created
Predictive power	• (−) The model represents effort relationships that are true for the multi-organizational projects on which it was built, but not necessarily for other contexts. In consequence, there is no guarantee that COCOMO II will fit a particular organization's style of development, data definitions, and set of operating assumptions—there is a high risk of failed estimates • (−) Empirical evaluations of COCOMO II confirm this observation by showing wide dispersion between estimation accuracy of COCOCMO II when validated on various data sets • (+) COCOMO II produces the same outputs when provided with the same inputs
Informative power	• (−) COCOMO II provides very limited insight into context-specific effort relationships. The model—effort drivers and associated effort multipliers—has actually been fixed upon multi organizational projects the model has been developed on. Simple calibration of the model's parameters A and B does not improve the model's informativeness
Handling uncertainty	• (−) COCOMO II only takes deterministic values as input and thus cannot explicitly assess the estimation uncertainty caused by the uncertainty of effort drivers

(continued)

Table 9.4   (continued)

Aspect	Strengths (+) and weaknesses (–)
Estimation scope	• (–) The type and scope of project activities for which COCOMO II estimates effort are fixed within the model. The model allows for estimating the total amount of effort required for developing the software project
Availability	• (–) Availability of the estimates is determined by the fixed set of metrics required for input to the COCOMO II model
	• (+) Yet, two different COCOMO II models are available (Post-Architecture and Early-Design) for estimating in different phases of a software development life cycle
Empirical evidence	• (+) Related literature documents a number of field studies where COCOMO II has been applied for the purpose of software effort estimation and compared to other estimation methods

are related to the way of counting project effort. Here we need to consider such issues as the type of project activities for which we count effort or how we account for uncompensated overtime. The COCOMO model considers, in addition to engineering activities, effort spent for configuration management, quality assurance, and project management. Moreover, it does not account for project overtime.

Tip

▶ Ensure that counting rules you use for collecting software size, effort, and effort driver data do not differ from those used to develop and calibrate the estimation models. In the case of COCOMO, make sure that your definition and understanding of the model's parameters do not differ from those upon which COCOMO has been founded.

9.3   Strengths and Weaknesses of COCOMO

COCOMO II represents a statistical regression method in which the estimation model has already been developed (fixed) using multi organizational data and is provided "as-is" for the purpose of estimation. Consequently, it shares a number of characteristics with the statistical regression approach. It solves several weaknesses of the define-your-own-model paradigm represented by the statistical regression method and has a few weaknesses typical of fixed regression models. Table 9.4 summarizes the strengths and weaknesses of COCOMO II.

Further Reading

• B.W. Boehm, C. Abts, A.W. Brown, S. Chulani, B.K. Clark, E. Horowitz, R. Madachy, D. Reifer, and B. Steece (2000), *Software Cost Estimation with COCOMO II*, Upper Saddle river, New Jersey: Prentice-Hall

This book is a source reference for the COCOMO II method. It provides comprehensive description of the COCOMO II effort estimation model and its calibration using Bayes' Theorem.

- S. Chulani, B. Boehm, and B. Steece (1999), "Bayesian Analysis of Empirical Software Engineering Cost Models," *IEEE Transactions on Software Engineering*, vol. 25, no. 4, pp. 573–583
    The article provides an in-depth description of different variants of calibration of the COCOMO model. As an alternative approach authors propose a g-prior calibration, in which weights are assigned to sample information in order to reflect believed reliability of this information against a priori knowledge acquired from human experts.

Classification and Regression Trees

10

> It is very difficult to make a vigorous, plausible, and job-risking defense of an estimate that is derived by no quantitative method, supported by little data, and certified chiefly by the hunches of the managers.
>
> —Frederick P. Brooks

Classification and Regression Trees (CART) represents a data-driven, model-based, nonparametric estimation method that implements the define-your-own-model approach. In other words, CART is a method that provides mechanisms for building a custom-specific, nonparametric estimation model based solely on the analysis of measurement project data, called training data.

In general, CART belongs to a wider group of machine learning methods that deal with building decision trees. The most well-known classification tree method is C4.5[1] proposed by Quinlan (1992, 1996).

10.1 Principles

10.1.1 The CART Model

Basically, a decision tree (Fig. 10.1) forms a stepwise partition of the data set on which it was developed. Each node of a tree specifies a condition based on one of the predictor variables. Each branch corresponds to possible values or range of values this variable may take.

The paths through the decision tree leading from the root to terminal nodes represent a collection of decision rules in the form:

IF (Condition₁ AND Condition₂ AND...AND Condition) THEN Decision

---

[1] The most recent version of the Quinlan's C4.5 method is called C5.0 and is not revealed to the public. It is implemented in the commercial proprietary software tool named RuleQuest (http://www.rulequest.com/).

A. Trendowicz and R. Jeffery, *Software Project Effort Estimation*,
DOI 10.1007/978-3-319-03629-8_10, © Springer International Publishing Switzerland 2014

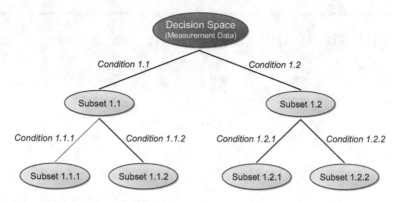

Fig. 10.1 Structure of a decision tree

where decision represents the value of a predicted variable determined on the basis
of data in the particular terminal node. For example, in the example tree presented
in Fig. 10.1, the example decision rule would be:

    IF (Condition1.1 AND Condition1.1.2) THEN Subset1.1.2

which would indicate that for a new project that meets *Condition1.1* and
Condition1.1.2 on its independent variables (effort drivers), the value of the dependent variable (effort) should be predicted using the historical projects in the
Subset1.1.2; for example, effort estimate for the new project can be computed as
mean over actual effort of projects in the *Subset1.1.2*.

Traditionally, decision tree methods were limited to either regression-type
problems or classification-type problems. In the regression-type problem, a decision tree is created for predicting the values of a continuous dependent variable
based on the one or more continuous and/or categorical predictor variables. In the
classification-type problem, a decision tree is developed for predicting the values of
a categorical dependent variable based on the one or more continuous and/or
categorical predictor variables.

Proposed by Breiman et al. (1984), the CART method overcomes this limitation
and can deal with both, regression and classification problems, meaning it deals
with any mixture of continuous and categorical predictor and predicted variables.

10.2 Usage Scenarios

10.2.1 Developing the CART Model

The CART develops classification and regression (C&R) tree models in two phases:

- *Generating Tree*: The tree model is developed based on the training data, which
  consists of measurement data from already completed (historical) projects.
  Generating the model involves recursively splitting the data set until certain

stop criteria are satisfied. In CART, univariate binary splits are considered, that is, each split depends on the value of one predictor variable (*univariate*) and results in two partitions[2] (*binary*).

- *Pruning Tree*: In order to avoid overfit, the model resulting from the "Generating tree" phase needs to be adjusted. The tree-generating process typically results in a "maximal" model, meaning a model that is very specific to the characteristics of the training set. In order to generalize the model for projects outside the training set, that is, for predicting new projects, an optimal sub tree of the maximal tree needs to be identified. In the pruning phase, such a sub tree is identified, and the maximal tree is reduced by cutting off its overfitted parts appropriately.

Generating Tree

The CART tree-generation procedure consists of several abstract steps[3]:

1. *Binary Splitting*: Starting with the first variable in the training data set, a variable is split at all of its possible split points. A variable's *split points* are determined by values the variable takes in the training set. For example, for a categorical variable, split points are defined by all categories the variable takes in the training set. At each possible split point of the variable, the project data sample is partitioned into two subsets represented by two nodes creating left and right branches in a tree. A single split is defined by a condition in the form: *IF Variable = Value THEN left branch ELSE right branch*. Notice that in CART, splits can also be based on linear combinations of variables.
2. *Evaluating Split*: Each possible split is evaluated using a "goodness of split" criterion. The *goodness of split* is quantified as reduction of sub node's *impurity* relative to its parent node. The node's impurity refers to the heterogeneity level in the distribution of the predicted variable's values observed in the node.
3. *Selecting Variable Split*: The best split on the variable in terms of the goodness of split (e.g., highest reduction in the partition's impurity) is selected, and the appropriate two subsets (branches) are created in the tree.
4. *Repeating Splitting*: Steps 1–3 are repeated for each of the remaining variables at the root node of the tree, that is, for each remaining variable in the training set.
5. *Ranking Splits*: All of the "best" splits on each variable are ranked according to the reduction of the node's impurity.
6. *Selecting Best Split*: The best split across all variables is selected based on the ranking results.
7. *Assigning Classes*: Tree nodes associated with the best split selected in the previous step are assigned classes according to a rule that minimizes

---

[2] Although CART generates binary partitions, other approaches have also been proposed for generating decision trees (Porter and Selby 1990).

[3] The detailed description of the procedure for building a C&R tree is beyond the scope of this book and can be found in Breiman et al. (1984).

misclassification costs.[4] In other words, each node resulting from the best split is assigned a decision regarding the value of the predicted variable (class). For each potential value of the predictor variable, a prediction error of the resulting tree model (misclassification cost) is computed. The value that results in the lowest prediction error is then assigned to the node.

8. *Repeat Recursively*: Steps 1–7 are repeated for each nonterminal tree node until the tree is complete, that is, until it cannot be grown any further.

Pruning a Tree

One of the major issues that arises when building C&R tree models is how to avoid their overfit. Overfitting generally occurs when an excessively complex, "maximal" model is generated to adjust it exactly to the characteristics of a specific training set. In the extreme case, a tree model encompasses all variables provided in the training set, and each terminal node includes only one project. Such a "maximal" model, although performing perfectly for projects in the training set, is typically not able to accurately predict projects from beyond the training set, yet similar to training projects. In such a case, it is said that the model does not generalize to situations not represented in the training data. In general, a model is considered to be overfitted relative to a simple one if it is more accurate in predicting known projects but less accurate in predicting new projects.

A major strategy to avoid overfit of a tree model is called *pruning*, and it can be implemented in two ways:

- *In-Process Pruning*: The tree-growing process is stopped in the middle based on a set of pruning criteria. In this approach, the node-splitting process is allowed to continue until certain stop criteria are met. An example instantiation of this idea is to continue the tree-generation process until subsequent splits (1) result only in a very little overall improvement in the tree's prediction performance or (2) contain fewer projects than the user-specified minimum threshold.

- *Post-Process Pruning*: The tree-growing process is allowed to continue until a maximal tree is built and a pruning procedure is applied on it afterward. The CART method actually uses this pruning strategy. At first, CART allows for growing a maximal possible tree. Then it examines sub trees obtained by pruning away branches of the maximal tree in order to select the one that is most likely to perform best on new projects. CART avoids stopping in the middle of the tree-growing process in order not to miss important information that might be discovered at lower levels of the tree.

Building a decision tree is a computationally intensive process and is laborious to perform manually even for small data sets. Therefore, a number of software tools to support building and applying CART exist.

---

[4] The CART method uses special algorithms for minimizing misclassification costs.

Software Tools Supporting the CART Method

Although the CART method has been revealed to the public (Breiman et al. 1984), "CART" is a trademarked name reserved for the Salford Systems software tool that implements the original CART method (http://www. salford-systems.com/). However, several other data analysis software tools have reimplemented the CART method. Examples include research tools such as CARTX (Srinivasan and Fisher 1995), as well as commercial tools such as Statistica (http://www.statsoft.com/), where it was implemented under the name GC&RT.

10.2.2 Applying the CART Model

A CART model can be applied for a number of purposes related to software effort estimation. On the one hand, a decision tree can be used to predict the effort of a new project. On the other hand, the tree can be analyzed in order to identify the most important factors and their dependencies affecting development effort for the purpose of planning the project and process improvement actions. Let us discuss these aspects of applying CART on a simple example.

Example 10.1. Predicting the Productivity of ESA Projects with CART

Let us consider an example decision tree in Fig. 10.2. It was developed by Briand et al. (1998) for estimating the productivity of software development projects in the context of the European Space Agency (ESA).

Estimating Productivity and Estimating Effort

In principle, it is beneficial to consider development productivity instead of project effort when utilizing CART for learning about the factors influencing a project's performance. In practice, software size is the main determinant of development effort. Therefore, the size will typically (if not always) be identified as the "top" most important factor influencing development effort. Yet, as we might be interested in the influence of other project factors on effort, we need to exclude size from the analysis. One option is to build a decision tree for multiple projects of the same size—yet this is difficult because projects are typically of different sizes. Another option is to build a decision tree for software productivity, which already incorporates effort in relation to size: *Productivity = Size/Effort*. In this case, we are interested in factors that make productivity differ across analyzed development projects. These are the factors that make the effort required for completing software of the same size differ in different project environments.

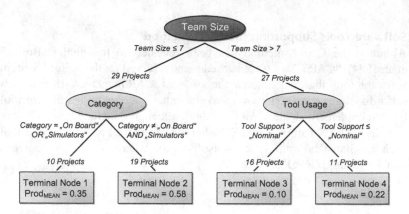

Fig. 10.2 Example decision tree

Each terminal node in the example tree represents the average productivity of projects that are characterized by the path from the root node. Each node represents an individual project factor, upon which *If–Then* decision criteria are defined. The tree represents binary splits, that is, for each node there are two outgoing arcs that represent splitting the underlying project data into two disjunctive sets based on two conditions. Depending on which condition is true for a particular project, the left or the right path is taken.

On the first level of the tree, projects are first split according to their "Team Size." If the team size is lower or equal to seven persons, then these projects are split further according to their *Category*; otherwise, projects are split further according to the "Tool Usage." In the context of ESA, in 29 projects the team size was lower or equal to seven persons, whereas in 27 projects, team size was greater than seven persons.

Following the *Category* branch: Ten projects falling into the "On board systems" or "Simulators" category have an average productivity of 0.35 kLOC/PM (thousand lines of source code per person-month). The remaining 19 projects falling in other categories have an average productivity of 0.58 kLOC/PM.

Following the *Tool Usage* branch: Eleven projects where tool usage is between "Low" and "Nominal" have a predicted average productivity of 0.10 kLOC/PM, whereby "Nominal" tool usage means no tool or basic lower CASE tools. The 16 projects with higher than "Nominal" tool usage—that is, with extensive use of upper CASE, project management, and documentation tools—have predicted an average productivity of 0.22 kLOC/PM.

Prediction: Productivity of a new project can be estimated by classifying the project into one of the tree terminal nodes. For this purpose, one would go through the decision tree starting at its root node and selecting its subsequent branches based on the project's specific factor value, until a terminal node is reached. The mean productivity computed for the historical projects in the node can then be used as the predicted productivity of the new project. Other statistics such as median, quartiles, or standard deviation can be computed additionally for each node as an indicator of potential uncertainty associated with the mean productivity estimate. Notice that building a decision tree for the purpose of prediction requires that the data on the factors considered in the tree model can be acquired at the beginning of a project—otherwise a new project cannot be estimated because the information on factors required as input for the tree model are not known at the time of estimation.

Risk Management and Performance Improvement: The decision tree allows for drawing some conclusions about the relative importance of factors (predictor variables) covered by the training data set. Factors selected on top levels of the tree hierarchy are typically more important than factors below them, when considered individually. In the example tree (Fig. 10.2), the size of a development team was selected as the most relevant factor influencing development productivity. This information can, for instance, be used to avoid short-term project risks and plan long-term process improvements. For example, large projects should be split into smaller ones in order to ensure optimal team size and, in consequence, optimal development productivity.

Furthermore, decision trees allow, to some extent, for learning about reciprocal dependencies between factors. This is accomplished by analyzing paths in a tree model. Selection of the factor to be considered in a particular node, on a certain tree level, depends on the value of factors considered on the path from the tree root to this node. In the example tree presented in Fig. 10.2, factors considered on the second level of the tree depend on the size of the development team. For projects with a team larger than seven persons, usage of tools plays a more important role than for projects with a team up to seven persons; for the small projects, the category of a project is a more important factor influencing development productivity than tool support. This information can be an additional guide for risk management and improvement activities. For instance, if it is not feasible to split large projects into smaller ones to ensure optimal performance, then one may consider alleviating the negative effect of a large team on productivity by ensuring appropriate tool usage.

Process Improvement: The goodness of a decision tree can be evaluated by comparing predicted against actual project data. For example, after classifying a project into a particular terminal node, one may determine whether a project's productivity varies significantly from the node's mean productivity value, where mean corresponds to a typical productivity for the class of projects represented by this very node. If this is the case, potential reasons for deviation should be investigated. It may, for example, occur that some relevant factor that makes the productivity of the new project differ from historical projects has not been measured so far and, thus, has not been considered in the decision tree. This would call for improving measurement processes and revising the tree model.   ∎

10.3   Strengths and Weaknesses

In principle, the CART method shares, to a large extent, general characteristics with other data-driven, model-based estimation methods, for example, in that it requires significant amounts of quantitative data. Table 10.1 summarizes the most relevant strengths and weaknesses specific to the CART method.

Table 10.1 Strengths and weaknesses of CART

Aspect	Strengths (+) and weaknesses (−)
Expert involvement	• (+) CART does not require much expert involvement. It requires an expert knowledgeable in using the method and interpreting its outputs • (+) Once a CART model is created, its use for estimation purposes is reduced to providing characteristics of the new project on its input and interpreting output (estimates) it provides • (−) Developing a CART model requires expertise in setting up the method's parameters
Required data	• (−) CART requires quite large amounts of data in order to produce reliable outputs • (−) The more effort drivers that are considered and the more different values they have across historical projects, the more historical data is required by CART to reliably "learn" effort dependencies represented by the data—i.e., to develop a reliable estimation model
Robustness	• (+) CART handles missing data • (+) CART makes no distributional assumptions of any kind, either on dependent or independent variables. No variable in CART is assumed to follow any kind of statistical distribution • (+) The explanatory variables in CART can be a mixture of categorical, interval, and continuous • (+) CART is not at all affected by outliers, collinearities, heteroscedasticity, or distributional error structures that affect parametric estimation methods such as regression analysis. Outliers are isolated into a node and do not have any effect on splitting. Contrary to parametric methods, CART handles and makes use of collinear data • (+) CART is invariant under monotone transformation of independent variables; i.e., the transformation of explanatory variables to logarithms or squares or square roots has no effect on the tree produced • (+) CART deals effectively with multidimensional project data; i.e., from a large number of project characteristics provided on CART's input, it can produce useful results using only a few characteristics that are most relevant from the perspective of project effort
Flexibility	• (+) CART does not require any specific information on its input • (+) Once developed, a CART model can be used multiple times for estimation without the necessity of accessing the base of historical projects • (+) A CART model can be easily rebuilt for a new situation using appropriate project data—under the condition that modeling is supported by a software tool
Complexity	• (−) CART has a complex theoretical basis; it uses elements of statistics and information theory • (−) CART requires setting up a few parameters, the meaning of which needs to be known by the person operating CART

(continued)

Table 10.1 (continued)

Aspect	Strengths (+) and weaknesses (−)
Support level	• (+) The CART method is well documented in multiple sources such as books and articles • (+) CART is supported by several software tools
Reusability	• (+) Estimation models created with CART are reusable for similar situations • (+) The CART model can be easily rebuilt for a new situation using appropriate project data—under the condition that appropriate tool support is available
Predictive power	• (+) CART produces the same outputs when provided with the same inputs • (−) The predictive power of CART depends on the similarity of the estimated project to historical projects on which the CART model was developed • (−) CART cannot estimate a value along a dimension that is outside the range of values encountered in the underlying data set (extrapolation)
Informative power	• (+) CART provides significant insight into project effort dependencies. For example, it has the ability to detect and reveal interactions between effort drivers represented in the input project data • (+) A CART tree allows for making conclusions about the relative importance of effort drivers. Effort drivers selected on top levels of the tree are considered more important than effort drivers below them • (−) Yet, binary trees do not allow for considering multiple factors in a single tree node. It might happen that two factors that are considered as less relevant when considered individually might be very important when considered in combination. This weakness can be solved by applying additional techniques for exploring relationships between effort drivers • (−) CART cannot reveal any effort relationships beyond that represented by available measurement data
Handling uncertainty	• (−) CART provides little support for handling estimation uncertainty. It does not accept uncertain inputs. Estimation uncertainty can be assessed using the distribution of effort across historical projects in the tree leaf in which the estimated project has been classified
Estimation scope	• (+) CART is, principally, applicable to any type of project activities at any granularity level. The only requirement for estimating effort associated with particular project activities is that historical data regarding these very activities are available for building the CART model
Availability	• (+) The availability of the estimates provided by CART depends on the availability of information on effort drivers covered by the CART model. For example, if a CART model requires information on effort drivers that are available late in the development cycle, it cannot be used for estimation before appropriate measurements can be collected. In order to estimate earlier, effort drivers need to be estimated. Yet, as CART does not support uncertain inputs, using estimates as a basis for estimation may lead to highly unreliable effort predictions
Empirical evidence	• (+) CART has been empirically validated in a number of field studies for effort estimation and predictions in other areas

Further Reading

- L. Breiman, J. Friedman, C. J. Stone, and R. A. Olshen (1984), *Classification and Regression Trees*. Chapman & Hall.

  This book provides a detailed overview of the theory and methodology of CART.

Case-Based Reasoning

11

We know nothing of what will happen in future, but by the analogy of experience.

—Abraham Lincoln

Case-based reasoning represents a memory-based, data-driven estimation method. In other words, it is an estimation method in which estimates are based solely on the analysis of quantitative project data and in which the data need to be available at the time of estimation.

11.1 Principles

The Case-based Reasoning (CBR) method literally implements the basic principle of the memory-based estimation paradigm. It estimates a new project (so-called *target*) by adapting the effort of the most similar historical projects (so-called *analogs*). Figure 11.1 illustrates this idea.

In order to find project analogs, CBR first selects the most relevant characteristics of a software project (effort drivers) and defines a project similarity metric upon it. The most commonly used measure of similarity is based on distance metrics such as Euclidian distance. Based on the distance metric k, nearest analogs to the target project are then selected.

The effort of selected analogs is then used to predict the target project. Simple approaches for adapting the effort of several analogs include median, mean, or distance-weighted mean over their actual effort.

Case-Based Reasoning is based on the intuition that new problems are often similar to previously encountered problems and, therefore, that past solutions may be of use in the current situation. In other words, the method solves a *new problem* by adapting solutions that were used to solve similar problems in the

A. Trendowicz and R. Jeffery, *Software Project Effort Estimation*,
DOI 10.1007/978-3-319-03629-8_11, © Springer International Publishing Switzerland 2014

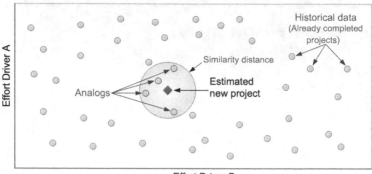

Fig. 11.1   Analogs in the case-based reasoning estimation

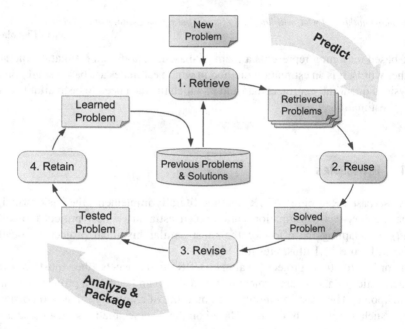

Fig. 11.2   The process of case-based reasoning

past—*previous problems.* Aamodt and Plaza (1994) present CBR as a four-step process (Fig. 11.2):

1. *Retrieve*: One or more problems that are similar to the new problem are retrieved from the base of previously solved problems, and one attempts to modify them to fit the new problem parameters.
2. *Reuse*: The solutions of the selected previous problems are reused to solve the new one.
3. *Revise*: The solved new problem is then revised against the actual solution.
4. *Retain*: When successfully tested, it is added to the base of previous problems to be reused for solving future problems.

In the context of software prediction, the retrieve and reuse phases represent a prediction method, that is, a process of coming up with estimates. The latter revise and retain phases represent a postmortem analysis of estimates and packaging project data for future reuse. The predictive performance of the estimation method is revised, in that estimates are compared against actual project outcomes observed at completion, and actual project data are stored in the measurement repository.

In fact, revise and retain phases should belong to every estimation process, independently of the particular method used to obtain estimates, as a part of organization improvement. In order to become and remain effective, effort estimation, as with any other process or technology within an organization, needs to be subject to continuous monitoring and improvement. We discuss these aspects in Chap. 16 as part of the continuous improvement of software effort estimation. The "revise" and "retain" steps of CBR correspond to the "Analyze Outcomes" and "Package Improvements" phases of the six-phase continuous improvement framework we propose in Sect. 16.3 for continuously improving an estimation approach. In the case of CBR estimation, retain and revise steps can, for example, include checking whether retrieved analogs were actually similar to the target project and whether all relevant project attributes were properly considered during the retrieval process.

In this chapter, we focus on the retrieve and reuse phases, which distinguish CBR from other estimation methods with respect to the way of obtaining effort estimates.

11.2 Estimation Process

In this section, we provide a brief overview of basic decisions that need to be made across retrieve and reuse phases while applying CBR for producing effort estimates. For each decision, we discuss supportive techniques that are typically applied in the software engineering context. Shepperd and Kadoda (2001) list several decisions that need to be made while applying CBR for the purpose of software effort estimation:

- *Selecting attributes*: Characteristics of the project environment that are believed to be relevant for differentiating projects with respect to productivity and effort are identified.
- *Scaling attributes*: In order to ensure an equal influence of selected attributes on the decision on which projects are similar, attributes needs to be normalized onto the same scale.
- *Identifying analogs*: Already completed projects (analogs) similar to the new project (target) are identified.
- *Selecting analogs*: The number of analogs to be used for estimating the effort of the target project is determined.
- *Adapting analogs*: The method for adapting the actual effort of analog projects in order to derive an estimated effort of the target project is defined.

11.2.1 Selecting Attributes

The first decision that needs to be made when applying CBR for effort estimation is what project attributes should be considered when searching through already completed projects for those that are most similar to the new project. Potential attributes may relate to any elements of the project environment such as processes, products, personnel, and resources.

Selecting vs. Weighting Attributes

In the context of software effort estimation, it was observed that relevant project attributes are often not equally relevant, and it is beneficial to differentiate the level of their relevancy. In consequence, selecting relevant project attribute factors has over the years been generalized to weighting attributes with respect to their relevancy. Notice that selecting or excluding an attribute corresponds to assigning it a dichotomous weight of 1 or 0, respectively. The predictive power of the CBR estimation is largely determined by the proper selection and weighting, of the relevance of project attributes influencing effort.

Suboptimal Approaches

In order to determine the weights, various techniques have been proposed. Mendes et al. (2002) propose deriving the weights based on the experience of human experts. A major critique regarding this approach is that weights depend largely on the subjective opinions of experts.

Alternatively to human judgment, several different analytical approaches for weighting attributes in CBR-based effort estimation have been proposed. Mendes et al. (2003a) proposed using correlation analysis for assignment of objective weights within similarity metrics. In this method, project attributes were simply categorized into two groups through assignment of dichotomous weights 1 or 2. Li and Ruhe (2008) in their AQUA+ method compute weights for different project attributes depending on their type; that is, whether an attribute represents a category, an ordinal or continuous number, a set, or a fuzzy number.

Optimal Approaches

Finally, a group of approaches have been proposed that attempt to determine an optimal set of project attributes through exhaustive search over a set of project measurements. Example techniques have been proposed by Shepperd and Schofield (1997) in their ANGEL[1] tool and by Auer et al. (2006). Yet, due to high computational complexity, the applicability of this approach is limited to small sets of attributes.

---

[1] Later version of the tool can also be found under the name ArchANGEL.

11.2.2 Identifying Analogs

The most relevant attributes identified in the previous step are then used to search for similar projects. Similarity between two projects is typically defined as a function of the distance between them. The most commonly used similarity metric is based on distance metrics such as the well-known *Euclidian distance* (Shepperd and Schofield 1997), *Manhattan distance* (Emam et al. 2001), and *Minkowski distance* (Stamelos et al. 2003b).

Alternative to using a single similarity metric, several authors propose considering multiple similarity metrics. For example, Walkerden and Jeffery (1997, 1999) use an average similarity computed over several distance metrics. Stamelos and Angelis (2001) analyze through simulation each alternative similarity metric and select the one that entails optimal estimation performance of CBR.

11.2.3 Scaling Attributes

An important issue to bear in mind when identifying project analogs with the help of similarity metrics is that all project characteristics under consideration must have the same degree of influence on the overall project similarity, independent of the units they are measured with. In order to address this issue, scaling techniques are used to transform the values of project characteristics before computing project similarity. For numerical scales, scaling may be realized by normalizing all project characteristics to the same range of values, for example, to [0, 1].

11.2.4 Selecting Analogs

Based on their similarity to the new target project, analog projects are selected from among already completed projects. As the number of analogs may significantly influence the performance of CBR estimation (e.g., Kadoda et al. 2001), selection of proper analogs should be considered carefully. In general, the number of analogs depends on the size of the available historical project data set.

One strategy is to fix the number analogs prior to estimation using information on the amount of available historical project data. For instance, Angelis and Stamelos (2000) recommend that for small data sets it is reasonable to consider a small number of analogs. In practice, the number of selected analogs varies between one and three (e.g., Myrtveit and Stensrud 1999; Jeffery et al. 2000, 2001; Mendes et al. 2003a; Martino et al. 2007).

Another strategy involves determining an optimal number of analogies in a cross-validation analysis. In this approach, different numbers of analogs are investigated using the past project data with respect to the predictive performance they provide. The number of analogs that provides the best estimation accuracy on the historical data is then adopted to estimate new projects. Example effort estimation methods that implement this strategy include BRACE (Stamelos and Angelis 2001) and AQUA (Li and Ruhe 2006).

11.2.5 Adapting Analogs

After selecting the most similar case(s), an adaptation method has to be selected to derive the final estimate. Adapting analogs to derive estimates is another activity that has significant impact on the overall performance of the CBR estimation process. There are several alternatives for adapting the nearest analogs for estimating the effort of a new, target project. We briefly discuss selected adaptation approaches that are most commonly used in the context of software effort estimation as follows:

- *Nearest neighbor*: This is the simplest case in which a single analog project is selected, and its actual effort is used as an estimate of the new project's effort.
- *Mean over selected analogs*: The statistical mean over the actual effort of selected analog projects is used as an estimate of the new project's effort.
- *Median over selected analogs*: The statistical median over the actual effort of selected analog projects is used as an estimate of the new project's effort. As compared to the "mean," the median moderates the impact of potential outlier effort on the final estimate.

In the context of these approaches, additional adjustments to estimated effort are typically applied in order to account for the differences between the estimated target project and the retrieved analogs. Most common adjustment approaches include:

- *Linear adjustment on project size*: The ratio between size of the analog and target projects is used to adjust effort (e.g., Mendes et al. 2003b, c; Ohsugi et al. 2007). For example, assume that the system size of the new project is 150 units, the system size of the most similar project is 200 units, and its effort is 1,000 units. With the application of an adaptation rule, the predicted effort is $150/200 \times 1,000 = 750$ units, rather than 1,000 units that would be estimated without applying the adaptation rule.
- *Linear adjustment on all project characteristics*: This approach represents a refinement of the linear adjustment on project size. Here, all factors with equal weights are used to adjust effort (Mendes et al. 2003b, c).
- *Weighted adjustment on all project characteristics*: This approach represents further refinement of the linear adjustment on all project characteristics. Here, all factors with various weights applied are used to adjust effort. The weight could be the same as those used in the weighted similarity metric (e.g., Mendes et al. 2003b, c). In another approach, weights represent ranks of analog projects sorted according to their similarity to the estimated target project. The higher-ranked analogs are then assigned higher weights to have more influence on the final estimate than lower-ranked ones (Kadoda et al. 2000; Mendes et al. 2003a, b).

Instead of deciding on a particular adaptation and adjustment approach, some estimation methods analyze several alternative adaptation approaches to determine the optimal one. An example of such a method is BRACE (Stamelos and Angelis 2001), which uses mechanisms of random simulation for selecting the optimal adaptation approach.

11.3 Strengths and Weaknesses

To a large extent, the CBR method shares general characteristics with other data-driven methods, yet it solves several weaknesses of the model-based approaches, especially parametric methods. Table 11.1 summarizes the strengths and weaknesses of the CBR method.

Table 11.1 Strengths and weaknesses of CBR

Aspect	Strengths (+) and weaknesses (−)
Expert involvement	• (+) CBR does not require much expert involvement. It solely requires an expert knowledgeable in using the method and interpreting its outputs
Required data	• (−) The amount and variety of project data required by CBR depend strongly on the range of different project situations that should be encompassed by estimation. If estimation takes place in a very homogeneous context, then very few historical projects would be sufficient for accurate estimation; in such cases, there is a good chance that a new project will be similar to one of the few historical ones
Robustness	• (+) CBR can deal with data on both continuous (i.e., interval, ratio, or absolute) as well as categorical (i.e., nominal or ordinal) measurement scales • (+) CBR deals well with collinearities in the underlying project data • (+) CBR does not require calibrating a single model to suit different estimation situations—the estimation process is simply repeated for each new project (target) using the complete set of historical projects • (+) CBR is able to deal with poorly understood domains (such as software projects), where the domain is difficult to model. In other words, CBR can be used successfully without having a clear model of how effort is related to different project characteristics • (+) CBR might be influenced by data outliers • (−) Dealing with missing data is still a rather difficult issue for CBR methods. Yet, typical implementations of CBR provide several ways to handle incomplete project data
Flexibility	• (+) CBR does not require any specific information on its input; that is, it does not require the input data to cover any specific effort factors or use any particular metric (e.g., software size can be measured using any metric as long as it is consistently used across all historical projects) • (−) CBR requires accessing the set of historical projects each time estimation needs to be performed. The complete data set needs to be available at the time of estimation
Complexity	• (+) CBR represents a way of reasoning similar to that of human estimators. In consequence, users of CBR may be more willing to accept estimates it provides

(continued)

Table 11.1 (continued)

Aspect	Strengths (+) and weaknesses (−)
	• (−) CBR requires setting up a few parameters, for which little guidance exists; a trial-and-error approach is typically necessary • (−) Factor selection/weighting techniques are typically computationally intensive
Support level	• (+) CBR is well-documented by a number of publications (e.g., books and journal articles) in the machine learning and software engineering domains • (+) CBR is supported by a number of tools, both free and commercial. Besides dedicated tools, CBR is typically implemented as a part of machine learning tools or machine learning modules of data analysis tools
Reusability	• (−) CBR has to be reapplied on the historical project data set each time an estimate is needed • (+) Once assigned, CBR parameters, such as weights on effort drivers, can be reused for multiple estimates in a similar context
Predictive power	• (+) An advantage of CBR over the model-based estimation methods is that it avoids the need to model the causal effort dependencies in a certain context based on sample data from this context (which is difficult without comprehensive data sets) • (−) The predictive power of CBR strongly relies on the available historical data. Accurate effort estimates for a new project are extremely dependent on the existence of analogs (similar projects) in the historical project data set • (−) Unless heuristics are used for selecting or weighting effort drivers, CBR provides repeatable estimates each time it is applied on the same inputs and with the same parameters • (−) CBR is not able to extrapolate, i.e., provide estimates for situations beyond those represented in the historical project data set • (−) Similarity metrics that assign effort drivers with equal importance, applied to search for similar cases, are intolerant of irrelevant effort drivers. This problem can be overcome by applying weighting techniques for prioritizing effort drivers
Informative power	• (+) CBR provides insight into its reasoning in that project analogs and the way they are adapted to derive effort estimates are explicitly visible • (+) CBR may provide insight into selected project effort relationships. Using techniques for selecting and/or weighting effort drivers provided in the project data set allows for drawing conclusions about the relative importance of particular effort drivers • (−) Factor selection/weighting techniques cannot identify relevant factors for which measurement data are not provided • (−) CBR is typically unable to provide information on the mutual relationships between considered effort drivers. Provided information is limited to the impact of individual effort factors on effort
Handling uncertainty	• (−) CBR typically does not accept uncertain information on its input • (−) Evaluating the uncertainty of estimates requires applying additional analysis. For example, distribution of actual effort across multiple project analogs (similar historical projects) can be used as an indicator of estimation uncertainty
Estimation scope	• (+) CBR is, principally, applicable to any type of project activities at any granularity level. The only requirement for estimating effort associated with particular project activities is that historical data regarding these very activities are provided in the base of historical projects

(continued)

Table 11.1 (continued)

Aspect	Strengths (+) and weaknesses (−)
Availability	• (+) Availability of the estimates provided by CBR depends on the availability of information on effort factors covered by the historical project base. If historical project data cover project characteristics that can be determined early in the project life cycle, then estimation can be performed early, based upon this subset of characteristics
Empirical evidence	• (+) CBR has been evaluated in a number of empirical studies in both academic and industrial contexts

Further Reading

• S.J. Delany and P. Cunningham (2000), *The Application of Case-Based Reasoning to Early Software Project Cost Estimation and Risk Assessment*, Report TCD-CS-2000-10, Department of Computer Science, UCD School of Computer Science and Informatics, Dublin, Ireland.

This report investigates the applicability of case-based reasoning for estimating software project effort in the early phases of the software development life cycle. The authors analyze the relevant strengths and weaknesses of CBR and discuss the issue of effort factors and their incomplete knowledge in the early stages of software development projects. They investigate the impact that missing and uncertain effort factors may have on the predictive performance of CBR.

• E. Mendes, N. Mosley, and S. Counsell (2003), "Replicated Assessment of the Use of Adaptation Rules to Improve Web Cost Estimation," *Proceedings of the 2nd International Symposium on Empirical Software Engineering*, September 29 – October 4, Rome, Italy.

E. Mendes, S. Counsell, N. Mosley, "Do Adaptation Rules Improve Web Cost Estimation," *Proceedings of the 14th Conference on Hypertext and Hypermedia*, Nottingham, UK, 2003, pp. 173–183.

These two publications present an empirical comparison of various approaches for adapting analogs in the context of CBR effort estimation. Authors investigate the impact of various adaptation rules on the estimation accuracy of CBR. Additionally, they analyze the impact of applying feature subset selection on the predictive performance of CBR. Authors perform their study in the context of "messy" project data, that is, data containing outliers and collinearities.

Wideband Delphi

12

It is not the majority vote, but the process that forms the majority that matters.

—John Dewey

Wideband Delphi represents expert-based estimation with a structured group consensus approach. Unlike most of the known effort estimation methods, it does not actually require a detailed description of the problem being estimated—that is, the scope of the project to be estimated. Determination of the exact project work items as well as their breakdown into detailed activities and tasks can be a part of the estimation process.

12.1 Principles

The method originates from the Delphi method developed at Rand Corporation in the late 1940s, in which a small team of experts provided their individual estimates based on the problem description and then reached consensus on a final estimate through feedback iteration. However, instead of open discussion, written feedback on individual estimates was summarized and provided back to estimators by a coordinator.

Farquhar (1970) observed that written feedback in the standard Delphi method does not provide a sufficiently broad communications bandwidth for the participants to exchange the volume of information necessary to calibrate their estimates with those of the other participants. This criticism led to the formulation of the modified Wideband[1] Delphi method, which was then popularized by Boehm (1981).

Finally, Mary Sakry and Neil Potter of The Process Group extended the Wideband Delphi procedure to seven steps (Fig. 12.1):

---

[1] The "Wideband" adjective underlines the widening of the communication channels in the original Delphi method.

A. Trendowicz and R. Jeffery, *Software Project Effort Estimation*,
DOI 10.1007/978-3-319-03629-8_12, © Springer International Publishing Switzerland 2014

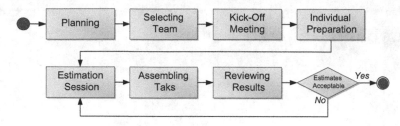

Fig. 12.1 Estimation procedure of Wideband Delphi method

1. *Planning*: The project manager defines the problem and plans estimation. Problem definition includes specifying project scope, constraints, and assumptions. In this step, work items (e.g., in a form of work breakdown structure) are identified. Moreover, supporting inputs for estimation such as historical project data are collected. Finally, the project manager specifies and schedules estimation activities.
2. *Selecting a team*: The project manager selects the coordinator and the estimation team (typically 2–7 estimators). The coordinator is responsible for moderating estimation sessions and integrating estimation results. It could be a project manager or a person delegated by him. Estimators should be knowledgeable in the estimated software product and represent perspectives of different project stakeholders (insofar as possible including sponsor, customer, and end user). In closing, the project manager supplies the estimation team with inputs to estimation collected in the planning step.
3. *Kickoff meeting*: The coordinator introduces the estimation procedure to the team and discusses inputs for estimation that were provided before the meeting (project scope, constraints, and assumptions). Finally, the team agrees on the estimation goal and consistent estimation units (e.g., person-hours, person-months, etc.)
4. *Individual preparation*: After the kickoff meeting, each member of the team estimates anonymously and independently of other estimators. Estimates as well as associated open questions and assumptions are documented in the estimation form (Fig. 12.2).
5. *Estimation session*: The coordinator calls a group meeting, in which he collects individual estimates and presents them (anonymously) to all team members. Estimators discuss open issues with the coordinator and with each other. At the end of each discussion round, each team member revises their estimates individually, yet without revealing them to the others. The discussion–revision cycles repeat until (1) the team accepts the range of estimates, (2) no estimator wants to change his/her individual estimates, or (3) the time planned for the session (e.g., 2 h) has elapsed.
6. *Assembling estimates*: The coordinator collects tasks, estimates, assumptions, and any other relevant information documented by estimators at the end of the estimation session and integrates (merges) them into the estimation output.

7. *Reviewing results*: The coordinator calls a group meeting, where estimators review the integrated estimation outcomes and reach consensus on final project estimates. In this session, a retrospective analysis of the applied estimation procedure (i.e., Wideband Delphi) is done, and potential improvements are identified.

12.2 Estimation Process

12.2.1 Planning

The goal of this step is to plan estimation work. Similar to overall project planning, a project manager identifies individual estimation activities, assigns necessary resources, and determines the estimation schedule. In the planning step, the problem being estimated is specified and scoped. The project manager breaks down large project activities into smaller, more manageable pieces of work that are also easier to estimate accurately. Furthermore, the project manager gathers any known project constraints, assumptions, and other information that might be relevant for creating credible estimates. Finally, historical project data that may support estimators' judgments are collected. The main inputs for this step are project charter and project data repository, if such a repository is available.

12.2.2 Selecting the Team

The goal of this step is to create an estimation team capable of providing accurate and credible project estimates. The project manager selects a coordinator, members of the estimation team, and any additional observers.

Coordinator

The role of the coordinator is to moderate and facilitate estimation meetings. For this purpose, a coordinator should be familiar with (and experienced in) the Wideband Delphi process and should possess the necessary leadership skills, such as conflict resolution capabilities, for example. The function of a coordinator is to objectively listen to the discussions, ask open-ended questions, challenge the team to address important project aspects they may have forgotten, calm down discussions when they get hot, and ensure that everyone in the team is contributing to the final outcome. The coordinator should be unprejudiced with respect to the estimated project and remain unbiased by opinions and estimates provided by estimators.

Tip

▶ In Wideband Delphi estimation, avoid the project manager taking the role of coordinator. Project managers should, at best, be a part of the estimation team.

Estimators

The role of estimators is to provide estimates for the problem defined by the project manager. While selecting estimators, several aspects should be considered. First of all, picking qualified estimators is a crucial element of generating credible estimates. Estimators should be knowledgeable about the estimation problem (project, domain, etc.), while being qualified in estimation, at the same time. Estimators should also cover a wide spectrum of development roles such as managers, developers, designers, architects, QA engineers, requirements analysts, technical writers, and so on. Moreover, sociological aspects should be considered to ensure that estimators are willing to provide honest predictions and feel comfortable while working with other team members. Summarizing, estimators should ideally represent a mixture of various skills, experiences, development functions, and personality types.

Observers

Observers are other project stakeholders, such as sponsors or customers, who introduce a "project-external," nonengineering perspective on the estimation problem. They should be encouraged to attend the meeting as they may provide valuable information not covered by the problem specification, for example, external project constraints. Their involvement may, and should, contribute to mutual understanding and trust between engineers, management, and customers. Yet, the presence of higher authorities, having political interests in the concrete estimation outcomes, may influence (bias) individual and group estimates. Therefore, involving observers should be considered with care.

Finally, in order to ensure high motivation, each person involved in the estimation should be personally interested in a good estimation outcome, not a particular outcome, because this will make them direct (intentionally or unintentionally) the estimation outcomes toward their personal expectations.

12.2.3 Kickoff Meeting

The goal of a kickoff meeting is to prepare the selected estimation team for applying the estimation procedure. Before the meeting, each member of the estimation team is provided with relevant project documents; that is, the problem definition as well as other information that may help in better understanding the project and, in the end, contribute to better estimates.

The kickoff meeting includes in particular the following activities:

1. Team reviews, discusses and agrees on the goals and scope of the estimation. The goal of estimation may, for example, be systematically determined using the goal template proposed by Basili et al. (1994b) in their Goal-Question-Metric (GQM) approach.

2. The coordinator explains the Wideband Delphi estimation procedure to the estimators.
3. If any estimation team member has not yet read the project documents distributed before the meeting, the coordinator reviews them with the team.
4. The team discusses project goals and the scope of the project to be estimated.
5. The team goes through and discusses the project work breakdown structure (WBS). The team decides initially on the list of 10–20 major activities from the top level of the WBS as the basis for the estimates. If necessary, these work activities can be further broken down into detailed tasks in the next steps of the estimation process.
6. The team discusses project scope, identifies missing information, and documents necessary assumptions.
7. Finally, the team agrees on a consistent unit of estimates (person-hours, person-days, etc.).

After the kickoff meeting, the coordinator consolidates and documents the outcomes and distributes them to the estimators as the basis for individual estimates. The inputs for estimation include project objectives, work items defined in the WBS, assumptions, and constraints.

12.2.4 Individual Preparation

The goal of the individual preparation is to produce initial estimates. Based on the outputs of the kickoff meeting, each estimator individually provides estimates for the identified project work items. Moreover, team members document any assumptions they need to additionally take in order to create estimates and any additional work items (e.g., project activities or tasks) they included into the WBS initially produced during the kickoff meeting. Figure 12.2 illustrates an example form of documents produced during the individual preparation step.

In practice, estimators may find it difficult to provide crisp estimates, particularly for the tasks with which they are not familiar. In order to handle the uncertainty of estimates, experts may be allowed to provide three numbers representing respectively best-case (minimal), most-likely-case, and worst-case (maximal) estimates.

Before estimating the effort required to accomplish particular project activities they can be grouped with respect to their main purpose. For example, as illustrated in Fig. 12.2, in addition to *constructive activities* for creating software products and *analytical activities* for assuring the quality of products, supporting *overhead activities* (e.g., training) can be distinguished.

Moreover, each estimator may break down the major activities identified initially during the kickoff meeting into tasks that are small enough to estimate accurately.

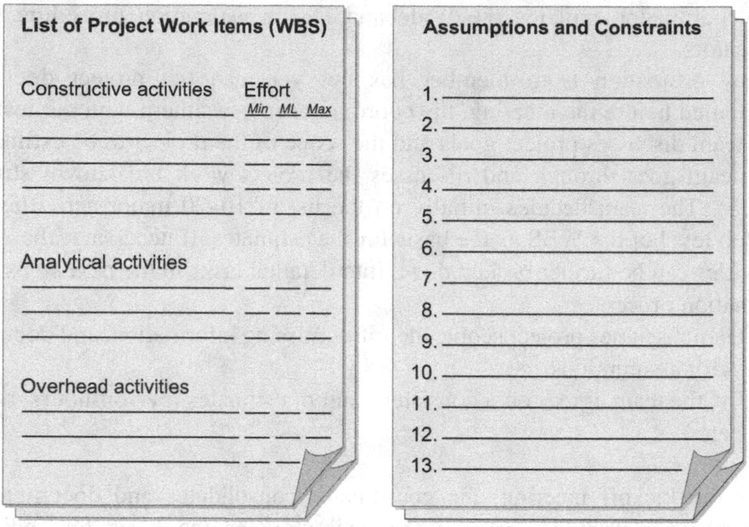

Fig. 12.2 Example Wideband Delphi individual preparation forms

Tip

▶ Make sure that during individual preparation, estimators are not biased in their predictions toward what the other project stakeholders want to hear. Ensure that estimators are free from external pressures.

12.2.5 Estimation Session

The goal of the estimation session is to come up with agreement among the estimators with respect to project scope (tasks), assumptions, and effort estimates.

At the beginning of the session, the coordinator leads a brief discussion, and estimators agree upon the essential changes they introduced during individual preparation to the project activities and assumptions defined during the kickoff meeting. The agreed changes create a basis for the further estimation process.

After initial discussion, team members obtain an estimation form (Fig. 12.3) where they put their initial estimates generated during the individual preparation phase. The estimation form can be used for estimating work items of any type and at any level of abstraction. For example, the form can document major project activities as well as detailed tasks for constructing software products, assuring the quality of software products, or for managing project work. The form will be used later in the session for documenting changes in personal estimates and the rationale behind particular changes. Typical rationales include known project constraints as well as assumptions that need to be made wherever information relevant to estimation is required but missing.

Team members input their best-case, most-likely, and worst-case estimates for each project activity and sum them up to the total project estimate.

Estimator _John Smith_   Date: _01 / 05 / 2010_   Form No. _01_

Estimation Goal

Object_ Software module X_   Perspective _Programmer_

Focus _Effort_   Context_Project Y_

Estimation Unit _Person-days_

	Work Items		Estimates - Min/ML/Max				Context & Assumptions
#	Name	Type	Initial	2nd	3rd	Final	
1	Code module X	Construc	9/10/12	7/9/10			Java, use of COTS
2	Review module X	Analyze	1/2/3	1/2/3			Review by peer
		Total	10/12/15	8/11/13			
		Delta	/////	-2/-1/-2			

Fig. 12.3 Example Wideband Delphi estimation form

At this point, an iterative process starts where, in each cycle, experts are presented total estimates, discuss them, and update their individual estimates based upon the discussion results. Because considering three values for each individual estimate may be difficult and confusing, a "compact" way of presenting total estimates to the team members, for the purpose of discussion, is necessary. One way is to represent each triple of estimates combined, in a form of probability distribution. We discuss representing triple estimates as Triangular or Beta-PERT distributions in Sect. 4.4. Although being an exact approach, representing estimates in the form of a probabilistic distribution might not be intuitive to the team members who are not familiar with and/or do not feel comfortable with probability theory. A simpler approach would be to compute statistical means for each triple estimate and present this value as a form of crisp estimate for the purpose of the discussion round. In this case, the range between the best-case and worst-case estimate can optionally be used as additional information on the uncertainty of a particular "mean" estimate. In order to compute the mean, one of the following formulas for appropriate probability distributions can be used:

- *Triangular*: Mean = (min + ML + max)/3
- *Beta-PERT*: Mean = (min + 4 ML + max)/6
- *Beta-PERT modified* (Stutzke 2005): Mean = (min + 3 ML + 2 max)/6

Raw Estimates

Estimator Id	Estimates		
	Min *Most Likely*	ML *Best Case*	Max *Worst Case*
Estimator 1	10	15	30
Estimator 2	30	35	40
Estimator 3	30	40	60
Estimator 4	50	60	60
Estimator 5	50	70	90

**Probability
Distribution**

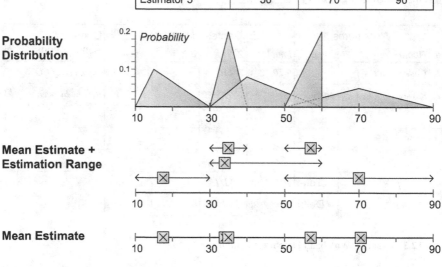

**Mean Estimate +
Estimation Range**

Mean Estimate

Fig. 12.4 Presentation of individual estimates

It is important that one formula should be consistently used for all estimates throughout the entire estimation session. Figure 12.4 illustrates the alternative ways of presenting individual estimates to the team members during the discussion rounds.

After discussing the "mean" estimates, team members can revise their estimate by providing again the best-case, the most-likely, and the worst-case predictions. In order to facilitate the process of deriving mean values, the estimation form should, at best, be provided in an electronic form, for example, as a calculation sheet where all derived values are automatically computed on the basis of individual triple estimates.

The typical estimation cycle consists of the following steps:

1. The coordinator collects all of the estimation forms and presents individual total estimates to the team. The forms are then returned to the estimators.
2. Estimators present to the rest of the group any changes they made to the task list and/or assumptions initially documented in the estimation form. Any open questions that occurred during individual preparation are raised and discussed

in the group. Specific estimates are not discussed, and estimators may remain anonymous if they wish to.

3. The team resolves open questions as well as any discrepancies in the tasks and assumptions taken individually by different team members. After achieving an agreement with respect to a particular issue, such as adding a new task or assumption, all team members modify their estimation forms in an appropriate and consistent manner, for example, by writing down appropriate tasks and assumptions. This step should typically take about 40 min for the first round and 20 min for the subsequent rounds.

4. Based on the changes to the tasks and assumptions made in the previous step, all estimators revise their individual estimates. This could be accomplished by, for example, providing the difference ("delta") between the previous and new estimate. For instance, an adjustment of "+5" or "−2" would respectively mean increasing the previous estimate, by 5 or decreasing it by 2. Alternatively, estimators may just provide new estimates, and "deltas" are computed afterward, if necessary. After the estimates for all tasks are revised, the new total estimates are computed for the next discussion and revision round.

The estimation session is typically finished when one of the following conditions is met:

- Individual estimates have converged to an acceptably narrow range. The acceptable range can either be quantitatively set up before the session or be decided ad hoc during the meeting by team members as the estimates converge.
- The consensus, that is, an acceptable convergence of estimates, cannot be achieved because, for example, team members are unwilling to modify their estimates any more.
- The scheduled number of estimation rounds has been reached (e.g., four rounds) or the scheduled meeting time has expired (e.g., 2 h). Still, an additional estimation session can be planned if required and agreed upon with all team members.

12.2.6 Assembling Estimates

The objective of assembling is to create the final list of project tasks and their estimates. The coordinator and project manager gather outputs of individual preparation and estimation sessions. They identify a unified list of project work items, for example, by removing redundant tasks, and resolve remaining differences in the individual estimates. Figure 12.5 illustrates an example assembly form.

For each work activity, its estimate is obtained by considering alternative estimates provided by different estimators. A formal way to aggregate alternative estimates might be to compute their average, for example, the average of probability distributions represented by triple estimates of individual estimators. An informal way of aggregating alternative effort estimates might be by taking the largest estimate as the worst-case effort, the lowest as the best-case effort, and the average

Estimation Goal					Date: _01 / 05 / 2010_

Object_ Software module X_   Perspective _Programmers, Testers_

Focus_ Effort_   Context _Project Y_

Estimators _J. Smith, M. White, S. Black_   Estimation Unit _Person-days_

	Work Items		Individual Estimates - Min/ML/Max				
#	Name	Type	Smith	White	Black	Final	Notes
1	Code module X	Construc	7/9/10	8/9/10	7/9/11	7/9/10	-
2	Review module X	Analyze	1/2/3	1/1/2	1/3/3	1/2/3	White has low experience in reviews
		Total	9/11/13	9/10/12	8/12/14	8/11/13	

Fig. 12.5 Typical Delphi task assembly form

from all alternative estimates as the most likely project effort. In Sect. 5.6, we discuss several potential approaches for integrating multiple alternative estimates.

Yet, before blindly aggregating widely different estimates, the project manager and coordinator should first consider handling outlier estimates. If there are good reasons to do it, for example, the relative inexperience of the estimator who provided estimates, outlier estimates should be excluded from the assembling.

Tip

▶ If estimates provided by individual experts differ widely, investigate the reasons of this discrepancy, and if you find good reasons, consider excluding them from the assembling.

The final project estimate is then obtained by summing up component estimates provided for all work activities identified during the estimation session. In Sect. 5.3, we discuss several approaches for aggregating component "bottom" estimates.

12.2.7 Reviewing Results

The goal of the review is to determine whether the assembled estimates are acceptable for all team members with respect to the achievement of estimation goals, such as planning and managing software project risks. The estimation team determines whether final estimates make sense and are within an acceptable range. Moreover, the team assesses if the integrated list of project work items is complete and corresponds to their vision of project work. If any critical deficiencies are identified, the team may decide to hold an additional estimation session where the issues identified during review will be resolved. For example, work activities, for which a wide discrepancy between best-case and worst-case estimates has been observed, might require more detailed consideration by decomposing them into detailed tasks and repeating the estimation on a lower level of abstraction.

12.3 Strengths and Weaknesses

In principle, the Wideband Delphi method shares, to a large extent, general characteristics with other group estimation methods, for example, in that it requires significant human overhead each time estimates are needed but deals with the low credibility of estimates based on the judgment of a single human expert. Table 12.1 summarizes the strengths and weaknesses of the Wideband Delphi method.

Table 12.1 Strengths and weaknesses of Wideband Delphi

Aspect	Strengths (+) and weaknesses (−)
Expert involvement	• (−) Wideband Delphi, similar to other group estimation methods, requires extensive involvement of multiple experts, who should represent a variety of expertise and viewpoints on the developed software. This makes group estimation methods relatively expensive
	• (−) The laborious estimation procedure must be repeated each time estimates are needed
Required data	• (+) Wideband Delphi does not require any historical project data
Robustness	• (−) Expert judgments can be biased by irrelevant and misleading information. For example, a customer's requirements regarding the project budget may bias estimators (willing to satisfy customer) toward this budget
	• (+) The structured group consensus procedure of Wideband Delphi contributes to lower bias than observed in estimation based on the judgment of a single expert or unstructured group estimation
Flexibility	• (+) Wideband Delphi does not require any particular information for its input
	• (+) Wideband Delphi does not require any adjustments when applied in different situations and contexts
Complexity	• (+) Wideband Delphi is intuitive and easy to apply
Support level	• (+) Wideband Delphi is well documented. It does not require any sophisticated tool support—beyond standard office software such as word processor and calculation spreadsheets
Reusability	• (−) Wideband Delphi does not provide an estimation model that can be reused across similar projects. The estimation procedure has to be completely reapplied each time estimates are needed

(continued)

Table 12.1 (continued)

Aspect	Strengths (+) and weaknesses (−)
Predictive power	• (+) Human experts can factor (yet implicitly) exceptional and unique project characteristics and their interactions. For example, experts are able to deal with the differences between past project experiences and the new techniques, architectures, or applications involved in the new project
	• (−) Human experts involved in the estimation procedure may vary largely with respect to their individual estimates. Although the group estimation process is supposed to compensate for the effect of a single expert, the group estimates may remain unstable
	• (−) Estimates based on human judgment can be biased by a number of factors such as individual expertise, experiences and preferences of the human expert, as well as influence of other experts participating in the estimation process and irrelevant and misleading information. For example, human estimators tend to provide underestimations for tasks perceived as easy, and overestimations for those perceived as difficult
Informative power	• (−) Expert estimation fails to provide an objective and quantitative analysis of project effort dependencies, for example, what project characteristics affect effort and to what extent
	• (+) As a side effect, estimation based on group discussion typically contributes to better understanding of software development problems; it also allows for identifying weaknesses in software requirements and design
Handling uncertainty	• (+) Wideband Delphi has the ability to operate on uncertain information (i.e., expertise of human experts). It may also provide information regarding the uncertainty of estimates, for example, in that experts provide their estimates in the form of three values: minimal, maximal, and most likely
	• (−) Yet, the method does not provide any systematic techniques for handling uncertainty; additional analysis techniques, such as operations on simple probability distributions, need to be used for this purpose
Estimation scope	• (−) Applicability of Wideband Delphi for estimating different type of activities is limited by the expertise of involved domain experts. In practice, estimation is limited to those project activities with which involved human estimators have experience
Availability	• (+) Wideband Delphi is applicable in any phase of software development. Also, here the general rule applies that the later in the development life cycle estimation is performed the more accurate estimates are because more is known about the project
Empirical evidence	• (+) Although Wideband Delphi specifically has not been widely investigated, group estimation methods have been validated in a number of empirical studies, in both research and industrial contexts

Further Reading

• A. Stellman and J. Greene (2005), *Applied software Project Management. 1st Edition.* O'Reilly Media Inc.

    In Chapter 3 ("Estimation"), the authors provide a detailed description of the Wideband Delphi procedure modified by Mary Sakry and Neil Potter from The Process Group.

Planning Poker

13

These days we do not program module by module; we program software feature by feature.
—Mary Poppendieck

Planning Poker represents expert-based estimation with a structured group consensus approach. The method originates from agile software development where it was created in order to provide a lightweight approach for estimating software development interactions and planning the scope of software releases. Unlike other alternative expert-based methods, Planning Poker explicitly makes use of historical project data. Actually, the method focuses on estimating the functional size of developed software and then uses historical data on development productivity to come up with the effort required to develop software of a given functionality.

13.1 Principles

13.1.1 Agile Estimation

The term Planning Poker—also known as Planning Game—was introduced by Grenning (2002) in the context of planning agile software development, in short, agile planning. Many of the principles of agile estimation are, in fact, derived from the expert-based group-consensus methods such as Wideband Delphi. Table 13.1 summarizes the most important principles of agile estimation defined by Cohn (2004, 2005). Actually, these principles go beyond agile development and apply to software effort estimation in general.

13.1.2 User Story

In Planning Poker, estimates are assigned to pieces of user-valued functionality (also called software features) that are specified in the form of one or two sentences in the everyday language of the user, the so-called user story. In agile planning, a

A. Trendowicz and R. Jeffery, *Software Project Effort Estimation*,
DOI 10.1007/978-3-319-03629-8_13, © Springer International Publishing Switzerland 2014

Table 13.1 Principles of agile estimation

Principle	Comment
Do not estimate waste and do not look too far into the future	Estimates should not go into the future more than two iterations on the fine-grain iteration planning level and not more than two releases on the coarse-grain release planning level
Estimate as a team (development + customer)	Both developers and customers should be involved in the estimation process as they represent different perspectives and different experiences and possess different information, typically not known to the others. If there are many people who should be involved in the estimation process, they may be split into several estimation subgroups
Estimate your own work	Software should be estimated by people committed to it. It means that at the level of the entire software (iteration or release planning), all members of the estimation team need to be interested in the software and good estimates. At the task level, developers responsible for completing the task should be providing their estimates
Base estimates on facts rather than on speculation	Estimates should be based upon actual data. The size of software features should be based on the size of similar features, and the effort required for implementing software features should be based on the delivery rates observed in the past
Estimate early	Estimation should start as soon as software features are initially specified in the form of user stories. If relevant information is missing for completing estimates for a particular user story, then this should be clarified in a question round with the author of the story
Estimate often. Learn from experience	Initial estimates generated at the beginning of an iteration should be revised on a daily basis. Notice that a typical iteration in the context of agile development spans from one to several weeks. For longer iterations, the frequency of estimation revisions should be adjusted appropriately
Estimate small features	A single software feature, represented by a user story, should be roughly between several days and 2 weeks of effort
Keep it simple. Use simple rules	Estimators involved in the agile planning are developers and customers who are typically not knowledgeable in software estimation. Therefore, the estimation process should be based on simple rules so that every estimator understands it and feels comfortable following it while creating individual estimates

(continued)

Table 13.1 (continued)

Principle	Comment
Communicate the constraints/assumptions of your estimates rather than just the numbers	The estimation process should contribute to better understanding and specification of the software system being developed. Therefore, any software project constraints and assumptions identified during the estimation process should be documented in addition to estimates
Estimate total effort for implementing a story (development, testing, documentation, etc.)	Different from other expert-based estimation methods, such as Wideband Delphi, where individual WBS activities are the subject of estimation. In agile planning, all tasks required for implementing a software feature are considered. In other words, an estimate for a user story covers all kinds of development activities such as design, coding, testing, and documentation
Do not bring initial estimates from release planning into sessions for detailed estimates, e.g., iteration planning	On the release planning level, initial coarse-grained estimates are assigned to complete software features in order to determine the rough scope of an individual release. On the iteration planning level, detailed estimates are created for the feature-related and technical tasks in order to plan the exact scope of the next development iteration. Using release planning estimates as a basis for iteration planning may bias task estimates so that the sum of task estimates fit a corresponding story estimate. As during detailed planning, additional constraints and assumptions can be identified, and as technical tasks are considered in addition to purely functional ones, the task estimates will typically not sum up to the initial feature estimates
While tracking effort, do not consider the percentage of feature implementation—count feature as implemented when all related tasks are completed	While tracking software development, only the effort spent on completed features should be counted as consumed—do not count partial effort consumption, e.g., by referring to the percentage of feature completion. A software feature is considered as completed when all its development activities are completed, e.g., design, coding, documentation, acceptance testing

user story is a unit of software functionality, and it represents a chunk of software functionality—software feature—which is (Beck and Fowler 2000)

- Valuable to the customer, that is it has a particular business value to the customer
- Understandable to both customers/users and developers

- Independent of one another
- Testable
- Small enough so that (1) it can be easily compared, regarding its size and complexity, to several stories developed in the past, and (2) developers can work out several user stories in a single development iteration

An example of two user stories might be (Beck and Fowler 2000): (1) *Present to the customer the ten lowest fares for a particular route,* or (2) *When you are showing the flights, sort them by convenience: time of journey, number of changes, closeness to desired departure, and arrival time.* User stories are not technical tasks—and they are written in business language, so they can be prioritized by the customer with respect to the business value they represent to the customer.

User Story
User stories are neither use cases nor requirement statements. User stories are written so that each can be given an estimate of how difficult or time-consuming it will be to develop; use cases, on the other hand, are generally too large to be given useful estimates. Also, a story is implemented in a single iteration of an agile project, while it is common to split a use case across multiple iterations (even though those iterations are usually longer than on a story-driven project).

13.1.3 Product Backlog

User stories are typically stored in a so-called *Product Backlog*, which is a list of all product features sought by the customer.

13.1.4 Story Point

The actual subject of estimation in Planning Poker is not effort but the size of the user story measured in terms of so-called story points. *Story Point* is an abstract unit of size that represents an intuitive mixture of effort and complexity. The size of user stories is then an input for further planning activities where project effort and schedule are planned.

Story points are assigned according to a *Fibonacci number sequence*, where each number is the sum of the previous two. For example, in Planning Poker story points may start from 0 and continue as 1, 1, 2, 3, 5, 8, 13, and so on. Using the Fibonacci sequence, where the distance between subsequent numbers increases, reflects the assumption that the larger the size of a user story, the greater is the uncertainty.

13.1.5 Triangulation

The basic principle behind estimating the size of a user story in Planning Poker is so-called triangulation. It refers (Cohn 2005) to the process of estimating the size of a user story relative to two other user stories with the purpose of increasing the reliability of the estimate. An example logic of triangulation may be as follows: *I am estimating the size of user story US-2 being equal to 2 story points because it looks to me somewhat larger than user story US-1, which I have already estimated at 1 story point, and somewhat smaller than user story US-3, which I already estimated at 3 story points.*

New user stories can be estimated in analogy to (1) the actual size of similar user stories already implemented in the past or (2) the estimated size of similar new stories already estimated in the same estimation session. Note that the latter approach can and should start as soon as a few user stories have already been estimated—estimates of next stories can then be based or validated relative to already estimated ones. Although not exact, triangulation is also quite an effective way for the estimation team to verify and control that they are not gradually changing the meaning of the story point unit over time.

Sizing User Stories Using Pair-Wise Comparisons

Miranda et al. (2009) observed that using triangulation principles for user stories is not good enough to produce reliable estimates.

First, triangulation is vulnerable to inconsistent judgments. Consistent sizing requires that if user story a is x times larger than user story b, and user story b is y times larger than user story c, then user story a is xy times larger than user story c, for all stories a, b, and c.

Second, in the case of multiple user stories, it is not clear which user story should be selected as the reference point for estimating other stories. Yet, the choice of a particular story affects estimates. Reliable sizing requires the structure of story comparisons is balanced and connected—balanced in that every user story should appear in as many comparisons as any other user story; connected in that any user story is compared, directly or indirectly, to every other user story.

In order to address these issues, the authors propose the use of incomplete cyclic designs to identify which user stories to compare with to reach desired estimation accuracy and the use of the paired comparison method to deal with judgment inconsistencies among estimators. Please refer to Miranda et al. (2009) for the detailed estimation procedure.

13.1.6 Disaggregation

In order to increase the chances of finding similar user stories for the purpose of triangulation, their size should be kept at a similar magnitude. As typical user stories are quite small, any extraordinarily large user story should be broken into smaller substories. In addition to the increased probability of finding analogous stories, substories are also principally easier to estimate by human experts—due to the relatively small scope of work associated with implementing a small story.

13.2   Estimation Process

Similar to Wideband Delphi and unlike most of the other known effort estimation methods, Planning Poker does not require a detailed description of the estimated problem, that is, of the scope of the project being estimated. It is a full planning process that combines estimation with identifying the scope of the project and the tasks required to complete the software development. Effort estimation in planning poker starts with estimating the size of user stories. After that, data on the effort needed to implement a user story within a single iteration in historical projects or in previous iterations of the new project is used to predict the effort for estimated user stories. The effort consumed per story unit is called velocity and, it corresponds to the development productivity of an agile team.

13.2.1   Estimation Team

Similar to the Wideband Delphi technique, different project stakeholders, such as developers and product owners, may and should be involved in the estimation. Yet, estimates are collaboratively created by developers only, where developers include all analysts, designers, programmers, testers, and so on. Other project stakeholders participate in estimation in the role of observers who represent another viewpoint on the software product and project. Observers may provide information the developers are not aware of, which is relevant for estimation. A coordinator, who does not estimate and is supported/advised by the project manager, moderates the estimation session. The coordinator is typically a person knowledgeable in software functionality such as the product owner or analyst.

13.2.2   Estimating the Size of User Stories

The procedure of Planning Poker for estimating user stories consists of several steps:

1. *Planning*: Although this step is not explicitly named in the Planning Poker process, it is necessary to prepare the estimation session. In this planning step, the project manager defines the problem and plans the estimation session. Problem definition includes specifying the project scope in terms of user stories, as well as any project constraints and assumptions that should be considered

during estimation. Finally, the project manager selects an estimation team and specifies the schedule for estimation.

2. *Preparation*: At the start of an estimation session, each estimator is given a deck of cards with valid estimates written on them. The valid estimates are represented by the number of story points in an increasing order, according to a Fibonacci sequence.

3. *Question Round*: For each user story to be estimated, the coordinator or the person most knowledgeable in the corresponding chunk of functionality presents it to the estimation team. Next, the estimation team is given an opportunity to raise questions and open issues for classifying potential assumptions and risks. A summary of the discussion is recorded by the project manager.

4. *Individual Estimation*: After potential issues have been clarified, estimators secretly assign their individual estimates to the user story by selecting the card with an appropriate number. After that, each estimator lays the selected card facedown on the table.

5. *Discussion*: After all estimators have decided on their individual estimates for the considered user story, they call their cards simultaneously by turning them over and revealing their estimates to other estimators. If estimates differ widely, the estimators who provided extremely low and high estimates are given an opportunity to justify their decision by explaining to the others the rationale behind particular estimates. The objective of this step is not to attack authors of outlier estimates but to allow learning of what the information and assumptions considered during the estimation were that they probably did not take into account. The group then discusses, for a few minutes, the user story as well as the estimates they provided and the rationale they took. During the discussion, the coordinator should document any information that may be relevant for implementing the user story. The coordinator also takes care that time limits set for the discussion round are strictly obeyed.

6. *Revision*: After the discussion, estimators revise their individual estimates by selecting an appropriate card. Again, cards are kept hidden until all estimators are done with reestimation, at which point they again show their estimates to the others. If estimates still differ widely, then the discussion and revision steps are repeated. The process of discussing and revising estimates is iterated until a consensus is reached. Typically, estimates provided by the developer who is likely to be assigned for implementing the user story have the largest weight for the overall consensus.

An estimated story point size of user-valued software functionality is used for further project planning, which in agile development includes two levels of planning: *iteration planning* and *release planning* (Fig. 13.1).

User stories and their estimated size are one of several inputs for project planning. In order to plan effort, estimators additionally need to know the productivity rate for user stories that are going to be developed. For this purpose, they first determine the length of a single development iteration and then look at historical projects (or previous iterations in the current project) for how many user stories the

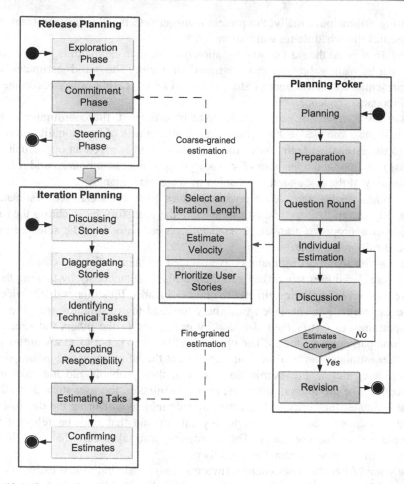

Fig. 13.1 Levels of project planning in the context of agile software development

team was able to develop within a single iteration of the selected length. This
number is referred to as *velocity*. Knowing the iteration length and velocity, one can
then estimate the total amount of effort required to develop all user stories. As
additional input to planning, priorities are assigned to user stories. This helps select
user stories that need to be developed first or to select a subset of user stories in case
product scope (functionality) needs to be downsized because of limited project
resources (budget).

13.2.3 Release Planning

Release planning focuses on coarse-grained planning of which user stories are to be
included in which release of the software product and when the product is going to

be delivered. In the case of fixed-date projects, the project planner starts with a delivery date and looks at how much work can be finished by this date. In the case of fixed-content projects, the project planner starts with required user stories and looks at how long it will take to develop them. The objective of release planning is not to create a plan that says which team members will work on which user stories or tasks, or in what sequence work activities will be performed in each iteration (this is the subject of iteration planning). Moreover, release planning focuses on user stories, not on work tasks. Customers and developers are both involved in the release planning process that consists of three main phases:

- *Exploration Phase*: In this phase, the customer gives all his requirements for the system, which are written down in the form of short sentences (*user stories*) on so-called *user story cards*. This is an iterative process where, based on business problems, corresponding solution requirements are gathered and their impact on work effort is estimated. If developers are not able to estimate some story, for example, due to its complexity, they split it up and write it down again. The process ends when all business problems are covered with requirements.
- *Commitment Phase*: Within the commitment phase, representatives of the business and development side commit themselves to the functionality that will be included in the software and the date of the next release. This is a typical release planning process where the customer prioritizes requirements, whereas developers assign risks and effort (requirements represent benefit, whereas risk and effort represent cost). The scope of the next release is agreed upon for the optimization of benefits and required cost. Based on the planned number of iterations per release and the estimated number of user stories per iteration (i.e., velocity), the total amount of work that can be accomplished within the release is estimated.
- *Steering Phase*: In this phase, the plan can be adjusted, new requirements can be added, and/or existing requirements can be changed or removed.

13.2.4 Iteration Planning

Iteration planning focuses on fine-grained planning of the work activities and tasks of the developers. It should be done at the beginning of each development iteration, and it is the time for clarifying details on how to implement each user story. The planning process involves the customer, and it consists of three phases:

- *Discussing Stories*: The customer reads the stories foreseen for a given iteration to developers who ask questions and give opinions regarding the difficulty of implementing particular stories. In order to facilitate better understanding of a story, the customer may provide additional information such as a detailed description of the story's acceptance criteria. During discussion, the customer may change the priority initially assigned to each story. The highest-priority stories should be developed first to deliver the highest business value. On the other hand, the highest-risk stories should be addressed earlier rather than later.

- *Disaggregating Stories*: As stories refer solely to software functionality, they are often difficult to estimate. In order to support developers in estimation, individual stories may be decomposed into a set of different tasks that are then recorded on so-called *task cards*. These tasks are then used by developers for detailed effort estimation. If a developer cannot estimate the task because it is too big or too small, then he can split it or combine it with other tasks, respectively.

- *Identifying Technical Tasks*: In addition to implementing user stories, a software development project also involves some purely technical tasks that are not directly related to software functionality. Examples of such tasks are installing necessary infrastructure, providing training, or adjusting specific development processes. As estimation requires considering all types of project activities, technical tasks need to be identified.

- *Accepting Responsibility*: The functional and technical tasks identified in the previous steps are then assigned to the developers who will estimate the effort or time needed to complete the task.

- *Estimating Tasks*: Developers estimate the effort or time required to complete tasks they are assigned. Individual estimates are based on the developer's velocity observed in the most recent development iterations. The estimation is based on so-called Yesterday's Weather principles, which says that in the current iteration a developer can implement exactly as many story points as he did in the last iteration. For example, if the historical velocity was 40 story points per iteration, tasks that are worth 40 story points should be planned per iteration.

- *Confirming Estimates*: This is actually a postmortem phase, which takes place after the iteration is finished. After all tasks planned for the iteration are completed, the end result is matched with the original user story and the actual effort or time is compared to the plan.

13.3   Strengths and Weaknesses

In principle, the Planning Poker method shares, to a large extent, general characteristics with other group estimation methods. For example, it requires extensive involvement of human experts. Yet, it minimizes the overhead required for estimation through lightweight estimation procedures and the use of historical project data on development productivity. Table 13.2 summarizes the strengths and weaknesses of the Planning Poker method.

Table 13.2 Strengths and weaknesses of Planning Poker

Aspect	Strengths (+) and weaknesses (−)
Expert involvement	• (−) Planning Poker, similar to other group estimation methods, requires extensive involvement of multiple experts—who should represent a variety of expertise and viewpoints on the developed software. This makes group estimation methods relatively expensive
Required data	• (+) Planning Poker does, principally, not require any historical project data. Information on the development velocity from previous iterations are however needed for predicting the effort required for developing estimated user stories
Robustness	• (−) Similar to other expert-based estimation methods, in Planning Poker expert judgments can be biased by irrelevant and misleading information. For example, a customer's requirements regarding the project budget may bias estimators who are willing to satisfy a customer, toward this budget
Flexibility	• (+) Planning Poker does not require any particular input information (besides software specification) • (+) Planning Poker does not require any adjustments when applied in different situations
Complexity	• (+) Planning Poker is intuitive and easy to apply
Support level	• (+) Planning Poker is well documented and does not require any sophisticated tool support. Standard office software such as word processor and calculation sheets suffice to support estimation steps, such as preparing estimation cards and collecting estimates
Reusability	• (−) Similar to other expert-based methods, Planning Poker does not provide any estimation model that can be reused across similar projects. The estimation procedure has to be completely reapplied each time estimates are needed • (+) Development velocity numbers can be reused for estimating user stories across similar projects and iterations of the same project
Predictive power	• (+) Human experts can factor (yet only implicitly) exceptional and unique project characteristics and their interactions. For example, experts are able to deal with the differences between past project experiences and the new techniques, architectures, or applications involved in the new project • (−) Estimates based on human judgment can be biased by a number of factors such as individual expertise, experiences and preferences of human experts, as well as the influence of other experts participating in the estimation process and irrelevant and misleading information • (−) Human experts vary largely with respect to their estimates. Although the group estimation process implemented in Planning Poker is supposed to compensate for this effect, the group estimates remain unstable—e.g., due to mutual influences of group members on each other's estimates
Informative power	• (−) Expert estimation within Planning Poker, rather fails to provide an objective and quantitative analysis of project effort dependencies; e.g., what project characteristics affect effort and to what extent • (+) As a side effect, estimation based on group discussion typically contributes to a better understanding of software development problems; it also allows for identifying weaknesses in software requirements and design
Handling uncertainty	• (+) In the context of agile development, uncertainty is tackled by incremental development. Development teams learn about product and project characteristics and revise estimates as they develop individual product features

(continued)

Table 13.2 (continued)

Aspect	Strengths (+) and weaknesses (−)
	• (−) Planning Poker provides limited support for handling uncertainty. It recommends using ranges for reflecting uncertain development velocity; yet, it principally leaves estimators free of selecting a specific method for defining the range. An example approach recommended by Cohn (2009) is to provide 50 % or 90 % confidence estimates and compute an uncertainty buffer using the standard deviation statistic
Estimation scope	• (−) Applicability of Planning Poker for estimating different types of activities is limited by the expertise of involved domain experts. In practice, only the activities that experts have experience with can be estimated
Availability	• (+) Planning Poker is applicable at any time—any increment or release—in the software development process
Empirical evidence	• (−) There is little empirical evidence regarding the Planning Poker method. Most of the available publications report on subjective experiences gained while using the method rather than any systematic empirical evidence of the method's effectiveness

Further Reading

• M. Cohn (2005), *Agile Estimating and Planning. 1st Edition.* Prentice Hall PTR.
    The book presents comprehensive discussion of estimation and planning agile software development projects.

• E. Miranda, P. Bourque, and A. Abran (2009), "Sizing user stories using paired comparisons." *Information and Software Technology*, vol. 51, no. 9, pp. 1327–1337.
    Authors provide a systematic way for estimating the size of user story using triangulation.

Bayesian Belief Networks (BBN)

14

Shallow men believe in luck. Strong men believe in cause and effect.
—Ralph Waldo Emerson

Bayesian Belief Networks (BBN) is a hybrid estimation method. It represents a model-based, parametric[1] estimation method that implements a define-your-own-model approach. Actually, for the purpose of software effort estimation, the method adapts the concept of Bayesian Networks, which has been evolving for many years in probability theory. The approach was recently adapted to software estimation due to its ability to combine knowledge based on quantitative measurement data and human judgment into intuitive graphical models with a sound theoretical basis. These applications include estimation of software development productivity (Stewart 2002; Pendharkar et al. 2005) and effort (Moses and Clifford 2000; Stamelos et al. 2003a; Mendes 2007; Hamdan et al. 2009). This ability is particularly attractive in the software engineering context where measurement data are scarce and much knowledge is hidden in the heads of human experts.

14.1 Principles

14.1.1 The BBN Model

Bayesian Belief Network (*BBN*) or simply *Belief Network* is a directed acyclic graph (DAG), in which nodes represent random variables (discrete or continuous) and edges express probabilistic dependency among the linked variables. Note that although BBNs are typically used to represent causal relationships, this does not need to always be the case; they can represent simple correlation. Each direct relationship is described by an *edge* starting from the influencing variable (*parent*

---

[1] Nodes in the parametric BBNs represent discrete or continuous (typically Gaussian) univariate random variables. In general, nonparametric BBNs have also been proposed, in which no joint probability distribution is assumed for variables.

A. Trendowicz and R. Jeffery, *Software Project Effort Estimation*,
DOI 10.1007/978-3-319-03629-8_14, © Springer International Publishing Switzerland 2014

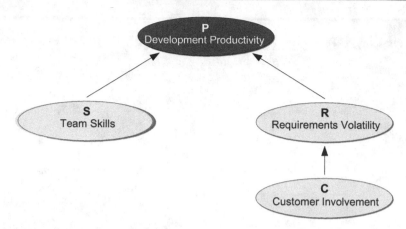

Fig. 14.1 Example Bayesian Belief Network

node) and terminating on the influenced variable (*child node*), where "influence" is understood as statistical dependency. The example network in Fig. 14.1 represents believed causal dependencies between software development productivity and selected characteristics of the software development environment. The root node "Development Productivity" has two child nodes: "Team Skills" and "Requirements volatility." These relationships represent the belief (typically based on empirical observations) that development productivity is influenced by the skills of the development team and the volatility of software requirements. In particular, the more skilled the team, the more productive it is, and the more volatile the requirements are, the less productive is development (e.g., because effort is spent on rework resulting from changing requirements). Finally, the "Requirements volatility" node has one child node "Customer Involvement." This association represents the belief that the more a customer is involved in software development (especially requirements specification), the more volatile are his or her requirements.

BBNs represent knowledge about an uncertain domain and are mainly used in situations that require statistical inference, that is, situations where beliefs regarding the likelihood of the events that have not yet been observed need to be updated in the light of other events that have actually been observed. In the context of BBNs, the events that have not yet been observed are called *hypotheses* (*H*), whereas the observed events are called *evidence* (*E*). BBNs use probability calculus and Bayes' Theorem (14.1) for propagating the evidence throughout the belief network, thereby updating the strength of beliefs regarding the likelihood of the events that have not been observed yet.

$$P(H|E) = \frac{P(H) \cdot P(E|H)}{P(E)} \tag{14.1}$$

where

- $P(H \mid E)$ represents the posterior probability of H given E
- $P(H)$ represents the prior probability that H is a correct hypothesis in the absence of evidence E

- $P(E / H)$ represents the conditional probability of the evidence E occurring if the hypothesis H is true; it is also called a likelihood function of H for fixed E
- $P(E)$ represents the marginal probability of E, that is, the a priori probability of witnessing the new evidence E (under all possible hypotheses)

14.1.2 Conditional Independence

An essential assumption underlying BBNs is *conditional independence* of variables it represents. It says that each variable is independent of its nondescendants (nonchildren) given the state of its direct parents. Thanks to this property, it is often possible to reduce (sometimes significantly) the number of parameters that are required to characterize the *joint probability distribution* (*JPD*) of the variables in a BBN. In consequence, BBNs provide an efficient way to compute the posterior probabilities given the evidence. For instance, computing JPD for all variables in the example BBN in Fig. 14.1 by the probabilistic chain rule, assuming that each factor is measured using <u>two</u> values "High" and "Low" would require $2^4 - 1 = 15$ parameters, whereas employing a conditional independence assumption would reduce this number to 8 parameters.

- *Chain rule: $P(P, R, C, S) = P(P \mid R, C, S) \cdot P(R \mid C, S) \cdot P(C \mid S) \cdot P(S)$*
- *BBN: $P(P, R, C, S) = P(P \mid C, S) \cdot P(R \mid C) \cdot P(S)$*

Depending on the structure of dependencies in the BBN, the reduction in the number of parameters that need to be considered compared to the simple chain rule may differ.

Chain Rule
In probability theory, the chain rule permits the calculation of any member of the joint distribution of a set of random variables using only conditional probabilities. Chain rule for a sequence of n events A:

$$P\left(\bigcap_{i=1}^{n} A_i\right) = P(A_1) \cdot P(A_2 | A_1) \cdot P(A_3 | A_2 \cap A_1) \cdot \ldots \cdot P\left(A_k \Big| \bigcap_{i=1}^{n-1} A_i\right)$$

14.2 Usage Scenarios

One of the very useful properties of BBNs is that they allow inference in any direction on the path between related nodes, thus supporting two basic purposes of estimation:

- *Predictive (causal) inference*: The hypothesis regarding the value of node X is updated based on evidence nodes connected to X through its parent node. This process is also referred to as a *top-down* or *forward* inference.
- *Diagnostic inference*: The hypothesis regarding the value of node X is verified in the light of evidence for nodes connected to X through its children nodes. This process is also referred to as a *bottom-up* or *backward* inference.

Due to the relatively high difficulty of acquiring parameters of a continuous probability distribution and the necessity of applying complex inference computations, continuous variables are rather rarely considered when constructing BBNs in the context of software effort estimation. Typically, discrete events are considered, whereby each particular state has an associated likelihood of occurrence.

Each discrete node in a BBN has an associated $N \times M$ *Node Probability Table* (*NPT*), where N is the number of node states and M is the product of its parent nodes states. In NPT, each column or row, depending on how NPTs are constructed, represents a conditional probability distribution, and, consequently, its values should sum up to 1. In Example 14.1, conditional probability distributions are represented by rows.

Cognitive and Computational Complexity of BBN

The size of the probability matrices of each node grows exponentially, as the values and the cause-nodes increase. In order to reduce the size and mental complexity of the NPTs, the values of each node must be as few as possible (e.g., up to eight). Moreover, the cause-nodes of each effect-node must also be as few as possible (e.g., up to four). One of the methods to keep the number of nodes and arcs low is grouping nodes that represent a certain concept and building a separate sub-BBN for them. Finally, exact inference (i.e., computation of joint probability distributions) is known to be an NP-hard problem.

Example 14.1. Applying Discrete BBN for Estimating Project Effort

Figure 14.2 presents a simple example of a *causal effort model*, that is, a model that represents cause–effect effort dependencies within a software project. The BBN has three nodes: "Total Effort" (dependent variable) and two effort factors: "Skilled Team" and "Requirements Volatility."

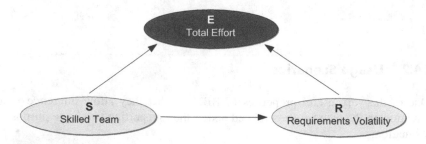

Fig. 14.2 Example effort estimation Bayesian Belief Network

For the sake of simplicity, each factor considered in our network is measured with very few discrete values. "Total Effort" has two discrete values: "low" and "high." "Skilled Team" is a binary variable ("true," "false"), and "Requirements Volatility" is measured on the ordinal scale: "low," "medium," and "high."

Joint Probability Distribution: $P(E, S, R) = P(E \mid S, R) \cdot P(S \mid R) \cdot P(R)$

Tables 14.1, 14.2, and 14.3 present respective node probability tables where initial probabilities are defined by domain experts based on their past experience.

Table 14.1 Node probability table for the "Skilled Team" variable

Skilled staff ("S")	
True ("t")	False ("f")
0.8	0.2

Table 14.2 Node probability table for the "Requirements Volatility" variable

Skilled team ("S")	Requirements volatility ("R")		
	Low ("l")	Medium ("m")	High ("h")
True ("t")	0.5	0.3	0.2
False ("f")	0.1	0.2	0.7

Table 14.3 Node probability table for the "Total Effort" variable

Skilled team (S)	Requirements volatility ("R")	Total effort ("E")	
		High ("h")	Low ("l")
True ("t")	Low ("l")	0.1	0.9
	Medium ("m")	0.3	0.7
	High ("h")	0.5	0.5
False ("f")	Low ("l")	0.4	0.6
	Medium ("m")	0.6	0.4
	High ("h")	0.9	0.1

Computing Marginal Probabilities: First let us compute unconditional (marginal) probabilities of a certain value of "Total Effort":

$$P(E = l) = \sum_{S \in \{t, f\}, R \in \{l, m, h\}} P(S) \cdot P(R) \cdot P(E = l \mid S, R) = 0.65$$

And since "Total Effort" has only two states, the probability of the "high" state can be easily computed as one minus the probability of the "low" state:

$$P(E = h) = 1 - P(E = l) = 0.35$$

In an analogical way, we compute marginal probabilities for the "Requirements Volatility" variable:

$$P(R = l) = \sum_{S \in \{t,f\}} P(S) \cdot P(R = l|S) = 0.42$$

$$P(R = m) = \sum_{S \in \{t,f\}} P(S) \cdot P(R = m|S) = 0.28$$

$$P(R = h) = \sum_{S \in \{t,f\}} P(S) \cdot P(R = h|S) = 0.30$$

Predictive Inference: Now let us update our initial beliefs regarding total effort in the light of evidence on skilled staff ("Skilled Team" = "true"). In this case, the conditional probability table (Table 14.2) already tells us the probabilities for the levels of requirements volatility.

- $P(R = l \: / \: S = t) = 0.5$
- $P(R = m \: / \: S = t) = 0.3$
- $P(R = h \: / \: S = t) = 0.2$

Total Effort is inferred from evidence on "Skilled Team" and updated beliefs on "Requirements Volatility":

$$P(E = l|S = t) = \frac{P(E = l|S = t)}{P(S = t)} = \frac{\sum_{R \in \{l,m,h\}} P(E = l, S = t, R)}{\sum_{E \in \{l,h\}, R \in \{l,m,h\}} P(E, S = t, R)} = 0.76$$

$$P(E = h|S = t) = \frac{P(E = h|S = t)}{P(S = t)} = \frac{\sum_{R \in \{l,m,h\}} P(E = h, S = t, R)}{\sum_{E \in \{l,h\}, R \in \{l,m,h\}} P(E, S = t, R)} = 0.24$$

Or, since "Total Effort" has only two states, the probability of the "high" state can be easily computed as one minus the probability of the "low" state:

$$P(E = h) = 1 - P(E = l) = 0.24$$

Notice that if we would know for sure, for instance, later in development, that "Requirements Volatility" is actually "low," then the probability of Total Effort being "low" would increase to 0.9 as specified in Table 14.3. The probability of "Total Effort" being "high" would be appropriately reduced to 0.1.

Diagnostic Inference: Another scenario might be that we want to adjust our initial belief, taken at the beginning of the project, that we have a highly skilled development team. The observation has been made as the project progresses that total effort is trending toward actually being high. We may formulate the initial belief and actual observation as follows:

- Initial belief: $P(Skilled \: Team = t) = 0.8$
- Evidence: $P(Total \: Effort = h) = 1.0$

Using diagnostic inference, we can then update our initial belief of the project staff being skilled in the light of evidence regarding total project effort:

$$P(S = t|E = h) = \frac{P(S = t|E = h)}{P(E = h)} = \frac{\sum_{R \in \{l,m,h\}} P(E = h, S = t, R)}{\sum_{S \in \{t,f\}, R \in \{l,m,h\}} P(E = h, S, R)} = 0.76$$

where

$$P(E, S, R) = P(E|S, R) \cdot P(S|R) \cdot P(R)$$

The resulting probability is:

- Adjusted belief: $P(Skilled\ Team = t) = 0.55$

As we see, the probability of skilled team decreased. Consequently, the likelihood of volatile requirements decreased also:

- $P(R = l\ /\ E = h) = 0.14$
- $P(R = m\ /\ E = h) = 0.27$
- $P(R = h\ /\ E = h) = 0.59$

In other words, evidence on "Total Effort" being actually "high" contributes to increased likelihood of variables that have a negative impact on "Total Effort," namely, unskilled team and volatile requirements. ∎

14.3 Strengths and Weaknesses

BBNs provide useful mechanisms for integrating quantitative techniques and expert judgment for the purpose of making predictions. In particular:

- BBNs are both mathematically rigorous and intuitively understandable.
- BBNs adopt probabilistic mechanisms for representing and operating on uncertain information.
- An inference mechanism in BBNs allows for testing various trade-off scenarios by introducing various evidence values.

Yet, their practical application is still limited by sophisticated theoretical background, restrictions on the use of continuous and mixed (continuous and discrete) variables, and exponential growth in complexity of acquiring conditional probability data and inference computations as the size of a causal model grows. Table 14.4 summarizes the strengths and weaknesses of the BBN method.

Table 14.4 Strengths and weaknesses of BBN

Aspect	Strengths (+) and weaknesses (−)
Expert involvement	• (+) Simple Bayesian network based on discrete variables does not require much expert involvement • (−) Dependent on which elements of the estimation model are to be based on human judgment, complex Bayesian networks require moderate to large involvement of human experts • (−) Creating a BBN model requires an expert to know basic principles of Bayesian Belief Networks, which is not covered by standard curricula in software engineering • (−) The structure of a BBN model can be constructed fairly easily. However, it should be constructed carefully because of the need to elicit the conditional probability values. For continuous probability functions, distribution parameters need to be provided, which might be difficult for experts not familiar with probability theory. For discrete probability functions, the number of conditional probabilities that need to be specified by experts increases exponentially as the number of possible values and the cause-nodes increase
Required data	• (+) BBN does not principally require any historical project data • (−) If a BBN model is to be elicited from the measurement data, then a significant amount of historical project data is required. This amount depends on which elements of the model are predefined and which need to be inferred from data: model structure or model parameters, or both
Robustness	• (+) BBN allows decision makers to combine partial empirical knowledge (collected through historical projects) with subjective human expertise • (−) BBN does not provide explicit support for dealing with multiple inputs, e.g., as provided by multiple experts. Handling multiple inputs requires application of additional techniques, such as group consensus techniques for combining judgments of multiple human experts
Flexibility	• (+) BBN does not require any particular data or specific metrics on its input • (+) Adapting a model to a new situation is quite straightforward and requires adjusting either the complete BBN model or its selected parts. The extent of adjustments depends on how much the target situation differs from the one for which the source BBN model was built
Complexity	• (−) BBN has a strong, yet relatively complex, theoretical background • (−) For discrete probability functions, the size of the node probability table (NPT) in each node of the BBN model grows exponentially, as the values and the cause-nodes increase. There is a trade-off between the granularity of the estimation output and the manageability of the BBN: the smaller the size of the NPTs, the more manageable the BBNs become and the larger will be the final interval estimates of the output of the BBN
Support level	• (+) Bayes' Theorem and Bayesian Belief Networks are widely documented in a number of books and publications from probability theory and causal modeling areas • (+) Modeling Bayesian Belief Networks is supported by a number of commercial and free software packages. Yet, features provided by different software tools differ widely
Reusability	• (+) BBN models can be reused "as is" across similar projects • (+) Elements of the BBN model, such as the structure of causal effort dependencies, can be reused (partially or as whole) for building BBN models in other contexts

(continued)

Table 14.4 (continued)

Aspect	Strengths (+) and weaknesses (−)
	• (+) For example, the values in the node probability tables assigned to intermediate nodes (i.e., those that have cause nodes) will typically not vary for each project because they reflect the expert opinion about the way the nodes affect each other in general. Therefore, the BBN can be reused across similar projects
Predictive power	• (+) BBN provides repeatable estimates when applied on the same inputs • (−) Empirical studies show rather poor predictive performance of the BBN when applied for the purpose of software effort estimation. When applied in the same situation, alternative methods such as multivariate stepwise regression or case-based reasoning outperform BBN methods (e.g., Mendes and Mosley 2008) • (−) Since the BBN model is based (at least partially) on human judgment, it is burdened by judgmental biases. BBN does not provide explicit ways to cope with judgmental biases
Informative power	• (+) The BBN model provides information on causal effort dependencies in a transparent and intuitive manner. It specifies the most relevant factors influencing project effort, their causal interdependencies, and the strength of these relationships
Handling uncertainty	• (+) BBN is powerful at representing and modeling uncertainty: (1) the input of the BBN can be probabilistic values, and the output is a joint probability distribution and not a point forecast; a decision maker can use the joint probability distribution information to estimate the probability or risk that a budget will overrun; (2) BBN provides a capability of updating the probability distribution • (+) The BBN method allows for risk estimation and can be used for "what if" analysis to explore the impact of changes in some project characteristics on other characteristics. In that sense, BBN facilitates considering multiple project scenarios and trade-offs between resources used in the project and outcomes it delivers • (+) BBN handles both continuous and discrete probability distributions • (−) Considering continuous probability distributions requires specifying a priori the distribution function and requires that experts provide their judgments regarding causal effort dependencies in terms of parameters of this function • (−) Using mixed (continuous and discrete) probability distributions within BBN requires involving advanced analysis techniques and is supported by a limited number of tools
Estimation scope	• (+) BBN is, principally, applicable to any type of project activities at any granularity level. The only requirement for estimating the effort associated with particular project activities is that appropriate factors are considered in the causal model; learning the BBN model from quantitative data requires that historical project data regarding appropriate project activities are available
Availability	• (+) The availability of the estimates provided by BBN depends on the availability of information on effort drivers covered by the BBN model. Yet, even if a BBN model requires information on effort drivers that are actually available late in the development cycle, early predictions can be based on estimated values of inputs. Later, when actual data are available, they are used as so-called facts for revising initial estimates
Empirical evidence	• (−) There is relatively little empirical evidence on applying BBNs to software effort estimation. Much of it is limited to the context of web applications

Further Reading

- I. Ben-Gal (2007), "Bayesian Networks", in F. Ruggeri, F. Faltin, and R. Kenett (eds.) *Encyclopedia of Statistics in Quality & Reliability*, Wiley & Sons.

  This short chapter provides a well-written compact introduction to Bayes' Theorem and Bayesian Belief Networks. It presents all relevant concepts in a concise and clear way and supports them with intuitive examples.

- A. Darwiche (2010), "Bayesian Networks. What are Bayesian networks and why are their applications growing across all fields" *Communications of the ACM*, vol. 53, no. 12, pp. 80–90.

  The article provides a lightweight introduction to the Bayesian Belief Networks. Using very simple language, the author explains the basic concepts of BBN and illustrates them on intuitive everyday and domain-specific examples. The author shows how example problems from various domains, such as medicine, systems engineering, genetic linkage analysis, or image processing, can be transformed to and solved (at least partially) with a BBN. Moreover, the article briefly discusses different usage scenarios of a BBN and the issue of its scalability. Finally, author compares BBN existing alternative probabilistic graphical models.

- C. Glymour and G.F. Cooper (eds.) (1999), *Computation, Causation, and Discovery*. AAAI Press.

  This book provides in-depth knowledge on causation and discovering causal dependencies based upon analysis of quantitative data and human expertise. Authors provide the theoretical background and discusses typical challenges and controversies with respect to causal discovery. Finally, they shows typical application domains for causal discovery.

- P. Spirtes, C. Glymour, and R. Scheines (2001), *Causation, Prediction, and Search, 2nd Edition*. New York, N.Y.: Springer-Verlag, MIT Press.

  This book provides in-depth knowledge on causal models, in particular Bayesian Belief Networks. Authors present theoretical background, specifically graph theory to display joint and conditional probability structure. Moreover, they discuss the relationship between probability and causation and describe several alternative algorithms for discovering causal structures from quantitative data. Finally, they review typical application domains of causal models.

CoBRA

15

The world is richer in associations than meanings, and it is the part of wisdom to differentiate the two.

—John Barth

Cost estimation, benchmarking, and risk assessment (CoBRA) method is a hybrid effort estimation method. It represents a model-based, parametric estimation method that implements a define-your-own-model approach. Briand et al. (1998) developed it specifically for the purpose of software effort estimation, and it considers the most relevant constraints and capabilities of software engineering contexts. The method has the capability of combining typically scarce measurement data with the expertise of human experts into an intuitive graphical effort model. These three aspects—little requirements on available measurement data, capability of utilizing humans, and a simple theoretical basis—make this method especially attractive in software engineering contexts.

15.1 Principles

15.1.1 The CoBRA Model

The core idea of CoBRA is to model software development effort as consisting of two elements: nominal effort and effort overhead.

Nominal effort is the engineering and management effort spent on developing a software product of a certain size in the context of a nominal project. *Nominal project* is a hypothetical "ideal" project in a certain environment of an organization (or business unit). It is a project that runs under optimal conditions, that is, a project where all environmental characteristics having an impact on project effort are at "the best" levels ("perfect") from the start of the project. Note that "the best" refers to realistic levels that are possible in a certain context, not to the best imaginable levels. For instance, the project objectives are well defined and understood by all

A. Trendowicz and R. Jeffery, *Software Project Effort Estimation*,
DOI 10.1007/978-3-319-03629-8_15, © Springer International Publishing Switzerland 2014

staff members and the customer and all key people in the project have appropriate skills to successfully conduct the project.

Effort overhead (*EO*) is the additional effort spent on overcoming imperfections of a real project environment, such as insufficient skills of the project team. Effort overhead refers to nonproductive project effort spent in addition to the nominal effort. In CoBRA, effort overhead is quantified as the percentage of additional effort over nominal. For example, a project's EO = 50 % would mean that the project actually requires 150 % of nominal effort, that is, 50 % more than it would require if it was a nominal project.

Nominal productivity (P_{Nom}) refers to development productivity under optimal project conditions, that is, productivity of a nominal project where all effort factors have their best levels. In general, productivity refers (IEEE-1045 1993) to the ratio between a project's output and input. In the concrete case of software projects, development productivity is computed as the ratio between the size of delivered software products and the effort consumed to develop these products (15.1).

$$\mathrm{Productivity} = \frac{\mathrm{Size}}{\mathrm{Effort}} \tag{15.1}$$

In real software projects, actual development productivity (P_{Act}) is decreased by nonproductive effort spent on overcoming any imperfect characteristics of the project. For example, a certain effort must be expended to train a development team. The factor by which productivity is decreased depends on specific characteristics of an individual project. The difference between nominal and actual productivity (called *productivity loss*) is proportional to the proportion of additional nonproductive effort, and in CoBRA, it is accounted for through effort overhead. In general, the higher the effort overhead, the higher the actual project effort and the lower the actual development productivity. CoBRA implements the idea of nominal project effort and effort overhead through two basic components of an effort model (Fig. 15.1): effort overhead model and productivity model.

15.1.2 Effort Overhead Model

Effort overhead model (or *causal effort model*) consists of factors affecting the project effort within a certain context (so-called *effort factors* or *effort drivers*). The causal model is obtained through expert knowledge acquisition (e.g., involving experienced project managers). An example is presented in Fig. 15.2. The arrows indicate direct relationships. The "+" indicates a positive relationship, and the "–" indicates a negative relationship. One arrow pointing to another indicates an interaction effect. For example, an interaction exists between "disciplined requirements management" and "requirements volatility". In this case, a decreased level of disciplined requirements management magnifies the negative influence of volatile requirements on project effort. In CoBRA, we refer to effort factors directly linked to effort as *direct effort factors* and to the effort factors linked to direct

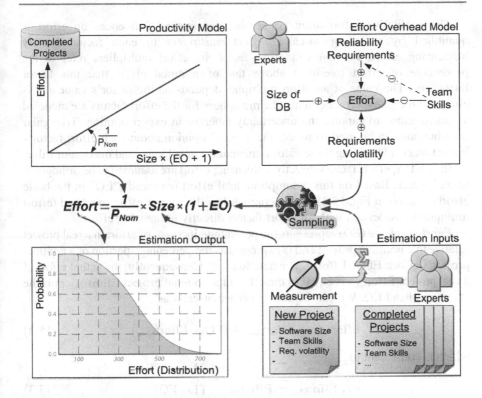

Fig. 15.1 Overview of the CoBRA method

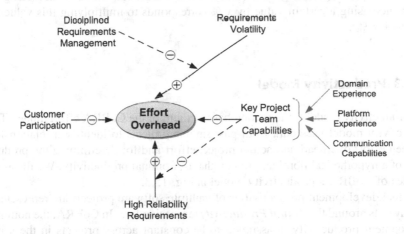

Fig. 15.2 Example of effort overhead model

factors as *indirect effort factors*. In the aforementioned example, "requirements volatility" is a direct effort factor, whereas "disciplined requirements management" is an indirect effort factor.

The qualitative information concerning the factors' influences on effort is quantified by assigning so-called *effort multipliers* to each factor directly influencing effort. For a given effort factor, its effort multipliers refer to the percentage of effort overhead above that of nominal effort that this factor introduces. The value of an effort multiplier depends on the factor's value and is elicited through expert judgment. The multipliers for the effort factors are modeled as distributions to capture the uncertainty inherent in expert opinion. Triangular distributions can be used to reflect the experts' opinion about each effort factor's impact on cost by giving three values: minimum, most likely, and maximum value.

In CoBRA, effort factors directly influencing effort are assumed to be orthogonal to each other. Based on this assumption, total effort overhead ("EO" in the basic effort equation in Fig. 15.1) can be computed as the sum of effort overhead (effort multipliers) associated with all effort factors directly influencing effort.

Effort overhead (*EO*) represents the percentage increase of effort in a real project relative to a nominal project and is expressed as the percentage portion of a nominal project's effort: $EO \times Effort_{Nom}$, where $EO \geq 0$. Consequently, the actual effort of a real project $Effort_{Act}$ is equal to the effort of a nominal project $Effort_{Nom}$ plus the effort overhead EO. We can express it mathematically as

$$Effort_{Act} = Effort_{Nom} + (EO \times Effort_{Nom}) \tag{15.2}$$

which is equivalent to

$$Effort_{Act} = Effort_{Nom} \times (1 + EO) \tag{15.3}$$

Simply speaking, (15.2) and (15.3) reflect basic mathematics, according to which increasing a certain value by x % corresponds to multiplying this value by (100 % + x %).

15.1.3 Productivity Model

The productivity model is the second base element of the CoBRA effort model. The productivity model uses data from past similar projects to identify a relationship between effort overhead and actual project effort and for determining the productivity of a hypothetical nominal project, that is, nominal productivity. We illustrate the idea of CoBRA's productivity model in Fig. 15.3.

Actual development productivities of multiple software projects are represented by gray dots around the *Actual Productivity* regression line. In CoBRA, the nominal development productivity is assumed to be constant across projects in the same context and is used as a baseline for estimating new projects. Therefore, we can theoretically determine nominal productivity using actual development productivity and actual effort overhead of any project. We need to solely increase the project's actual development productivity by the factor represented by its actual effort overhead (15.4).

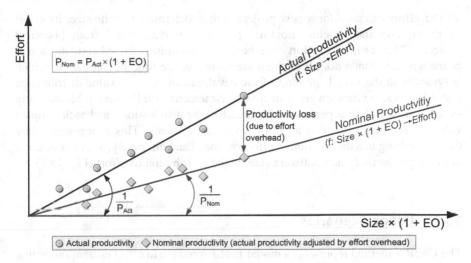

Fig. 15.3 Nominal productivity (P_{Nom}) and actual productivity (P_{Act})

$$P_{\text{Act}} = \frac{P_{\text{Nom}}}{1 + \text{EO}} \qquad (15.4)$$

In real software projects, computing nominal productivity using project-specific actual productivity and effort overhead will lead to nominal productivities that vary across projects. This phenomenon is represented in Fig. 15.3 by diamond-shaped dots spread around the *Nominal Productivity* regression line. It is because the effort overhead computed using CoBRA's effort overhead model does not account for the true project's effort overhead. Main causes of this deviation are (1) modeling error, in that an imperfect effort overhead model does not correctly and completely cover all true causal effort dependencies, and (2) measurement error in project data used for computing nominal productivity.

In order to determine *baseline productivity* for estimating future projects, CoBRA synthesizes project-specific nominal productivities computed across multiple historical projects, for which actual development productivity and effort overhead are already known. Traditionally, this is accomplished using a linear regression model f : Size $\times$ (1 + EO) $\rightarrow$ Effort. The model represents the basic idea of the CoBRA method that nominal effort is linearly dependent on size and that actual nonlinearity is caused by environmental influencing characteristics represented by effort factors. The slope of the regression line of the model approximates the inverse hypothetical nominal development productivity and is used in CoBRA as a baseline for estimating new projects.

Notice that the nominal productivity regression line represents a simple bivariate relationship that does not require a large data set. This is important, as it explains why CoBRA does not have demanding data requirements, as opposed to data-driven estimation techniques. In order to build up such a regression model, data from merely about ten historical projects are needed.

The effort estimate for a new project is then determined by its size, its effort overhead, and the baseline nominal productivity determined from historical projects. The project's effort overhead is determined based on its actual characteristics. Since not all of them are known at the time of estimation, which is typically at the very beginning of the development process, value distributions instead of exact values are given to cover their uncertainty. Running a Monte Carlo simulation, sampling is performed from each of the distributions, and each sampled value is summed, obtaining an effort overhead estimate. This is repeated many times, resulting in a distribution of effort overhead and ultimately, after considering nominal productivity and software size, in the distribution of effort (Fig. 15.1).

15.2   Usage Scenarios

The CoBRA method represents a model-based approach to effort estimation, in that an effort model is developed prior to estimation. Like other model-based estimation methods, it includes three basic processes: developing an estimation model, applying the model to obtain estimates, and maintaining the model in order to preserve or improve its performance. Figure 15.4 shows an abstract view of these processes and their relationships within the CoBRA method.

An initial effort model is developed from scratch, but it may reuse elements of already existing models that have been used in similar contexts and proved to provide effective support for achieving similar estimation objectives. In traditional effort modeling approaches, a complete model is created in the initial iteration and is then revised in the following iterations based upon results of its validation using historical project data. In consequence, in the first iteration, a complex model would typically be developed. In practice, estimators have difficulty in focusing on the most relevant effort factors and tend to consider a number of factors that have minimal or even no impact on project effort. Analyzing and improving such complex models is difficult and brings more cost than benefits. Inspired by Agile approaches to software development, CoBRA develops an effort model in a series of small increments. In each increment, only a very limited part of the model is changed, where changes include additions, deletions, and modifications of basic model elements. After the initial model has successfully been developed, it is

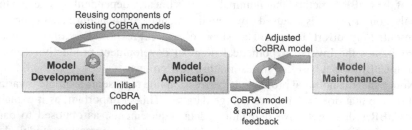

Fig. 15.4 Major processes of the CoBRA method

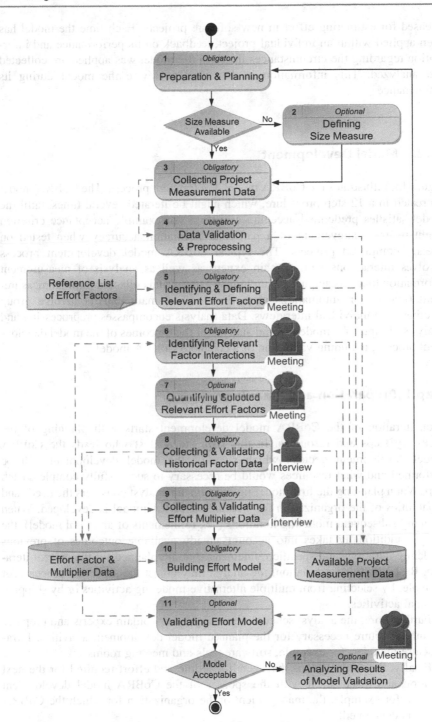

Fig. 15.5 Major steps of the CoBRA model development process

released for estimating effort in new software projects. Each time the model has been applied within an individual project, feedback on its performance and information regarding the circumstances in which the model was applied are collected and analyzed. This information is then used to revise the model during its maintenance.

15.2.1 Model Development

Figure 15.5 illustrates the CoBRA model development process. The CoBRA model is created in a 12-step procedure, which might be iterated several times, until the model satisfies predefined acceptance criteria. An example acceptance criterion might be the achievement of a particular estimation accuracy when tested on already completed projects. The typical CoBRA model development process involves interactions with domain experts as well as analysis of measurement information that was acquired from human experts and collected through measurement (manual or automatic). Interactions with domain experts involve group meetings and individual interviews. Data analysis encompasses preprocessing and analysis of inputs for modeling and analysis of the outcomes of the model development process, including validation of a complete CoBRA model.

Step 1. Preparation and Planning

Each iteration of the CoBRA model development starts with planning of the necessary steps and resources. In this step, the analyst who leads the CoBRA model development decides which steps of the model development will be performed and what resources would be necessary to successfully complete each step. When planning the first modeling iteration, an analyst considers the needs and capabilities of the organization for which the CoBRA model is developed. When planning subsequent modeling iterations (i.e., refinements of an initial model), the analyst additionally takes into account already available outcomes of previous modeling iterations and specific refinements that are planned for the current iteration. Based on this information, the analyst may adjust the modeling process, for example, by selecting from multiple alternative modeling activities or by skipping optional activities.

Furthermore, the analyst schedules meetings with domain experts and prepares the infrastructure necessary for the planned model development activities. Infrastructure includes, for example, software tools and meeting rooms.

Finally, the analyst plans the overall schedule and effort required for the next iteration and discusses it with the sponsor of the CoBRA model development process, for example, the management of the organization for which the CoBRA model is developed.

Step 2. Defining the Size Metric

Software size is one of the critical inputs for estimation with the CoBRA method (see basic CoBRA equation in Fig. 15.1). In order to build a CoBRA model, the data on software size from about at least ten already completed—historical—projects are needed for developing the CoBRA model. For this purpose, a consistently measured software size must be available for the historical projects and for the future projects that are to be estimated using the developed CoBRA model. If an appropriate size metric is not already defined or the software size has been inconsistently measured across historical projects, then an appropriate size metric is defined in this step of the model development process. Otherwise, this step can be omitted.

In order to define an appropriate size metric, the analyst identifies software artifacts produced by the processes, for which effort is going to be estimated using CoBRA. For these artifacts, a size metric is then defined. An appropriate size metric does not have to be restricted to one artifact. It may consider the volume of multiple artifacts. A classic example is measuring the size of software code in the context of enhancement projects. In order to reflect the effort required for developing code, the size metric considers four different types of code: the newly developed code, the existing code that has been modified, the existing code that has been removed, and the existing code that has been adapted without changes.

An important requirement regarding the size metric is that reliable and consistent size data can be retrospectively collected for the historical projects considered in the CoBRA model development.

Step 3. Collecting Project Measurement Data

In this step, the analyst collects measurement data that are necessary and data that can be useful for building a CoBRA effort model. The absolutely necessary data include actual software size and development effort from the historical projects upon which the CoBRA model is developed.

In addition to size and effort, the analyst may collect any measurement data that are already available for the considered historical projects. These data can then be used as an additional source of information when developing CoBRA. For example, the analyst may use additional project measurement data to complement and/or validate information acquired using expert judgment.

Step 4. Data Validation and Preprocessing

In this step, the analyst validates measurement data collected across historical projects and prepares the data for use in further steps of CoBRA modeling. Data validation includes checking correctness and consistency of measurement data. Any identified defects need to be resolved before the data can be passed to subsequent model development steps. Data preprocessing, on the other hand, includes adjusting the format accepted by the tools employed to support CoBRA model development activities.

Step 5. Identifying and Defining Relevant Effort Factors

In this step, the analyst determines the most relevant effort factors to be considered in the CoBRA model. Usually, the analyst organizes a group meeting with domain experts. During the meeting, experts first brainstorm potentially relevant factors influencing project effort, discuss their rationale, and agree on their consistent definition. The analyst can support domain experts by explaining to them the concept of effort factors and by presenting to them a set of example effort factors. At the end of the session, experts individually prioritize the identified effort factors with respect to their relevancy. Prioritization might be realized by simply rank ordering the factors or by assigning them numerical importance scores.

After the session, the analyst synthesizes the outcomes of factor prioritization and prepares analysis results for presentation to the domain experts. If appropriate data are available, the analyst may combine expert-based factor prioritization with prioritization based on the analysis of project measurement data.

Step 6. Identifying Relevant Factor Interactions

In this step, the analyst identifies potential interactions between effort factors that have been selected to consider in the CoBRA model. Similar to the factor identification step, factor interactions are typically identified by domain experts in a group meeting. During a brainstorming session, domain experts identify factors that have an indirect influence on effort. Indirect effort factors are factors that influence the strength of the impact direct effort factors have on effort. During the group session, experts are allowed to consider new factors, which go beyond the ones they already selected as most relevant in previous steps of the modeling process. After discussing the relevancy of identified factor interactions, experts agree on the most relevant indirect effort factors to consider in the CoBRA model.

The analyst can support the identification of factor interactions through the analysis of available project data. On the one hand, the analyst may investigate project data collected in the previous model development iterations for the existence of potentially relevant factor interactions. On the other hand, the analyst may apply analogical analysis to whatever additional project measurement data are available from the historical projects considered during CoBRA model development.

Step 7. Quantifying Selected Relevant Effort Factors

In this step, metrics are defined for the most relevant effort factors selected for the inclusion into the CoBRA effort model. Usually, this step is realized during a group meeting with domain experts. At the beginning, the analyst presents to the experts the results of factor prioritization performed in Step 5. Experts discuss these results and decide on the final set of effort factors to consider in the CoBRA model. Afterward, experts define metrics for the selected effort factors. Usually, effort factors are measured using a four-point approximate interval scale. In such a case, the analyst asks experts to define each level on the scale so that it is consistently understood by all experts. Ensuring consistent interpretation of defined metrics is critical for collecting consistent factor data for developing a CoBRA model.

Step 8. Collecting and Validating Historical Factor Data

In this step, the analyst collects project data for the selected effort factors across historical projects upon which the CoBRA model is to be developed and initially validated. In the typical case, where appropriate measurement data are not available, the factor data are acquired from human experts. Experts who are familiar with one or more historical projects provide the factors' values they observed in their projects. The analyst acquires factor data either during individual interviews with experts or via an offline survey sent to experts. Since expert judgment is typically biased by subjective perception of a particular person, it is recommended to acquire the same factor data from at least two experts.

Next, the analyst validates the acquired effort factor data with respect to their credibility. There are several possibilities of validating factor data. The simplest one is to compare data inputs that multiple experts provided for the same factor and the same historical project. If they are inconsistent, then the analyst must investigate probable reasons for discovered inconsistencies and correct the data appropriately. Another data validation approach is to verify the collected factor data against the corresponding or related measurement data, if such data are available. Again, the analyst should investigate sources of potential inconsistencies between measurement data and expert judgments and correct the data appropriately.

Step 9. Collecting and Validating Effort Multiplier Data

In this step, the analyst collects data regarding the impact on project effort of each effort factor considered in the CoBRA model, the so-called effort multiplier. Typically, a factor's impact on effort is measured in terms of the percentage increase in project effort introduced by an effort factor in the worst case, that is, when it has the worst value on the associated metric. The analyst acquires effort multipliers during individual interviews with one or more domain experts. Typically, effort multipliers are acquired from multiple domain experts in order to account for a potentially wide spectrum of project experiences and to identify possibly incorrect data. The analyst may also acquire effort multiplier data in an offline survey, yet only if domain experts are already familiar with the CoBRA model development procedure. In order to account for uncertainty in expert judgment and for the variance of factors' impact on effort across different projects, domain experts provide three multiplier values for each effort factor: minimal, maximal, and most likely effort multiplier.

After collecting effort multiplier data, the analyst validates them with respect to completeness and consistency. Regarding consistency, if some expert differs significantly with respect to the judged effort multipliers from other experts, then the analyst should clarify the rationale behind such outlier multipliers. Potential actions the analyst may take encompass recollecting multiplier data or excluding the outlier expert and associated project data from the model development data set.

Step 10. Building Effort Models

In this step, the analyst uses the causal effort model and historical project data collected in the previous steps of the model development to derive a productivity model. The productivity model represents the baseline development productivity, which is used for estimating the effort of future projects. The analyst computes the actual effort overhead (EO) of each historical project using the effort overhead model, effort multipliers, and the project's actual values of effort factors considered in the causal effort model. Using the actual effort overhead and software size from multiple historical projects, the analyst determines the baseline productivity for estimating future projects. For this purpose, the analyst constructs a regression line ("productivity model" in Fig. 15.1) and takes the line's slope ($1/P_{Nom}$) as inverse baseline productivity. For a comprehensive explanation of developing the CoBRA model, refer to the "Software Cost Estimation, Benchmarking, and Risk Assessment" book (Trendowicz 2013) we also briefly describe in the "Further Reading" to this chapter.

Step 11. Validating Effort Models

Model development iterations end with validating the performance of the constructed CoBRA effort model. The performance of the effort model is evaluated in a cross-validation experiment, using the set of historical projects upon which the model has been developed. If the model's performance is accepted, then it can be released for estimating the effort of new software projects.

Step 12. Analyzing the Results of Model Validation

If the CoBRA model failed the validation step, then the analyst investigates it with respect to possible weaknesses and corresponding improvement actions. The investigation focuses on analyzing the results of model validation and is performed from the perspective of inputs to the model development and – in the case of subsequent development iterations—changes made to the model. After identifying the most promising model improvements, the analyst implements them in the next iteration of the model development process.

15.2.2 Model Application

After developing a CoBRA effort model, it can be applied within individual software projects for estimating and managing their effort. The CoBRA effort model can be used for multiple purposes. In practice, the most common scenarios of applying a CoBRA model include

- *Effort Estimation*: The CoBRA model is used to produce distribution of effort needed to successfully complete specific project activities. Using the distribution of predicted effort, an estimator can determine the appropriate value of project effort. In addition, the distribution allows for estimation of the risk of exceeding the particular effort value, which is not possible for estimation methods that solely provide point estimates.
- *Risk Management*: The CoBRA model is used to assess resource-related risks and opportunities for a particular software project. For this purpose, the distribution of estimated effort and the CoBRA effort overhead model are analyzed. On the one hand, the estimator may use the distribution of estimated effort to assess the probability of exceeding the planned project effort. On the other hand, based on the impact of individual effort factors on the effort of the specific project, the estimator may identify project characteristics which are inexpensive to improve but will then contribute to significant reduction in project effort. Moreover, estimators and project planners may assess the relative risk of a specific project by comparing its effort distribution to the effort distributions of successfully completed historical projects.
- *Project Scope Negotiation*: The CoBRA model is used to support negotiating and/or justifying estimated effort. In this scenario, the analyst performs a sensitivity analysis, in which the actual impact of effort factors on effort in specific software projects is computed. The estimator (project manager) may then use this information to justify and negotiate particular effort estimates with the project owner or customer. For instance, if bad values of some effort factors depend on the customer and cannot be affected by the software provider, then the project planner may argue that high project effort is beyond his responsibility. Furthermore, the project manager may negotiate reducing effort estimates under the condition that the customer commits to ensure better values of considered effort factors. A typical example might be an increase in project effort due to low quality and high volatility of software requirements caused by little engagement of the customer in the requirements specification phase. In order to improve these aspects and reduce project effort, the customer must improve his engagement in software requirements specification activities.
- *Benchmarking*: The CoBRA model is used to benchmark software projects with respect to the efficiency of their particular development processes, that is, with respect to their productivity. In this scenario, the CoBRA model is employed to determine the impact of effort factors across compared software projects. Factor impacts indicate the causes of the differences with respect to actual development productivity observed for the considered projects.

- *Process and Productivity Improvement*: The CoBRA model is used to plan process improvements. In this scenario, outcomes of the sensitivity analysis for multiple projects are combined in order to find effort factors that consistently have the greatest negative impact on project effort across considered projects. Process areas indicated by these effort factors are then candidates for improvement. One of the objectives of such process improvement is the long-term increase in development productivity and, in consequence, reduction of development effort.

15.2.3 Model Maintenance

In order to preserve and/or improve the performance of CoBRA, it needs to be subject to systematic maintenance. Maintenance of the CoBRA model adopts the generic approach we present in Chap. 16.

15.3 Strengths and Weaknesses

The CoBRA method combines elements of data-driven and expert-based effort estimation in order to exploit the strengths of these two paradigms and mitigate their weaknesses. Table 15.1 summarizes the strengths and weaknesses of the CoBRA method.

Table 15.1 Strengths and weaknesses of CoBRA

Aspect	Strengths (+) and weaknesses (−)
Expert involvement	• (−) CoBRA requires moderate involvement of human experts. Usually, 2-3 domain experts suffice to provide information necessary for creating a CoBRA model. Domain experts need solely to have domain experience and know historical projects on which a CoBRA model is developed. The expert leading the model development needs to know the CoBRA method, which is based on a few simple principles from mathematics and probability theory • (+) Creating CoBRA is quite intuitive and requires knowledge of only a few principles of statistics and probability distributions
Required data	• (+) CoBRA requires historical project data regarding project size and effort from about ten already completed projects. Even though these data are not available, they are typically possible to elicit postmortem—effort spent on projects is usually documented, and software size can be measured from delivered software products
Robustness	• (+) CoBRA allows decision-makers to combine partial empirical knowledge collected throughout historical projects with subjective human expertise • (+) CoBRA provides explicit support for dealing with multiple inputs, for example, as provided by multiple experts. The method provides mechanisms to deal with redundant and inconsistent information • (−) CoBRA does not handle missing information. Once created, the model requires complete data for estimation

(continued)

Table 15.1   (continued)

Aspect	Strengths (+) and weaknesses (−)
Flexibility	• (+) CoBRA does not require any particular data or metrics as its input. As with many other effort estimation methods, it requires size as the most relevant effort driver • (+) Adapting a CoBRA model to a new situation is quite straightforward and requires adjusting either the complete model or selected parts. The extent of adjustments depends on how much the target situation differs from the one for which the source CoBRA model was built
Complexity	• (+) CoBRA has a sound but relatively simple theoretical background
Support level	• (+) CoBRA is documented in a dedicated book (see the "Further Reading" section at the end of this chapter) and a few publications • (−) CoBRA is supported by a few noncommercial freely available tools
Reusability	• (+) CoBRA models can be reused "as-is" across similar projects • (+) Elements of the CoBRA model, such as the structure of effort dependencies, can be reused (partially or as whole) for building effort models in other situations. For example, impacts of particular effort drivers can be reused
Predictive power	• (+) Empirical studies show high predictive performance of the CoBRA method. Estimation error observed in different situations varies between 5 % and 20 % • (+) Application of random simulation techniques introduces small variance in the CoBRA estimates even though the method is applied on the same inputs; yet, the variance introduced by simulation is so small that it can, in practice, be ignored • (−) Since the CoBRA model is based (at least partially) on human judgment, it is burdened by judgmental biases. Yet, the CoBRA method includes group consensus techniques that support dealing with judgmental biases
Informative power	• (+) The CoBRA model provides information on causal effort dependencies in a transparent and intuitive manner. It specifies the most relevant factors influencing project effort, their causal interdependencies, and the strength of these relationships
Handling uncertainty	• (+) CoBRA handles uncertainty in probabilistic terms; both inputs to estimation and output estimates are specified in a form of probability distribution. The uncertainty of project characteristics is modeled by the use of intuitive triangular distributions • (+) CoBRA allows for risk estimation and can be used for "what-if" analysis to explore the impact of changes in some project characteristics on other characteristics. In that sense, CoBRA facilitates considering multiple project scenarios and trade-offs between resources used in the project and outcomes it delivers
Estimation scope	• (+) CoBRA is, principally, applicable to any type of project activities at any granularity level. The only requirement for estimating effort associated with particular project activities is that appropriate factors are considered in the causal effort model
Availability	• (+) The availability of the estimates provided by CoBRA depends on the availability of information on effort drivers covered by the causal effort model
Empirical evidence	• (+) Several studies have been published on CoBRA application in different industrial contexts

Further Reading

- A. Trendowicz (2013), *Software Cost Estimation, Benchmarking, and Risk Assessment. Software Decision Makers' Guide for Predictable Software Development*. Springer Verlag.

  In this book, we provide a detailed description of the CoBRA method. The book provides a comprehensive specification of processes for developing a CoBRA effort model and for applying the model in a number of different project management scenarios. For each of these processes, we describe detailed activities that need to be performed and associated techniques. We illustrate the presented concepts through a number of examples and graphical illustrations. Moreover, we provide a number of practical guidelines on applying these processes, based on industrial experiences regarding project effort estimation, in general, and using the CoBRA method, in particular. Furthermore, we present several real-world cases of applying the CoBRA method in various industrial contexts for illustrating the practical usage of the method.

Part IV

Establishing Sustainable Effort Estimation

Even if we aren't good at it, we know how to get better.

—Edward Yourdon

Human beings, who are almost unique [among animals] in having the ability learn from the experience of others, are also remarkable for their apparent disinclination to do so.

—Douglas Adams

In this part, we discuss how to effectively apply and improve effort estimation. Like any other technology or process within a software organization, in order to work effectively, effort estimation requires systematic deployment, controlled application, and continuous improvement. Moreover, lessons learned during effort estimation in a specific context should be used to guide future application of an estimation approach.

Chapter 16 discusses an approach for continuously improving an effort estimation approach. We show how a basic improvement cycle is used for controlling and improving performance of effort estimation in a software organization.

Chapter 17 summarizes best practices of effort estimation. In this chapter, we discuss do's and don'ts of effort estimation with respect to such aspects and estimation inputs, outputs, resources, and processes.

Continuously Improving Effort Estimation

16

> No matter how well developed a thing or system becomes, however, it will never be without limitations. [...] Therefore, there will always be room for improvement.
>
> —Henry Petroski

> Take chances, make mistakes. That's how you grow.
>
> —Mary Tyler Moore

Mistaken is he who hopes that a new effort estimation will work right from the outset. Effort estimation, as with any other technology, needs to be introduced gradually into an organization and requires continuous improvement. A "Big Bang" approach to deploying new technology typically ends up with a big disappointment. Changing multiple internal processes at once usually hits upon great resistance from people who are not willing to change their behavior. Mistaken is also he who hopes that a new effort estimation, once successfully introduced, will work forever. As the context of estimation changes, its performance must be monitored, and it needs to be amended to changing conditions.

In effort estimation, as anywhere else in software engineering, if you do not continuously improve, you continuously worsen. Three key questions of continuous improvement are: (1) Where am I now? (2) Where do I want to be? and (3) How do I get there? In this chapter, we briefly present a systematic approach that guides to the answers to these three questions.

16.1 Objects of Continuous Improvement

> Good judgment comes from experience, and experience comes from poor judgment.
>
> —Mulla Nasrudin

As an integral part of the software organization, effort estimation is associated with learning and continuous improvement. Pedler et al. (1998) described the learning organization as "*an organization that facilitates the learning of all its members and continuously transforms itself.*" In terms of transformations, an organization adapts itself to changing environments, in terms of technological advances, evolving

A. Trendowicz and R. Jeffery, *Software Project Effort Estimation*,
DOI 10.1007/978-3-319-03629-8_16, © Springer International Publishing Switzerland 2014

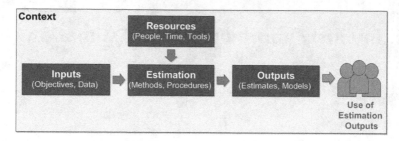

Fig. 16.1 Basic elements of effort estimation process

market demands, and legal constraints, etc. In terms of learning, people learn new technologies and new processes, gain expertise in the domain and project work, learn about their capabilities and limitations, and adapt their behavior appropriately.

In the following sections, we briefly discuss how continuous improvement in terms of continual transformation and learning refers to effort estimation. Let us start by identifying the basic elements of effort estimation that are subject to continuous improvement. Software effort estimation is one of the project management processes. As with any process, it is defined as an activity that takes inputs and produces outputs using certain resources (Fig. 16.1).

In principle, all these elements of effort estimation should be considered when continuously improving effort estimation. In particular,

- *Inputs* upon which we base estimates, particularly quantitative project data from already completed projects
- *Estimation* methods and techniques used for estimation
- *Outputs* of estimation, in particular effort models we can use for estimating other projects
- *Resources*, in particular, people (their skills and capabilities) and tools involved in the estimation
- *Context* of estimation (optionally), in that we adjust those aspects of an estimation environment that facilitate or hinder estimation

16.1.1 Inputs

In order to be effective, effort estimation requires knowledge of the relevant project's effort effects. This knowledge is obtained from the quantitative information and human expertise gained through already completed projects (so-called *historical projects*). Both quantitative information and expertise can, and should, be measured and maintained in an organization repository of historical project data. However, more data does not mean more information and more knowledge. On the one hand, large datasets are more likely to include redundant and irrelevant

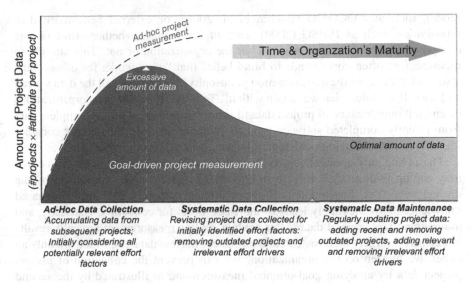

Fig. 16.2 Improving input data for effort estimation

information. On the other hand, rapid changes (e.g., technological) in the software engineering environments will quickly outdate the gathered information. Redundant, irrelevant, and outdated information is very likely to mislead effort estimation and will, for sure, make estimation more expensive.

Tip

▶ Poor inputs to estimation are a common cause of failed estimates. When looking for potential causes of poor estimates, start with validating estimation inputs before analyzing the estimation approach itself.

Figure 16.2 illustrates briefly the idea of maintaining an organization's project data repository in the context of effort estimation. The curve represents the total amount of project data collected in the organization. The amount of data includes both the number of projects for which data has been gathered and the number of project characteristics (attributes) collected for each project.

We divide the curve into three parts, each representing a particular measurement approach we often observe in industrial contexts.

Ad Hoc Data Collection

The first part of the curve represents ad hoc measurement, where an organization collects extensive amounts of project data for arbitrarily selected effort factors. Examples of arbitrary selection of effort factors might be the situation where an organization decides to collect data on effort factors proposed by an external effort model, such as COCOMO (Boehm et al. 2000), or external benchmark data repositories, such as ISBSG (2009), without considering whether effort factors comprised by these sets are relevant for the organization or not. This attitude to measurement often corresponds to blind belief that "what works for others must also work for me" or the quite common philosophy, "let's collect all the data we can and we will see later what we can do with it". To make matters worse, organizations often limit maintenance of project data to simply throwing into it the complete data from recently completed software projects. When doing this, they do not consider identifying and removing outdated, redundant, or irrelevant project data.

The ad hoc measurement approach represented by the first part of the data curve may end up with a large increase in historical project data as represented by the dashed curve. Yet, large amounts of information do not necessarily imply increased knowledge. This inevitably leads to increased costs for collecting, analyzing, and maintaining large sets of data. After a while, ad hoc measurement typically results in extensive, largely inconsistent, and ultimately useless datasets, which are only an expensive burden on the organization. We can prevent the collection of useless project data by applying goal-oriented measurement, as illustrated by the second and third parts of the data curve in the figure.

Systematic Data Collection

The second part of the curve reflects the collection of project data when introducing structured effort estimation, where effort factors are typically based on human judgment and include some irrelevant factors while missing some relevant ones. Initially, effort estimation tends to consider an extensive set of effort factors that typically can be reduced after analyzing the performance of the estimation method. At the same time, we can revise data for outdated projects, that is, projects that do not correspond to the current estimation context (i.e., the actual situation of a software project). Outdated projects are, for example, those that involved development processes, paradigms, and technologies that are not used anymore and thus no longer have any impact on project effort. Retaining such data in the repository contributes to increased data maintenance and analysis costs without adding any benefit in terms of improved estimates. Worse yet, obsolete data represents project effort effects that are not true anymore and thus may mislead estimation and result in unreliable estimates. Effort estimation optimization and the revision of extensive amounts of initially collected project data are both represented in the curve by the decreasing amount of project data.

Systematic Data Maintenance

The third part of the curve represents systematic maintenance of project data, where we (1) add data from the most recent projects and remove the complete datasets for outdated projects and (2) add and remove data on individual effort factors based on their contribution to the goodness of the estimates. For example, in the case of model-based estimation, we revise the effort models by removing effort factors that did not prove to have any impact on project effort and by adding new, potentially relevant factors (to be checked for actual relevancy in subsequent model applications). For a particular estimation context, we can try to keep the amount of added and removed project data at approximately the same level, thus keeping the overall size of the project data repository roughly constant. How much data is needed depends, for example, on how many projects we complete in the given context (i.e., how many data we are able to collect before they become outdated). Increasing amounts of historical project data can, however, be legitimate when a number of projects are completed over a period of time without significant changes in context. Recall that when talking of the project, we mean the scope of the estimated work activity. For the sake of simplicity and for historical reasons, we will refer to a project as the typical scope of work effort. Yet, it can also be a project phase in waterfall software development life cycle, or sprint in Agile Scrum development life cycle.

16.1.2 Estimation

In order to be effective, estimation methods and procedures should typically be adjusted to a specific context and goals of effort estimation. We may be lucky and find a method that perfectly suits our particular needs and constraints. In practice, however, estimation methods need some adjustments, at least when first introduced into a specific organization. Typically, method adjustments are limited to minor adaptations of estimation procedures to the capabilities and constraints of a particular organization. Major adaptations are rather rare in practice because they require appropriate expertise regarding the method and the underlying theories. For example, we may adjust an estimation method by selecting optional and/or by choosing between alternative elements of the method. Thus, analogy-based estimation (e.g., Chap. 11) offers multiple alternative distance metrics for finding analog historical projects. Or, another example is group consensus estimation (e.g., Chap. 12) that offers different consensus metrics for quantifying disagreement between multiple human experts. Yet, modifying an estimation method would require appropriate knowledge. Moreover, the modified method should be empirically validated before it can be reliably used in real-life projects. Such modifications could, for instance, be realized in cooperation with external research institutions.

16.1.3 Outputs

A number of estimation methods deliver an explicit effort model, which documents the most relevant relationships between work effort and one or more characteristics of the work environment (modeled as effort factors). The model is derived from the information provided on the inputs to estimation in the form of quantitative project data and/or human judgment. The advantage of an effort model is that it can be used to learn about effort dependencies in a specific context and it can be used for estimation without the need to analyze input information (e.g., historical project data) each time estimates are required.

In order to reliably reflect the current estimation context, an effort model must be subject to continuous improvement; that is, monitoring the model's performance and adjusting the model if necessary. In practice, the model will require adjustments in response to some change. On the one hand, the change may refer to decreased performance of the estimation model, for example, manifested by decreased estimation accuracy observed when the model is applied for estimating multiple projects. In this case, the model needs to be corrected in order to provide reliable estimates. On the other hand, the change may refer to changes in the estimation context and/or estimation objectives. In this case, the model potentially must be adjusted in order to adhere to a changed environment to avoid poor performance of the model.

A typical example of such an adjustment is calibration of external effort models, such as COCOMO, that have been fixed on project data from multiple external organizations. Such project data, and thus the resulting model, represent a context that differs from the one in which the model is intended to be used. Therefore, prior to its application in a particular context, the model should be calibrated using context-specific project data. In practice, calibration is not as easy as it sounds, and the success of calibration is not guaranteed. For instance, Lum et al. (2006) observed that "*current approaches to model calibration often produce sub-optimal models because of the large variance problem inherent in cost data and by including far more effort multipliers than the data supports.*" In other words, software projects vary on multiple aspects that are rather difficult to reliably model in an effort model; therefore, only the most relevant factors influencing effort should be considered. Yet, factors that are important in one context do not have to be relevant in other contexts. Thus, generic effort models, such as COCOMO, typically consider many factors that are not relevant in a specific context, while missing factors that are relevant. In consequence, a simple adjustment of model parameters is ineffective. Instead, a major model calibration would be necessary in that irrelevant effort factors are excluded and relevant ones are included in the model. Yet, such calibration requires much project data and work, and thus does not differ much from developing a custom-specific effort model, which typically gives better results than adapting external models.

Changes in the context of estimation may, however, not always be manifested explicitly. Therefore, it is a good practice to revise effort models on a regular basis, at best after completing a project or (few projects, if they are small)—after historical project data has been updated and/or experts gain new experiences. This new information may bring new knowledge that has not been considered by the estimation model, or it can also reflect changes in the estimation context that have not been observed explicitly. In any case, the information should be considered in the effort model, and thus the model needs to be adjusted appropriately.

16.1.4 Resources

People and tools must improve in order to keep up with an evolving environment. New software technologies and development paradigms require new tools. People must learn new processes and tools and adjust their behaviors appropriately. A changing environment requires adjusted estimation methods and models, which in turn requires improved skills of estimators using estimation methods, models, and tools. Finally, a changing environment of software development implies new experiences with respect to work performance and associated work effort; these experiences should be collected and utilized in improved estimation capabilities (e.g., integrated into estimation models and/or used to adapt measurement processes for collecting data for estimation).

16.1.5 Context

Usually, it is the estimation method and/or model that should be adjusted to changing contexts. Yet, not every change in the estimation context is reasonable and thus should automatically lead to changes in the estimation approach. If the development environment of an individual project deviates from the context within which an available effort model was developed (and used so far), then we may also consider adjusting the project context in order to avoid failed estimations, in particular if we suspect that the project is rather exceptional and the context deviation it represents will not occur again. A typical example might be in the measurement process. If, within a particular project, measurement procedures are rather poor and are likely to provide unreliable data for estimation, we may beforehand plan alternative ways of obtaining appropriate data or undertake extra activities in order to improve the measurement processes, if, for example, we introduced new processes for which a new, still immature, measurement process was established. In this case, we should adjust the effort estimation approach, for example, by involving experts for collecting information that could not be reliably collected by means of quantitative measurement. For example, if we used data-driven estimation, we may, in such a situation, shift toward a hybrid estimation approach and evolve it systematically back in the direction of a data-driven method as we improve measurement processes (i.e., adapt them to changed development processes).

16.2   Basic Improvement Scenarios

Change is inevitable, growth is optional.

—Walt Disney

Improvement of software project estimation may be initiated by different events (*triggers*) and requires different actions (*responses*). Inspired by the maintenance of software products, we distinguish four scenarios for improving a software estimation approach: preventive, perfective, adaptive, and corrective. Similar to maintaining software products, maintaining effort estimation focuses on modifying an existing estimation approach (including estimation method, effort models, historical data, etc.) in order to keep it up with a changing environment.

Types of Software Maintenance According to ISO 14764
The ISO14764 (2006) distinguishes two major classes of software mainte-nance, correction and enhancement, depending on the type of modification the maintenance involves.

Corrections aim at removing defects in a software product that already caused problems or that may cause problems during software operation. In particular, corrections may involve two types of modifications:

- *Corrective modification*: A reactive modification of a software product performed after delivery to correct discovered problems.
- *Preventive modification*: A modification of a software product after deliv-ery to detect and correct latent faults in the software product before they become operational faults.

Enhancements aim at adjusting a software product to changes in its environment or requirements. In particular, enhancements may involve two types of modifications:

- *Adaptive modification*: An enhancement of a software product, performed after delivery, to keep a software product usable in a changed or changing environment.
- *Perfective modification*: An enhancement of a software product after delivery to detect and correct latent faults in the software product before they are manifested as failures in operation.

Inspired by ISO14764 (2006), we distinguish between two major scenarios of adjusting an effort estimation approach: corrections and enhancements. These two differ with respect to the exact rationale.

Corrections comprise improvements of those elements of an effort estimation approach (including associated data and personnel's capabilities) that may poten-tially manifest or have already been manifested in poor estimates. In particular, corrections may involve two types of adjustments:

- *Corrective improvements*, which refer to adjustments of an estimation approach in response to actual poor estimates already delivered. The objective of these improvements is to eliminate weaknesses of the estimation approach, which has already been manifested in poor predictive performance.
- *Preventive improvements*, which refer to adjustments in response to potentially poor estimates an approach may deliver. The objective of these improvements is to eliminate perceived weaknesses of the estimation approach, which we expect will result in poor predictive performance.

Enhancements comprise improvements of the estimation approach that aim to improve its capabilities. In particular, enhancements may involve two types of adjustments:

- *Adaptive improvements*, which refer to adjustments to an estimation approach in response to a changed estimation context. The objective of adaptive improvements is to modify the estimation approach in order to (1) tailor it to changed characteristics of the project environment, (2) meet new objectives with respect to effort estimation, and/or (3) adhere to changed capabilities and constraints of the organization.
- *Perfective adjustments*, which refer to adjustments of an estimation approach performed on a regular basis in order to optimize its estimation performance— although the estimation context has not changed explicitly. The objective of perfective improvements is to (1) optimize effectiveness and/or efficacy of the estimation approach and (2) tailor the estimation approach to context changes that have not been explicitly observed and addressed through adaptive maintenance.

For each improvement scenario, we distinguish a different rationale (*trigger*) that leads to corresponding adjustments (*responses*). Table 16.1 summarizes the typical rationales and responses for the four aforementioned improvement scenarios. Thereby, we distinguish responses to be made at the <u>level of the individual project</u> (in which potential or an actual issue with estimation has been manifested) and at the <u>level of the organization</u> where the estimation approach is maintained and deployed to individual projects. The simple reason for this centralization, as for any technology employed within an organization, is to avoid multiple, project-specific implementations of a technology, which are difficult and expensive to monitor and maintain. For example, distributing project-specific variants of an effort estimation model may quickly lead to all kinds of problems related to ad hoc management of multiple models—the problems that are known from the area of software configuration management (Abran et al. 2004, Chap. 7). An example issue here might be the large overhead to maintain multiple effort models.

Note that adjusting the available estimation approach might not always be reasonable or even possible. In such a case, an alternative estimation approach should be considered, especially if a more appropriate approach exists and could be adopted at relatively low cost. We can also consider using an alternative estimation approach temporarily. For instance, after major change in the organizational environment, most of the historical project data cannot be used for estimation because

Table 16.1 Improvement scenarios of effort estimation approach

Scenario	Rationale (Trigger)	Actions (Response)
Corrective	Decrease in actual performance of the estimation approach observed in an individual project (i.e., estimation goals are not fulfilled). Neither the context of estimation nor the estimation objectives have changed	Within an individual project, • Consider potential causes of poor estimation performance in the project • Propose appropriate improvements to the estimation approach • Report estimation results and associated information (e.g., estimation inputs and context) to the person responsible for maintaining the estimation approach in the organization For the whole organization, • Validate the estimation method on available historical project data • Investigate causes of poor estimates for selected project(s); consider feedback from projects where estimation performed poorly • Adjust appropriate elements of the estimation approach if necessary. For example, if estimation failed because input information was incorrectly collected in a specific project, then no modifications are needed; solely execution of data collection at the project level must be improved
Preventive	Change in the project's estimation environment. The estimation approach is going to be applied to a project, in which the context deviates from the range of estimation contexts for which the approach has been intended (created/adjusted and validated)	Within an individual project, • Adjust project context and/or objectives, to fit the estimation approach if appropriate (e.g., improve project's conformity to data collection processes in order to ensure that all inputs required by estimation are available) • Adjust (quick fix) estimation approach to fit the project-specific context • Report project-specific estimation context and potential adjustments of the estimation technology to the person responsible for maintaining estimation approach in the organization
Adaptive	Change in organization environment (context and/or estimation objectives). The estimation approach is going to be applied in contexts that differ from those intended because • Estimation context, in which the estimation approach has been used so far, has changed over time • The estimation approach is going to be used (ported) to another context (e.g., another organization)	For the whole organization, • Determine exact differences in the organization's target context/objectives and the context/objectives for which the estimation approach was designed • If possible, consider adjusting the context/objectives before modifying the estimation approach (e.g., introduce measurement processes to collect required inputs for estimation or set less stringent objectives for estimation)

(continued)

Table 16.1 (continued)

Scenario	Rationale (Trigger)	Actions (Response)
		• Adjust historical project data to reflect changes in the estimation context (e.g., remove data that does not reflect changed context) • Use updated historical data and/or expert judgment for adjusting and validating the estimation approach (e.g., rebuilding the effort estimation model)
Perfective	Regular model revision. The estimation approach is reviewed on a regular basis and can be refined, although neither estimation context nor estimation objectives have changed. The revisions aim at optimizing the estimation approach, for example, reducing overhead required for estimation while maintaining estimation performance Yet, if a regular review discovers significant change in estimation performance or estimation context, then the appropriate corrective or adaptive adjustment scenario should be triggered	For the whole organization, • Update historical project data; make sure it contains most recent projects in which the estimation approach was used • Review historical project data for potential changes in estimation context • Validate the current estimation approach on an updated set of historical project data. Look closer into projects for which estimates are significantly worse than for others; look for potential causes. Check actual relevancy of considered effort factors (e.g., by excluding selected factors from consideration and observing their effect on estimates performance); try including new factors you believe may become important • Adjust the estimation approach if (1) it does not perform satisfactorily, (2) estimation context has changed and the approach may not perform satisfactorily when used in the future, and (3) model performs satisfactorily but it can be improved easily at minimal cost

they reflect the context prior to the change. In this case, we may consider using expert-based estimation until we collect a sufficient amount of data in order to get back to hybrid or data-driven estimation used prior to the change in organizational context.

16.3 Continuous Improvement Cycle

The time for action is now. It's never too late to do something.

—Antoine de Saint-Exupéry

Fig. 16.3 Quality improvement paradigm and plan-do-check-act paradigms

Quality improvement paradigm (QIP) was originally proposed by Basili and others (Basili 1985; Basili et al. 1994a) and revised by Basili et al. (2014) to support the continuous improvement of software organizations. Instead of improvement approaches based on reference "maturity" models, such as CMMI (2010), QIP uses internal assessment against the organization's own goals and status (rather than predefined process areas) to improve products and services through process improvement. QIP compares evolving organizational goals against the current status and derives appropriate improvements to close any identified gaps. Note that the QIP improvement cycle corresponds, in general, to the popular *Plan-Do-Check-Act* (*PDCA*) improvement cycle proposed by Shewhart (1939) and widely popularized by Deming (1986). Figure 16.3 illustrates approximate mapping between the phases of QIP and PDCA. The major difference between these two improvement paradigms (Basili 1993) is that PDCA aims at optimizing a single production process for which sufficient amount of data can be collected when continually repeating this process, whereas QIP aims at development processes which are rarely replicable, for example, due to the unique character of each software development project and significant involvement of human factors.

QIP defines two feedback and improvement loops, project and organization loops. The organizational loop consists of six steps:

1. *Characterize environment (plan)*: The current organizational situation is characterized from the perspective of the organization's estimation capabilities and constraints.
2. *Define goals, strategies, and measurement (plan)*: The goals of estimation and associated process changes are specified. Means are planned for measuring estimation performance and collecting project feedback regarding estimation.

3. *Plan implementation (plan)*: Plans for implementing and deploying estimation strategies and measurement are developed in order to attain estimation goals. Appropriate estimation processes, methods, and tools are adapted to the specific needs and capabilities of the organization.

4. *Execute plans (do)*: Estimation processes, methods, and tools are deployed in individual software development projects, and data regarding the performance of the estimation are collected. Actually, in this phase of QIP, the complete PDCA cycle will be repeated on the level of the individual project. At this level, estimation approach designed in "plan implementation" phase are adjusted to the context of a specific project (plan) and used for estimating the project (do); estimates are compared to actual project performance (check) and revised appropriately as the project progresses (act).

5. *Analyze outcomes (check)*: Results of the estimation (performance data, project feedback) are analyzed, and improvement potentials are identified.

6. *Package improvements (act)*: Selected improvements are implemented and packaged together with the associated lessons learned.

16.3.1 Characterize the Environment

Each improvement cycle starts with characterizing and comprehending the environment of continuous improvement and establishing quantifiable baselines for existing processes, in our case processes related to effort estimation. Typically, this phase is accomplished using the models and data available within the organization as well as the intuition of human experts. The characterization phase provides a context for defining relevant estimation goals, creating reusable experiences and artifacts, selecting appropriate estimation processes and methods, and, finally, evaluating, comparing, and predicting organizational performance with respect to defined estimation goals.

Context characteristics encompass a large variety of people-, process-, product-, and problem-related factors that may determine the feasible estimation approach and its performance when applied to estimate work effort in this context. Example people factors include the number of people who can be involved in estimation, their estimation skills and expertise, or technological and domain experience. Important human factors that may hinder a rational estimation process are personal interests and "political games" of estimation stakeholders. Example process factors include development life cycle, software engineering processes, measurement and data collection processes, etc. Example product factors include number and type of artifacts delivered during software development, as well as their size, complexity, quality, etc. Finally, example problem factors include application domain, internal and external constraints, etc.

Whereas context refers to those factors we know, assumptions refer to those context characteristics that we are not sure about but which should be considered when selecting, introducing, and continuously improving an estimation approach. The benefit of considering assumptions explicitly is that when an estimation approach does not perform as expected due to wrong assumptions, we immediately find out by simply checking which of our initial assumptions turn out to be false.

Tip

▶ Document and communicate <u>explicitly</u> the context of estimation and assumptions you take in your estimation process.

16.3.2 Define Goals, Strategies, and Measurement

The next step of understanding the estimation problem, after comprehending the estimation environment, is the specification of estimation goals. In his "Seven Habits of Highly Effective People", Stephen Covey (2004) suggested as one key to success to *"begin with the end in mind"*. This habit also applies to highly effective effort estimation—it has to start with the end in mind, specified in terms of goals we want to attain with estimation. Proper goals let us monitor the performance of the employed estimation approach and give a basis for its continuous improvement.

The basis for specifying estimation goals are expectations of the intended users of estimates. For example, if the owner of a software development project expects estimation to support negotiating the project scope, the estimation method should allow explicit assessment of the impact of both software provider's and acquirer's characteristics on the effort required to complete the project.

Tip

▶ In order to clearly attain your goals, you should first define your goals clearly (paraphrasing Tom Gilb).

One of the widely acknowledged principles for defining goals is the SMART principle. According to this principle, goals should be specific, measurable, attainable, relevant, and timely. "Specific" stresses the need for goals to be specific versus generic and abstract goals. "Measurable" stresses the need for quantitative criteria for verifying the attainment of goals. "Attainable" stresses the importance of goals to be realistic. "Relevant" stresses the need for goals that matter to the specific organization. "Timely" stresses the importance of placing goals within a time frame, giving them a target date. One of the approaches for defining SMART goals might be GQM$^+$Strategies proposed by Basili et al. (2010, 2014).

The GQM$^+$Strategies Approach

The GQM$^+$Strategies approach supports (1) explicitly considering organizational goals and strategies, (2) aligning them at all levels of the organization, (3) making them visible to be shared and analyzed by all stakeholders, and (4) establishing the

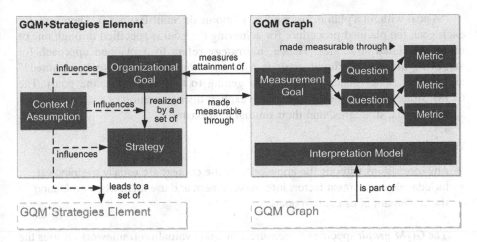

Fig. 16.4 GQM⁺Strategies Grid

Table 16.2 Basic aspects of an organizational goal

Organizational goal	
Object	What is the object under consideration? Object refers to artifacts, processes, or personnel addressed by the goal. *Examples*: effort estimation method, estimators, IT infrastructure, etc.
Focus	What characteristic of the object is considered? Focus refers to the object's attribute, for which a certain state is going to be attained. *Examples*: predictive power, informative power, availability, cost, skills, etc.
Magnitude	What is the quantity (measure) of the goal to be attained? *Examples*: percentage of change relative to current state (50 %), absolute value (20), etc.
Time frame	When should the goal be attained? *Examples*: 6 months, next fiscal year, etc.
Organizational scope	Who or what organizations are responsible for the goal attainment? *Examples*: a particular set of projects, company, business unit, division, department, etc.
Constraints	What are the relevant constraints that may prevent attainment of the goal? *Examples*: legal regulations, obligatory standards, available resources, available measurement data, etc.
Relationships	What are other goals the goal is related to? Goals are related due to a strategy that leads to both goals: Goals are in agreement given certain strategy if the strategy supports attainment of both goals. Goals are conflicting given certain strategy if the strategy supports attainment of one goal while having negative impact on the other goal. *Example*: Introducing a new estimation approach in order to achieve increased predictive and informative power goals will require additional investments and thus contradict a cost reduction goal

connection between organizational goals/strategies and measurement goals. The outcome of GQM⁺Strategies is a model of organizational goals, strategies, and associated measurement models—so-called GQM⁺Strategies Grid (Fig. 16.4).

The *GQM⁺Strategies element* specifies goals and strategies and their mutual relationships. Table 16.2 specifies the aspects of an organizational goal in more detail.

"A goal without a plan is just a wish" (Antoine de Saint-Exupéry). Therefore, for each goal, the planned procedure for achieving the goal is specified through one or more associated strategies. Hence, a *strategy* refers to a planned approach for achieving an organizational goal. It answers "How is the goal to be attained?" and defines rather general "means" of getting to the "end" (i.e., the goal). The GQM⁺Strategies approach enforces the explicit documentation of the rationale for specific goals, strategies, and their mutual relationships.

Tip

▶ Any conclusions without the knowledge of the context are usually meaningless. Include relevant context factors into measurement and use them when evaluating the attainment of estimation goals.

The *GQM graph* specifies a measurement and evaluation framework. It uses the classical GQM approach to specify what data needs to be collected and how that data should be interpreted in order to make informed decisions about the success of strategies and attainment of the organizational goals defined in the GQM⁺Strategies element. Each GQM graph consists of a measurement goal, questions, metrics, and interpretation model.

Tip

▶ "Goals begin behaviors, consequences maintain behaviors" (Kenneth Blanchard and Spenser Johnson]. Set goals and strategies in order to know how you should behave, and measure goal attainment in order to maintain right behavior and eliminate wrong behavior.

Typically, one GQM graph should be defined for each organizational goal in order to quantitatively evaluate its attainment. Each organizational goal in the GQM⁺Strategies element may have several associated measurement goals, each of which is the basis for an entire GQM graph. However, it is expected that different GQM structures will share several questions and metrics. Table 16.3 briefly explains the meaning of all key elements of GQM⁺Strategies that we have discussed in the paragraphs above.

Summarizing, the GQM⁺Strategies approach addresses the aspects of a SMART goal in the following way:

- *Specific*: GQM⁺Strategies specifies what exactly is to be achieved by indicating the object (e.g., "estimation method") and the focus of the goal (e.g., "prediction accuracy"). Moreover, it specifies the magnitude (e.g., "+10 %"), time frame (e.g., "in the next year"), scope (e.g., "software development department"), constraints (e.g., "available resources"), and relationships to other goals (e.g., "potential conflicts with the goal of reduced estimation overhead"). The complete example goal would be then to increase "prediction accuracy of effort estimation method by 10 % within the next 6 months in the software development department.

Table 16.3 Key elements of a GQM$^+$Strategies grid

Organizational goal	An anticipated state in the future that an organization wants to attain. It answers the question: "What is to be attained?" The goal is formalized by using a goal template and quantified by using GQM
Strategy	A planned procedure for achieving an organizational goal. It answers the question: "How is the goal to be attained?" Strategy refers to the "means" of getting to the "end" (i.e., goal), and it can be refined by a set of concrete activities (i.e., business or development processes)
Context factor	A factual characteristic of an organization or its environment that affects the models and data that need to be used
Assumption	A presumed (expected, yet uncertain) characteristic of an organization, its environment, or the availability of data that affect the kind of models and data that needs to be used
Measurement goal	An objective of measurement derived from a particular information need. Information need refers to the information that the organization needs in order to make certain decisions (e.g., if organizational goals are attained). The measurement goal is formalized using GQM goal template
GQM graph	A hierarchy of measurement goals, questions, metrics, and interpretation models provided as the result of applying the GQM method. Questions are derived from measurement goals and lead to metrics

- *Measurable*: GQM$^+$Strategies associates each goal with one or more metrics and an appropriate interpretation model in order to interpret collected data and decide whether the goal has been attained or not.
- *Attainable*: GQM$^+$Strategies accomplishes this requirement of SMART goal definition by explicitly considering the rationale for the goal, in the form of characteristics of the context and assumptions that led to goal definition.
- *Relevant*: GQM$^+$Strategies ensures this by aligning goals in an organization to each other and to associated strategies. Moreover, it requires explicitly specifying the rationale for goals and for their linkages to other goals in the organization.
- *Timely*: GQM$^+$Strategies realizes this aspect by explicitly defining the time frame for achieving the goal (through associated strategies) and for validating its attainment (using the associated measurement).

16.3.3 Plan Implementation

After defining goals, strategies, and metrics, we need to plan who will implement them and how, when and where. The result of this planning is one or more strategy implementation projects (*strategic projects* for short). The objective of each strategic project is to implement and deploy one or more estimation strategies and associated measurement. One strategic project should encompass closely related strategies, for instance, those that are derived from the same goal and affect the same organizational unit.

For example, if a strategy is to support an estimation approach with analysis of quantitative measurement data, one strategic project may be devoted to implementing and deploying the appropriate estimation approach, whereas another project may be devoted to implementing and deploying appropriate measurement processes (i.e., processes that will provide quantitative data for estimation).

As for any project in an organization, a strategic project's plan should, in addition to scope (i.e., implemented strategies and measurement), specify at least such elements as major work activities, human and material resources, budget, and milestone schedule. Detailed discussion of project planning is beyond the scope of this book. For more details on planning, directing, and controlling project work, refer to project management literature—for example, best-practice guides such as *PMBOK—Project Management Body of Knowledge* (PMI 2013) or *PRINCE2—PRojects IN Controlled Environments 2* (OGC 2009).

Tip

▶ The problems of software process change are often complicated by the fact that no one is responsible to make it happen. If software process improvement isn't anybody's job, it is not surprising that it doesn't get done! If it is important enough to do, however, someone must be assigned the responsibility and given the necessary resources. Until this is done, software process development will remain a nice thing to do someday, but never today.—Watts S. Humphrey (1999)

16.3.4 Execute Plans

The objective of the fourth phase of the continuous improvement cycle is to implement the strategies and measurement defined in the grid. Implementation of strategies takes place in one or more strategy implementation projects (*strategic projects*), each of which represents a three-phase feedback loop: (4.1) new or adjusted estimation processes, methods, techniques, and tools are planned in detail and deployed and measurement data on their performance are collected, (4.2) the measurement data are analyzed, and the estimation process is assessed with respect to the attainment of estimation goals, and (4.3) feedback regarding the performance of the estimation approach is provided, and necessary improvements to the approach are made in real time (Fig. 16.5).

Execute Strategies

Planning. Executing effort estimation strategies within each strategic project starts with preparing detailed plans (1) for implementing and deploying strategies (*strategy plans* for short) and (2) for measuring the impact of the strategies on the attainment of organizational goals (*measurement plans* for short). Figure 16.6 illustrates the approach to preparing strategy and measurement plans.

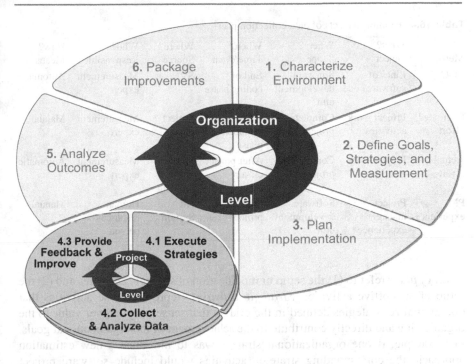

Fig. 16.5 Continuous improvement cycle: execute plans

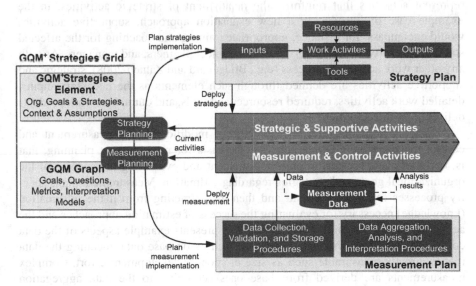

Fig. 16.6 Preparing strategy and measurement plans

Table 16.4 Example aspects of data collection plan

Metric	What? Object	Where? Scope	When? Time/event	Where? Source	Who? Responsible	How? Means
LOC	Lines of software code	Software development unit	End of coding phase	SVN	Measurement expert	Automatic
Estimated effort	Project work activities	Complete project	After project initiation phase	Project plan	Measurement expert	Manual
Actual effort	Project work activities	Complete project	After project closure	Project effort tracking	Measurement expert	Automatic
PM experience	Project manager's experience	Software development unit	Start of project	HR System	Human resources person	Manual

Strategy plans refer to (1) the setup or modification of strategic activities and (2) the setup of supportive activities. *Strategic activities* represent those activities that operationalize strategies defined in the grid. In that sense, they deliver value to the organization and directly contribute to the achievement of the organizational goals. For example, if one organizational strategy was to introduce a new estimation approach, the corresponding strategic activities would include software project management processes that are associated with estimation. *Supportive activities* represent activities that reinforce the deployment of strategic activities. In the example case of introducing a new estimation approach, supportive activities would encompass, for instance, appropriate training and coaching for the affected staff such as software estimators, software project planners, and managers. As with any other work activity or process (e.g., Bridgeland and Zahavi 2008), strategic and supportive activities are defined through such elements as the necessary inputs, detailed work activities, required resources and tools, and outputs or work products delivered by the activities.

Measurement plans refer to the setup or modification of measurement and control mechanisms. GQM graphs are the basis for measurement planning, that is, deriving plans for performing measurement and evaluating the success of the organizational goals and strategies regarding estimation. Measurement plans specify processes for acquiring data and then for extracting from it the information (knowledge) necessary for evaluating the success of estimation approaches and the achievement of estimation goals. Table 16.4 presents example aspects of the data collection plan. Note that data collection focuses on base data, meaning the data that is directly measurable such as size of code or development effort. Complex measurements are derived from base ones according to the data aggregation mechanism; for example, estimation accuracy is derived using measurements of estimated and actual development effort.

Measurement plans are then used for adjusting existing measurement and control activities in the organization.

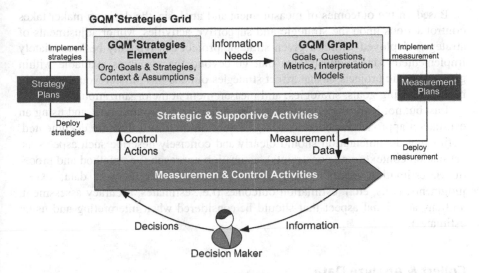

Fig. 16.7 Usage of strategy and measurement plans

Tip

▶ While planning estimation and measurement, try to reuse as much as possible the processes and tools that already exist in your organization. Start small by focusing process changes on the most important ones and focusing measurement on the most relevant metrics. Evolutionary (instead of revolutionary) improvement will allow to keep changes at a limited level and thus to increase the chance of being accepted by involved personnel.

Deployment. Planned estimation and measurement activities (strategy and measurement plans) are deployed in the context of individual software projects—first pilot and then real ones. During the transition period of introducing a new or changed estimation approach, appropriate supporting activities, such as training and coaching, are also executed. Figure 16.7 illustrates the integration of preparing and executing strategy and measurement plans. Measurement plans are employed (1) within strategic and supportive work activities for collecting measurement data and (2) within measurement and control activities for extracting information (knowledge) needed by the decision makers for deciding about the performance of the estimation activities, that is, the success of the organizational goals and strategies regarding effort estimation.

Tip

▶ Support team members with tools for easily collecting and validating project data. The more overhead the measurement and analysis will bring upon people, the less acceptance these activities will gain.

Based on the outcomes of measurement and analysis, the decision maker takes control actions upon the strategic and supportive activities. Minor adjustments of strategies deployed within a given strategic project can typically be immediately implemented. Major adjustments that go beyond the resources available within given strategic projects or that affect strategies outside this project would typically require revising goals, strategies, and measurement at the organizational level.

Last but not least, the effectiveness of validating, communicating, and using an estimation approach depends to a large extent on how well they are documented. Estimating documentation should clearly and concisely describe such aspects as: estimation context (e.g., constraints), estimation approach (i.e., method and procedure), estimation inputs (e.g., project documents, measurement data, expert judgments, risks, etc.), estimation outcomes (i.e., estimates, accuracy assessment, and any additional aspect that should be considered when interpreting and using estimates).

Collect & Analyze Data

During estimation, its outcomes should be reviewed by estimators, engineers responsible for performing the estimated work, and the stakeholders who will use estimates for decision-making purposes. The goal of a review is to ensure that estimation methods, procedures, techniques, data, and guidelines have been properly used.

Finally, after the estimated work is completed, the estimates should be evaluated against actual outcomes of the work (e.g., actual consumed effort or actual impact of effort factors on the work effort). Note that by evaluation, we mean tracking estimates against actual resource consumption as the project progresses, rather than solely checking the overall estimate after project completion. In practice, we would evaluate estimates after completing project phase, work package, or iteration and revise estimates for remaining work based on the results of the evaluation.

It is good if the estimates were accurate enough and estimation goals were attained—the estimation approach works and we can keep using it without change. If, however, the estimates were not accurate and estimation goals were not attained, then corrective action needs to be taken. But before that, the estimator must investigate the exact cause of the failed estimation. Two potential causes are

- *Inadequacy of the estimation approach*: The estimation approach was not adequate in terms of available data, project and personnel constraints, etc.). In such a case, the estimator must consider whether the project-specific context was one of the causes that is rather unlikely to reoccur or it is going to reoccur in the future.
  - *Exceptional project*: If the project is an exceptional one, we can make a recommendation for the future that prior to employing the estimation approach, we should evaluate its feasibility and appropriateness for a specific project. In such a case, the adjusted or another estimation approach should be

employed, and/or the project environment should be adjusted in order to ensure reliable estimation.

– *Typical project*: If the project is a typical one and is expected to reoccur in the future, then we should consider adjusting the estimation approach on an organizational level in order to be able to reliably apply it in the future. In such a case, we should stop execution of the estimation process and continue with the "analyze outcomes" of the continuous improvement cycle.

- *Unstable project scope and environment*: The scope and characteristics of the project changed so often and so much that in the end, the project's scope and/or characteristics differed from those considered during the project when estimating its effort. In this case, we should consider if we were reestimating frequently enough to account for the project changes and to reflect them through adjusted estimates.

Tip

▶ "Validating estimates requires honesty, courage and wisdom: the honesty to accept and understand that early estimates may not be accurate, the courage to review in the face of a human desire not to be shown to have "failed", and the wisdom to understand that estimate review and validation isn't about apportioning blame or finding mistakes, but is in fact a very effective tool for improving project efficiency and performance."—Matthew Kabik

Provide Feedback and Improve

Based on the results of deploying and applying the estimation approach (i.e., processes, methods, tools, etc.) and associated measurement activities, they are adjusted appropriately, and feedback is given to the organizational level (e.g., responsible for improving the estimation approach). Feedback should include information on what problems were faced during executing estimation processes and how these problems are addressed. Improvements may not only apply to core effort estimation processes. They may apply to the supporting processes (e.g., effort estimation training), measurement and analysis processes (e.g., measurement of estimation error), or the project environment (e.g., availability of measurement data).

16.3.5 Analyze Outcomes

Performance data and feedback regarding the effort estimation approach gathered across multiple projects in the "execute plans" phase are analyzed in order to assess attainment of the estimation goals. During the analysis phase, gathered data are validated, formatted, aggregated, visualized, and, finally, interpreted in order to decide about accomplishment of estimation goals. In the following paragraphs, we briefly discuss these analysis activities.

Validate Measurement Data

Before analyzing the measurement data collected across multiple software projects, it should be validated regarding its credibility. Example data issues include

- *Completeness*: Not all data are collected as planned, which results in missing data in the database.
- *Consistency*: Data points for the same attribute of the same object are not in a meaningful relation to each other. For example, total project effort measured in different projects encompasses inconsistent development phases.
- *Plausibility*: Data points for different attributes of the same object are not in a meaningful relation to each other. For example, the number of nonfunctional requirements could not be larger than the total number of requirements.
- *Abnormal data*: Measurement data include outlier data.

Prepare Measurement Data

Prior to any analysis, validated measurement data typically require preparation and aggregation. The objective of data preparation is to adjust the measurement data to the format acceptable by the tools used for data aggregation and analysis. Example preparation activities include

- *Changing representation format*: Changing data representation, for example, changing the date from European (day-month-year) to US (month-day-year) format.
- *Capitalization*: Changing the case of data strings.
- *Concatenation and splitting*: Joining multiple data fields into one, or splitting one complex data field into several, for example, splitting "programming language" attribute "Java, C++" into "primary language" ("Java") and "secondary Language" ("C++").
- *Character clean-up*: Removing extraneous characters that are not accepted by automatic analysis tools, for example, currency symbols such as dollar (\$), euro (€), or yen (¥).

Aggregate Measurement Data

Following the preparation step, the base measurements are aggregated in order to derive meaningful insights. Aggregation corresponds to deriving complex measurements from the base metrics using the formulas defined for complex metrics in the GQM graphs. For example, if complex metric "*productivity*" is defined as "*productivity = size/effort*", then measurement data for productivity are derived using this formula from sets of directly collected base data: "*size*" and "*effort*" measurements.

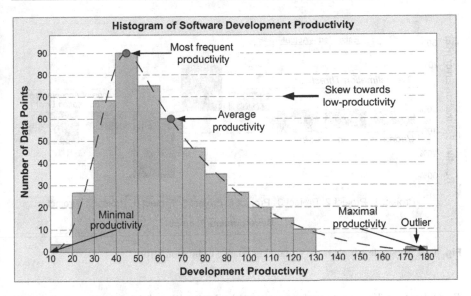

Fig. 16.8 Example descriptive statistics illustrated on the data histogram

Analyze and Visualize Measurement Data

Measurement data are analyzed in order to check whether estimation goals were attained or not and to find out potential causes for goals not attained. On the one hand, we should use visualization to look at the rough measurement data. This gives a quick look into the "nature" of the data and shows potential threats to proper data interpretation. Descriptive statistics are a helpful and easy-to-use tool that supports this quick look at the rough data. Example descriptive statistics include

- The range of values, that is, minimum and maximum value
- Distribution of values across the range, for example, in terms of its variance, standard deviation, and skewness
- Central tendency of the data, for example, in terms of average value (statistical mean) or most frequent values (statistical mode)

Descriptive statistics help, for example, in identifying data outliers (e.g., through analyzing data distribution) and aggregating the data (e.g., by computing average value). Figure 16.8 illustrates example descriptive statistics on an example data histogram.

Appropriate visualization can greatly improve quick and accurate insights into the nature of both base and derived measurement data. Examples of basic visualization means include histograms, scatter plots, bar charts, pie charts, and box plots. We briefly explain the most common visualization means in the next few paragraphs.

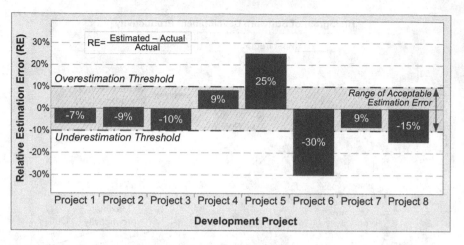

Fig. 16.9 Example bar chart for visualizing relative estimation error

Bar Chart. A bar chart displays rectangular bars with heights (for vertical bars) or lengths (for horizontal bars) proportional to the values that they represent. Bar charts provide a visual presentation of categorical (nominal) data, which is a grouping of data into discrete groups. For example, Fig. 16.9 present values of *relative estimation error (RE)* across multiple projects. This simple visualization gives an immediate answer to such questions as: Are we tending to over- or underestimate? Are we consistent in the magnitude of estimation error, or are any projects extremely over- or underestimated? Did we achieve expected estimation accuracy? If not, how many projects and about how much did we exceed the acceptable error thresholds?

Notice that bar charts look similar to histograms, which we present later in this section. Yet, unlike histograms, bars on a bar chart are separated to indicate that values they represent are independent of each other.

Pie Chart. A pie chart is a circle divided into distinct sectors, each of which represents a proportion of data illustrated by the chart. Notice that all sectors sum up to the total amount of defects (i.e., to 100 %). The size of each sector (determined by the arc length of each sector and measured by a sector's area) is proportional to the quantity it represents. For example, Fig. 16.10 presents a combination of a pie chart and a bar chart for visualizing example project context characteristics. The chart shows what portion of development projects were new development, enhancement, or redevelopment projects. Moreover, for the new development projects, the chart presents what programming was used and what portion of software code has been developed using respective programming languages.

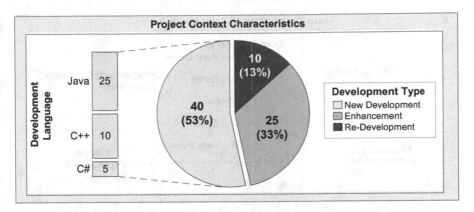

Fig. 16.10 Example pie chart for visualizing project context characteristics

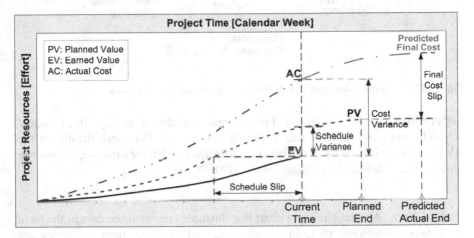

Fig. 16.11 Example run chart for visualizing project effort consumption

Run Chart. A run chart (run-sequence plot) displays the observed data in a time sequence. The horizontal axis in a run chart represents time, and the vertical axis represents a variable of interest. The interval value represents the time elapsed between these values. Subsequent (in time) values of this variable of interest are connected with a curve. A trend plot offers quick insight into trends of the variable over time. For example, Fig. 16.11 illustrates visualization of the basic parameters of the *earned value project management (EVM)*. The *planned value PV* (also known as *budgeted cost of work scheduled, BCWS*) represents planned cumulative amount of resources (e.g., effort or budget) spent on completing project work tasks as a project progresses. The *earned value EV* (also known as *budgeted cost of work performed, BCWP*) represents planned resource consumption of project tasks actually completed up to a given point in time. The *actual cost AC* (also known as *actual cost of work performed, ACWP*) represents resources actually consumed until a given point in time. Based on three indicators, project cost and schedule

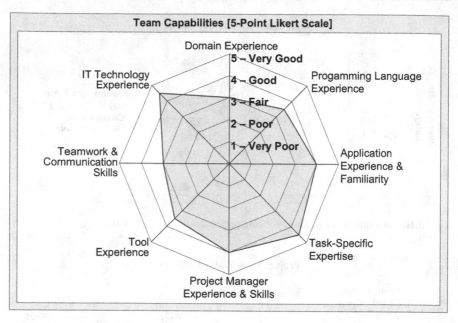

Fig. 16.12 Example radar chart visualizing team capabilities (effort factors)

performance can be monitored. For example, as shown in Fig. 16.11, actual schedule and cost variance can be easily determined. For more details on the EVM and associated project performance indicators, refer, for example, to *Practice Standard for Earned Value Management* (PMI 2011).

Radar Chart. A radar chart is a chart that illustrates multivariate data in the form of a two-dimensional plot, in which values of three or more variables are represented by equiangular axes that start from the same point. For a single vector of data (i.e., single observation), individual values are connected with a line. Figure 16.12 illustrates an example radar chart that visualizes team capability, where the most relevant team qualifications (from the perspective of project effort) are combined in one graph.

Scatter Plot. A scatter plot displays, on Cartesian coordinates, the values of two variables for a set of data. The data is displayed as a collection of points, each having the value of one variable determining the position on the horizontal axis and the value of the other variable determining the position on the vertical axis. Scatter plots are useful for identifying potential correlations between two variables, including functional relationships. It can also indicate data clusters and outliers. Figure 16.13 illustrates an exemplary scatter plot for software size and effort. The horizontal axis represents the size of a software module measured in 1,000 lines of code (kLOC), and the vertical axis represents the project effort consumed to deliver

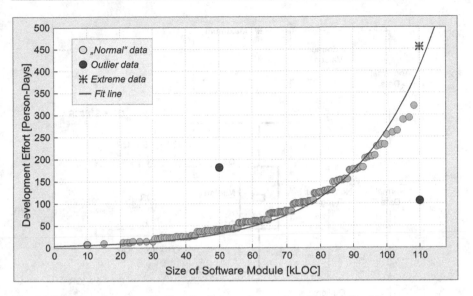

Fig. 16.13 Example scatter plot for visualizing software size-effort relationship

software products of a given size. Looking at the plot, we may immediately say that there is a correlation between software size and project effort. Moreover, the relationship is not linear, meaning that development effort increases disproportionally to the increase of software size. We discuss this phenomenon (called diseconomies of scale) in Sect. 3.2.1. Finally, the plot shows three data outliers. Data outliers can be investigated further by using box plots. In Fig. 16.15, we visualize the same set of data using a box plot, and there, we can see that the three outliers are actually two outliers and one extreme value.

Box Plot. A box plot graphically represents groups of numerical data through their five descriptive statistics (Fig. 16.14): minimal value (*min*), lower quartile (*Q*1), median (*Q*2), upper quartile (*Q*3), and maximum value (*max*). A box plot may also indicate which observations, if any, might be considered outliers and extreme values (Fig. 16.8 illustrates how to determine these values). In this sense, a box plot implements an important principle of visualization, which is to focus the viewer's attention on what should be seen in the data. Figure 16.15 illustrates a box plot combined with a histogram, which shows software development productivity data. This is the same dataset as in the scatter plot in Fig. 16.13, but the software size and effort data were aggregated to development productivity such that *productivity = size/effort*. The box plot clearly shows the two data outliers and one extreme value we already could see in the scatter plot.

Histogram. A histogram displays adjacent bars representing the distribution of data. The bars are of equal width, which represents intervals (bins) of the data for

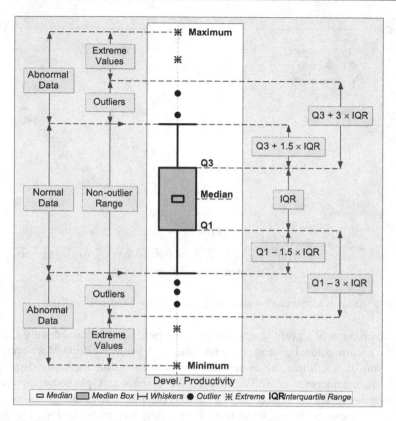

Fig. 16.14 Basic elements of box plot

the variable of interest. The height of the bars represents frequency of data points in the interval (bin) represented by bars. A histogram may also be normalized displaying relative frequencies. A normalized histogram displays the proportion of data that fall into each interval, with the total area equaling 1 or 100 %. Figure 16.15 illustrates an example histogram combined with a box plot for software development productivity data—the same data we visualized in Fig. 16.13. We can see that the distribution of productivity data has a bell-like shape, yet it is skewed toward small values. We can also identify outlier data represented by low bars located outside the main body of data. Yet, already, the associated box plot clearly highlights these observations as two outliers and one extreme value.

Interpret Analysis Results

Finally, measurement data are interpreted using the predefined interpretation models and baselines. For example, consider an interpretation model associated with the measurement goal of evaluating the reduction of estimation error within

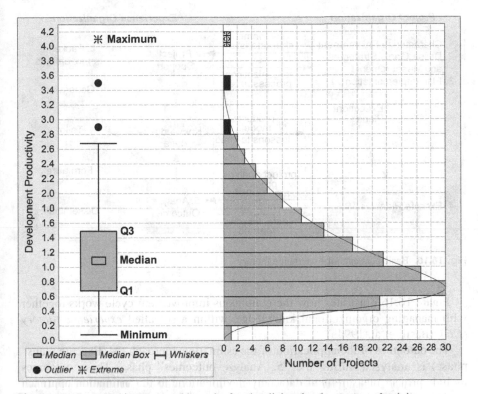

Fig. 16.15 Example histogram and box plot for visualizing development productivity

the next year to 10 % or less. The interpretation model would compare the *target* estimation error achieved in development projects performed in a recent year against the *baseline* estimation error in subsequent years. Simple analysis would check if average (or maximal) estimation error across target projects is 10 % or lower than the average (or maximal) error across baseline projects.

16.3.6 Package Improvements

In the last phase of the continuous improvement cycle, appropriate improvements to the effort estimation approach are made based on the results of the analysis phase. Afterward, all changed organizational process assets and knowledge gained during application of the estimation approach are packaged and stored in the organizational knowledge base. *Organizational process assets* include processes, procedures, templates, guidelines, and policies related to the effort estimation approach. *Organizational knowledge* includes measurement data, project deliverables and documentation, as well as lessons learned. These assets are then used to facilitate improved effort estimation in future projects.

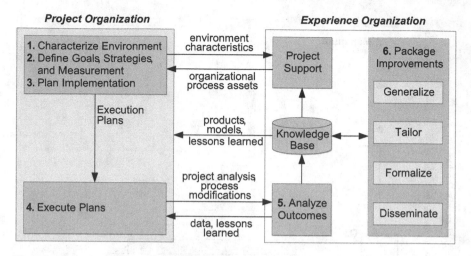

Fig. 16.16   Basic concepts of experience factory

Figure 16.16 illustrates how the continuous improvement cycle works together with managing organizational knowledge, within a so-called *experience factory (EF)* (Basili et al. 1994a).

The outcomes of the application of the estimation approach ("4. Execute plans" phase) is analyzed during the "5. Analyze outcomes" phase. These outcomes include project measurement data, any modifications to the estimation approach made locally within individual software projects, and lessons learned during application of the estimation approach. Together with results of the analysis phase, all this information is stored in the organizational knowledge base. The content of the knowledge base is then processed (in the "6. Package improvements" phase) in order to generalize, tailor, formalize, and disseminate reusable organizational knowledge. For example, an estimation approach's improvement potentials and lessons learned are used to tailor organizational process assets such as effort estimation models, estimating processes, guidelines, and templates. Reusable knowledge is then available in the subsequent improvement cycle when it facilitates planning and implementing the improved effort estimation approach in future projects.

Further Reading

- V. Basili, A. Trendowicz, M. Kowalczyk, J. Heidrich, C. Seaman, J. Münch, and D. Rombach (2014), *Aligning Organizations through Measurement. The GQM⁺Strategies Approach*. The Fraunhofer IESE Series on Software and Systems Engineering. Springer Verlag.
  This book presents the GQM⁺Strategies approach for aligning organizational goals and strategies through measurement. In particular, the book specifies

methodological concepts (goals, strategies, context, assumptions, measurements, interpretations) and the steps for developing their hierarchy. It also provides examples of its application based upon experience with various organizations.

- D. Pyle (1999), *Data Preparation for Data Mining*. Morgan Kaufmann.

  This book synthesizes best practices in the area of data preparation and exploration. Author provides background knowledge needed for recognizing and eliminating the source of problems with data. With respect to data preparation, the book presents comprehensive information on the purposes, overall process, and common techniques of data cleansing.

- N. Yau (2011), *Visualize This: The FlowingData Guide to Design, Visualization, and Statistics*, Wiley & Sons.

  This book introduces various means of data visualization to support basic data analysis purposes such as visualizing patterns, trends over time, proportions, and relationships. Author explains how to design visualization and select the best visualization means in order to make the data tell its full story. Moreover, the author provides a brief introduction to preparing the data for analysis and visualization. Author illustrates proposed visualization means with many full-color figures.

Effort Estimation Best Practices

17

Given the faults of human nature, coupled with the complexity of the design of everything, from lectures to bridges, it behooves us to beware of the lure of success and listen to the lessons of failure.

—Henry Petroski

You are making progress if each mistake is a new one.

—Anonymous

It is a human thing to err. Yet, we should learn from mistakes in order not to repeat them. At best, when we learn from others' mistakes, we do not have to bear their consequences; others already did it.

In this chapter, we synthesize success and failure lessons that we and other software practitioners have learned about software effort estimation. We synthesize these estimation "patterns" and "antipatterns" into a set of "do" and "don't" recommendations. We group these recommendations according to the basic elements of the estimation process. We distinguish the following elements of the estimation process (Fig. 17.1):

- *Inputs* refers to estimation objectives and quantitative project data from already completed projects.
- *Context* refers to characteristics of the estimation environment that may facilitate or hinder estimation.
- *Resources* refers to people involved in the estimation, the cost of estimation (e.g., in terms of time), and tools used to support the estimation procedure.
- *Estimation* includes methods and procedures used in estimation. It also encompasses characteristics of estimators who set up and apply estimation methods, processes, and tools.
- *Outputs* refers to products of estimation such as effort estimates or estimation models.
- *Use of estimation outputs* refers to the way in which estimation outputs are employed for project decision-making purposes (e.g., resource planning, risk analysis, benchmarking, etc.).

A. Trendowicz and R. Jeffery, *Software Project Effort Estimation*,
DOI 10.1007/978-3-319-03629-8_17, © Springer International Publishing Switzerland 2014

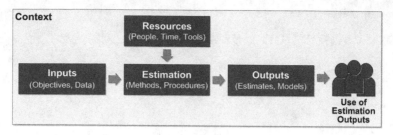

Fig. 17.1 Simplified view of the basic elements of effort estimation

17.1 Ensure Appropriate Inputs

Data has no meaning apart from its context. Data contains both signal and noise. To be able to extract information, one must separate the signal from the noise within the data.
—Walter Shewhart

Information upon which estimates are based is the very first success factor of project effort estimation. In practice, even the best estimation method cannot derive reliable estimates from unreliable inputs. Inputs include not only facts about the estimated project but also information on estimation objectives and experiences from already completed projects. In this section, we gather best-practice recommendations regarding various inputs to effort estimation.

17.1.1 Clearly Define Estimation Purpose and Goals

If you don't know where you are going, you'll end up someplace else.
—Yogi Berra

The purposes and goals of effort estimation can vary. Typically, estimation is expected to serve more purposes than simple project resource planning and to achieve more goals than simple accuracy of predictions. In order to be an effective project management tool, project estimation must accomplish more; it should support project decision making throughout the complete project lifetime, beginning from project bidding and negotiations until project closing and retrospective analysis (including goodness of estimates).

Estimation purpose and goals determine other elements of estimation such as the estimation method used, the input project data, and the outcomes of estimation. Therefore, explicitly and clearly specifying the estimation purpose and goals should be the starting point for project estimation.

17.1.2 Clearly Identify Activities You Estimate

A problem well stated is a problem half solved.
—Charles F. Kettering

One of the prominent reasons for project underestimation is omitted or strongly underestimated project activities. Typical examples include documentation activities, which are depreciated or completely forgotten.

For example, the US Government Accountability Office, in their Cost Estimating and Assessment Guide (GAO 2009), require that an estimator is provided with and reviews the system description, its ground rules and assumptions, and technical and performance characteristics. The GAO indicates this as a best practice for ensuring reliable and well-documented estimates.

One important prerequisite for identifying all relevant project activities is a complete requirements specification for the developed software system. This can be achieved through broad participation of all project stakeholders in specifying requirements and in defining system parameters and its other characteristics. Another prerequisite is a systematic derivation of work activities based on the requirements regarding expected project outcomes, which include a wide variety of artifacts (e.g., requirements, specification, system, software code, test case specification, executable software system, and user manuals). Project management best practice for systematically deriving project activities is to break down work activities. We discuss this practice in the next section.

17.1.3 Structure Work Activities Prior to Estimation

Divide et impera [Divide and Conquer].
—Julius Caesar

Well-structured work activities are the best way to avoid the problem of unclear, misunderstood, redundant, or missing project activities. Work breakdown structure (WBS) is the most recommended approach for systematically structuring project work activities. In the essence (PMI 2013, 2006), "WBS is a deliverable-oriented hierarchical decomposition of the work to be executed by the project team to accomplish project objectives and create the required deliverables, with each descending level of the WBS representing the increasingly detailed definition of the project work." One advantage of WBS is that in can be used directly within a bottom-up estimation strategy (see Sect. 5.2). The effort for accomplishing the work specified at the bottom level of a WBS can be estimated and aggregated, using the WBS structure, into the overall effort required for completing the project.

Well-structured specification of the project work ensures that no portions of the estimate are omitted. Moreover, smaller pieces of work defined at the bottom level of a work breakdown structure are easier to understand and more likely to be comparable to work already done in other projects—thus easier to estimate.

17.1.4 Use Your Own Data and Expertise

The best data for comparison is your own.

—Lawrence H. Putnam

I have but one lamp by which my feet are guided and that is the lamp of experience. I know of no way of judging the future but by the past experience.

—Patrick Henry

Predicting the future is always based on past experiences and is best done when these experiences originate from the same environment in which the predictions are made. This applies to any domain, including software effort estimation. But different factors may have a different impact on effort in various contexts. For example, factors that are important determinants of effort required for developing embedded software systems may be (and typically are) completely irrelevant in the context of developing a web application. So in order to learn the various impacts on project effort, in order to later use this knowledge for estimation on new projects, we need data from already completed projects in the same or at least in very similar contexts.

Yet, in reality, there are an infinite number of factors influencing project effort, and it is not possible to consider all of them; moreover, it is economically unfeasible to consider more than a dozen of them. Using data from the same or a similar context gives us the advantage that even though we do not explicitly consider many of the relevant effects on project effort, there is a great chance that by using the data from the same context, we will implicitly consider these effects. For instance, in the context of analogy-based estimation, if we explicitly consider only the application domain and take as the basis for estimates the development productivity of external software organizations from the same domain, we risk poor estimates, as external organizations are very likely to differ from ours with respect to many relevant aspects affecting development effort. These aspects include capabilities of the development team, maturity and type of development processes, and technologies employed. By using our own data, we have quite a good chance that these aspects will not differ much between already completed projects and new projects.

Organization-specific data forms a composite picture of how an organization develops software, with both its strengths and its weaknesses. External data can be useful for comparisons; yet, it cannot tell us how particular organizations produce software. Most organizations run software development projects in very specific ways. If no project history is kept, either in the form of the expertise of human experts or quantitative measurement data, very valuable information about the specific organization remains unknown. As a consequence, such organizations cannot tell how much effort it will require to produce software of certain functional and nonfunctional characteristics. Therefore, it is crucial for estimation to keep and use its own project knowledge.

However, having their own data and experience does not necessarily mean having knowledge upon which reliable project estimates can be derived. In this matter, we agree with W.E. Deming according to whom[1] *"Experience by itself teaches nothing."* Deming disagreed with the simplified interpretation of the old proverb saying that "experience is the best teacher." Raw experiences and observations without proper understanding and interpretation can be misleading in that they are open to misuse and misinterpretation. The advantage of collecting one's own project information and experience is that we have access to context information and can use it to derive useful and correct knowledge.

17.1.5　Combine Expertise with Quantitative Data

Never ignore a gut feeling, but never believe that it's enough.

—Robert Heller

The common industrial approach is to base estimation on human judgment, and the common research approach is to base estimation on measurement data. Which approach is right? None and both at the same time; none when used alone and both when used in combination. In the end, reliable estimation requires solid knowledge of the software development environment; in particular, knowledge of which of its aspects are important and how they affect development effort. Without such knowledge, we may invest a lot of work into estimation without getting even close to reliable estimates.

In principle, we would agree with Ed Yourdon (2003), according to whom one of the most common best practices for a successful project is to base estimates and plans on measurement data from already completed projects. Yet, basing estimation solely on measurement data is rather unrealistic in practice. We first need to know which project characteristics to measure. Either we determine these using human expertise or we need to blindly measure an extensive set of project aspects for a sufficiently large number of projects in order to be able to analytically determine those aspects that are relevant for effort estimation. Besides being economically unacceptable, the idea of collecting extensive sets of project data is in reality rarely feasible. During the time, we would need to measure a sufficient number of projects their context will most likely change. In consequence, only a part of the most recently collected project data will reflect the current situation and thus be useful for estimating new projects; the rest of the data will only confuse estimation, leading to unreliable estimates.

So the question is not whether to combine data with expertise but how to do it effectively. Unfortunately, estimation methods that support such combination are still rather unpopular. Section 6.5 presents an overview of example hybrid effort estimation methods, including their common strengths and weaknesses. As an alternative to using a hybrid estimation method, one may use a data-driven method and an expert-based method individually and then combine their outcomes. Yet,

---

[1] Scott M. Paton, "Four Days with W. Edwards Deming", The W. Edwards Deming Institute, available at http://deming.org/index.cfm?content=653.

this solution is more expensive than using a single method on mixed measurement data and human expertise. Moreover, combining outcomes of independent estimation methods may be complex. We discuss usage of multiple estimation methods and combining their outcomes in Sects. 5.5 and 5.6, respectively.

In the end, successful estimation is based on sound knowledge. And this comes from a combination of different sources. As William Edwards Deming pointed, *"there is no substitute for knowledge [. . .] a small amount of knowledge could save many hours of hard work."*

17.1.6 Ensure Appropriate Quality of Project Data

More is not better; better is better.

—Jade Teta

Quantitative project data comprise, besides human expertise, a very important input to estimation. Quantitative data represents objective information and can be automatically analyzed to acquire knowledge upon which to base estimates. Yet, all the advantages of using quantitative project data for estimation are based on the assumption that these data are valid. Even if we use a great estimation method and reliably perform the estimation process, we will not get error-free estimation if the input data are not free from errors. Some estimation methods may provide support for handling selected data deficits, but most commonly, multiple errors in estimation inputs are accumulated throughout the estimation process into large errors in the estimation outputs.

The most common cause of invalid project data are defective or/and poorly implemented data collection and preparation processes. Jørgensen et al. (2009), gurus of software project estimation, point to invalid measurement processes as the prominent cause of invalid estimates. For example, measurement rules used for software size and project effort might differ from those used for estimation purposes. Examples of common issues with respect to software size and project effort measurement include

- *Inconsistent definition of software size*: Different definitions are used for apparently the same size metric. For example, lines of code (LOC) may comprise logical and physical lines of code, counting of nonexecutable statements, counting nongenerated code only, or even counting support software such as deliverable tools and test drivers.
- *Inconsistent scope of size measurement*: Different software artifacts are included in size measurement across historical projects. For example, measurement of software lines of code for some projects included generated software code, while for other projects not.
- *Inconsistent definition of project effort*: Different work activities are covered by apparently the same effort metrics. For example, effort measurement may consider different phases of the development life cycle, different types of work

time (training, checking personal e-mail, and overtime), and different types of activities (development, management, quality assurance).

- *Inconsistent scope of effort measurement*: Different work activities are included in project effort measurement across historical projects. For example, total project effort is measured for projects that consist of different phases. In consequence, effort of projects that included requirements analysis and system testing is compared with effort of projects in which these phases were not included (e.g., because the requirements specification was prepared by a customer and system testing was done by an independent verification & validation authority).

With respect to inconsistent definition of metrics, Jørgensen and his colleagues found factor-of-three differences between the data collected for the COCOMO model in an example study and the data conforming to COCOMO's published definitions. With respect to the scope of measurement, we observed a factor-of-two drop in the accuracy of the estimates provided by hybrid estimation with the CoBRA method when size measurement across historical projects encompassed inconsistent software artifacts; for instance, in some projects, the automatically generated code of the graphical user interface was included in size measurement whereas in other projects it was not.

17.1.7 Ensure Appropriate Quantity of Project Data

You need less data than you think, you have more data than you think.
—Douglas W. Hubbard

The amount of data used for estimation is another important aspect to consider when striving for reliable estimates. In this context, more does not mean better.

Project data encompass two dimensions and are thus usually represented as a two-dimensional matrix. One dimension represents already completed projects that can potentially be used for estimating a new project. The second dimension represents characteristics of a project and its environment; they constitute a set of potential context or effort factors (we discuss context and effort factors in Chap. 3). In data exploration terminology, projects and their characteristics are referred to as cases and attributes, respectively. Data quantity refers to both number of projects and the number of characteristics per project. Both extremes, too much or too little data, can jeopardize estimation. What counts in the end is how much useful knowledge we can extract from the data for the purpose of reliable estimation.

Too Much Data

In the rapidly changing context of software engineering, large amounts of project data collected within a specific context (e.g., one software organization) are very rare. Even though a software organization performs multiple projects, changes in the application domain and technologies mean that data collected even a short time ago do not reflect the current characteristics of development projects and thus are of limited or no use for estimating current projects. In the end, larger data does not necessarily mean more knowledge. Yet for sure, increased amounts of data do contribute to higher cost of estimation because larger sets of data are more expensive to collect, to maintain, and to prepare for estimation. Summarizing, although more data always means higher cost of usage, it often does not mean higher benefit for estimation.

Too Little Data

Little data implies little information and may—yet does not have to—mean insufficient knowledge for reliable estimation.

Data-driven methods analyze data for a sample of projects from a certain context in order to infer effort dependencies in this context. The underlying assumption is that the dependencies represented by the sample project data reflect real dependencies in this context. In such a case, the more data we have, the more likely they are to cover true effect dependencies and the more likely they are to be discovered by the estimation method. For example, for statistical regression best practice is to provide 10–30 projects for each unique project characteristic.

In the case of insufficient information on which to base estimates, we may "buy information." There are several approaches to buying information. In the context of data-driven methods, one of the most popular approaches is augmenting available project data by means of sampling techniques such as bootstrapping. In Sect. 4.4.1, we discuss the application of bootstrapping for handling estimation uncertainty ("Prediction Intervals Based on Bootstrapping" paragraph). Another way of buying information is to combine different sources of information. In the case of scarce project data, we may involve human experts and acquire their expertise in order to complement quantitative project data. An example approach for combining quantitative data with human expertise might be the hybrid estimation methods such as CoBRA (which we present in Chap. 15). Human expertise can already be used before we start collecting project data for the purpose of effort estimation. Experts may indicate a set of project factors that are most likely to have significant impact on project effort and for which corresponding quantitative data should thus be initially collected. The Pareto rule seems to apply here in that a minority of effort factors is responsible for a majority of project effort. Finding these factors is the key to successful estimation.

17.1.8 Avoid Irrelevant and Misleading Information

In anything at all, perfection is finally attained, not when there is no longer anything to add,
but when there is no longer anything to take away.

—Antoine de Saint-Exupéry

This practice is related to the aspect of data quantity we discussed in the previous section. However, here, we do not limit ourselves to project data but to any information that may jeopardize estimation performance. As noted by Walter Andrew Shewhart (see Sect. 17.1), one of the key points of estimation is to separate the signal part of the information from the noise and turn the signal into knowledge useful for estimation purposes. In the estimation context, "information noise" includes mainly irrelevant and misleading information. This noise information might come with the project data or experiences, or the estimation process may also be affected by noise information beyond the explicit, intended estimation inputs. Unintentional information includes interests and expectations of estimators and project stakeholders. Thus, noise information will affect expert-based and hybrid estimation. But it will also affect data-driven estimation in that the estimator who interprets outcomes of analytical estimation may also adjust the final estimates toward the noise information he has been exposed to.

Information Misleading Effort Estimates

Jørgensen and Grimstad (2008, 2011) observe, in the context of expert-based estimation, that "eliminating irrelevant and misleading information can help avoid inaccurate, overly optimistic software development effort estimates." In the course of their investigation, they identified several types of information that misleads effort estimates:

- *Clients' cost expectations*: Customers' or project owners' expectations regarding project costs often affect estimates in that estimators try to satisfy these expectations by appropriately adjusting unbiased outcomes of estimation. In this case, expectations change estimates into a self-fulfilling prophecy. Jørgensen and Grimstad (2008) observed up to a 500 % difference in estimations due to customer's expectations.
- *Length and wording of work specification*: The way work is specified may affect estimation. One aspect is the amount of documentation used for specifying the work. The length of requirements specification alone (without changing its content) may significantly change estimates. In this case, the amount of documentation is used as a determinant of the amount of work. Another aspect is the wording used for specifying the work. Using suggestive wording, the same amount of actual work may be communicated as more or less effort-consuming. For example, adding the same new functionality to an existing software system may be communicated as "minor extension," "extension," or simply "new functionality." In each case, the perceived amount of work will probably be different and will have a corresponding effect on effort estimates.
- *Schedule pressure*: Information on unrealistically short project schedules creates pressure on estimators to downsize their estimates in order to fit to the predefined schedule.

(continued)

Information Misleading Effort Estimates (continued)

- *Future opportunities*: The perspective of potential future benefits affect estimation in that estimators try to ensure these benefits. A typical situation is project bidding, when estimators underestimate in order to increase their chances of winning the tender (assuming that project cost is most important or the only criterion for assessing alternative bids). Jørgensen and Grimstad (2008) observed up to a 150 % difference in estimations due to future opportunities.

In terms of the simplified view of estimation we presented at the beginning of this chapter (Fig. 17.1), the following actions can be undertaken to reduce the negative impact of irrelevant or misleading information:

Estimation Inputs

- *Exclude irrelevant information from the estimation*. This would be very difficult in practice because it would mean isolating the estimation team from the outer world. Jørgensen and Grimstad (2008) made an interesting observation that highlighting relevant information (i.e., separating irrelevant and relevant information) does not reduce the negative effect of irrelevant information on estimates.
- *Explicitly list and assess the relevancy of information used for estimation*. Experts and estimators involved in the estimation process should present the way they came up with estimates and list information they used for estimation.
- *Clearly define goals and purpose of estimation*. All persons involved in the estimation should understand what estimation is about and what estimation goals are to be achieved. For example, they should understand the difference between estimate, target, and bid.

Estimation Method

- *Use formal effort estimation methods and models*. In the case of data-driven methods, estimates are based on formal analysis of objective project data. This is free from the impact of typical misleading information, which has a qualitative and subjective character. Only at the time of interpreting estimation outcomes can misleading information lead to original estimate adjustment toward a less realistic one. In the case of expert-based estimation, misleading information typically affects the source of estimates, that is, the human experts who provide estimates. Applying systematic estimation based on group consensus may reduce this negative effect in that members of the group may be differently affected by misleading information and must justify and discuss their individual estimates in the group.

Estimation Resources

- *Select the most competent experts and estimators.* Involve highly skilled and experienced experts (e.g., senior developers and project managers).
- *Exclude personnel from estimation who are likely to be affected by misleading information.* As an alternative to eliminating irrelevant information from estimation, we may exclude people who are likely to be affected by the information.
- *Create an atmosphere of trust between the project team and managers.* The project team and estimators should be assured by their managers that their objective is to provide the most likely, realistic project estimate and that they will need to justify their estimates, to reestimate if the scope of the project changes, and most importantly, that they will not be punished if they make an honest mistake in estimation or of their estimate will not fulfill the management's expectations.

Estimation Outputs

- *Separate estimation from project targeting and bidding processes.* This is especially important when estimations do not achieve predefined project targets or bids. In this case, project owners should use realistic estimates and decide on how to achieve their goals. They may decide on adjusting the project scope or environment (relevant effort drivers) to meet a target budget or on consciously reducing the project bid in order to win a bid.

17.2 Ensure Appropriate Resources

> *It is very difficult to make a vigorous, plausible, and job-risking defense of an estimate that is derived by no quantitative method, supported by little data, and certified chiefly by the hunches of the managers.*
>
> —Frederick P. Brooks

Software engineering is a human-intensive activity, and its success relies largely on the skills of people involved. Betts (2003) felicitously points out that, in practice, every problem in the context of software development can be boiled down to a people problem. For instance, calling something a technical problem is a convenient label to say "It's not something I can handle." In this section, we discuss best estimation practices related to human resources involved in estimation. We focus on human experts providing inputs to estimation and estimators responsible for running estimation.

17.2.1 Create Specialized Role of Estimator

My guess is that most technology managers tasked with estimating the cost of a project have no experience or training in the use of formal methods based on empirical research to compute the time, cost and resources required by a software project.

—Samuel Prasad

Effort estimation should be assigned to dedicated roles (responsibilities) of estimators in the organization. It does not mean that the estimator will deal only with effort estimation. This is unrealistic in small software organizations. Yet, an estimator should not have any personal interest in estimation outcomes, and he/she should be independent of both developers and project owners. At best, an estimator should also play other project- or process-improvement activities in the organization; for example, be a member group of a software engineering process group responsible for project measurement and governance.

In order to build up estimation skills, an estimator should perform, or at least lead, estimation for different projects within an organization—at best for all projects if it is within the estimator's capabilities. Moreover, an estimator should have somebody to check and to consult with concerning his/her ideas and estimation results.

17.2.2 Train Estimators

Accurate software estimation has long been a headache for software developers. Much of the problem stems from lack of estimation training and practice.

—David Henry

Robert Glass (2002) points out that "Software estimation is usually done by the wrong people." In practice, software organizations do not have a specialized role of estimator. Typically, project managers do the job in addition to their main activities. Yet, they are usually missing any appropriate training and resources to do proper estimation. For example, they get 10 % or less of the time they would need to do it right. Finally, as they estimate only those projects they manage, it is not rare that they do estimation merely once or twice a year and thus have little opportunity to get appropriate practice in estimating.

Successful estimation requires that all parties involved in the estimation obtain appropriate training and opportunity to practice. Developers who provide inputs to estimation should learn the principles of estimation, their role in the process, and tasks they are supposed to accomplish. Estimators should obtain comprehensive training on software effort estimation, in particular selecting and using appropriate estimation methods.

17.2.3 Motivate Estimators

If the estimator has no stake in success or failure of the project, what is left as his/her motivation? What constitutes success for the estimator?

—Tom DeMarco

Creating a separate role of estimator exposes the risk that the estimator will have little motivation because he has no stake in successful estimation. Therefore, along with entrusting estimation to a dedicated role, we should take care of appropriate motivation. In small- and medium-size organizations, the estimator role is combined with other process or project responsibilities. For example, the estimator is responsible for measurement and quantitative process control. Or he can be responsible for project portfolio management. In these cases, he would have a personal interest in "good" estimates since they would help him in his work (managing development processes or managing projects).

Note that the estimator should have a stake in successful estimation, not in a particular outcome of estimation. This is an important difference because interest in a particular estimation outcome will most probably bias estimates. For example, if we entrusted estimation to developers, they might typically tend to overestimate in order to ensure more resources for themselves; yet, if we entrusted estimation to management, they might typically tend to underestimate in order to achieve their target of completing the project with minimal resources (e.g., to satisfy project owners and/or customers). Therefore, estimation should involve both groups of stakeholders but should be done by people knowledgeable in estimation and the domain, yet having no personal interest in a particular outcome but only in estimation quality.

In general, success of estimation should be measured in terms of achieving estimation goals. We would not entirely agree with Tom DeMarco that *"success for the estimator must be defined as a function of convergence of the estimate to the actual, and nothing else"* because convergence of estimates to actual is only one aspect of "good" estimation. Another aspect is the extent to which estimates support decision making. Estimation fails if it provides information that is far from the true project situation, and it fails when it provides true but useless information for project decision making. For example, estimation that only provides an accurate number for the effort required to complete the project would be considered successful by the project manager who needs to simply plan project resources, but as a failure by the project manager who needs to justify estimates to a customer.

17.2.4 Make the Estimator Responsible for Measurement

You can't control what you can't measure.

—Tom DeMarco

One of the key elements of successful estimation is the use of quantitative project data (preferably combined with human expertise). An estimator must have insight and influence on the measurement processes related to estimation. Whatever measurements are needed for estimation, potential measurement error produces estimation error, independent of how good are the estimation methods used. An estimator should, for example, control measurement of software effort, size, and most relevant effort drivers.

An estimator should also ensure that project characteristics that are relevant for estimation are actually measurable. This means that selected project activities, methods, resources, and products must be quantifiable.

17.2.5 Involve People Doing the Work and Having Done the Work

It is people who estimate not machines.

—Thomsett International[2]

Software project scoping and planning should involve the people who have already done a similar job in the past and the people who are going to do the job. In particular, identifying and breaking down work activities and estimating effort needed for their completion should not be done by a team that have never done a similar job before. If we do so, we risk that important work activities might be omitted and that effort for their completion will be estimated blindly.

People who have done the work before not only know the exact scope of the work but also important aspects that influenced the effort required to get the work done in the past. People doing the work, on the other hand, know their capabilities and thus can better assess the effort needed to accomplish the work (after they know the work scope and influencing factors).

The entire process of project scoping and estimation should be managed by an independent estimator who collects and verifies inputs from involved people and who prepares final estimates.

17.2.6 Provide Appropriate Resources

One valid definition of an "out of control" project is one that doesn't have time to plan—large projects should expect to devote ~5 % of total effort to planning and status tracking.

—Gary A. Gack

Estimation, as with any other project task, requires appropriate resources. Successful estimation needs time and money. Project owners often ignore this fact until one project fails and the corresponding loss exceeds what they would have needed to invest in proper planning and tracking in order to avoid the project failure.

When we talk to project estimators about estimation overhead, they claim that what they usually get for the purpose of project estimation is 10–15 % of what they would actually need. In consequence, they cannot afford to collect proper information or involve appropriate people but need to limit estimation to rule-of-thumb predictions.

---

[2] http://www.thomsettinternational.com/main/articles/hot/games.htm.

Project planning and tracking needs estimation resources to successfully complete it. General numbers such as 5 % of total project effort might be a good starting point, but one needs to adjust it to the situation of a particular organization by considering relevant context factors. The cost of estimation would differ depending on such aspects as project size, estimation approach, or capabilities of involved personnel (especially the estimator). Large projects require identifying more relevant activities and would involve more people than small projects. Using expert-based estimation would involve much more overhead than using data-driven estimation.

One would probably never be able to assess exactly the estimation overhead because it needs to be done before the size of the project (and the size of estimation task) is known.

17.2.7 Use Independent Estimators

When you can't afford to fail, always get an independent expert estimate.
                                                                —Gary A. Gack

In order to avoid estimation bias, estimators should be independent of the projects they estimate; independent in the sense that they have no personal interest in a particular estimation outcome. Yet, the dedicated and independent role of estimators also has negative aspects. As pointed out by Tom DeMarco, even the very largest projects can hardly afford more than one estimator, so most estimators would work alone. In that situation, estimators would be working in a vacuum with no one to react to their ideas and no one to check their work. In order to avoid relying on the opinion of one man, we should consider getting estimates from another, independent estimator. For example, the United States Government Accountability Office (2009) recommends conducting an independent review of estimates as crucial to establishing confidence in the estimate. In their Cost Estimating and Assessment Guide, GAO advises that an independent reviewer should verify, modify, and correct an estimate to ensure its realism, completeness, and consistency.

17.3 Use Appropriate Estimation Methods and Models

You can't expect to meet the challenges of today with yesterday's tools and expect to be in business tomorrow.
                                                                —Unknown author

A proper estimation approach is, after the human factor, another important factor influencing the success or failure of effort estimation. There are a number of detailed questions to answer when deciding on an appropriate estimation approach. Which estimation strategy should we use? What estimation method is the best in our situation? In Chaps. 5 and 6, we discuss specific estimation strategies and methods, respectively. Moreover, in Chap. 7, we specify a detailed framework for selecting the most suitable estimation method.

In this section, we summarize the general best practices regarding the use of estimation approaches.

17.3.1 Avoid Ad Hoc On-Demand Estimation

Projects that aim from the beginning at achieving the shortest possible schedules regardless of quality considerations tend to have the fairly high frequencies of both schedule and cost overruns.

—Capers Jones

A common problem of software effort prediction is giving immediate estimates, like in the elevator or on a napkin during a lunch. This kind of estimate would not be a problem if they were treated as seriously as the conditions under which they had been created. Yet, in practice, napkin estimates are taken as commitments. The best practice is to beware of "napkin" and "guts" estimates. And this refers to both those who ask for such estimates and those who give them. Before we ask for or give immediate estimates, we need to realize that they are typically ad hoc predictions based on good feelings rather than on facts resulting from a systematic process.

17.3.2 Use a Systematic and Structured Approach

Good ideas are not adopted automatically. They must be driven into practice with courageous patience.

– Hyman Rickover

As with any other software engineering activity, estimation should follow a systematic and repeatable process. Using a systematic approach increases repeatability of estimates and reduces estimation error. Even if we decide on estimation based on human judgment, we should use structured rather than unstructured methods and follow systematic estimation processes. For example, the structured group consensus estimation procedure of the Wideband Delphi method supports avoiding estimation biases that are inevitable in ad hoc estimation based on human judgment. Refer to Sect. 6.4.3 for a discussion of biases in expert-based estimation and to Chap. 12 for a description of the Wideband Delphi method.

17.3.3 Fit Estimation Methods to Your Needs and Capabilities

Like in all other engineering disciplines, there is no one-solution-fits-all answer to the question of which process to choose. The earlier we acknowledge this fact, the earlier we can focus our efforts on determining relationships between contexts and processes.

—Ove Armbrust and Dieter Rombach

Common software estimation practice is the arbitrary choice of an estimation method. Guided by marketing information or accidentally found opinions of others, software estimators select "the best" estimation method without verifying its applicability (feasibility and usefulness) in their particular situation.

Applying democracy and the voice of the majority is not a good idea when selecting a suitable effort estimation method. The fact that the majority considers something as right does not mean that it is actually right. The estimation method that worked for other software organizations will not necessarily work for me.

When selecting a suitable effort estimation method, we should focus on looking for the method that is most likely to work well for us; that is, fulfill the particular needs under consideration for our particular capabilities and constraints. The most we can do is to consider, as additional information, which methods worked for others whose context is the same or very similar to ours, that is, similar enough to reliably convey experiences gained there to our context. In practice, however, such similarity across various software organizations happens rather rarely. We recommend using the systematic selection procedure we present in Chap. 7.

17.3.4 Introduce Estimation Methods Iteratively

Companies should define their own processes beginning with what is broken and critical to their business.

—Sarah A. Sheard

Known rules like "start small" and "keep it simple" seem to be applicable to software effort estimation. And "small and simple" does not contradict "structured and systematic" that we recommend as one best practice of effort estimation.

Introducing systematic effort estimation into an organization means change; change to processes, but first and foremost, change to the behavior of involved personnel. Similar to any other change in an organization, doing it in a "big bang" manner typically will not work because

- Effects of multiple changes introduced at once are difficult to predict and control due to their potential interactions.
- Software estimation is a human-intensive activity (involves many stakeholders), and they are typically reluctant to change their behavior, especially when the change is large.

Therefore, change should be introduced in small steps, and people should be supported to adapt their behavior to the change. Example strategies include piloting new estimation processes in selected projects and building estimation models in an incremental manner.

In Chap. 16, we present a general framework for introducing and continuously improving effort estimation within an organization.

17.3.5 Analyze Estimates, Learn, and Continuously Improve

The most successful improvements ultimately are those that focus on the limitations—on the failures.

—Henry Petroski

As with any process or technology, estimation requires systematic integration into existing organizational processes, regular performance assessments, and continuous improvement. Software organizations often fail to improve their estimation because they expect a new estimation approach to work right at the outset. If it does not, the software organization jumps to another solution or goes back to the old one without asking about the causes of the failure and improvement potentials.

Successful effort estimation is not limited to the effort estimation method. It requires systematic mechanisms to monitor its performance, identify causes of deficiencies, and improve it continuously. Dysert and Eliott (2002) propose comprehensive guidelines for reviewing and validating project estimates from the product contractor's and owner's points of view.

In order to provide objective indication of the estimation performance, corresponding control mechanisms should be based on quantitative metrics and structured analysis. As pointed by Tom DeMarco, *"If you don't measure, then you're left with only one reason to believe that you are still in control: hysterical optimism."* For example, in the context of expert-based estimation, Jørgensen and Gruschke (2009) observed that ad hoc feedback sessions may contribute to even more bias in estimates.

In principle, measures of estimation performance should check the achievement of estimation goals. Assigning goals with quantitative metrics makes it possible to verify their achievement. For example, saying that estimation should be accurate and should support improving development productivity is not of much of a help when it comes to objectively assessing performance of a particular estimation method. Making these two goals verifiable would require specifying what "estimation accuracy" and "support for productivity improvement" exactly mean and how to measure it. For example, we can define "estimation accuracy" as the difference between estimated and actual work effort and "support for productivity improvement" as the percentage of productivity improvement gained though factors indicated by the effort estimation method (i.e., effort factors). An example approach for assigning goals with quantitative metrics includes the well-known goal-question-metric (GQM) method (Basili et al. 1994b).

Performance of an effort estimation method should be monitored within one project and across multiple projects. For example, within a project, we may monitor whether reestimated effort converges or diverges. Across multiple projects, we may look at the discrepancy between estimated and actual work effort. For underachieved goals, we should perform root-cause analysis in order to get to the reasons for the failed estimates, to find counter measures to solve the problem, and to improve our estimation capability.

Barry Boehm and Magne Jørgensen (2009), although promoting alternative estimation paradigms—data-driven and expert-based—both underline that

successful effort estimation requires initial investment and continuous improvement. Refer to Chap. 16 for a detailed discussion of continuously improving
software effort estimation capabilities.

17.3.6 Use Causal Rather Than Naive Methods

It is easy and almost inherent in us to look for and find solutions. It takes discipline to first
stop and look for causes.

—Tony Burns

The software estimation literature, especially research publications, promotes an
accuracy oriented view of successful effort estimation. The accuracy of effort
estimates (measured as the difference between estimated and actual project effort)
dominates the criteria for assessing goodness of estimation. In practice, however,
estimation is expected (often tacitly) to provide a comprehensive support for project
decision making. For example, it should support analyzing effort-related project
risks, justifying effort estimates to project owners, and finding sources of potential
effort savings in order to reduce overall work effort.

Naive methods, even though able to provide accurate estimates in terms of effort
required to complete the work, do not provide much support for project decision
making. Therefore, before deciding on a particular effort estimation method, goals
of estimation should be considered and explicitly specified. In Chap. 7, we present a
systematic procedure for selecting a suitable estimation method based upon specific
estimation goals.

17.3.7 Combine Multiple Alternative Estimates

There is no such thing as judgment-free estimation. [. . .] The organizations I've seen that
have had the most success at meeting cost and schedule commitments use a mix of
parametric models and expert judgment.

—Barry Boehm

Each and every estimation method has its specific strengths and limitations, which
depend on the particular situation in which the method is used. And each and every
human estimator differs with respect to expertise and experience. In consequence,
they will provide different estimates even though applied in the same situation.
Moreover, depending on the estimation context, their estimation quality will vary.

In order to increase the reliability of estimates, we should consider using
multiple alternative estimation methods. Having multiple estimates gives us an
opportunity to better assess estimation uncertainty and the associated project risks.
There are several situations where employing multiple alternative estimation
methods is particularly recommended:

- It is uncertain which forecasting method is most suitable: In this situation, a search for the most suitable estimation method indicates that more than one reasonable method is available. For example, after using a systematic method selection approach as proposed in Chap. 7, multiple methods are identified as equally suitable.
- It is uncertain in which context the estimation method is to be employed: For example, we may not be sure, or simply do not know, certain information necessary for selecting the most suitable estimation method. In such a case, known context characteristics will most likely point to multiple estimation methods that are equally suitable for such a context.
- It is critical to avoid large estimation error: In this situation, potential cost of failed estimates is much higher than the overhead required for multiple alternative estimation methods. In such a case, it is better to spend more on estimation with multiple methods to mitigate the risk of failed estimates, and the associated loss.

There are also several recommendations with respect to alternative methods to select and combine:

- Use at least two alternative estimation methods.
- Use estimation methods that differ substantially with respect to the estimation approach (e.g., analogy-based vs. model based) and that use different information sources (e.g., measurements data and human judgment).
- Investigate sources of potential discrepancies between multiple estimates before combining them (improve estimates if possible, and combine them first when they start to converge).
- Use a structured and systematic approach to combine multiple estimates.

In Sect. 5.5, we discuss in more detail the strategy of using multiple alternative estimation methods and in Sect. 5.6, approaches for combining multiple estimates provided by these methods.

17.3.8 Estimate Early and Keep Estimates Up-to-Date

A good plan today is better than a perfect plan tomorrow.

—George S. Patton

Effort prediction is inherently burdened with error because prediction refers to events that have not yet happened.

At the very beginning of a project, estimators do not have all of the information they need to produce reliable estimates. Nevertheless, they need to come up with at least initial estimates to allow project planning, for example. To deal with incomplete and uncertain information, estimators must make assumptions about the project work to be done and the project environment. By making such assumptions, estimators leave placeholders for information that can be corrected later in order to make the estimate more exact. The common mistake is that these placeholders are never filled with correct information and estimates are not revised.

To be effective, estimation should include reestimation. Estimators should explicitly document knowns and unknowns (assumptions) regarding project work and the environment. Moreover, they should communicate to relevant stakeholders the uncertain nature of estimates and agree with stakeholders on regular revisions of initial estimates during the project lifetime, especially after each significant change to project scope and environment. Example changes include modifications to requirements specification, change in the capabilities of the development team (e.g., due to staff turnover), or introduction of new development technology during the project lifetime.

Several sources give detailed guidelines on when to reestimate and when not. For example, US Government Accountability Office (2009), in their Cost Estimating and Assessment Guide, require reestimation after each change to a software system's requirements specification. Cohn (2005, Chap. 7) discusses reestimation in the context of Agile project estimation and planning. The author considers several scenarios for do and don't reestimate depending on the discrepancy between assumed and actual development velocity (in terms of the story points completed per iteration). This discrepancy may be caused by incorrect assumptions regarding the complexity of user stories (measured in terms of story points) or development velocity. For example, if one wrongly estimates the complexity of story points, reestimation should include revising estimated complexity of the remaining stories (i.e., backlog) and revising the iterations' plan using originally assumed velocity. If, however, one wrongly assumed velocity, reestimation should include revising the iterations' plan using the originally estimated complexity of user stories and revised velocity. Cohn warns against uncritically revising both complexity of user stories and velocity. This may lead to mixing original and revised estimates and result in incorrect iterations' plan.

17.3.9 Expect Change and Consider It While Estimating

In short, the software product is embedded in a cultural matrix of applications, users, laws, and machine vehicles. These all change continually, and their changes force change upon the software product.
—Frederick P. Brooks

Heraclitus of Ephesus said, "*Nothing is permanent except change*," and software projects are the best example of this phenomenon. Software project decision makers should be prepared for the unexpected to almost certainly happen. People get sick or leave the organization, development teams run into technical problems, customers change their requirements, or subcontractors do not meet their obligations. Morgenshtern et al. (2007) observed in their study among over 40 IT projects in a large government organization that a high level of project uncertainty is a more important factor influencing effort estimation error than the use of estimation processes or skills of the estimator.

Therefore, effort estimators should expect and consider change. They should attempt to give well-informed assessment of the effort required to complete work giving consideration to the estimation uncertainty associated with possible changes to the project scope and environment. The job of effort estimation is to identify project variations that have already occurred in the past, showed relevant impact on project effort, are likely to occur in the future, and can be systematically considered during estimations, for instance, in a form of an effort factor. For example, past project experiences indicated that changes to software requirements increase project effort and that this effect can be considered in the form of an effort factor "requirements volatility" measured in terms of the percentage of requirements changed after the requirements specification phase. However, effort estimation should not involve handling events that do not have direct impact on effort. These events are typically considered during project planning and risk management. For example, delay on the subcontractor side would lead to project delay; yet, since it implies nonproductive waiting time, it does not have impact on project effort. It may have indirect influence on effort if other tasks are undertaken while waiting on a subcontractor; in this case, switching between work tasks will have a negative impact on productivity and effort (Rubinstein et al. 2001; Meyer 2001; Averill-Snell 2007; Lohr 2007).

17.3.10 Involve Risk Analysis

The most important figures that one needs for management are unknown or unknowable (Lloyd S. Nelson), but successful management must nevertheless take account of them.
—W. Edwards Deming

Effort estimation and risk management should be closely related (see Fig. 2.4 in Sect. 2.4). On the one hand, project risks identified during risk analysis can be inputs to estimation as the most relevant effort factors. A simple process for considering expected risks during effort estimation might be as follows:

- Estimate the "nominal" effort (e.g., the most likely effort assuming normal productivity and no substantial problems).
- Identify risks and their expected impact on development effort.
- Add the expected impact of each of the identified risks on the use of effort.

On the other hand, effort estimation may provide information to project risk analysis regarding the likely impact of considered effort factors on project effort, which can further be used to undertake appropriate risk response activities. Yet, estimation should not substitute for risk planning and management. For example, it should not account for project risks by arbitrarily increasing effort estimates. This may easily lead to double counting of project risks if project managers consider the same risk again to increase a project's contingency reserves. Jørgensen and Grimstad (2010) list several potential threats of performing risk analysis in the context of expert-based estimation. One of the threats is that human experts tend to overemphasize the relevance of the risks they have most recently been exposed to. In consequence, they are inclined to consider irrelevant risks or overemphasize the impact of risks only because they have recently been experienced.

17.3.11 Support Estimation with Proper Tools

The expectations of life depend upon diligence; the mechanic that would perfect his work must first sharpen his tools.

—Confucius

Using proper tools may greatly improve the effectiveness and efficiency of estimation. A common argument against systematic software effort estimation is its large cost. In consequence, software organizations either do not use systematic estimation or do not provide sufficient resources for proper estimation. With proper tools, many sophisticated and laborious estimation activities can be automated, thus significantly reducing the estimation overhead. Moreover, automating the estimation method contributes to increased repeatability and reliability of estimates, especially when estimation involves computationally complex algorithms. In particular, tools can support the following elements of software effort estimation:

- Collecting, storing, and maintaining information used for estimation, specifically:
    - Measurement data from already completed projects used in data-driven and hybrid estimation methods and
    - Expert judgments used in expert-based and hybrid estimation methods (particularly when multiple human experts are involved).
- Documenting characteristics of the estimation environment and assumptions made during estimation.
- Deriving effort models and effort estimates, particularity when they involve sophisticated theories and techniques.
- Presenting, interpreting, and communicating estimation outcomes to relevant stakeholders.
- Storing estimation outcomes for future reuse, specifically
    - Effort models for reestimating effort during the project runtime and for estimating similar future projects and
    - Effort estimates for analyzing goodness of estimates (i.e., estimated vs. actual project performance) for one or multiple completed projects.

17.4   Use Appropriate Estimation Outcomes

It is of paramount importance to provide reliable evidence in order to be able to make sound, fact-based decisions.

—Ove Armbrust and Dieter Rombach

In practice, effort estimation is expected to support a number of different organizational objectives. The most common goals of effort estimation include planning project resources, negotiating project scope and cost, managing project risks, improving processes, and benchmarking development productivity. Achieving these goals requires not only selecting and applying appropriate estimation methods but also proper interpretation of estimation outcomes. This section provides several guidelines on how best to use outcomes of estimation rather than misuse them (either consciously or not).

17.4.1 Interpret Outcomes of Estimation

The best use of a cost model is to treat its results as input to the estimating process, not as its final output.

—Tom DeMarco

An estimation method is not an oracle, and estimates should always be interpreted by a human expert. Outcomes of estimation should at least be interpreted against expert experience and common sense. In the best case, outcomes of multiple alternative estimation approaches should be considered (we discuss this aspect in Sects. 17.3.7 and 17.1.5). Moreover, in order to properly interpret estimation outputs, the context of estimation needs to be taken into account (as we point in the next practice; Sect. 17.4.2).

Finally, as effort estimation is only one element of software project management, its outcomes should be interpreted with consideration of other inputs and specific purposes. For example, project time management requires (besides work effort) such information as sequencing of work activities and availability of necessary resources. It is not an infrequent mistake to assume that developers can spend 100 % of their work time on productive work tasks—if they did, they would not be human.

17.4.2 Consider the Estimation Context

The context for any value will always determine how that value should be analyzed and how it should be interpreted.

—Donald J. Wheeler

Without context, outcomes of effort estimation are hard to interpret properly, even though they are considered to be the true ones. Let us consider a simple example. Two estimators used the same estimation method to predict effort required for completing the same work, and they provided significantly different estimates. Without any additional context information, we may, for instance, interpret these outcomes as highly unreliable and reject the estimation method. Now, our interpretation might have been quite different if we knew that estimation took place in the early phase of the project and that one estimator assumed best-case project characteristics, whereas the other estimator assumed the worst-case characteristics. In this case, the method may actually be reliable, and apparently contradicting estimates should be considered as lower- and upper-bound estimates for the best- and worst-case project characteristics. A number of other examples can be given that show how important it is to consider context of estimation while interpreting estimation outcomes.

17.4.3 Avoid Using Estimates for Finger-Pointing

When you point one accusing finger at someone; three of your own fingers point back at you.

—Louis Nizer

As for any other initiative that involves measurement, effort estimation will fail as soon as it is used for finger-pointing purposes. Finger-pointing refers to using estimation—consciously or not—to evaluate performance of particular projects, teams, or team members. The only thing we can achieve by doing this is that affected individuals reject involvement in the estimation or (if forced to) instead of true inputs, will make up data which make them look good and avoid finger-pointing.

Effort estimation should thus be used in a constructive manner, and its outcomes should never be considered at the level of individual persons or projects. Personnel involved in estimation should keep in mind that the primary objective of estimation is organizational learning and improvement. For this purpose, estimation outcomes should be analyzed in an aggregated form, and improvement potential should refer to organizational processes and environment, instead of to individual persons.

17.4.4 Avoid Estimates Becoming Commitments

The 'future' is not a 'present' to come.

—Bernard Roy

The objective of effort estimation is not to predict the future but to give well-informed assessment of the effort required to complete work based on the available information of known and expected project characteristics and of past experiences gained in already completed projects. By definition, uncertainty is an inherent aspect of effort estimation. At the time of estimation, information about the work to be estimated and its environment is incomplete and ambiguous. Moreover, both scope and context of the work may change as the work progresses. Finally, past experiences may not be transferable to new work tasks because they are more or less dissimilar. In this situation, effort estimates should never be committed to as the definitive effort that will be actually required to complete the work. Estimators should always make clear to relevant stakeholders the uncertain and volatile nature of estimates and the conditions upon which estimates can change and thus require appropriate revisions.

17.4.5 Consider the Uncertainty of Estimates

It is better to be roughly right than precisely wrong.

—John Maynard Keynes

One of the basic problems of software development is that *"The most important business decisions about a software product are made at the time of minimum knowledge and maximum uncertainty"* (Michel A. Ross). Effort estimation is one of the key means to support software project decision making at the time when little is known about the project; that is, before it actually starts. In order to effectively support decision makers, useful effort estimates must be associated with information about their uncertainty—at best in a quantitative manner.

In practice, the phrase "accurate estimate" is an oxymoron, and point effort estimates are virtually never correct. Estimates without accompanying information of uncertainty are simply incomplete and should be avoided as potentially dangerous to project success. Useful estimates inform about their uncertainty. A simple way of quantifying estimation uncertainty is to provide estimated effort in the form of a range with associated probabilities. Chapter 4 provides comprehensive discussion of estimation uncertainty. Among others, it presents different kinds of estimation uncertainty and example ways of representing, quantifying, and reducing estimation uncertainty.

17.4.6 Avoid Padding Estimates

Cost and schedule estimations are poorly developed and reflect an unstated assumption that all will go well.

—Frederick P. Brooks

Padding estimates refers to adding extra effort on top of realistic and honest estimates just to be on the safe side when it comes to project risks and exceeding planned effort and schedule (Verzuh 2011).

In practice, inflated estimates are counterproductive and risky. They undermine sound project management in several ways:

- *Undermine trust.* Padded estimates may, and typically are, not accepted by a project owner and/or customer because (a) they are too high and (b) they are not supported by a reasonable rationale, which, in the case of padding, is simply nonexistent.
- *Undermines other projects.* Extra resources planned with padding are often taken away from projects that really need them—according to realistic and honest estimates. When such a "padded" project is of high priority and is accepted, it may jeopardize the success of other, less important, projects.
- *Undermines the opportunity to learn.* Padded estimates may, and often do, lead to project effort shortages. Let us consider a simple example. The project manager keeps realistically estimated project effort of 3 person-months for the development team but communicates to the project owner a padded estimate

of 5 person-months. If the project owner accepts the inflated estimate, the project manager obtains budget for 5 person-months, while the development team will strive to complete the work within 4 person-months. When the team eventually finish the work within 4 person-months (or a few person-days more), they will be glad to have got the project done within plan (or with a little overrun), and the project owner will be happy with the saved budget of about 1 person-month. In the end, the two-faced project manager will look like a highly skilled estimator. Yet, eventually, the project owner will notice that the development team never consumes the complete budget allocated to the work and will start to cut the budget communicated by the project manager. At the same time, the development team notices that they consume a little more effort than they have officially been assigned and start making this little budget overrun their regular practice. Under the pressure of the developer requiring more effort and project owners cutting the effort, the project manager starts padding estimates even more than before. At some time, it becomes clear that the project manager is not such a skilled estimator after all. The padding game between estimators, developers, and project owners does not allow appropriate learning and improvement for any of these parties and the whole organization.

Padding at the level of effort estimation actually corresponds to "planning contingency reserves" at the level of project budgeting. Both mechanisms attempt to achieve the same thing: allow for risk. Yet, padding is an ad hoc and uncontrolled way of addressing unnamed risks. Effort estimation can address project risks as long as they are "expected" and can be explicitly and systematically considered, for instance, by naming specific effort factors that represent certain risks. An example way of addressing explicit project risks is to explicitly acknowledge optimistic, pessimistic, and realistic project scenarios through considering best-case, worst-case, and most likely values of the relevant factors influencing project effort.

Unnamed risks, however, should be addressed by risk analysis, where probability and impact of unexpected events are systematically analyzed and addressed by contingency reserves; that is, an extra amount of effort, time, or money justified to and approved by project owners.

17.4.7 Distinguish Effort from Time and Duration

The worst case of poor estimating is when the manager doing the final estimate does not allow any time for false starts or even bathroom breaks. This is almost as bad as missing Christmas because you did not get the memo indicating the date!
—James E. Tomayko and Orit Hazzan

The job of effort estimation is to plan the effort required to complete work and should not be confused with estimating time and project duration. These are often confused due to interchangeable use of work effort, time, and duration and due to the similarity of associated measurement units. In essence, the difference between them is as follows:

- *Effort* refers to manpower required to complete work and is measured in terms of person-hours, person-months, person-years, etc.
- *Productive Time* refers to working time required for completing the work under the assumption of nonstop, 100 % productive work of a certain number of persons. Time is a direct derivative of effort and staffing. For example, time required by one person to complete 1 person-day work task would be 1 day.
  - Effort = 1 person-day = 8 person-hours;
  - Productive Time = 8 person-hour work/8 h of normative work per day = 1 day.
- *Total Time* refers to the sum of productive and nonproductive time (so-called slack) spent while completing the work. For example, people usually do not work 8 h per day even though it is their "working" time. Continuing our example, if we assume that 1 person-day equals 8 person-hours but that a person works productively for only 7 h per day, then the person would require more than 1 working day to complete a 1 person-day work task:
  - Total Time = 8 person-hour work/7 h of productive work per day = 1.1 days.
- *Duration* refers to calendar time spent on completing work. Duration includes productive time, slack, and work breaks related to scheduling of work tasks (e.g., breaks due to task dependencies or unavailable resources). Continuing the example of 1 person-day work task, if a person who is supposed to perform the task is available for the task for only 50 % per day and must take in between 1 day off, then the work will be completed in 3.3 days
  - Duration = (8 person-hour work/0.5 × 7 h of productive work) + 1 day off = 3.3 days.

17.5   Ensure a Proper Estimation Environment

Is fact the truth? Yes, but without the context it is not the whole truth, and it can even have connotation that is opposite to its actual meaning.

—Ryszard Kapuściński

Software effort estimation is influenced by a number of external factors that may facilitate or hinder effective estimation. Therefore, prior to estimation, all relevant constraints and conditions should be clearly identified and taken into account to ensure reliable estimation. In this section, we list several practices that should be considered with respect to external influences on estimation.

17.5.1 Avoid Overoptimism

A sure path to failure in software development is to plan on a best case scenario which is really an exercise in self-deception.

—Lawrence H. Putnam

When you care a lot about the result [of estimation], the quality of your estimate approaches zero.

—Tom DeMarco

Overoptimism is one of the most frequent reasons for unrealistic estimates. Overoptimism of estimators is their belief that the work being estimated will run under optimal (best-case) conditions. Estimation based on human judgment is particularly endangered by overoptimism. Human experts not only assume best-case scenarios but also—as it is generally observed in psychology—tend to be overconfident about their personal capabilities. Tversky and Kahneman (1974), in their psychological research, observed that people tend to be overoptimistic when asked to make predictions regarding complex matters. In the case of software estimation, developers tend to underestimate effort required to complete complex tasks.

Overoptimism can be avoided by a careful, reflective approach to estimation—as opposed to a "quick and dirty" or intuitive one. A careful and reflective approach eliminates bias by reducing the effect of individual judgments. Example approaches to avoid over optimism include

- Use of structured estimation procedures based on well-founded theories instead of ad hoc off-the-cuff estimation.
- Base estimates on quantitative, objective information from similar tasks already completed in the past.
- Involve independent experts to do the estimation.
- Employ bottom-up estimation, in which complex work tasks are broken down into smaller and better manageable work activities.
- Use multipoint estimates including worst-case, best-case, and most likely scenarios.

17.5.2 Avoid Expectation-Driven Estimates

Software types tend to be optimists, and leaders tend to be in a hurry—a deadly combination that leads to planned schedules and budgets that never had any chance to be realized.

—Gary A. Gack

The issue of expectation-driven estimates is related to overoptimism and a lack of realism in estimation; yet, it refers not to the estimators themselves but to the people that have influence on the estimators. These could be project owners, company marketing, or customers that have particular interests in decreasing project effort. In practice, pressure and political games often make estimators willing to please project stakeholders through meeting their unrealistic expectations. This inevitably leads to unrealistic estimates. Politics is one of the major biases of expert-based estimation, even in the group estimation process, when different attitudes to estimation games are represented (stronger players typically win and convince others to their political option). Another example of a frequent situation that leads to unrealistic estimates is project bidding. Jørgensen and Grimstadt (2005) give examples of contractors who typically select software providers from among those who offer the lowest bid—so actually, those that tend toward the highest level of overoptimism and lower level of realism. In this situation, bidders are susceptible to so-called "winner's curse" and tend to reduce their estimates below a reasonable level. Jørgensen (2009) lists several recommendations on how to avoid selecting providers with bids based on overoptimistic cost estimates.

In order to avoid the effect of expectation-driven estimates, estimators should be independent of the estimated project, be aware of potential influences aiming toward reducing realistic estimates, and resist these influences. For example, estimators should base effort prediction on objective project information and avoid an overoptimistic view from management or unrealistic demands from the customer. The best solution would be to create an estimation environment free from interpersonal games and politics. Yet, in reality, this is not always possible. Thomsett International concludes their experiences on expectation-driven estimates in the following way[3]: "I.T. people are pretty good at estimating. Further, our research has shown that the major precondition for improving estimation accuracy is the existence of an estimation environment free of inter-personal politics and political games".

17.6 Last But Not Least...

17.6.1 Keep It Small and Simple

Simple models typically perform just as well as more advanced models and that more sophisticated models are vulnerable to overfitting to outdated or unrepresentative data sets.
—Magne Jørgensen

Use Simple Methods and Models

Many years of experience gained over multiple studies and context show that simple estimation methods work at least as effectively as complex ones. Yet, the cost of introducing, using, and improving complex methods is incomparably higher than simple methods. As noted by Boehm and Jørgensen (2009), improvement potentials for complex estimation models is likely to be quite low as compared to simple models.

---

[3] Web article "Estimation Games" published by Thomsett International. Last visited in June 2010. http://www.thomsettinternational.com/main/articles/hot/games.htm.

We should consider relatively simple estimation methods and a limited number of the most important effort factors. Moreover, we should avoid building a universal model for a large context encompassing a wide variety of domains, technologies, and development paradigms—instead, small, comprehensible models for limited contexts should be considered. For example, Mendes and Mosley (2008) compared several estimation models using multiorganizational project data. They compared several complex models based on Bayesian belief networks (BBN), with case-based reasoning (CBR), and simple manual stepwise regression (MSWR). The MSWR method presented significantly better predictions than any of the BBN models. Estimates provided by any of the complex BBN models were significantly better than simple medians of effort measured in historical projects.

Use Simple Information

In order to provide reliable forecasts, effort estimation must be based on sufficient and reliable information. As we already pointed out in the recommendation regarding data quantity (Sect. 17.1.7), too much information is as undesired as too little information. Large amounts of information are more likely to contain irrelevant and redundant information that may mislead estimation. Besides that, large information is expensive to acquire, maintain, and analyze. For example, developers do not typically enjoy providing data and are likely to provide unreliable data if overwhelmed by data collection requests.

When collecting inputs to estimation, we should not get lost in the details. Input data for estimation should capture only what we need and can use. Moreover, the data collection should be as unobtrusive as possible in order to facilitate getting credible data. Last but not least, when starting systematic estimation, we should consider collecting data incrementally. We should start with few effort factors (e.g., we consider most relevant) and incrementally build up the estimation repository. Each increment (i.e., revision of data repository) is driven by the goodness of estimates delivered based upon the data. In Sect. 16.1.1, we briefly discuss the issue of maintaining and improving project data for the purpose of effort estimation.

17.6.2 Think Out of the Box

> *Thanks to my isolation, I would do things differently than people subjected to the standard pressures of conformity. I was a free man.*
> —Edsger W. Dijkstra

Every software development undertaking is to some extent unique and, as such, requires a unique approach. This also counts for estimation. Using approaches that worked for others does not usually mean they will work for us. This is why we should be open to tailoring existing estimation approaches to our specific needs and capabilities as we learn about their strengths and weaknesses. We should be open to new ideas and to change our estimation habits as the ever-changing environment of software engineering requires it.

Further Reading

- K. El Emam and A. Koru (2008), "A Replicated Survey of IT Software Project Failures," *IEEE Software*, vol. 25, no. 5, pp. 84–90.

  This article provides an overview of the studies presenting the rates and common causes of software project failures.

- C. T. Jones (2006), "Social and Technical Reasons for Software Project Failures," *Cross-Talk: The Journal of Defense Software Engineering*, vol. 19, no. 6, pp. 4–9.

  This article discusses the most common causes of failures in software development projects. Two of them are failed estimates and project changes as sources of failed projects. Author goes deeper and analyzes the detailed root causes of the reasons of failed projects.

- J. S. Armstrong (2001), *Principles of forecasting: A handbook for researchers and practitioners*. Kluwer Academic Publishers, Dordrecht, The Netherlands.

  In Chap. 20 of his book, author specifies 139 principles of forecasting. He groups them into 16 categories including formulating forecasting problems, collecting necessary information, implementing forecasting methods, evaluating these methods, using these methods for prediction, and utilizing the predictions these methods deliver. For each practice, the author provides its description and specifies its purpose, conditions, as well as the strength and source of evidence behind the practice.

- M. Jørgensen and K. Moløkken-Østvold (2003), "A Preliminary Checklist for Software Cost Management," in *Proceedings of the 3rd International Conference on Quality Software*, p. 134.

  This paper presents a checklist of best-practice software effort estimation activities. The checklist is a synthesis of experiences gained by multiple software estimation experts, including the authors of the paper. The checklist is structured according to 12 basic effort estimation activities, grouped into 4 major phases of project estimation: preparing for estimation, estimating, applying estimates, and learning from estimation feedback.

- Wikipedia: *List of cognitive biases*

  This Wikipedia page briefly lists cognitive biases considered in psychology. It is worth reading and considering which of them can affect the estimation approach we use and how to avoid them.

Appendix A: Measuring Software Size

Software size matters and you should measure it.

—Mary Gerush and Dave West

Software size is the major determinant of software project effort. Effectively measuring software size is thus a key element of successful effort estimation. Failed software sizing is often the main contributor to failed effort estimates and, in consequence, failed projects.

Measuring software size is a challenging task. A number of methods for measuring software size have been proposed over the years. Yet, none of them seems to be the "silver bullet" that solves all problems and serves all purposes. Depending on the particular situation different size metrics should typically be used.

In this appendix we provide a brief overview of the common software sizing approaches: functional and structural. These approaches represent two, often-confused, perspectives on software size: customer perspective and developer perspective. The first perspective represents value of software, whereas the second perspective represents the cost (work) of creating this value. We summarize the most relevant strengths and weaknesses of the two most popular sizing methods that represent these perspectives: function point analysis (FPA) and lines of code (LOC). In technical terms, FPA represents "what" whereas LOC represent "how" in software development. Finally, we provide guidelines for selecting appropriate sizing methods for the purpose of effort estimation.

A.1 Introduction

There are two aspects to sizing a system: what is the count, and what is the meaning or definition of the unit being counted?

—Phillip G. Armour

A. Trendowicz and R. Jeffery, *Software Project Effort Estimation*,
DOI 10.1007/978-3-319-03629-8, © Springer International Publishing Switzerland 2014

A.1.1   What Is Software Size?

One of the key questions project managers need to answer is "how big is my development project going to be?" The key to answering this question is software size. The size of software is the major determinant of project volume, and thus it is commonly used as a proxy for project's size. It is a basis for essential project management activities, such as planning, tracking, and controlling project scope and productivity.

But what constitutes software size? In order to answer this question we need to answer two simple questions: what is software and what is size of software?

The first question addresses multiple facets of software that need to be considered. Is software the executable code delivered to the customer? Does it include user documentation? Or does software encompass all products created during the whole software development project?

The second question addresses multiple abstractions of software. Is size referring to abstract properties of software such as functionality or to physical properties of software project outcomes such as code and documentation? This multiple nature of software makes measuring its size an extremely challenging task. A number of software sizing metrics have been proposed to address this challenge. Yet, practitioners criticize traditional sizing techniques as being too complex and expensive. In consequence, very few organizations measure size of software or of a project in a consistent and systematic way. The software sizing solution depends on the specific situation in which we need to measure size, and in particular our needs and capabilities.

Tip

▶ Choose the right sizing method based on your objectives and capabilities. As with any other technology, software sizing requires associated introduction, application, and continuous optimization processes.

A.1.2   Types of Size Metrics

Briand and Wieczorek (2002) group software sizing methods into two types: problem-oriented and solution-oriented. *Problem-oriented metrics* represent the size of the problem that the future software product will solve, i.e., the target functionality of the system. Since these metrics typically focus on measuring elements of software functionality they are also commonly referred to as functional size metrics. *Solution-oriented metrics* represent the size of the software development outcomes such as specifications, the design, or implementation of software system. Since they typically focus on measuring structural properties of software products they are also commonly referred to as structural size metrics. In principle, we may say that while problem-oriented measurement methods represent a customer perspective, the solution-oriented methods represent a developer perspective.

Table A.1 Methods for estimating the functional size of software

Sizing method	Description
Function points	Introduced by Albrecht (1979) the function point method measures the relative size of software functions based on the amount of different data types processed (enter, leave, read and written to storage) by a software function. Albrecht's approach evolved into several variants of functional size measurement methods. Several of them have been published as ISO standards:
	• IFPUG: ISO-20926 (ISO 2009)
	• NESMA: ISO-24570 (ISO 2005)
	• FiSMA: ISO-29881 (ISO 2008)
	• COSMIC: ISO-19761 (ISO 2003)
	• Mk II: ISO-20968 (ISO 2002)
Feature points	Introduced by Jones (1996) "The SPR Feature Point Method" extended Albrecht's function point method by additionally counting algorithms and multiplying this count by relative complexity of an algorithm. This method suffers from imprecise description and lack of reference applications. It has been largely abandoned in practice
Use-case points	Introduced by Karner (1993) Use-Case Points (UCP) are inspired and based on function point analysis and founded on its philosophy. Inputs for UCP are use-case specifications. UCP counts instances of two elements: actors and use cases. Similar to FPA each instance is evaluated with respect to its complexity and assigned an appropriate weight. The unadjusted CUP count is equal to the weighted sum of individual counts. Similar to FPA unadjusted UCP can be modified using an adjustment factor, which is determined on the basis of several technical complexity and environmental factors
Story points	Introduced by Cohn (2004, 2005) for the purpose of estimating the size of agile software projects. Story Point is an abstract unit of software size that represents an intuitive mixture of development effort and complexity. Story points are assigned according to a Fibonacci number sequence, where each number is the sum of the previous two. As noted earlier, in planning poker story points may start from 1/2 and continue as 1, 2, 3, 5, 8, 13, and so on
Object points	A number of different object point metrics have been proposed for measuring software size. Two example measurement methods are:
	• *Predictive Object Points* (*POP*): Introduced by Minkiewicz (1997) predictive object points are based on counts of classes and weighted methods per class, with adjustments for the average depth of the inheritance tree and the average number of children per class. Methods are weighted by considering their type (constructor, destructor, modifier, selector, iterator) and complexity (low, average, high), giving a number of POPs in a way analogous to traditional FPs
	• *Object Points* (*OP*): Introduced by Banker et al. (1992) object points measure software size by counting visual widgets of the fourth generation languages in integrated CASE environments. Widgets are (1) logical system components, (2) constructs of the third generation language that is used to supplement fourth generation language code, (3) user interface screens, and (4) user report. Widgets counts are adjusted by complexity and reuse multipliers, and summed to total object points count. Other than POP object points do not consider such object-oriented concepts as inheritance or encapsulation. Instead OP considers elements of user interface

(continued)

Table A.1 (continued)

Sizing method	Description
Web objects	Introduced by Reifer (2000) the Web Objects method extends the well-known Function Point Analysis in that, in addition to the five elements already considered in FPA, it counts four elements specific to Web application: multimedia files, web building blocks, scripts, and links. Web objects are measured on user requirements and Web page designs. The counting procedure is analogical to FPA and comprises counting instances of the nine elements and weighting them according to their complexity. Total size is computed as weighted sum of all individual counts

Problem-Oriented Size Metrics

Problem-oriented software sizing methods identify the elements of the problem, and count their instances. These instances can additionally be weighted with respect to their complexity. Total software size is then a result of the weighted sum over individual instance counts.

Several methods provide an opportunity to adjust software size with respect to the particular context in which the software is developed. For this purpose they consider a set of project context factors, commonly referred to as technical or environmental factors. The method rates each factor based on the associated weights and constants defined within the method. The total adjustment coefficient is then computed as a weighted sum of ratings for all factors. Software size is then adjusted by multiplying it by the adjustment coefficient. Table A.1 provides a brief overview of common problem-oriented software size measurement methods.

Solution-Oriented Size Metrics

Solution-oriented software sizing methods identify key components of the software solutions. Typical components of the software solution comprise project

Table A.2 Methods for estimating structural size of software

Sizing method	Description
Lines of code	Lines of code (LOC) method measures software size by counting the number of lines in the text of the program's source code. There are many variations of the LOC metric. They differ principally on what is counted as a line of code. Park (1992) provides an example checklist for measuring different variants of the LOC metric[a]. Example definitions of the LOC metric are:
	• *Physical LOC (pLOC)*: This method measures all lines of code that end with an "end of line" character; including comments and blanks
	• *Effective LOC (eLOC)*: This method measures all lines of code that end with an "end of line" symbol except for comments, blanks, or stand-alone braces or parenthesis

(continued)

Table A.2 (continued)

Sizing method	Description
	• *Logical LOC* (*lLOC*): This method measures lines of code which form code statements. These statements end with a termination symbol specific to a particular programming language, e.g., a semi-colon
	• *Enhancement LOC* (*EnhLOC*): This method measures the size of modified software. It separately counts lines of code that have been added, deleted, or modified
Halstead's science	Introduced by Halstead (1977) science measure comprises several metrics of software code size and complexity
	The size metrics include:
	• *Halstead's Length*: The program length (N) is the sum of the total number of operators ($N1$) and total number of operands ($N2$) in the software program's code
	• *Halstead's Volume*: The program volume (V) represents the information content of the program, measured in mathematical bits. It is calculated as the Halstead's Length (N) times the 2-base logarithm of the vocabulary size (n); where vocabulary (n) is the sum of all unique—distinct—operators ($n1$) and the number of unique—distinct—operands ($n2$). Halstead's volume describes the size of the implementation of an algorithm
	The Halstead's science metrics have rather rarely been used in practice
Primitive count metrics	These methods comprise simple counting of structural elements of a software artifact. Example incarnations of this approach include measuring the number of files within software source code, number of requirements in the requirements specification, or the number of activities in the UML software specifications

[a]Note that definitions provided here of different variants of the LOC metric are for illustration purposes only. They are not precise and may differ from definitions provided in the related literature

deliverables such as requirements specification documents, design documents, source code, test cases, and user documentation. Table A.2 provides a brief overview of common solution-oriented software size measurement methods.

A.2   Sizing Methods in Software Effort Estimation

> *Where SLOC represents something tangible that may or may not relate directly to value, function points attempt to measure the intangible of end user value.*
> —Arlene F. Minkiewicz

Function point analysis (FPA) and source lines of code (LOC) methods are two common, and competing, software sizing methods in the context of managing software development productivity and effort. The principle difference is the abstraction level at which they operate. While LOC measure structural properties of specific physical artifacts, FPA estimates functionality of software. In this respect, FPA represents the customers' and managers' perspective on software, whereas LOC represents the developers' view.

Both FPA and LOC have their advantages and disadvantages when used for effort estimation. In principle, LOC have an advantage over FP in terms of ease of automation and calculation, availability of measured artifacts, intuitiveness, and understandability. FPA has an advantage over LOC in that it is independent of technologies used—in particular programming language—it is applicable from the very beginning and throughout the whole life cycle, and that it is more normative.

Technological Independence: FPA—Yes, Effort—No

Function point analysis (FPA) has an advantage over lines of code in that it is independent of project environmental factors such as skills of developers and technologies used.

But in the context of effort estimation, this advantage of FPA should be taken with care. This is because effective effort estimation requires consideration of project environmental factors that have relevant impact on development productivity and thus on project effort.

To make productivity comparable between different environments, the effect of environmental factors needs to be excluded when measuring development productivity. In this case FPA would be better choice. As pointed by Bill Gates, "*Measuring software productivity by lines of code is like measuring progress on an airplane by how much it weighs.*"

When estimating effort, the impact of the environment factors should, again be taken into consideration to account for resultant differences in development productivity. For example, the effort required to develop software of a certain functional size will depend on the programming language selected; although functional size will not. Therefore, programming language should be considered when estimating effort.

Popularity of both LOC and FPA in the context of software effort estimation created demand for formulating relationships between these two metrics. A body of literature has been devoted to this subject. Finally, several authors provided rules and coefficients for converting between LOC and FPA for particular FPA methods and programming languages. Since then there has been much controversy in applying simple conversion coefficient to change between LOC and FPA. We dissuade from using them as the ratio between LOC and FPA—if any consistency exists—depends on many factors other than solely programming language.

Backfiring—Converting Between LOC and FP

Backfiring refers to converting between lines of code and function points. A number of organizations have provided conversion ratios for different programming languages. Unfortunately, these ratios are inconsistent even though they refer to the same metrics and the same programming languages.

(continued)

> **Backfiring—Converting Between LOC and FP** (continued)
>
> The problem with backfiring is that the conversion ratio depends on many aspects other than programming language, which is the only one typically considered for published backfiring factors.
>
> It is commonly recommended to avoid using backfiring, especially when conversion ratios originate from external sources (Galorath and Evans 2006). If unavoidable, backfiring should be based on conversion ratios computed in the same context they are used in. This, however, requires large sets of project data including both LOC and FP metrics, which reduces feasibility of such an approach in industrial practice.

We recommend selecting a sizing method—or methods—that best fits organizational needs and capabilities and maintaining it within this organization. Any method adaptations from external contexts are bound to risk unreliable outputs.

A.3 Strengths and Weaknesses of Lines of Code

For all its deficiencies, a LOC is a fairly precise unit of knowledge.

—Phillip G. Armour

[but]

You can't count lines of code at the beginning of a project; you have to estimate it. Most people are not much better at estimating line counts than they are at estimating resultant development costs

—Tom DeMarco

In this section, we summarize briefly common strengths and weaknesses of software sizing methods based on counting lines of code compared to function point analysis. We base our summary on related literature and our own professional experiences.

In principle, LOC have an advantage over FPA in terms of ease of automation and calculation, availability of measured artifacts, intuitiveness, and understandability. Major disadvantages of LOC include its dependency on technologies, applicability late in development life cycle, and lack of standardized measurement procedure.

A.3.1 Strengths of LOC

Major strengths of lines of code are related to relatively low abstraction level of this metric (Table A.3). It operates on tangible, physical development output and measures its tangible properties. The fact that LOC have been present in the

Table A.3 Strengths of lines of code as software sizing method

Strength of LOC metric	Description
Easy to measure	Since lines of code have a physical representation LOC are among the easiest measurements to make
Measurable postmortem	Lines of code are easily measured at any time after software development completion
Require minimal measurement overhead	Counting LOC can easily be automated. A number of LOC measurement tools exist. Yet, a LOC measurement tool that is developed for a specific language cannot be used for other languages due to the syntactical and structural differences among languages
Measurements are objective and repeatable	Since LOC counting can be defined by a set of unambiguous rules (and thus automated) and since it is run on a physical entity (source code), the measurements are objective and repeatable
Measurement data are typically available or can be easily collected postmortem, based on project deliverables (software source code)	Many software organizations that have stable measurement processes in place have historical databases containing LOC data. In consequence, although LOC are relatively difficult to estimate in early phases of software development (e.g., requirements specification), organizations that have large sets of historical LOC measurement data can often successfully estimate LOC early within their specific context
	Moreover, most of the publicly available effort models are directly based on LOC. Although some of such models offer the possibility of using functional software size, it is internally converted to LOC anyway before estimating
Commonly used for effort estimation purpose	Lines of code are used in most of the fixed effort estimation models
Reusable for numerous purposes	Lines of code are also used for a number of other purposes such as, e.g., defect measurement when comparing defect rates
Intuitive and easy to interpret for technical staff	Lines of code are easier to understand and estimate for technical project staff, especially software developers

software industry for much longer than FPA has probably impacted its perceived benefits.

A.3.2 Weaknesses of LOC

Major weaknesses of LOC sizing method are connected with its "technical" character and focus on a selected software development artifact (Table A.4).

Table A.4 Weaknesses of lines of code as a software sizing method

Weakness of LOC	Description
Lack of accountability	LOC might be an inappropriate proxy for software size in the context of software effort modeling because the implementation phase, in which code it is mainly produced, typically accounts for only one third of the overall software engineering effort
Poor reflection of the value delivered to the customer (lack of cohesion with functionality)	Although LOC is highly correlated with development effort, software functionality, which is the major value from the customer's perspective, is less well-correlated with LOC. For example, skilled developers may provide the same functionality with less code, which means that they may be productive in terms of delivered software functionality although they are unproductive in terms of delivered software code. In consequence, development productivity in terms of delivering a value to a customer may not be well-measured using LOC
Vulnerable to developer's experience	The number of LOC required to implement certain software functionality depends significantly on the skills of developers. An experienced developer may implement certain functionality using fewer lines of code than does another developer of relatively less experience, although they use the same language
Vulnerable to programming languages	The number of measured lines of source code depends on the programming language used. In consequence, the amount of effort required to develop the application would be different for different programming languages, though delivered software functionality (value to customers) would remain the same. The problem with measuring LOC becomes even more severe when multiple programming languages are used to implement software
Lack of counting standards (inconsistent definitions)	There is no standard definition of the LOC metric. Although organizations such as SEI and IEEE have published some guidelines for LOC counting, they are rarely followed in practice. In consequence every organization measuring LOC typically follows its own definition
	For example, definitions of logical and physical LOC differ among organizations and make software size measurements incomparable. Furthermore, even within each of these definitions, there are questions as to how to deal with blanks, comments, and non-executable statements, such as data declarations

(continued)

Table A.4 (continued)

Weakness of LOC	Description
Requires distinguishing generated vs. manually implemented code	Measuring lines of code requires distinguishing between generated code and handcrafted code. For example, in the context of effort estimation generated code implies much less effort than manually created code
Late availability	Since source code is available late in the software development life cycle, it needs to be estimated at the time effort predictions are needed (early development phases). In consequence, effort estimates are burdened from the very beginning by uncertainty of its major component, size

A.4 Strengths and Weaknesses of Function Point Analysis

While function points were good for measuring organizational productivity, they weren't really fitting the bill for estimating cost and effort.

—Arlene F. Minkiewicz

In this section, we summarize briefly the common strengths and weaknesses of function point analysis compared to lines of code. We base our summary on related literature and our own professional experiences.

FPA has an advantage over LOC in that it is independent of technologies used—in particular programming language—is applicable from the very beginning and throughout the whole life cycle, and is more normative. Major disadvantages of FPA comprise significant measurement subjectivity, relatively high complexity of calculation and thus limited feasibility of automation, and low intuitiveness to software developers.

A.4.1 Strengths of FPA

Major strengths of FPA are connected with its orientation on the value delivered to a customer (Table A.5). The metric focuses on functionality as the aspect of software that counts to a customer.

Table A.5 Strengths of function point analysis as a software sizing method

Strengths of FPA	Description
Reflects software value to the customer	FPA better reflects software value from the customer viewpoint. In that sense, FPA is more appropriate for specifying and negotiating project scope in terms of delivered software functionality. For example, in the context of fixed price contracts FPA can be used (1) for specifying what exactly should be delivered and (2) for estimating and tracking effort across the entire life cycle. In contrast, LOC measurement is limited to merely one development phase

(continued)

Table A.5 (continued)

Strengths of FPA	Description
Independent of language and technology	Since FPA measures software from a functional perspective, they are independent of technology. Regardless of language, development method, or developer skills, the number of FP for a system will remain constant
	Since the only variable that remains is the amount of effort needed to deliver a given functionality, FPA can be used to determine whether a certain technology (e.g., tool or language) is more productive compared with others within or across software organizations. Yet, estimating effort requires considering factors that influence the amount of effort required to deliver the same unit of function points. Finally, since results of FPA do not depend on technology, projects that use FPA are principally better candidates for benchmarking—within and across software organizations
Applicable throughout development life cycle	Since FPA measures abstract functionality (specified or already implemented), it can be applied at each point of the software development life cycle. The FP measurements reflect the current status of requirements. If new features are added to the software, the total FP count will go up accordingly. If some features are removed or postponed to the next release, the FPA will also reflect this state of software functionality. FPA is thus useful to monitor changes in project scope (in terms of functionality of software to be delivered) throughout the project lifetime. The amount of variance in an FP count reflects requirements volatility, which in turn, is an indicator of potential problems regarding requirements management
Intuitive and easy to interpret for nontechnical staff	Since FPA reflects software value in terms of delivered functionality (rather that its technical details) it is a much better mean for communicating with nontechnical staff. This includes especially senior management, on both the developer and customer side
Supports removing uncertainty	Counting function points forces a review of system specifications in a search for elements that are countable by the function point method. Anyone who wants to measure function points must parse through the system specification and look for evidence of discrete entities considered by the function points method—in the case of the IFPUG approach these are inputs, outputs, inquiries, and files. While doing this a counter needs to face and remove uncertainty existing in the specification. This does not take place when measuring structural software size

A.4.2 Weaknesses of FPA

The main source of FPA weaknesses is its abstract character (Table A.6). This causes troubles with implementing and understanding the method, especially by software developers.

Table A.6 Weaknesses of function point analysis as a software sizing method

Weaknesses of FPA	Description
Complex counting rules	The FPA counting methodology consists of many steps accompanied by a number of guidelines and examples. Furthermore, some elements of particular FPA approaches do not seem to be mathematically sound, which is a source of common criticism
Large measurement overhead; lack of measurement automation	Counting FP is still a manual, human-intensive process that requires much overhead and involvement of experienced (certified) counters. These elements contribute to the overall high cost of applying FPA. Until now, no effective automation for FPA is available
Equally difficult to measure at any project time	The difficulty of measuring function points does not change much during project lifetime. The only advantage of measuring function points in late phases of development is that more is known about the software—in consequence, inputs for counting are easily available and counts are more accurate. Measuring FP upon project completion might be difficult, especially long after development is finished, since it requires investigating software functionality that might have already been forgotten (specification documents must be analyzed)
Significant level of detail	A high level of detail is required for FPA. Information on inputs, outputs, external and internal data, and even individual data records and fields are needed for counting FP accurately. In consequence, FP counts may differ across development phases not only because of the change in the requirements but also because of the change in the level of detail in the specification of requirements. For example, initial requirements available at the beginning of the project are typically lacking the details required for accurate FPA
Significant subjectivity and low repeatability	Although well-documented rules exist for counting function points, there is still room allowed for subjective interpretation of these rules. Studies performed in the industry show that results of FPA, even though performed by experienced counters, may deviate from 10 % up to 30 %
Vulnerable to capabilities of FP counters	In order to provide reliable results FPA requires large experience of the counters. On the one hand FPA requires good knowledge of the numerous and complex counting rules. On the other hand it requires practical experience in applying them in an industrial reality. This includes the ability to find relevant information in the requirements documentation and proper interpretation of this information according to FPA counting rules
Vulnerable to the quality of requirements specification and documentation	The quality (consistency, completeness, etc.) of the requirements specification and documentation determines the ability of producing precise and correct

(continued)

Table A.6 (continued)

Weaknesses of FPA	Description
	FPA counts. In that sense, FPA is indirectly vulnerable to capabilities of a development team, in particular personnel responsible for specifying and documenting software requirements
Unintuitive and difficult to interpret to technical staff	FPA is an abstract metric of software functionality, which is a quite high-level, nonphysical property of software. Therefore, it is difficult to interpret (visualize), especially by software developers
Complexity weights are arbitrary and not up to date	Complexity weights associated with functional elements counted in function points do not necessarily reflect the overhead required to implement them in a particular situation. Moreover, once set up they have not changed over the years—particularly in case of IFPUG function points. Weakness can be overcome by calibrating the complexity weights, for example, as proposed by Xia et al. (2008). Yet, this solution suffers from two significant weaknesses (1) calibration methods proposed so far require much project data and use sophisticated analysis techniques and (2) once adjusted function point metrics no longer conform to standard function points—therefore, cannot be compared to external benchmark data
Does not address algorithmic data transformations	Function point methods measure the relative size of software functions based on the amount of different data types processed by software functions. They do not consider intermediate algorithmic transformations of data but solely the actual data movements from one form to another. A common way to overcome this problem is to include an effort driver related to algorithmic complexity of the software into effort estimation

A.5 Selecting Appropriate Sizing Method

Predicting the size of a software system becomes progressively easier as the project advances.

—Robert T. Futrell, Donald F. Shafer, and Linda Shafer

In this section, we define a set for criteria for selecting a sizing method that is most suitable for effort estimation. We also rate each criterion with respect to its relevance in the context of software effort estimation.

We based the selection criteria on the characteristics of the software sizing methods that are typical subjects of criticism in the related literature and desirable properties of software sizing methods defined by Sheetz et al. (2009). Table A.7 defines these criteria and their relevancy for the purpose of software effort estimation.

Table A.7 Criteria for selecting an appropriate software sizing method

Criteria	Definition	Relevancy
Automation	The degree to which the process of collecting input data and calculating size metric can—and already is—automated	Medium
Calculation ease	The degree to which the value of the size metric is easy to calculate based on the collected input data	High
Objectivity	The degree to which measurement results are independent of the individual perception and skills of the person using the method—excluding the case of intentional misuse of the method	High
Data availability	The degree to which the data required to calculate the measure are readily available given the software products and processes currently used	Medium
Context independence	The degree to which results of measurement do not depend on project context. This includes independence of project environmental and technological factors	Low
Life cycle applicability	The degree to which the metric can be continuously applied throughout the entire software development life cycle. Particularly important is the degree to which the method can be applied in early phases of the software life cycle	High
Standardization	The degree to which the measurement method and process are formalized and standardized. This aspect becomes very important when it comes to benchmarking software projects with respect to development productivity	Low
Problem identification	The degree to which the measurement method facilitates review of products and processes and supports identifying potential deficits. For example, during size measurement incompleteness or inconsistencies in project scope can be identified	Medium
Improvement support	The degree to which the measurement method suggests solutions to the problems it helped to identify	Medium
Sensitivity	The degree to which the metric is sensitive to changes in the scope of software project and provides the necessary feedback to adjust development processes	Medium
Intuitiveness	The degree to which the metric's behavior conforms to intuition of different software stakeholders, such as customers, managers, and developers	Low
Understandability	The degree to which the metric is easy to understand for different software stakeholders. Understandability refers also to complexity of the measurement method as whole; that is, how much mental effort it requires to understand	Medium
Validity	According to Kitchenham et al. (1995, 1997) validity criterion comprises two aspects: • *Theoretical validity* (*internal validity*): The degree to which software size metric assesses the attributes of software it purports to measure. This concerns intermediate elements under measurement and the software size itself • *Empirical validity* (*external validity*): The degree to which software size metric has been empirically evaluated and proved to be useful for the purpose of productivity and effort modeling; that is, the extent it is associated with productivity and effort	High

A.6 Summary

Our continued inability to make much progress in coming up with measures that are scientifically sound and reliably effective in dealing with a broad spectrum of problems has continued to frustrate the community. It is interesting to note, for example, that attempts to measure even the most rudimentary software dimension, the size of a body of software code, have been frustrating.

—Leon J. Osterweil

Despite massive criticism, LOC may still be a useful sizing method for the purpose of effort estimation—if we carefully consider its deficiencies. In many situations FPA offers a better solution but this method, too, does not come without weaknesses that need to be considered before use in particular situation. Table A.8 briefly compares the key attributes of FPA and LOC methods in the context of software effort estimation.

Table A.8 LOC vs. FPA: Overview of strengths and weaknesses

Aspect	Justification	LOC	FPA
Automation	Analyzing source code for the purpose of LOC measurement is easy to automate. Subjective counting procedures of FPA are difficult to automate especially when software requirements are specified in an informal or semi-formal way using natural language	++	—
Calculation ease	Calculating LOC requires solely summing up the counts of code lines for complete software. FPA requires weighting counts of data types processed by their relative complexity, which is determined by counting the number of associated data and record element types	+	—
Objectivity	LOC is more objective than FPA because it directly measures structural properties of a physical software artifact. Once it is defined what should be counted as a line of code, the metric provides repeatable measures for the same software code. FPA measures an abstract property of software—its functionality—based on physical artifacts such as requirements specifications. Identifying functional elements requires subjective interpretation of project-specific software artifacts. In consequence, outcomes of FPA are typically not repeatable and may deviate significantly for the same software depending on who performs FPA	++	—
Data availability	Data for LOC measurement can easily be obtained in any environment by analyzing text code of software. Data for FPA require analyzing software functional specifications that are typically documented in an informal way using natural language	+	—
Context independence	Outcomes from LOC counting depend to a large extent on who implemented the software under measurement and with what technologies. For example, different numbers of LOC depend on programmer skills and programming language used. FPA measures software functionality that does not depend on context	—	++
Life cycle applicability	FPA is applicable from the very early phases of software development when information on software functionality is known—independent of the form in which it is documented. FPA	—	++

(continued)

Table A.8 (continued)

Aspect	Justification	LOC	FPA
	can be then applied throughout the software life cycle using different artifacts to identify functional components of software. LOC is applicable only on software code. In consequence, they can be counted no earlier than at the end of the coding phase and later; yet always for software code only. This limits the usefulness of LOC for the purpose of estimation		
Standardization	FPA is documented by formalized procedures and has been published as an international standard. This allows comparison of FPA counts across organizations. LOC is missing any unified counting procedure. Definitions of LOC differ across software organizations, even though they are often referred to using the same terms	−	++
Problem identification	FPA facilitates the review of software requirements specifications and identification of incomplete or inconsistent project scope. Moreover, it facilitates monitoring scope creep and traces software functionality along development phases and products	−	++
Improvement support	FPA supports improvement in many ways. For example, tracking functional size throughout different life cycle phases and different artifacts allows for identifying potential scope creep and functional traceability problems. Moreover, context independence allows for cross-context comparison of development productivity and identifying potential deficits in this respect	—	+
Sensitivity	Both FPA and LOC are sensitive to changes in software requirements. LOC is additionally sensitive to changes in software technologies	−	−
Intuitiveness	LOC refers to a tangible property of a software artifact and thus is relatively intuitive for different project stakeholders. FPA refers to an abstract property of software and, as such, is more intuitive to software managers and customers than to software developers	+	−
Understandability	LOC is relatively easy to understand. Definition of code lines and counting processes are typically quite simple. In FPA the definition of the size metric and counting procedures are relatively complex and require significant effort to master	+	−
Validity	FPA has limited theoretical validity. For example, depending on the specific FPA method, size is not theoretically additive. Empirical validity of FPA is limited by differences between counts provided by different individuals; individual counts may differ up to 30 % even though they are provided by experienced counters. Although theoretically valid, LOC suffers from low empirical validity in the case where it needs to be estimated before the coding phase; in this case LOC estimates depend largely on the estimator. Large variation in software sizing limits its usefulness for the purpose of effort estimation	+	++

Summarizing, the benefits of FPA with respect to effort estimation suggest that software organizations interested in managing software development effort and productivity should focus on building expertise in FPA and integrate it into their standard measurement and quantitative project management processes.

Yet, even the strengths of FPA should be considered carefully when applying the method in context and for a particular purpose. Although, unlike LOC, the FPA counts are not burdened by the technology in which software is developed or the skills of personnel who develop it, these factors must still be considered when modeling development effort. The same amount of functionality will need different amounts of effort when developed in a different technology—for example, programming language—and by personnel with different skills. The LOC metric is much more tightly connected with the characteristics of the environment in which source code is created. In consequence, particular technologies used for programming software code and particular capabilities of the team that programmed it are an inherent part of size measurements.

Further Reading

- L. M. Laird and M. C. Brennan (2006), *Software Measurement and Estimation. A Practical Approach*. Quantitative Software Engineering Series. Wiley-IEEE Computer Society Press.

  This book provides a comprehensive overview of various approaches for measuring software size.

- C. Jones (2007), *Strengths and Weaknesses of Software Metrics. Version 5*. Software Productivity Research, March 22, 2006. Included in IT Metrics and Productivity Journal, September 4, 2007.

  The article discusses the strengths and weaknesses of common measures of software volume (size). The author summarizes the most important characteristics of software size metrics based on lines of source code and function points that were published in the related literature and complements it with his own experiences.

- S. L. Pfleeger, F. Wu, and R. Lewis (2005), *Software cost estimation and sizing methods: issues and guidelines*. RAND Corporation.

  In Chap. 3, authors overview the differences between seven popular methods for sizing software: lines of code; function points and feature points; object points; applications points; predictive objective points; analogies; and estimating from UML constructs. For each method, authors briefly present what the sizing method is about as well as when the method should, and when it should not, be used. In the following chapters, authors provide practical checklists for managing software sizing risks.

- P. Morris (2001), *Uses and Benefits of Function Points*, Total Metrics Pty. Ltd.
  In this short report, author lists the benefits of using function point size measurement for a number of purposes from industrial practice. She addresses two major areas of software engineering: managing project development and customizing packaged software. In the first domain, she considers three groups of software sizing purposes: project planning, project construction, and software implementation.

- ISO/IEC 14143-6 (2006), *Functional size measurement. Part 6: Guide for use of ISO/IEC 14143 series and related International Standards*, International Standardization Organization.
  The standard provides guidelines for selecting the functional size measurement method that is most appropriate for a particular situation. It considers such aspects as applicability to the domain of software, availability of equivalent industry data, availability of training and tools, and availability of trained experienced certified measurement experts.

- R. E. Park et al. (1992), *Software Size Measurement: A Framework for Counting Source Statements*. Pittsburgh, Pennsylvania, USA: Carnegie Mellon University.
  This technical report provides a comprehensive framework for constructing and communicating definitions of software size metrics. In particular, it formulates a checklist for defining two popular size metrics: source lines of code and logical source statements. It illustrates the checklist with example definitions for counts of physical source lines and logical source statements. Moreover, the report provides forms for recording and reporting measurement results.

- G. C. Low and D. R. Jeffery (1990), "Function Points in the Estimation and the Evaluation of the Software Process". *IEEE Transactions on Software Engineering*, vol. 16, no. 1, pp. 64–71.
  This article empirically evaluates the limitations of the function point size measurement and its consistency as compared to the LOC metric. It identifies the potential sources of variation in the function point counts obtained within—and across—organizations.

- A. Meneely, B. Smith, and L. Williams (2010), *Software Metrics Validation Criteria: A Systematic Literature Review*, Technical Report TR-2010-2, North Carolina State University, Raleigh, NC, USA.
  Meneely and colleagues provide a comprehensive list of criteria used in software engineering for proving the validity of metrics. They systematize aspects that should be considered when defining sound metrics. Moreover, authors identify commonalities and conflicts between validity criteria defined by different authors and provided by formal measurement theory. Finally, they group the criteria found in the review into those that are necessary, desirable, and sufficient for a given metric to be considered as being valid.

Bibliography

Aamodt A, Plaza E (1994) Case-based reasoning: foundational issues, methodological variations, and system approaches. AI Commun 7(1):39–59

Abran A, Moore JW, Bourque P, Dupuis R (2004) Guide to the software engineering body of knowledge - 2004 Version. IEEE Computer Society Press, Los Alamitos, CA

Agrawal M, Chari K (2007) Software effort, quality, and cycle time: a study of CMM level 5 projects. IEEE Trans Softw Eng 33(3):145–156

Albrecht AJ (1979) Measuring application development productivity. In: Proceedings of the IBM application development symposium, 14–17 Oct 1979. IBM Corporation, Monterey, CA, pp 83–92

Ambler SW (2004) Doomed from the start: what everyone but senior management seems to know. Cutter IT J 17(3):29–33

Angelis L, Stamelos I (2000) A simulation tool for efficient analogy based cost estimation. Empir Softw Eng 5(1):35–68

Arkes HR (2001) Overconfidence in judgmental forecasting. In: Armstrong JS (ed) Principles of forecasting. Kluwer Academic, Norwell, MA

Armour PG (2005) To plan, two plans. Commun ACM 48(9):15–19

Armour PG (2008) The inaccurate conception. Commun ACM 51(3):13–16

Armstrong JS (2001) Principles of forecasting: a handbook for researchers and practitioners. Kluwer Academic, Dordrecht

Auer M, Trendowicz A, Graser B, Haunschmid E, Biffl S (2006) Optimal project feature weights in analogy-based cost estimation: improvement and limitations. IEEE Trans Softw Eng 32 (2):83–92

Averill-Snell J (2007) Is multi-tasking counterproductive? White Paper, Institute for Corporate Productivity

Bachore Z, Zhou L (2009) A critical review of the role of user participation in IS success. In: Proceedings of the 15th Americas conference on information systems, San Francisco, CA

Bailey J, Basili V (1981) A meta-model for software development resource expenditures. In: Proceedings of the 5th international conference on software engineering, 9–12 March, San Diego, CA, pp 107–116 (Reprinted in Kemerer CF (1997), Software project management readings and cases, The McGraw-Hill Companies, pp 30–40)

Banker RD, Kauffman RJ, Kumar R (1992) An empirical test of object-based output measurement metrics in a computer aided software engineering (CASE) environment. J Manage Inform Syst 8(3):127–150

Barron FH, Barrett BE (1996) Decision quality using ranked attribute weights. Manage Sci 42 (11):1515–1523

Basili VR (1985) Quantitative evaluation of software methodology. In: Proceedings of the 1st pan pacific computer conference, vol 1, Melbourne, Australia, 10–13 Sept 1985, pp 379–398

Basili VR (1993) The experience factory and its relationship to other improvement paradigms. In: Proceedings of the 4th European software engineering conference on software engineering, Garmisch-Partenkirchen, Germany, 13–17 September, pp 68–83

Basili VR, Weiss DM (1984) A methodology for collecting valid software engineering data. IEEE Trans Softw Eng SE-10(6):728–738

Basili VR, Caldiera G, Rombach HD (1994a) The experience factory. In: Marciniak JJ (ed) Encyclopedia of software engineering, vol 1, 2nd edn. Wiley, Chichester, pp 469–476

Basili VR, Caldiera G, Rombach HD (1994b) The goal question metric approach. In: Marciniak JJ (ed) Encyclopedia of software engineering, vol 1, 2nd edn. Wiley, New York, pp 528–532

Basili VR, Lindvall M, Regardie M, Seaman C, Heidrich J, Münch J, Rombach D, Trendowicz A (2010) Linking software development and business strategy through measurement. IEEE Comput 43(4):57–65

Basili VR, Trendowicz A, Kowalczyk M, Heidrich J, Seaman C, Münch J, Rombach D (2014) Aligning organizations through measurement. The GQM+Strategies approach, The Fraunhofer IESE series on software and systems engineering. Springer, Heidelberg

Beck K, Fowler M (2000) Planning extreme programming. Addison-Wesley Longman Publishing Company, Boston, MA

Becker C, Huber E (2008) Die Bilanz des (Miss)-Erfolges in IT-Projekten Harte Fakten und weiche Faktoren [Summary of (Un)Successes in IT Projects. Hard Facts and Soft Factors]. White Paper, Pentaeder, Ludwigsburg, Germany

Bentley J (1988) More programming pearls: confessions of a coder. Addison-Wesley Professional, Reading, MA

Betts M (2003) Why IT projects fail. Computerworld 37(34):44

Biehl M (2007) Success factors for implementing global information systems. Commun ACM 50 (1):52–58

Boehm BW (1981) Software engineering economics. Prentice-Hall, Englewood Cliffs, NJ

Boehm B, Basili VR (2001) Software defect reduction top 10 list. IEEE Comput 34(1):135–137

Boehm BW, Abts C, Brown AW, Chulani S, Clark BK, Horowitz E, Madachy R, Reifer D, Steece B (2000) Software cost estimation with COCOMO II. Prentice Hall, Upper Saddle River, NJ

Breiman L, Friedman J, Stone CJ, Olshen RA (1984) Classification and regression trees. Chapman and Hall, New York

Briand LC, Wieczorek I (2002) Resource modeling in software engineering. In: Marciniak JJ (ed) Encyclopedia of software engineering, 2nd edn. Wiley, New York

Briand LC, El Emam K, Bomarius F (1998) COBRA: a hybrid method for software cost estimation, benchmarking, and risk assessment. In: Proceedings of the 20th international conference on software engineering, pp 390–399

Briand LC, Emam KE, Wieczorek I (1999) Explaining the cost of European space and military projects. In: Proceedings of the 21st international conference on software engineering, Los Angeles, CA, pp 303–312

Briand LC, Langley T, Wieczorek I (2000) A replicated assessment and comparison of common software cost modeling techniques. In: Proceedings of the 22nd international conference on software engineering, 4–11 June 2000. IEEE Computer Society, Limerick, pp 377–386

Bridgeland DM, Zahavi R (2008) Business modeling: a practical guide to realizing business value. Morgan Kaufmann, San Francisco, CA

Brooks FP (1995) The mythical man-month: essays on software engineering, 2nd edn. Addison-Wesley, Boston, MA

Carey JM, Kacmar CJ (1997) The impact of communication mode and task complexity on small group performance and member satisfaction. Comput Hum Behav 13(1):23–49

Cerpa N, Verner JM (2009) Why did your project fail? Commun ACM 52(12):130–134

Charette RN (2005) Why software fails [software failure]. IEEE Spectr 42(9):42–49

Chulani S, Boehm B, Steece B (1999) Bayesian analysis of empirical software engineering cost models. IEEE Trans Softw Eng 25(4):573–583

Clark BK (2000) Quantifying the effects on effort of process improvement. IEEE Softw 17(6):65–70

CMMI Product Team (2010) CMMI for development, Version 1.3. Software Engineering Institute, Carnegie Mellon University, Pittsburgh, PA, Technical Report CMU/SEI-2010-TR-033

Cohn M (2004) User stories applied: for agile software development. Addison-Wesley Professional, Boston, MA

Cohn M (2005) Agile estimating and planning. Prentice-Hall, Upper Saddle River, NJ

Cohn M (2009) Succeeding with agile: software development using scrum. Addison-Wesley Professional, Upper Saddle River, NJ

Conte SD, Dunsmore HE, Shen YE (1986) Software engineering metrics and models. Benjamin-Cummings Publishing Company, Menlo Park, CA

Covey SR (2004) The 7 habits of highly effective people. Free Press, New York

DeMarco T (1982) Controlling software projects: management, measurement, and estimates. Prentice-Hall, Englewood Cliffs, NJ

Deming WE (1986) Out of crisis. Massachusetts Institute of Technology, Center for Advance Education Services, Cambridge, MA

Diaz M, King J (2002) How CMM impacts quality, productivity, rework, and the bottom line. CrossTalk 15(3):9–14

Dillibabu R, Krishnaiah K (2005) Cost estimation of a software product using COCOMO II.2000 model – a case study. Int J Proj Manage 23(4):297–307

Dolado JJ (1999) Limits to the methods in software cost estimation. In: Proceedings of the 1st international workshop on soft computing applied to software engineering, 12–14 Apr 1999. Limerick University Press, Limerick, pp 63–68

Dolado JJ (2001) On the problem of the software cost function. Inform Softw Technol 43(1):61–72

Dysert L, Eliott BG (2002) The estimate review and validation process. Cost Eng 44(1):17–22

Ebert C, Man JD (2008) Effectively utilizing project, product and process knowledge. Inform Softw Technol 50(6):579–594

Efron B, Tibshirani RJ (1994) An introduction to the bootstrap. Chapman and Hall, New York

El Emam K, Koru AG (2008) A replicated survey of IT software project failures. IEEE Softw 25 (5):84–90

Elkjaer M (2000) Stochastic budget simulation. Int J Proj Manage 18(2):139–147

Emam KE, Benlarbi S, Goel N, Rai SN (2001) Comparing case-based reasoning classifiers for predicting high risk software components. J Syst Softw 55(3):301–320

Espinosa J, Slaughter S, Kraut R, Herbsleb J (2007) Team knowledge and coordination in geographically distributed software development. J Manage Inform Syst 24(1):135–169

Faraj S, Sproull L (2000) Coordinating expertise in software development teams. Manage Sci 46 (12):1554–1568

Farquhar JA (1970) A preliminary inquiry into the software estimation process. The Rand Corporation, Santa Monica, CA, Technical Report RM-6271-PR

Fitzmaurice G (2002) Sample size and power: how big is big enough? Nutrition 18(3):289–290

Flyvbjerg B (2006) From Nobel Prize to project management: getting risks right. Proj Manage J 37 (3):5–15

Foss T, Stensrud E, Kitchenham B, Myrtveit I (2003) A simulation study of the model evaluation criterion MMRE. IEEE Trans Softw 29(11):985–995

Frankenhaeuser M, Gardell B (1976) Underload and overload in working life: outline of a multidisciplinary approach. J Hum Stress 2(3):35–46

French S (1995) Uncertainty and imprecision: modelling and analysis. J Oper Res Soc 46:70–79

Galorath DD, Evans MW (2006) Software sizing, estimation, and risk management: when performance is measured performance improves. Auerbach, Boca Raton, FL

GAO (2009) GAO cost estimating and assessment guide. best practices for developing and managing capital program costs. Report GAO-09-3SP, United States Government Accountability Office, Washington, DC

Glass RL (2002) Facts and fallacies of software engineering. Addison-Wesley Professional, Boston, MA

Green SB (1991) How many subjects does it take to do a regression analysis? Multivar Behav Res 26(3):499–510

Green PJ, Silverman BW (1994) Nonparametric regression and generalized linear models: a roughness penalty approach, vol 58, Chapman & Hall/CRC monographs on statistics and applied probability. Chapman and Hall, London

Greene WH (2011) Econometric analysis, 7th edn. Prentice-Hall, New York

Grenning J (2002) Planning poker or how to avoid analysis paralysis while release planning. White Paper, Renaissance Software Consulting

Grimstad S, Jørgensen M (2006) A framework for the analysis of software cost estimation accuracy. In: Proceedings of the 2006 ACM/IEEE international symposium on empirical software engineering, 21–22 Sept 2006, Rio de Janeiro, Brazil. ACM Press, New York, pp 58–65

Grimstad S, Jørgensen M, Moløkken-Østvold K (2006) Software effort estimation terminology: the tower of Babel. Inform Softw Technol 48(4):302–310

Grinstead CM, Snell LJ (2003) Introduction to probability, 2nd edn. American Mathematical Society, Providence, RI

Guinan PJ, Cooprider JG, Sawyer S (1997) The effective use of automated application development tools. IBM Syst J 36(1):124–139

Halstead MH (1977) Elements of software science, Operating and programming systems series. Elsevier Science, New York

Hamdan K, Bibi S, Angelis L, Stamelos I (2009) A bayesian belief network cost estimation model that incorporates cultural and project leadership factors. In: IEEE symposium on industrial electronics and applications 2009. ISIEA 2009, vol 2. pp 985–989, 4

Haugan GT (2002) Effective work breakdown structures. Management Concepts, Vienna, VA

Haugen NC (2006) An empirical study of using planning poker for user story estimation. In: Proceedings to agile conference, Washington, DC, pp 23–34

He J, Butler B, King W (2007) Team cognition: development and evolution in software project teams. J Manage Inform Syst 24(2):261–292

Herbsleb JD, Mockus A (2003) An empirical study of speed and communication in globally distributed software development. IEEE Trans Softw Eng 29(6):481–494

Hsu JSC, Chang JYT, Klein G, Jiang JJ (2011) Exploring the impact of team mental models on information utilization and project performance in system development. Int J Proj Manage 29 (1):1–12

Huckman RS, Staats BR, Upton DM (2009) Team familiarity, role experience, and performance: evidence from indian software services. Manage Sci 55(1):85–100

Hughes RT (1996) Expert judgement as an estimating method. Inform Softw Technol 38(2):67–75

Humphrey WS (1995) A discipline for software engineering. Addison-Wesley Longman, Reading, MA

Humphrey WS (1999) Managing the software process. Addison-Wesley, Reading, MA

Humphrey WS (2001) The future of software engineering: I-V. Carnegie Mellon University, Software Engineering Institute, Pittsburgh, PA

IEEE (1993) IEEE standard for software productivity metrics, IEEE Std 1045-1992

ISBSG (2009) Estimating, benchmarking research suite release 10. International Software Benchmarking Standards Group, Hawthorn, VIC

ISO (2002) ISO/IEC 20968 - Mk II function point analysis. Counting practices manual, 1st edn. International Standardization Organization, Geneva

ISO (2003) ISO/IEC 19761 - COSMIC-FFP a functional size measurement method, 1st edn. International Standardization Organization, Geneva

ISO (2005) ISO/IEC 24570 - NESMA Functional Size Measurement Method Version 2.1. Definitions and counting guidelines for the application of function point analysis, 1st edn. International Standardization Organization, Geneva

ISO (2008) ISO/IEC 29881 - FiSMA 1.1 functional size measurement method, 1st edn. International Standardization Organization, Geneva

ISO (2009) ISO/IEC 20926 - IFPUG Functional Size Measurement Method 2009, 2nd edn. International Standardization Organization, Geneva

Jeffery R, Ruhe M, Wieczorek I (2000) A comparative study of two software development cost modeling techniques using multi-organizational and company-specific data. Inform Softw Technol 42(14):1009–1016

Jeffery R, Ruhe M, Wieczorek I (2001) Using public domain metrics to estimate software development effort. In: Proceedings of the 7th international symposium on software metrics, 4–6 Apr 2001. IEEE Computer Society, London, pp 16–27

Jensen RW (1983) An improved macrolevel software development resource estimation model. In: Proceedings of the fifth international society of parametric analysts conference, St. Louis, MO, pp 88–92

Jensen RW, Putnam LH, Roetzheim W (2006) Software estimating models: three viewpoints. CrossTalk 19(2):23–29

Jiang JJ, Klein G, Chen H-G, Lin L (2002) Reducing user-related risks during and prior to system development. Int J Proj Manage 20(7):507–515

Jones CT (1996) Applied software measurement: assuring productivity and quality, 2nd edn. McGraw Hill Osborne Media, New York

Jones CT (2006) Social and technical reasons for software project failures. CrossTalk 19(6):4–9

Jones CT (2007) Estimating software costs, 2nd edn. McGraw-Hill Osborne Media, New York

Jones CT (2009) Software engineering best practices: lessons from successful projects in the top companies. McGraw-Hill Osborne Media, New York

Jørgensen M (2004a) A review of studies on expert estimation of software development effort. J Syst Softw 70(1–2):37–60

Jørgensen M (2004b) Top-down and bottom-up expert estimation of software development effort. Inform Softw Technol 46(1):3–16

Jørgensen M (2004c) Realism in assessment of effort estimation uncertainty: it matters how you ask. IEEE Trans Softw Eng 30(4):209–217

Jørgensen M (2005a) Practical guidelines for expert-judgment-based software effort estimation. IEEE Softw 22(3):57–63

Jørgensen M (2005b) Evidence-based guidelines for assessment of software development cost uncertainty. IEEE Trans Softw Eng 31(11):942–954

Jørgensen M (2007) Forecasting of software development work effort: evidence on expert judgement and formal models. Int J Forecast 23(3):449–462

Jørgensen M (2009) How to avoid selecting bids based on overoptimistic cost estimates. IEEE Softw 26(3):79–84

Jørgensen M, Indahl U, Sjøberg D (2003) Software effort estimation by analogy and 'regression toward the mean'. J Syst Softw 68(3):253–262

Jørgensen M, Grimstad S (2005) Over-optimism in software development projects: 'the winner's curse. In: Proceedings of the 15th international conference on electronics, communications and computers, Puebla, Mexico, 28 February–2 March, pp 280–285

Jørgensen M, Grimstad S (2008) Avoiding irrelevant and misleading information when estimating development effort. IEEE Softw 25(3):78–83

Jørgensen M, Grimstad S (2010) Software development effort estimation: demystifying and improving expert estimation. In: Tveito A, Bruaset AM, Lysne O (eds) Simula research laboratory by thinking constantly about it. Springer, Berlin, pp 381–403

Jørgensen M, Grimstad S (2011) The impact of irrelevant and misleading information on software development effort estimates: a randomized controlled field experiment. IEEE Trans Softw Eng 37(5):695–707

Jørgensen M, Gruschke TM (2009) The impact of lessons-learned sessions on effort estimation and uncertainty assessments. IEEE Trans Softw Eng 35(3):368–383

Jørgensen M, Moløkken-Østvold K (2002) Combination of software development effort prediction intervals: why, when and how? In: Proceedings of the 14th international conference on software engineering and knowledge engineering, Ischia, Italy, pp 425–428

Jørgensen M, Sjøberg DIK (2001) Impact of effort estimates on software project work. Inform Softw Technol 43(15):939–948

Jørgensen M, Sjøberg DIK (2003) An effort prediction interval approach based on the empirical distribution of previous estimation accuracy. Inform Softw Technol 45(3):123–136

Jørgensen M, Sjøberg DIK (2004) The impact of customer expectation on software development effort estimates. Int J Proj Manage 22(4):317–325

Jørgensen M, Løvstad N, Moen L (2002) Combining quantitative software development cost estimation precision data with qualitative data from project experience reports at ericsson design center in Norway. In: Proceedings of the conference on empirical assessment in software engineering, Keele, UK, 8–10 April

Jørgensen M, Teigen KH, Moløkken-Østvold K (2004) Better sure than safe? Over-confidence in judgement based software development effort prediction intervals. J Syst Softw 70(1–2):79–93

Jørgensen M, Boehm B, Rifkin S (2009) Software development effort estimation: formal models or expert judgment? IEEE Softw 26(2):14–19

Kadoda G, Cartwright M, Chen L, Shepperd M (2000) Experiences using case-based reasoning to predict software project effort. In: Proceedings of the 4th international conference on empirical assessment and evaluation in software engineering, 17–19 Apr 2000. Keele University, Staffordshire, pp 23–28

Kadoda GF, Cartwright M, Shepperd MJ (2001) Issues on the effective use of CBR technology for software project prediction. In: Proceedings of the 4th international conference on case-based reasoning: case-based reasoning research and development, Vancouver, BC, Canada, 30 July–2 August, pp 276–290

Kahneman D (2011) Thinking, fast and slow. Farrar, Straus and Giroux, New York, 499 p

Karner (1993) Technical report, Objective systems SF AB, Kista, Sweden, 17 Sep 1993.

Kenney S. Top two factors that tank many IT projects. The project management hut, 21 Aug 2011. http://www.pmhut.com/top-two-factors-that-tank-many-it-projects

Kitchenham B, Jeffery R, Connaughton C (2007) Misleading metrics and unsound analyses. IEEE Softw 24(2):73–78

Kitchenham B, Linkman S (1997) Estimates, uncertainty, and risk. IEEE Softw 14(3):69–74

Kitchenham BA, Mendes E (2004) A comparison of cross-company and single-company effort estimation models for web applications. In: Proceedings of the international conference on empirical assessment in software engineering, Edinburgh, Ireland, 24–25 May, pp 47–55

Kitchenham BA, Pfleeger SL, Fenton N (1995) Towards a framework for software measurement validation. IEEE Trans Softw Eng 21(12):929–944

Kitchenham BA, Pfleeger SL, Fenton N (1997) Reply to: comments on 'towards a framework for software measurement validation'. IEEE Trans Softw Eng 23(3):189

Kitchenham BA, Pickard LM, MacDonell SG, Shepperd MJ (2001) What accuracy statistics really measure [software estimation]. IEE Proc Softw 148(3):81–85

Kitchenham BA, Pickard LM, Linkman S, Jones PW (2003) Modeling software bidding risks. IEEE Trans Softw Eng 29(6):542–554

Kitchenham BA, Pickard LM, Linkman S, Jones P (2005) A framework for evaluating a software bidding model. Inform Softw Technol 47(11):747–760

Klein C, DiazGranados D, Salas E, Le H, Burke CS, Lyons R, Goodwin GF (2009) Does team building work? Small Group Res 40(2):181–222

Kraut RE, Streeter LA (1995) Coordination in software development. Commun ACM 38(3):69–81

Lee S, Yong H-S (2010) Distributed agile: project management in a global environment. Empir Softw Eng 15(2):204–217

Leung HKN (2002) Estimating maintenance effort by analogy. Empir Softw Eng 7(2):157–175

Li J, Ruhe G (2006) A comparative study of attribute weighting heuristics for effort estimation by analogy. In: Proceedings of the international symposium on empirical software engineering, 21–22 September, Rio de Janeiro, Brazil, pp 66–74

Li J, Ruhe G (2008) Analysis of attribute weighting heuristics for analogy-based software effort estimation method AQUA+. Empir Softw Eng 13(1):63–96

Little T (2006) Schedule estimation and uncertainty surrounding the cone of uncertainty. IEEE Softw 23(3):48–54

Lohr S (2007) Slow down, brawe multitasker, and don't read this in traffic. New York Times, 25 March 2007

Lokan C (2005) What should you optimize when building an estimation model? In: Proceedings of the 11th international software metrics symposium, 19–22 September 2005, Como, Italy, p 34

Lum K, Hihn J, Menzies T (2006) Studies in software cost model behavior: do we really understand cost model performance? In: Presented at the 28th conference of the international society of parametric analysts, 23–26 May, Seattle, WA

MacDonell SG, Shepperd MJ (2003) Combining techniques to optimize effort predictions in software project management. J Syst Softw 66(2):91–98

MacDonell SG, Shepperd MJ (2007) Comparing local and global software effort estimation models – reflections on a systematic review. In: Proceedings of the 1st international symposium on empirical software engineering and measurement, Madrid, Spain, 20–21 Sept 2007. IEEE Computer Society, Washington, DC, pp 401–409

MacKinnon JG (1983) Model specification tests against non-nested alternatives. Econom Rev 2 (1):85–110

Martino SD, Ferrucci F, Gravino C, Mendes E (2007) Comparing size measures for predicting web application development effort: a case study. In: Proceedings of the 1st international symposium on empirical software engineering and measurement, 20–21 September, Madrid, Spain, pp 324–333

Maxwell SE (2000) Sample size and multiple regression analysis. Psychol Methods 5(4):434–458

McConnell S (1996) Rapid development: taming wild software schedules. Microsoft Press, Redmond, MA

McConnell S (2006) Software estimation: demystifying the black art. Microsoft Press, Redmond, MA

Mendes E (2007) A comparison of techniques for web effort estimation. In: Proceedings of the 1st international symposium on empirical software engineering and measurement, 20–21 September 2007, Madrid, Spain, pp 334–343

Mendes E, Kitchenham B (2004) Further comparison of cross-company and within-company effort estimation models for Web applications. In: Proceedings of the 10th international symposium on software metrics, 11–17 Sept 2004. IEEE Computer Society, Chicago, IL, pp 348–357

Mendes E, Lokan C (2008) Replicating studies on cross- vs. single-company effort models using the ISBSG database. Empir Softw Eng 13(1):3–37

Mendes E, Lokan C, Harrison R, Triggs C (2005) A replicated comparison of cross-company and within-company effort estimation models using the ISBSG database. In: Proceedings of the 11th IEEE international symposium on software metrics, 19–22 Sept 2005. IEEE Computer Society, Como, pp 27–36

Mendes E, Mosley N (2008) Bayesian network models for web effort prediction: a comparative study. IEEE Trans Softw Eng 34(6):723–737

Mendes E, Mosley N, Counsell S (2002) The application of case-based reasoning to early web project cost estimation. In: Proceedings of the 26th international computer software and applications conference on prolonging software life: development and redevelopment, 26–29 August 2002, Oxford, England, pp 393–398

Mendes E, Mosley N, Counsell S (2003a) A replicated assessment of the use of adaptation rules to improve web cost estimation. In: Proceedings of the 2nd international symposium on empirical software engineering, 30 September–1 October, Rome, Italy, p 100

Mendes E, Mosley N, Counsell S (2003b) Do adaptation rules improve web cost estimation? In: Proceedings of the 14th conference on hypertext and hypermedia, 26–30 August, Nottingham, pp 173–183

Mendes E, Watson I, Triggs C, Mosley N, Counsell S (2003c) A comparative study of cost estimation models for web hypermedia applications. Empir Softw Eng 8(2):163–196

Menzies T, Hihn J (2006) Evidence-based cost estimation for better-quality software. IEEE Softw 23(4):64–66

Meyer DE (2001) Multitasking has problems, study finds. CNN Tonight, 5 August, Sunday Transcript # 080502CN.V70, CNN

Minkiewicz AF (1997) Measuring object-oriented software with predictive object points. In: Proceedings of the 8th European software control and metrics conference, 26–28 May, Berlin, Germany

Miranda E, Bourque P, Abran A (2009) Sizing user stories using paired comparisons. Inform Softw Technol 51(9):1327–1337

Mittas N, Angelis L (2009) Bootstrap prediction intervals for a semi-parametric software cost estimation model. In: Proceedings of the 35th Euromicro conference on software engineering and advanced applications, 27–29 August, Patras, Greece, pp 293–299

Miyazaki Y, Takanou A, Nozaki H, Nakagawa N, Okada K (1991) Method to estimate parameter values in software prediction models. Inform Softw Technol 33(3):239–243

Moe NB, Dingsoyr D, Dybå D (2009) Overcoming barriers to self-management in software teams. IEEE Softw 26(6):20–26

Moløkken-Østvold K, Jørgensen M (2004) Group processes in software effort estimation. Empir Softw Eng 9(4):315–334

Moløkken-Østvold K, Jørgensen M, Tanilkan SS, Gallis H, Lien AC, Hove SE (2004) A survey on software estimation in the Norwegian industry. In: Proceedings of the 10th international symposium software metrics, 11–17 September, Chicago, IL, pp 208–219

Moløkken-Østvold K, Haugen NC, Benestad HC (2008) Using planning poker for combining expert estimates in software projects. J Syst Softw 81(12):2106–2117

Mookerjee VS, Chiang IR (2002) A dynamic coordination policy for software system construction. IEEE Trans Softw Eng 28(7):684–694

Morgenshtern O, Raz T, Dvir D (2007) Factors affecting duration and effort estimation errors in software development projects. Inform Softw Technol 49(8):827–837

Moses J, Clifford J (2000) Learning how to improve effort estimation in small software development companies. In: Proceedings of the 24th annual international computer software and applications conference, 25–28 October 2000, Taipei, Taiwan, pp 522–527

Myrtveit I, Stensrud E (1999) A controlled experiment to assess the benefits of estimating with analogy and regression models. IEEE Trans Softw Eng 25(4):510–525

Myrtveit I, Stensrud E, Shepperd M (2005) Reliability and validity in comparative studies of software prediction models. IEEE Trans Softw Eng 31(5):380–391

Norden PV (1958) Curve fitting for a model of applied research and development scheduling. IBM J Res Dev 2(3):232–248

O'Sullivan A, Sheffrin SM (2007) Economics: principles in action, 3rd edn. Pearson Prentice Hall, Boston, MA

Office of Government Commerce OGC (2009) Managing successful projects with PRINCE2 2009 Edition Manual. The Stationary Office

Ohsugi N, Tsunoda M, Monden A, Matsumoto K (2004) Effort estimation based on collaborative filtering. In: Proceedings of the 5th international conference on product focused software process improvement, Apr 2004, Kansai Science City, Japan. Springer, Berlin, pp 274–286

Ohsugi N, Monden A, Kikuchi N, Barker MD, Tsunoda M, Kakimoto T, Matsumoto K (2007) Is this cost estimate reliable? – The relationship between homogeneity of analogues and estimation reliability. In: Proceedings of the 1st international symposium on empirical software engineering and measurement, Madrid, Spain, pp 384–392

Ozernoy VM (1992) Choosing the 'best' multiple criteria decision-making method. Inform Syst Oper Res 30(2):159–171

Park RE (1992) Software size measurement: a framework for counting source statements. Technical Report CMU/SEI-92-TR-020, Carnegie Mellon University, Pittsburgh, PA

Parolia N, Goodman S, Li Y, Jiang JJ (2007) Mediators between coordination and IS project performance. Inform Manage 44(7):635–645

Parr FN (1980) An alternative to the Rayleigh Curve Model for software development effort. IEEE Trans Softw Eng SE-6(3):291–296

Pawlak Z (1982) Rough sets. Int J Inform Comput Sci 11(5):341–356

Pawlak Z (1991) Rough sets: theoretical aspects of reasoning about data. Kluwer, Dordrecht

Pawlak Z, Skowron A (2007) Rudiments of rough sets. Inform Sci 177(1):3–27

Pedler M, Burgoyne J, Boydell T (1998) The learning company: a strategy for sustainable development, 2nd edn. McGraw-Hill, London

Pendharkar PC, Subramanian GH, Rodger JA (2005) A probabilistic model for predicting software development effort. IEEE Trans Softw Eng 31(7):615–624

Pesaran MH, Deaton AS (1978) Testing non-nested regression models. Econometrica 46(3):677–694

Pesaran MH, Weeks M (1999) Non-nested hypothesis testing: an overview. Technical Report 9918, Faculty of Economics, University of Cambridge, Cambridge, MA

Pickard L, Kitchenham B, Linkman S (1999) An investigation of analysis techniques for software datasets. In: Proceedings of the 6th international symposium on software metrics, 4–6 Nov 1999, Boca Raton, FL. IEEE Computer Society, Washington, DC, pp 130–142

Pillai K, Sukumaran Nair VS (1997) A model for software development effort and cost estimation. IEEE Trans Softw Eng 23(8):485–497

PMI (2006) Practice standard for work breakdown structures, 2nd edn. Project Management Institute, Newtown Square, PA

PMI (2011) Practice standard for earned value management, 2nd edn. Project Management Institute, Newtown Square, PA

PMI (2013) A guide to the project management body of knowledge (PMBOK Guide), 5th edn. Project Management Institute, Newtown Square, PA

Port D, Korte M (2008) Comparative studies of the model evaluation criterions MMRE and PRED in software cost estimation research. In: Proceedings of the 2nd international symposium on empirical software engineering and measurement, Kaiserslautern, Germany, pp 51–60

Porter AA, Selby RW (1990) Evaluating techniques for generating metric-based classification trees. J Syst Softw 12(3):209–218

Putnam LH (1980) Software cost estimating and life-cycle control: getting the software numbers. IEEE Computer Society, New York

Putnam LH (2000) Linking the QSM productivity index with the SEI maturity level. Version 6. Quantitative Software Management, Inc., McLean, VA

Putnam LH, Myers W (1992) Measures for excellence: reliable software on time, within budget. Prentice-Hall Professional Technical Reference, Englewood Cliffs, NJ

Putnam LH, Myers W (2003) Five core metrics: the intelligence behind successful software management. Dorset House Publishing Company, New York

QSM (2013) Function point languages table. Version 5.0. Technical report, quantitative software management, Inc., 2013. Available online: http://www.qsm.com/resources/function-point-languages-table

Quinlan JR (1992) C4.5: programs for machine learning. Morgan Kaufmann, San Mateo, CA

Quinlan JR (1996) Learning decision tree classifiers. ACM Comput Surv 28(1):71–72

Reifer DJ (2000) Web development: estimating quick-to-market software. IEEE Softw 17(6):57–64

Rico DF (2000) Using cost benefit analyses to develop software process improvement (SPI) strategies. A DACS state-of-the-art report. ITT Industries, Advanced Engineering and Sciences Division, New York, NY

Rosencrance (2007) Survey: poor communication causes most IT project failures. Computerworld, 9 March 2007

Ross MA (2008) Next generation software estimating framework: 25 years and thousands of projects later. J Cost Anal Parametrics 1(2):7–30

Rousseeuw PJ, Leroy AM (2003) Robust regression and outlier detection. Wiley, Hoboken, NJ

Rubin DB, Little RJA (1983) Incomplete data. In: Kotz S, Johnson NL (eds) Encyclopedia of statistical sciences, vol 4. Wiley, New York, pp 46–53

Rubin KS (2012) Essential scrum: a practical guide to the most popular agile process. Addison-Wesley Professional, Upper Saddle River, NJ

Rubinstein JS, Meyer DE, Evans JE (2001) Executive control of cognitive processes in task switching. J Exp Psychol Hum Percept Perform 27(4):763–797

Saaty TL (1980) The analytic hierarchy process, planning, priority setting, resource allocation. McGraw-Hill, New York

Salas A (2004) Cost estimation: more than an analytical tool. In: Proceeding of the IEEE aerospace conference, Big Sky, Montana, vol 2. pp 1053–1060

Sauer C, Gemino A, Reich BH (2007) The impact of size and volatility on IT project performance. Commun ACM 50(11):79–84

Schafer JL (1997) Analysis of incomplete multivariate data, Monographs on statistics and applied probability. Chapman & Hall/CRC, London

Sheetz SD, Henderson D, Wallace L (2009) Understanding developer and manager perceptions of function points and source lines of code. J Syst Softw 82(9):1540–1549

Shepperd M (2005) Evaluating software project prediction systems. In: Proceedings of the 11th international software metrics symposium, 19–22 September 2005, Como, Italy, p 2

Shepperd M, Cartwright M (2001) Predicting with sparse data. IEEE Trans Softw Eng 27(11):987–998

Shepperd M, Cartwright M (2005) A replication of the use of regression towards the mean (R2M) as an adjustment to effort estimation models. In: Proceedings of the 11th IEEE international symposium on software metrics, 19–22 Sept 2005. IEEE Computer Society, Como, pp 38–47

Shepperd M, Kadoda G (2001) Comparing software prediction techniques using simulation. IEEE Trans Softw Eng 27(11):1014–1022

Shepperd M, Schofield C (1997) Estimating software project effort using analogies. IEEE Trans Softw Eng 23(11):736–743

Shepperd M, Cartwright M, Kadoda G (2000) On building prediction systems for software engineers. Empir Softw Eng 5(3):175–182

Shewhart WA (1939) Statistical method from the viewpoint of quality control. Dover, New York

Srinivasan K, Fisher D (1995) Machine learning approaches to estimating software development effort. IEEE Trans Softw Eng 21(2):126–137

Stamelos I, Angelis L (2001) Managing uncertainty in project portfolio cost estimation. Inform Softw Technol 43(13):759–768

Stamelos I, Angelis L, Dimou P, Sakellaris E (2003a) On the use of bayesian belief networks for the prediction of software productivity. Inform Softw Technol 45(1):51–60

Stamelos I, Angelis L, Morisio M, Sakellaris E, Bleris GL (2003b) Estimating the development cost of custom software. Inform Manage 40(8):729–741

Stevenson DH, Starkweather JA (2010) PM critical competency index: IT execs prefer soft skills. Int J Proj Manage 28(7):663–671

Stewart B (2002) Predicting project delivery rates using the Naive-Bayes classifier. J Softw Maint 14(3):161–179

Stutzke RD (2005) Estimating software-intensive systems: projects, products, and processes. Addison-Wesley Professional, Reading, MA

Tesch D, Sobol MG, Klein G, Jiang JJ (2009) User and developer common knowledge: effect on the success of information system development projects. Int J Proj Manage 27(7):657–664

Tiwana A (2008) Impact of classes of development coordination tools on software development performance: a multinational empirical study. ACM Trans Softw Eng Methodol 17(2):1–47

Tiwana A, Keil M (2004) The one-minute risk assessment tool. Commun ACM 47(11):73–77

Tiwana A, McLean ER (2003) The tightrope to e-business project success. Commun ACM 46 (12):345–350

Trendowicz A (2008) Software effort estimation with well-founded causal models. Ph.D. thesis, Technical University Kaiserslautern, Kaiserslautern, Germany

Trendowicz A, Münch J (2009) Factors influencing software development productivity – state-of-the-art and industrial experiences. In: Zelkowitz MV (ed) Advances in computers, vol 77. Elsevier Science, New York, pp 185–241

Trendowicz A (2013) Software cost estimation, benchmarking, and risk analysis. Software decision makers' guide for predictable software development. Springer, New York

Tversky A, Kahneman D (1974) Judgment under uncertainty: heuristics and biases. Science 185 (4157):1124–1131

Verzuh E (2011) The fast forward MBA in project management, 4th edn. Wiley, Hoboken, NJ

Vincke P (1992) Multicriteria decision-aid. Wiley, New York

Walkerden F, Jeffery R (1997) Software cost estimation: a review of models, process, and practice. In: Advances in Computers, vol 44. Elsevier Science, pp 59–125

Walkerden F, Jeffery R (1999) An empirical study of analogy-based software effort estimation. Empir Softw Eng 4(2):135–158

Wang Y (2007a) Software engineering foundations: a software science perspective, vol 2. Auerbach/CRC Press, New York

Wang Y (2007b) On laws of work organization in human cooperation. Int J Cogn Inform Nat Intell 1(2):1–15

Wang Y, King G (2000) Software engineering processes: principles and applications. CRC, Boca Raton, FL

Wang ETG, Ju P-H, Jiang JJ, Klein G (2008) The effects of change control and management review on software flexibility and project performance. Inform Manage 45(7):438–443

Weinberg GM (1986) Secrets of consulting: a guide to giving and getting advice successfully. Dorset House Publishing Company, New York NY, USA

Wieczorek I, Ruhe M (2002) How valuable is company-specific data compared to multi-company data for software cost estimation? In: Proceedings of the 8th international symposium on software metrics, 4–7 June 2002, Ottawa, Canada. IEEE Computer Society, Washington, DC, pp 237–246

Wohlin C, Runeson P, Höst M, Ohlsson MC, Regnell B, Wesslen A (2000) Experimentation in software engineering: an introduction. Kluwer, Norwell, MT

Xia W, Capretz LF, Ho D, Ahmed F (2008) A new calibration for function point complexity weights. Inform Softw Technol 50(7–8):670–683

Yang D, Wang Q, Li M, Yang Y, Ye K, Du J (2008) A survey on software cost estimation in the Chinese software industry. In: Proceedings of the 2nd ACM-IEEE international symposium on empirical software engineering and measurement, 9–10 Oct 2008, Kaiserslautern. ACM Press, Germany, pp 253–262

Yerkes RM, Dodson JD (1908) The relation of strength of stimulus to rapidity of habit-formation. J Comp Neurol Psychol 18(5):459–482

Yourdon E (2003) Death March. 2nd edn. Prentice-Hall, New York, NY, USA

Zadeh LA (1965) Fuzzy sets. Inform Control 8:338–353

Zhang H (2008) Qualitative and semi-quantitative modelling and simulation of the software engineering processes. Ph.D. thesis, University of New South Wales, 256 p

Index

A
Accuracy, 249
Actual, 16
Agile estimation
    principles, 324–325
Analogs, 301
Analogy with virtual neighbor (AVN), 161
Analytic hierarchy process (AHP), 168, 232
Anchoring, 172
ANGEL, 304
AQUA, 304
Artificial neural network (ANN), 167
Autocorrelation, 266–267

B
Backfiring, 279, 432
Backward elimination, 263
Backward inference. *See* Diagnostic inference
Balanced relative error (BRE), 98, 101
Bayesian belief network (BBN), 178, 180, 201,
    254, 335–343
    cognitive complexity, 338
    conditional independence, 337
    diagnostic inference, 337, 340
    diagnostic reasoning, 181
    evidence, 336
    hypothesis, 336
    joint probability distribution, 337
    node probability table, 338
    predictive inference, 337, 339–340
    predictive reasoning, 181
Bayesian calibration, 286
Bayesian inference, 179
Bayes' statistics, 286
Bayes' theorem, 178–181, 288
    conditional probability, 179, 336
    marginal probability, 179, 336
    posterior probability, 178–179, 336
    prior probability, 179, 336

Belief network. *See* Bayesian belief
    network (BBN)
Beta-PERT distribution, 92, 102, 134, 136, 317
Bias, 88, 249
Bid, 15
Bidirectional search, 264
Binary splitting, 293
Bottom-up estimation, 125–130
    advantages, 139
    method of proportions, 130
    process level, 125
    product level, 125
Bottom-up inference. *See* Diagnostic inference
BRACE, 306
BRE. *See* Balanced relative error (BRE)
Brook's law, 24
Budget, 49

C
Case-based reasoning (CBR), 254, 301–308
Causal effort model, 338
Chain rule, 337
Change
    acceptance, 120
    avoidance, 118
    change control, 119
    design for change, 119
    governance volatility, 117
    mitigation, 119–120
    process management, 118
    product management, 118
    resource management, 119
    target volatility, 117
    transfer, 119
Chebyshev's inequality, 101
Classical set theory, 111
Classification and Regression Trees (CART),
    163, 217, 223, 224, 251
    model, 291–299

Good ideas are not adopted automatically. They must be driven into practice with courageous patience.
– Hyman Rickover

Printed in the United States
By Bookmasters